DISCARDED

ISLAMISM

ISLAMISM

A Documentary and Reference Guide

John Calvert

Greenwood Press

Westport, Connecticut • London

Library of Congress Cataloging-in-Publication Data

Calvert, John, Dr.
    Islamism : a documentary and reference guide / By John Calvert.
        p. cm.
    Includes bibliographical references.
    ISBN 978-0-313-33856-4 (alk. paper)
    1. Islam—21st century. 2. Islam—Essence, genius, nature. 3. Islamic
renewal—Islamic countries. 4. Islam and politics—Islamic countries.
5. Religion and politics—Islamic countries. 6. Islamic countries—Politics
and government. I. Title.
    BP161.3.C35 2008
    320.5′57—dc22   2007026092

British Library Cataloguing in Publication Data is available.

Library of Congress Catalog Card Number: 2007026092
ISBN: 978-0-313-33856-4

First published in 2008

Greenwood Press, 88 Post Road West, Westport, CT 06881
An imprint of Greenwood Publishing Group, Inc.
www.greenwood.com

Printed in the United States of America

The paper used in this book complies with the
Permanent Paper Standard issued by the National
Information Standards Organization (Z39.48–1984).

10   9   8   7   6   5   4   3   2   1

Every reasonable effort has been made to trace the owners of copyright
materials in this book, but in some instances this has proven impossible.
The author and publisher will be glad to receive information leading to
more complete acknowledgments in subsequent printings of the book and
in the meantime extend their apologies for any omissions.

CONTENTS

READER'S GUIDE TO RELATED DOCUMENTS AND SIDEBARS

PREFACE

Since September 11, 2001, interest in and concern with things Islamic has reached unprecedented levels in the United States and much of the world. Academics and policymakers have been hauled in front of microphones and television cameras, looking very much like deer caught in headlights in their efforts to explain the context in which the Al Qaeda phenomena emerged. And it is a daunting task, both because of the complexity of the subject matter and because so little is known about Islam by the general population—despite the fact that in the United States Islam is now about comparable to Judaism in terms of numbers of adherents. One of the largest concentrated populations of Arabic-speaking Muslims outside of the Middle East is in Dearborn, Michigan.

Images of Islam available to Americans are generally negative and are products of centuries of conflict between the countries of the West and various Muslim states. Historically, Western and Muslim states rubbed against one another uneasily, if for no other reason than that they were contiguous. They glowered at one another from across a shifting frontier that cut through the Balkans and the Mediterranean Sea.

In 1529 and again in 1683 the Ottoman Turks besieged Vienna in the heart of Europe. All of Europe trembled at the specter of the so-called "Terrible Turk." German woodcuts of the period portray the Sultan as a cowering, demonic figure.

In the nineteenth century, negative images of Islam helped to justify Western imperialism in Africa and Asia. Europeans portrayed Muslim regions from Morocco to the Malay Archipelago as backward and barbaric, in need of Europe's expert tutelage and civilizing mission. Americans tended to buy into this imagery. One has only to look at certain passages in Mark Twain's *Innocents Abroad*, which chronicled his journey to the Islamic East, or issues of *National Geographic Magazine* from the 1920s and 1930s, to see how this was so. In each case we find images of American progress juxtaposed to Muslim "primitiveness."

The terrorist attacks in New York, Washington, Bali, Casablanca, Istanbul, Madrid, and London, carried out by radicalized Muslims in recent years, confirmed in the minds of many North Americans, Europeans, and Australians, Islam's putative violence. Despite the plea of U.S. President George W. Bush for Americans to distinguish carefully between "good" and "bad" Muslims, the terrorist attacks reinforced the long-standing stereotype, strong in the West since Medieval times, that Islam is a religion that condones intolerance and violent behavior.

Presently, in the United States and much of Europe, the distinction between a virtuous national self and a nefarious Muslim "other" has never been stronger. This is precisely the division that the global jihadis seek to perpetuate. Indeed, it is significant that in one of his

"Messages to the World" (the phrase is taken from Bruce Lawrence's book) Usama bin Laden endorses a vulgar understanding of Samuel Huntington's "Clash of Civilizations" thesis.

Since 9/11, serious students of Islam, Muslim and non-Muslim alike, have devoted considerable energy to challenging the ingrained assumption of Islamic fanaticism and intolerance. If violence occurs in the name of Islam, these critics say, it is because Islam has been hijacked by political or ideological zealots. In order to set the record straight, they remind people of Islam's core teachings of mutual respect, social justice, and equilibrium, values evident, for example, in the poetry of the thirteenth-century C.E. Persian mystic, Jalal al-Din Rumi. According to the experts, even among Islamists (Muslim activists) the prevailing trend is toward missionary activity and peaceful change through legal channels.

Yet, one cannot get away from the reality that extremist traits do exist in the Muslim world. To regard bin Laden and other radical Muslims as aberrations bereft of any connection to Islam is both to deny their self-understanding and their linkage to history.

What is it in the Islamic tradition, and in the experience of Muslims in the modern world, that fosters fundamentalist attitudes? What makes it attractive to believe that one monopolizes the truth, to engage in harsh rhetoric, to deny diversity and difference? To be sure, the Islamists of the Muslim world have their analogues in Christianity, Judaism, and Hinduism. Yet, due to the salience of the contemporary Islamic resurgence, it is the Islamists who command our attention.

This documentary and reference guide aims to enhance our understanding of the Islamist phenomenon by presenting forty-one documents, written by Islamists themselves, which shed light on the origins, goals, beliefs, and practices of Islamic-focused groups and movements throughout the Muslim world. Included in the collection are writings penned by Islamists active in Morocco, Algeria, Tunisia, Bosnia-Herzegovina, Chechnya, Egypt, Sudan, Syria, Palestine, Israel, Jordan, Saudi Arabia, Iraq, Iran, Afghanistan, Pakistan, and Indonesia. A number of these documents have been translated by qualified individuals into English specifically for this volume. Many of the documents are polished tractates that articulate in clear terms a distinct ideological vision. Others are little more than memos from the front lines of Islamist effort and struggle to create what they deem is a better world. All address issues at the heart of the relationship between the Muslim world and the West: Is Islamism necessarily antagonistic to the West and/or modernity? Are Islam and democracy incompatible? Is there a distinctive Islamist road to representative government or to the enhancement of women's rights? Should Western governments and populations be concerned or even afraid if an Islamist movement such as Egypt's Muslim Brotherhood gains political power? Do progressive aspects of Islamist thought and practice exist, or are all forms of the Islamist phenomenon retrograde and discriminatory?

The relationship between Islamists and the West is problematic. Yet, the alert reader will discern that the important conversation in these documents is among Muslims themselves. Islamists proffer solutions to the political, economic, and social blockages that prevent Muslims from attaining creativity and greatness in the modern era. But not all Muslims agree that the Islamists' central postulate—the necessity to establish an authentic Islamic state or social order—is feasible or even required in the present day. Islamists focus most of their attention on winning the hearts and minds of these Muslim skeptics, primarily through argument, but sometimes also by means of the "propaganda of the deed," violent actions meant to polarize populations and attract adherents to the cause.

One of the primary goals of this work is to communicate the diversity of views within the Islamist camp. It accomplishes this by drawing on representative examples of the various kinds of Islamist discourse extant in the world today. The documents are arranged in nine chapters. Each chapter highlights a specific theme important to the overall Islamist landscape. Within a chapter, each document is prefaced by brief contextual information that identifies it, provides the document's date of creation, indicates where it was written, and comments on its significance. The documents are followed by short essays that analyze the pieces and provide them with greater context, and by short lists of published works designed to aid the interested reader in pursuing specific subjects in greater depth. Many of the documents are supplemented by sidebars that provide additional information relevant to the specific document. Many of these include portions of other, related primary documents.

The volume opens with an expository essay that defines Islamism and traces its historical development. At the book's end is a reference section that provides an extensive list of published works relating to Islamism. These works are divided into regional or country categories. Thus, for example, there is a list of books and articles related to North Africa, one devoted to Egypt and Sudan (the "Nile Valley"), and another to Islamism in Southeast Asia. The bibliography is not exhaustive, but it does include what I consider to be the most important works on the topic. I have also included at the end a short list of electronic sources on Islamism that are available on the Internet, in addition to select radio and film documentaries.

Most of the documents presented here have been excerpted from lengthier writings. There is a practical necessity for this: the space available for any printed book such as this is limited. In making my selections, I have taken pains not to compromise the meaning of the original work. In cases where I include portions of works that have been previously translated, I have retained their original spellings and language. Therefore, the reader will notice that proper names, especially, are spelled differently from document to document (for example, "Husayn" and "Hussein").

I should mention that I did not come to this project with a political or ideological agenda. It is important to make this point because Islamism is a contentious topic that elicits strong feelings. As far as possible, I have taken pains to be fair to the topic, presenting documents that represent the plurality of views found within the phenomenon. That being said, I alone am responsible for any shortcomings that may exist in this book.

No currently published collection dealing exclusively with Islamism contains the present volume's scope of coverage. Every effort has been made to include documents that have not before appeared in published collections. It is expected that this documentary and source guide will be consulted by students (high school and up) and by academic researchers and members of the general public who seek answers to questions pertaining to the subject of Islamism.

When I first took on this project I assumed, in the most optimistic scholarly fashion, that it would be something I could finish in "reasonable time." I was quite wrong. Both the depth of the project and the work of translation stretched it out well beyond what I had anticipated. I owe debts to a number of people who helped me along the way. Kevin Downing, my editor at Greenwood, offered sound advice at every turn and patiently guided me through the maze of copyright regulations. I am grateful to Mohammed Zakaria, Fachrizal Halim, and David Vanderboegh for working on a number of the translations. Timothy Austin, Dean of Creighton University's College of Arts and Sciences, granted me a one course reduction to expedite the project. I am grateful also for the financial support provided by Ron Simkins, Director of Creighton's Kripke Center for the Study of Religion and Society. My greatest thanks are to my wife Im and son Sean who have always provided me with support whether I needed it or not. It is to them that I dedicate this book.

INTRODUCTION

WHAT IS ISLAMISM?

The past seventy five years have witnessed the appearance in the Middle East, Africa, Southeast Asia, and elsewhere of political parties and other formal organizations with Islamic agendas, a phenomenon that has both surprised and frightened many in the West. The last thirty years have been particularly active in this regard. Events from the Revolution of 1978–1979 in Iran to the attacks on New York and Washington of September 11, 2001, have led some to conclude that the United States and the European nations are on a collision course with Islam, the religion of one-fifth of the world's population. Although the view of a monolithic Islamic threat ranged against the West is problematic, not least because it ignores the many fruitful relationships that exist between Muslims and non-Muslims, it is true that in recent decades Muslim populations around the world have exhibited heightened religiosity within the context of doctrinally and socially conservative mass movements.

Western observers have used a number of terms to refer to the modern-era phenomenon of Islamic resurgence. One of the most widely used of these is *Islamic fundamentalism*. Other terms include *political Islam, Islamic revivalism, Islamic extremism*, and (more controversially), *Islamofascism*. Although all of these terms succeed in denoting an aspect of the phenomenon, none covers its entire meaning. A better term, one increasingly employed by scholars and journalists, and the one adopted for this volume, is *Islamism*. Like other "isms" of the modern era, for example communism and fascism, Islamist organizations subscribe to a dogmatic view that claims to supply answers to all of the problems of the world. Resting on what its adherents consider a solid foundation of truth, Islamism passes judgment on history. However, those whom we call "Islamists" do not apply that term to themselves. Islamists oppose the term because it suggests their philosophy to be a political extrapolation from Islam rather than a straightforward expression of Islam as a way of life. Indeed, most Islamists define themselves simply as concerned Muslims working for the restoration of authentic Islam. Nonetheless, the terms *"Islamist"* and *"Islamism"* are now widely used even among Muslims. Several publications in the Muslim world use the terms to describe domestic and transnational organizations seeking to implement Islamic teachings in society or state or both. This is true, for example, of the English Web sites for the newspapers *Al Jazeera* and *Asharq al-Awsat*.

It is important at the outset of our discussion that we understand something about the Islamic heritage, upon which Islamist movements draw for inspiration. Islam is the youngest of the major world religions. It is also the fastest growing. In many areas of the world, including Europe and North America, the number of Muslims is increasing rapidly. In this global context, Muslims exhibit as many differences among themselves as do the other great religions of the world. These differences are often formalized as sects, schools of thought, and attitudes toward politics. However, regardless of sectarian and other kinds of divisions, Muslims share core beliefs that bind them in a worldwide community.

Muslims believe in a single, all powerful deity (in Arabic, "Allah"), the same God revered by Jews and Christians. According to Muslims, God revealed his will to humankind through the agency of the Prophet Muhammad. The belief that God speaks through His prophets is central to the Semitic tradition to which Muhammad belonged; Muhammad's career unfolded in Arabia. Following the Prophet's death in 632 C.E., his companions collected the dozens of revelations that had come to him from God in a scripture called "The Noble Qur'an." Muslims regard the Qur'an to be the exact and unaltered Word of God. They regard Muhammad as the last in a great line of prophets that includes such figures as Abraham, Moses, and Jesus. After Muhammad, God will never again address His creation. God has left the world with the Qur'an and it is the responsibility of Muslims to follow its teachings. The word "*Islam*" is an Arabic verbal noun that means "submission"—submission to the will of God. A Muslim is one who submits to the divine will as revealed in the Qur'an.

The Qur'an imparts guidance by relating lesson-filled stories of the ancient prophets. Additionally, it provides advice and regulations for righteous and purposeful living. The Qur'an's teachings are fleshed out and provided with context by the hadith, the eye-witness reports of the words and deeds of the Prophet Muhammad, whose life Muslims consider to be exemplary and worthy of emulation. Together, the Qur'an and the hadith form the basis of Islamic law, known as the "Shari'a." The Shari'a is not a fixed legal code, but rather the path toward knowledge of God's will and the way to achieve God's justice on earth. Historically, the discernment of the divine "way" for humankind is the responsibility of the *'ulama* ("learned ones"), the class of scholars who are trained in Islamic theology and jurisprudence at *madrasas* (Islamic seminaries), such as the Azhar in Cairo, Egypt, or al-Qarawiyyin in Fez, Morocco.

Among the specific rulings of the Qur'an is the injunction to "command the right and forbid the wrong" (Q. 3:104). According to this stipulation, Muslims are duty-bound to correct beliefs and behaviors in society that are at odds with the Qur'an's mandate. The Qur'an also urges Muslims to strive to realize God's will on earth. Throughout history, Muslims have drawn on one or both of these injunctions in order to strengthen Islam against internal and external enemies through *jihad*. Specific examples of *jihad* movements include that of Usman dan Fodio who founded the Fulani Empire in what is now northern Nigeria in 1804–1808, and Muhammad Ahmad (d. 1885), the charismatic Sufi leader, who fought to rid the Sudan of the disruptive features of Egyptian colonialism. Generally, the leaders of such movements wanted to replace local rulers and enemies whom they considered not sufficiently Muslim, with truly Islamic ones.

Contemporary Islamists share many characteristics of earlier Islamic movements, but they differ in at least one important way. In contrast to medieval and early modern Islamic revivalists who focused solely on locally-generated sources of decline, Islamist movements implicitly or explicitly address challenges to Islam that stem from the power and secular culture of modern states.

The most satisfactory short definition of Islamism comes from the independent, nongovernmental International Crisis Group, which sees Islamism as "synonymous with 'Islamic activism,' the active assertion and promotion of beliefs, prescriptions, laws or policies that are held to be Islamic in character."[1] Islamists oppose forces in the modern world that, in their view, hinder the existence of authentic Islamic communities. Feeling their Islamic identity at risk, and angered by what they regard as the unfair treatment of Muslim populations by both Western states and westernized governmental and cultural elites in the Muslim world, Islamists seek to fortify their faith by deploying doctrines, beliefs, and practices taken from Islam's sacred past. In so doing, they often modify these doctrines in ways that address contemporary needs and situations, although they rarely acknowledge this accommodation. In the Islamist view, the revival of Islam in state and society will guarantee things like social justice, fair economic practice, and probity in public affairs. Empowered by these principles,

Muslim nations will find their God-given potential and assert their interests in the international arena as shining examples of modernity imbued with spiritual value.

The means by which Islamists attempt to accomplish their goals varies among groups and thinkers. Most Islamists focus on preaching and other kinds of nonviolent activity in order to build a modern Islamic society and state from the ground up. In Egypt, for example, Islamists have infiltrated professional syndicates. The Refah (Welfare) Party in Turkey and the Partai Keadilan Sejahtera (Prosperous Justice Party) in Indonesia are examples of Islamist organizations that work within existing political systems to attempt to produce change. Other "moderate" Islamists undertake missions of conversion in order to preserve Muslim identity against the forces of disbelief. An extremist minority, however, eschews the strategy of building a true Islamic society from the ground up and instead advocates violence in pursuit of Islamist goals. Throughout the world, "radical" Islamists combat nominally Muslim regimes, foreign occupiers of Muslim lands, and domineering Western states. What all varieties of Islamism have in common is the tendency to ground their activism in the teachings of the Qur'an and the example of the Prophet Muhammad with the aim of restoring the utopian condition that Islamists presume to have pertained before the alleged corruption of the faith. In referring to an unblemished past, Islamists attempt to undercut the claims to legitimacy of existing socio-political orders.

Islamists differ from mainstream Muslims who focus on matters of personal and community-oriented piety and do not have specific agendas for social and political change. Although some of these Muslims may well believe that in theory Islam is a political religion, they do not strive actively to impose an Islamic order on the state, society, or both. Islamists differ also from "ordinary" Muslims in their attitude toward outside influences on Islam. Whereas many Muslims are content to mingle their Islam with beliefs and practices derived from non-Muslim cultures, Islamists are careful to pattern their lives on scriptural and canonical sources only. In the Islamist view, traditional and popular practices such as visiting tombs of Muslim "saints" (awliya), no less than Western-generated practices like the free mixing of the sexes, are "innovations" that ought to be purged from the lives of Muslims. True Islam, Islamists emphasize, is adaptable to any population because it constructs religion not as local culture but on Qur'anic norms and values that are universal.

Despite the different strategies employed by Islamists, Islamism holds to a number of common features. Adherents of Islamism regard Islam not as a private affair but as a *nizam*, by which they mean an "integrated system" or "closed order" that includes all aspects of life, including public matters. The idea of Islamic holism is not pure invention. There is a good deal of legitimacy to the claim that Islam is intrinsically a public affair. Since the earliest days of Islam, Muslims have recognized that the divinely mandated vocation to implement God's will on earth is a communal as well as an individual responsibility. In practical terms this mandate is reflected in the Shari'a, which covers issues relating to social and economic transactions (*mu'amallat*) in addition to ritual, faith, and worship (*Ibadat*). In putting forward the idea of Islamic holism, the Islamists draw upon a concept of social order that is deeply rooted in Islamic thought and tradition. This being so, "there is a tendency for a large proportion of 'ordinary Muslims' to be responsive to the proposition of activist minorities that the prescriptions of their religion should be reflected in social mores, laws, and form the government of the states in which they live."[2]

According to Islamists, Muslims have a divinely-directed responsibility to challenge the secular, Western-inspired social and political order of the world. The injunction to act, they point out, comes from the Qur'an. Numerous, diverse, and even contradictory verses in the Qur'an enjoin Muslims to "strive in the way of God" (*jihad fi sabil Allah*). But the meaning and practical implications of this injunction have been much debated among Muslims. Traditionally, Muslims have distinguished between the "Greater Jihad," which is the personal struggle to be a better Muslim, and the "Lesser Jihad," the effort to spread Islam in the world and defend it from enemies. Today's Islamists, especially militant ones, tend to downplay understandings of *jihad* that limit it to the warding off of aggression or which define *jihad* as primarily an internal spiritual struggle. Rather, they resurrect and implement the medieval juridical discourses on *jihad* that press for Islam's worldly triumph against disbelievers. While most Islamists believe that Islam's forward march can be achieved through missionary activity, the "radicals" look to the "Sword Verses" of the Qur'an, for example, sura 9:29, which enjoins Muslims to "Fight those who do not believe in God and His Messenger, nor acknowledge the religion of truth from among the People of the Book, until they pay the poll tax out of hand, having been brought low." Even so, there is a debate among extreme, jihadist Islamists about who among the enemy may be legitimately targeted. At root, this is an argument about where the line lies between combatant and noncombatant.

Islamists look back to the example of the Prophet and the first generations of Muslims, but it would be wrong to consider them as being against the conveniences of the modern age. Very few Islamists want to return to the material and cultural conditions of the first Muslim community in seventh-century Arabia. Rather, most Islamists seek to impose the spiritual values expressed in the Qur'an and by the Prophet Muhammad on the technical and organizational aspects of modernity. In the Islamists' view, technology is neutral in terms of its moral value; what matters are the uses toward which it is put. Technology, they say, must be applied in ways that further the divine mandate. Today, for example, Islamists use the Internet and other electronic technologies to disseminate their messages to wider publics. In the late 1970s, the Ayatollah Khomeini sent his revolutionary message to the Iranian people via tape cassettes. Islamists harness technology in order to do "God's work." However, there are exceptions to the Islamists' comfort with technology. The radical Salafi-Islamist group led by Juhayman al-Utaybi, which attempted to take over the Mecca mosque in 1979, shunned modern society altogether, its members preferring to live simple "authentically Islamic" lives among the desert nomads.

Islamists tend to be critical of the 'ulama who they regard as peddlers of dry and irrelevant scholasticism, and as being generally out of touch with the modern world. Moreover, many Islamists regard the 'ulama negatively as the co-opted mouthpieces of corrupt and secular political leaders in the Muslim world; it is a fact that in modern history many Sunni 'ulama were absorbed into the state as salaried employees (their Shi'i counterparts maintained a greater degree of autonomy). In the view of most Islamists, the 'ulama's dependency on the state compromises any potential they might have as champions of the people's interests against the governing elite. It should come as no surprise, then, that many Islamist thinkers and activists are laymen who have by-passed the specialized juridical and theological training of the scholars. In fact, Islamists generally tend to be Western-educated and hold degrees in engineering and other technical fields. Many are self-schooled in Islamic studies, or else are renegade scholars who operate beyond the fringes of the official Islamic establishment. Shaykh 'Umar 'Abd al-Rahman, the spiritual guide of Egypt's al-Gama'a al-Islamiyya (The Islamic Group), is an example of a trained scholar (he is a graduate of the Azhar) who abandoned the religious establishment for a career of Islamist militancy.

But since the 1970s, even mainstream 'ulama have shared the Islamists' concern about the erosion of Islamic values in society. A few of the more dramatic cases include Indonesia's Muhammidiyya and Nahdatul Ulama (NU) movements, and the ascension to the presidency in 1999 of Abdurrahman Wahid, leader of the NU. In Malaysia, the Islamist PAS Party, which captured two provincial governments in the 1999 elections, has in its ranks several prominent scholars. Most of these Islamist-oriented 'ulama do not adopt a harsh and uncompromising stance toward the state, preferring to chastise rulers whose behavior they deem to be un-Islamic. Again, there are exceptions, the most notable being the Ayatollah Khomeini who in 1979 led the Islamic revolution against the Shah in Iran.

Another characteristic of Islamism is the expressed goal of its adherents to bring unity to the Muslim world. Islamists hold that, once "liberated," Muslim countries should cooperate closely to further the common interests of the umma—the worldwide community of Muslims. Some Islamists, however, want to erase existing national frontiers altogether so as to politically unite Muslims across geographic, ethnic, and state boundaries. For these Islamists, the aim is nothing less than resurrecting the universal Caliphate. But regardless of these goals, Muslims today are more aware of one another than at any time in the past. Just as the spread of literacy in eighteenth- and nineteenth-century Europe enabled the formation of national identities and the nation state, the spread of modern media has enabled Muslims the world over increasingly to see themselves as parts of the same community of shared interests, goals, concerns, achievements, and grievances.

HISTORICAL OVERVIEW

Islamism, as suggested above, is very much a product of modern history. It arose in the early and middle decades of the twentieth century in response to the long, slow decline of Muslim fortunes in the modern period. During the medieval era, Islam had been the dominant and outstanding civilization on earth. Muslim rulers sponsored cutting-edge scientific research and Muslim armies routinely defeated the armies of non-Muslims on the battle field. The pattern of Muslim success traces back to the origins of Islam. In 622 C.E. the Prophet Muhammad was forced to flee his native city of Mecca, only to return victorious eight years later as its ruler. In the decades that followed, the Caliphs assembled an empire that stretched from the Indus River to Spain and from the plains and mountains of Central Asia to the deserts of Africa. To be a Muslim meant to belong to a victorious civilization. Muslims saw a correlation between their worldly success and the Qur'an's pronouncement that Islam is "the best community raised for mankind" (Q 3:110).

However, beginning in the 1700s, if not before, the powerful new nation-states of Europe forcefully imposed degrees of control over much of Asia and Africa, including the swath of Muslim lands. Muslim sultanates and princedoms, which had once commanded resources and power, were incorporated as subordinates into a European order of culture and economic exchange. In India, Britain supplanted the Muslim Mughal Empire, while in North and West Africa the French held sway. Central Asia fell to the Russian Czars and the islands of the Malay Archipelago to the Dutch and British. In 1882 British forces attacked and occupied the Ottoman province of Egypt. Following World War I, British and French statesmen portioned the Ottoman Arabic-speaking provinces in Greater Syria and Mesopotamia and created the mandated states of Syria, Lebanon, Palestine, Transjordan (later, Jordan), and Iraq. By the 1920s, only the new state of Turkey and the interior and western regions of Arabia remained free of overt forms of European control.

The decline of Islam as a worldly force was a terrible blow to Muslims. In the view of many Muslims, "something [had] gone wrong with Islamic history." Concerned Muslims felt compelled to "set their history going again in full vigor, so that Islamic society may once again flourish as a divinely guided society should and must."[3]

One response to the malaise was the attempt to strengthen Islam by accommodating its principles to the requirements of global modernity. Throughout the Islamic world, but especially in Egypt, Istanbul, and India, modernist reformers emerged who sought to justify in Islamic terms the adoption by Muslims of Western political, economic, and civic institutions, which they regarded as necessary to the empowerment of Muslim states and societies. Often, the approach taken by the reformers was grounded in metaphorical and apologetic understandings of the Qur'an. Thus, for example, several reformers, including the Ottoman-Turkish Namik Kemal (d. 1888) and the Egyptian Muhammad 'Abduh (d. 1905), redefined the old Islamic principle of *shura* ("consultation") to legitimize the writing up of political constitutions in their countries. In India, the reformer Sir Sayyid Ahmad Khan (d. 1898) attempted to demonstrate the Qur'an's compatibility with reason and with "nature."

Secularism, the view that public life, including politics, should not be subjected to Islamic guidance or interpretation, was another Muslim response to the crisis of Muslim decline. Secularist discourses appeared in Egypt and India, but the most successful center of secularism in the Muslim world was Turkey, where Mustafa Kemal Ataturk undertook Europeanizing reforms and abolished religious institutions or put them firmly under government control. Ataturk shocked the Muslim world by abolishing the venerated institution of the caliphate in 1924.

Despite promising beginnings, the modernist approach was not given the opportunity to mature. By the mid-1930s it was matched and soon after superseded by the more vigorous and confrontational Islamist posture. In contrast to the Islamic modernists who admired much of what the West had to offer, the Islamists aimed to distance Islamic civilization from Europe and America, an approach that had broad appeal to Muslims who felt politically, culturally, and economically dominated by Western powers. Speaking the language of cultural authenticity, Islamists held that the failures experienced by Muslims in modern times were the result of Muslim peoples and leaders turning away from Qur'anic values. Islamists viewed Western ideologies such as capitalism, socialism, and liberalism as undermining the virtue of Muslim societies by promoting selfish individualism, moral relativism, and materialism. Although many Islamists accepted the Islamic modernist project of reinterpreting much tradition, they said this should be accomplished in an Islamic spirit and not as a cover for Europeanization.

Secular nationalism proved to be more resilient than Islamic modernism, although in many countries it, too, eventually succumbed to Islamism. During the 1940s and 1950s, Islamists struggled alongside more popular and powerful secular nationalist groups against the common enemy of European colonialism. Among these Islamist organizations was Egypt's Muslim Brotherhood, founded in the European-controlled Suez Canal Zone in 1928 by a primary school teacher named Hasan al-Banna. The Brotherhood, which began as an educational and social welfare organization, aimed to revive Islam among the people. By the 1940s it claimed in Egypt some 500,000 members and supporters. It was common at this time for Muslim Brothers to provide socialism, which was popular among all opposition factions at the time, with an Islamic pedigree by evoking the Qur'an-based concept of "mutual social responsibility" (*al-takaful al-ijtima'iyya*). In this and other ways the Muslim Brotherhood sought to accommodate Islam to the political temper of the time.

When Jamal 'Abd al-Nasser and the Free Officers came to power in Egypt in 1952 many Muslim Brothers supported them, assuming that the Officers might be convinced to implement Islamic law. Unhappily for the Muslim Brothers, however, 'Abd al-Nasser and the Free Officers displayed no interest in establishing an Islamic state in Egypt and in fact implemented policies that were clearly secular in orientation. Worried by the Brotherhood's close connection to the people, the Free Officers forcibly disbanded the movement, imprisoned many of its members, and executed four of its leaders.

Among those jailed was Sayyid Qutb (1906–1966), who, while incarcerated, developed a radical version of Islamism. In Qutb's view, submission to the supervision of secular authorities and humanly devised institutions meant surrender to the whims and selfish interests of imperfect worldly forces. Qutb underscored his denial of the legitimacy of the Egyptian and other Muslim regimes by equating their moral universe with that of the *jahiliyya*, the condition of disbelief and cultural barbarism characteristic of the Arabs of the Arabian Peninsula prior to the advent of the Prophet Muhammad. He held that all Muslim societies were, in fact, anti-Islamic—he described them as *jahili*, that is, "ignorant" of God's Will—because they were not governed according to Qur'anic principles and the Prophet Muhammad's example. Qutb explained how the restitution of God's sovereignty was dependent on the formation of a vanguard of believers who would remove themselves mentally from the corrupting influences of the surrounding culture. Once prepared, the vanguard would then strive to realize manifestly the Islamic conception of life. Accused of planning with others to overthrow the Egyptian government, Sayyid Qutb was executed in 1966. Yet his radical ideas lived on.

At the same time, Islamist movements arose in British India and Iran. In the former, a journalist named 'Abu al-A'la Maududi (1903–1979) founded a movement among the more modernized sectors of Muslim Indian society called Jama'at-e Islami in 1941. Maududi was strongly opposed to the idea of creating Pakistan, a separate Muslim country, both because the Muslim leaders of the Pakistan Movement were secular and because he did not believe Muslims should be isolated from one another in distinct nation states. However, after Pakistan came into being in 1947, Maududi accepted the reality of the situation and began working to build an Islamic society in the new state. He relentlessly criticized the secular policies of Pakistan's leaders and berated them for failing to create an Islamic political order.

In Iran the Shi'i religious scholars ('ulama) had managed since the eighteenth century to remain largely independent of the government. This was in contrast to their counterparts in the Sunni-dominated Ottoman Empire who, at an early date, were absorbed into the state bureaucracy. The relative independence of the scholars, however, diminished with the coming to the throne of Reza Shah Pahlavi, who imposed a nationalist ideology and implemented secular reforms. He advocated women's emancipation and outlawed the veil. In 1941 the British forced Reza Shah from power on account of his pro-German sympathies and replaced him with his son, Mohammed Reza Pahlavi. There followed a period of lively political activity as nationalists, communists, and Islamists contended for power. One of the Islamist groups, the Fida'yan-e Islami, turned to political assassination and was in contact with the Muslim Brotherhood in Egypt. Following the ouster of the populist Prime Minister Mohammad Mussadiq in 1953 by a U.S.- and U.K.-engineered coup, Mohammed Reza Shah consolidated his autocracy and proceeded with his secular modernization plans.

Secular nationalism in the Muslim World reached the peak of its popularity in the 1960s, as leaders such as 'Abd al-Nasser, Pakistan's Ayub Khan, and Indonesia's Sukarno forcibly limited the influence of Islam in the public realm. However, beginning in the 1970s Islamism once again began to command attention. By that time it had become painfully clear to Muslims that the material prosperity and full independence promised by the new national ruling elites had not materialized. All over the Muslim World populations felt crushed by failing economies, rising unemployment, and by the closed political systems imposed by dictatorships and monarchies. Moreover, they accused their governments of being under the thumbs of the Great Powers, especially the United States. The propagation of secularism by the leaders of the postcolonial order added to the growing discontent by challenging inherited values and practices. Many Muslims saw Israel's decisive defeat of the Arab armies during the June 1967 Arab-Israeli war as the inevitable outcome of national policies that served to sap the ethical strength of the people.

The failure of the political regimes to meet the expectations of their people reinvigorated Islamism and made it the primary expression of popular protest. Over the 1970s, Islamist activists revived moribund Islamist organizations and created new ones. Some of these were more militant and more narrowly focused than anything that had previously been seen. Whereas in the 1940s and 1950s Islamists primarily targeted Western imperialism, now they challenged Muslim governments also. But the resurgence was not only focused on the Islamization of the State. It was also manifested in increased religious observance. Not only the *hijab*, but also the *niqab* became widespread and a part of a national dress code of sorts for women, and popular preachers imparted conservative Islamic messages via the television. In Malaysia, for example, the Muslim Youth Movement, led by Anwar Ibrahim, set forth "to 'make better Muslims' of the young, to incite them to purge their faith of rustic 'superstitions' rooted in the original Hinduism of the peninsula, and generally to 'civilize' them."[4] Islamists in Egypt communicated their desire for change in a simple slogan, "Islam is the Solution," which provided an "orienting vision" of the sort of community the Islamists wanted to establish: one premised on the solid foundations of Qur'anic morality.

Islamism's greatest triumph during this period occurred not within the widespread Sunni tradition, but within Shi'i Iran where uneven economic development, dictatorship, forced westernization, and the support given the Shah by a foreign power, namely, the United States, combined to alienate significant sectors of the population from the regime. Beginning in the mid-1960s, two major streams of opposition emerged. One stream was represented by 'ulama and merchants and looked to the leadership of the Ayatollahs. The other was composed of members of the modernizing middle class and was influenced by the exhortations of modernizing intellectuals, such as 'Ali Shariati. Shariati, who had studied in France, combined the revolutionary ideas of Frantz Fanon and Che Guevera with powerful symbols taken from Shi'i Islam to create a revolutionary theology that had particular appeal to the students of the new universities. In 1978–1979 the two streams of opposition united under the conservative leadership of the Ayatollah Khomeini to overthrow the Shah and establish an Islamic Republic. In the years that followed, Khomeini actively encouraged Shi'is in other countries to assert themselves against the powers-that-be.

One of Iran's successes abroad was the formation of Hizballah (The Party of God) in Lebanon, which continues to be strong and operates a network of social agencies that serves the relatively disadvantaged Shi'i population in that country. Inspired by the Iranian revolutionary example, Hizballah engaged in terrorist martyrdom operations in the 1980s that prompted first the Americans and then the Israelis to withdraw their military forces from Lebanon. Subsequently, the tactic of martyrdom attacks was taken up by Palestinian organizations (notably the Islamist Hamas) and by Al Qaeda and Al Qaeda-inspired groups.

The success of Islamist revolutionaries in Iran and Lebanon had a major impact on Sunni Arab militants, although Sunni radicals also looked to sources of inspiration within their own tradition, for instance, the works of Sayyid Qutb. Throughout the 1970s, 1980s, and especially the 1990s, underground groups such as the Islamic Jihad, of which the (Al) Qaeda lieutenant Ayman al-Zawahiri was a member, waged a deadly campaign of terror and assassination against the regimes of Egyptian presidents Anwar Sadat and Husni Mubarak. In 1981 Islamic Jihad assassinated Sadat, justifying their attack by citing Taqi al-Din Ibn Taymiyya, a medieval Hanbali jurist who endorsed rebellion against Muslim rulers who failed to enforce the Shari'a in their countries. In Algeria the government's cancellation of the national election in 1991, which the grassroots Front Islamique du Salut (Islamic Salvation Front) was poised to win, prompted a savage outburst of violence spearheaded by radical Islamist organizations, such as the Armed Islamic Movement (MIA) and the Armed Islamic Group (GIA). Both the Egyptian and Algerian states acted vociferously against the Islamist insurgents, prompting many radicals to reconsider the effectiveness of tactics based on violence in meeting their goals.

Another source of Sunni radicalism emerged from within the distinctive milieu of Saudi Arabian Salafism, a conservative and puritanical interpretation of Islam that 'Abd al-'Aziz Ibn Saud, the founder of the Saudi state, spread forcefully throughout much of the Arabian Peninsula during the 1910s and 1920s. Against the tendency of religious tolerance and accommodation held by the majority of Muslims, the Saudi Salafis drew a sharp line of distinction between those who upheld what they considered to be the true and authentic understanding of Islam and "iniquitous" others, including Shi'is, Sufis (Islamic mystics), and "infidel" Jews and Christians. As the Saudi state consolidated, its ruling house abandoned the movement's original penchant for territorial conquest in favor of more peaceful methods of propagation.

Beginning in the 1960s, the Saudi royal house actively spread its conservative brand of Islam throughout the Middle East and South Asia. In so doing, it aimed to counter the Arab socialism spilling out of 'Abd al-Nasser's Egypt and, after 1979, the spread of the Shi'i Iranian Revolution; the latter, as we have noted, sought to maximize its influence in the region. In Pakistan, Salafism found favor especially among the school of the Deoband, whose core doctrines were in some respects similar. Yet there lurked the possibility that circumstances might reawaken the Salafi discourse of opposition and assertiveness, even against the house of Saud. Thus, for example, charges of corruption against the ruling house prompted a group of zealots led by Juhayman al-Utaybi briefly to take over the Mecca mosque in 1979.

The struggle of the Afghan people in the 1980s against the Soviet invasion of their country provided opportunities for Salafi Puritanism and radical Egyptian-style Islamism to commingle. Keen to prevent the spread of communism in South Asia and strengthen Sunni Islam against Iranian revolutionary Shi'ism, the Saudis funneled money and Salafi ideas into Afghanistan. The war attracted foreign volunteers, many of whom belonged to established Islamist opposition groups from all over the Middle East as well as South and South East Asia. Overwhelmingly, they were Arabs from Saudi Arabia, Egypt, and Algeria. They included, in addition to bin Laden, Ayman al-Zawahiri, who had just completed a prison term earned for his incidental role in the assassination of Egyptian president Anwar al-Sadat in 1981, the Algerian Sa'id Makhlufi, destined to become one of the founders of the Islamist Front Islamique du Salut (FIS), and the Indonesian 'Abdullah Sungkar, who went on to found the radical Jemaah Islamiyah. Blocked in their home countries by police action, these Islamist soldiers of fortune considered Afghanistan an appropriate and inviting location to engage the principle of *jihad*. The merging of conservative Salafi and radical jihadi trends was evident in the writings of the famous Palestinian advocate of the *jihad*, 'Abdallah 'Azzam, who took much of his inspiration from Qutb but was also a beneficiary of Saudi patronage.

The mix of Puritanism and *jihad* was potent. For the fighters in Afghanistan the war was a source of heroism, solidarity, and total devotion to Islam as defined in terms of the Shari'a. Many were already aware that the struggle against the Soviet Red Army was a school in which they might learn the violent techniques required to topple their governments at home. The list of such countries was long and included, in addition to Afghanistan, Palestine, Kashmir, and the Southern Philippines. Some even thought of "liberating" Spain—the fabled al-Andalus.

The Afghan war was the defining experience in the life of Usama bin Laden. A native Saudi who grew up in the devotional environment of Salafism, bin Laden was one of the first Arabs to join the *jihad*. He saw his role there as facilitator and spent his personal fortune to build roads and tunnels for the *mujahidin* and provide pensions to the families of the fallen. He is reputed to have been involved in at least one major battle. His personal piety and willingness to sacrifice comfort and wealth for the cause of Islam endeared him to his fellows.

After the Soviet withdrawal from Afghanistan in 1989, Usama bin Laden returned home in triumph with other Saudi veterans. When the Ba'thist regime in Iraq invaded Kuwait one year later, he approached the Saudi leadership with a plan to raise a new army of Muslims to resist Saddam Husayn. When the ruling house rejected the offer, bin Laden became increasingly alienated from the ruling stratum of his birth. His loathing for the Saudi ruling family deepened when it allowed the stationing of U.S. troops in the kingdom during and after the war. In bin Laden's mind, in aiding and abetting the U.S. "occupation" of the kingdom, the House of Sa'ud, whose legitimacy derived from its protection of Salafism, had entered the circle of iniquity.

In his criticisms of the Saudi royal family, bin Laden had at his disposal the articulations of anathema developed by Sayyid Qutb and the traditions of rebuke of the Salafi tradition in which he had been raised. Yet while bin Laden was willing to chastise the royal family, he chose instead to attack the alleged American puppet master operating from behind the throne. In so doing he reversed the order theorized by other extremist Islamist groups, which advocated as a first step the eradication of the perceived corruption at home. According to the standard view, the Western "other" should be engaged only once the Muslim world had been strengthened by the creation of a transnational Islamic state.

Bin Laden had a practical reason for desiring global confrontation sooner rather than later. By the late 1990s it had became clear to the Islamist militants that the regimes in Riyadh, Cairo, Algiers, and elsewhere were relatively strong and would not fall easily. The Muslim masses had failed to join the militants in their armed struggles against their "Godless" governments. Mainstream Islamist movements, like the Muslim Brotherhood, also decried violence, preferring the tried-and-true methods of political advocacy and missionary work in meeting their goals. In calling for attacks on U.S. citizens, bin Laden hoped to deflate Muslim complacency by provoking a massive American response that would galvanize the world's Muslim population against the secular governments in the Middle East, Africa, and South and South East Asia. His goal, some analysts say, was to provoke nothing less than a "clash of civilizations." As evidence of Western disregard for Muslim sensibilities, bin Laden and al-Zawahiri pointed to beleaguered Palestinian, Bosnian, Kashmiri, and Chechen Muslims, all of whom were seen to suffer as a consequence of policies implemented by Western states and their allies in the Muslim world and beyond.

As we all know, bin Laden ratcheted up his war against the "Crusader-Zionist" conspiracy by striking at the symbolic heart of American power and prestige in the world. Following the logic of bin Laden and al-Zawahiri, the 9/11 hijackers defined their actions as the ultimate act of *jihad*, which called into stark relief the chasm in their minds between the forces of virtue and disbelief. The attacks were spectacular acts of carnage and death designed to have a searing effect on the millions who witnessed them on television. Indeed, this reading of the events is confirmed by bin Laden who related in a videotape seized by American forces during the anti-Taliban and al-Qaeda campaign how the hijackers "said in deeds in New York and Washington, speeches that overshadowed all other speeches made anywhere in the world." Here is dramatic testimony of how the events were understood by the perpetrators themselves, as metaphors of the confrontation between an absolute good threatened with destruction by its absolute opposite.

Critical assessments of U.S. policy and Western values are common to Muslims (and others), who chafe at the imbalance of power in the world. It is a common belief among Muslims that the United States and other industrial nations of the West are prepared to prop up allegedly corrupt regimes in order to sustain Western influence and access to Middle Eastern oil. Many of these will support their positions on world affairs with reasoned arguments and dismiss the rhetoric of the Islamists as reductionist and hyperbolic, even while recognizing the kernels of "truth" lurking in their statements. Other Muslims might overtly sympathize with the radical Islamists' grievances against the West, yet shy away from outright activism on behalf of the Islamist cause. Indeed, many Muslims who expressed genuine horror at the 9/11 attacks nevertheless suggested gingerly, "America had it coming." Interviews conducted by the *Cairo Times* in the weeks following the attacks are indicative in this regard. Consistently the interviewees focused on what they considered to be the provocations of American foreign policy, especially regarding the Palestine issue.[5]

There is a small but crucial number, however, for whom the radical Al Qaeda discourse is especially compelling. The profiles of captured or killed lower-level Al Qaeda operatives suggest an ideal type: Young men of conservative religious and middle- or lower-middle-class backgrounds, caught between cultures and often living lives of alienation and anomie. The radical Islamist discourse created by the ideologues gives shape and direction to these outsiders' anger, which is as likely to have a personal source as derive from political grievances. In gravitating to radical Islamism, these young men are able to identify their activities with a "sacred and transcendent cause," thus insulating the propositions and preferences of the movement "against criticism by mere mortals."[6]

Jihadist attacks undertaken by Al Qaeda and Al Qaeda-inspired groups continued following 9/11. Terrorist bombings targeting Westerners occurred in Bali in 2002, Madrid in 2004, and London in 2005, while police and security agencies thwarted other attacks that were in their planning stages. In the Middle East, a group calling itself "Al Qaeda in the Arabian Peninsula" attacked Saudis and Western expatriates. In Iraq Abu Mus'ab Zarqawi unleashed a campaign of terror aimed at U.S. and Iraqi forces and the majority Shi'i population of the country; it is widely claimed that Zarqawi's aim was to create instability in Iraq by igniting a civil war between Sunnis and Shi'is. Zarqawi was killed by a U.S. air strike in June 2006, yet his jihadist supporters have continued the campaign of terror and assassination that he helped to initiate in Iraq.

The violence unleashed by Al Qaeda and its jihadi affiliates commands attention. Yet, as this introduction has made clear, Islamism is a complex phenomenon with many shades of expression, only a few of them militant. Indeed, new Islamist responses to the challenges facing Muslims today are emerging, as is the case in Iran where figures such as Abdol Karim Sorush are advocating a pluralist and inclusive trend within Shi'i Islamism, or in Egypt, where in the mid 1990s the Al-Wasat Party emerged as a progressive alternative to the Muslim Brotherhood. As with other ideological movements, Islamism is not a static phenomenon. Islamist activists and thinkers are compelled to reinvent and modify the theoretical bases and practical applications of Islamism to meet social, economic and political realities. Yet, despite modifications and divergences within the trend, Islamism maintains its basic coherency. Overall, it can be compared with fundamentalisms in other religious traditions, including Christianity and Judaism, all of which attempt to temper the perceived immorality and injustices of our time through recourse to scriptural principles.

We hope that the selections included in this sourcebook will provide readers with some insight into the broad range of Islamist responses that have issued from the Muslim world over the past three quarters of a century.

NOTES

1. "Understanding Islamism," *Crisis Group Middle East/North Africa Report*, 37, no. 2 (March 2005), 1.

2. Ibid., 2.

3. Wilfred Cantwell Smith, *Islam in Modern History* (Princeton, NJ: Princeton University Press, 1957), 41.

4. Gilles Kepel, *Jihad: The Trail of Political Islam* (Cambridge, MA: Harvard University Press, 2002), 90.

5. *Cairo Times*, September 27–October 3, 2001.

6. Bruce Lincoln, *Holy Terrors: Thinking about Religion after September 11* (Chicago: University of Chicago Press, 2003), 55.

1

ISLAMIST MOVEMENTS AND THINKERS

Adnan al-Dulaimi, leader of the Iraq Accordance Front, right, and Selem al-Falahat and Abdullah Farajallah of Jordan's Muslim Brotherhood sit with a portrait of Hasan al-Banna, behind, during the celebration of the one-hundredth anniversary of the birth of Hasan al-Banna, the founder of the Islamist movement the Muslim Brotherhood, in Amman, November 16, 2006. The Muslim Brotherhood was formed in 1928 and is the largest Sunni Islamist organization of the twentieth century. (AP photo/Nader Daoud. Courtesy of AP Images.)

INTRODUCTION

The most widespread form of Islamism is the effort to build an Islamic society from the ground up by means of advocacy, social mobilization, and preaching. Among the currents representative of this strategy, pride of place belongs to the political Islamists who organize in popular movements or parties. Eschewing violence, their chosen weapons are the clinics, co-ops, schools, legal-aid societies, and professional associations that they found and through which they spread their message of Islamic renewal to the wider population. By winning the hearts and minds of the majority Muslim population, political Islamists aim to pressure governments to accede to their demands. Although their stated goal is an Islamic state, they acknowledge that in no case does scripture provide a precise model and thus are flexible as to the form the sought-after Islamic state should take. Many political Islamists are content simply to graft Islamic values onto the existing political system, whether a constitutional monarchy or a self-declared republic.

Political Islamists are oftentimes tolerated by the state elite against whom they operate. In most cases, however, their existence is precarious, waffling between periods of relative freedom and outright suppression by the state authorities. In terms of ethical demeanor and tactical orientation, political Islamists may be compared to the Christian evangelicals who have organized politically in the United States. Both political Islamists and activist Christian evangelicals are interested in cleansing state and society of political corruption and individual selfishness by gaining influence within the political arena. Both view with alarm the rationalist cosmology that underlies and justifies modern forms of political sovereignty.

Political Islamism emerged in Egypt and South Asia during the first half of the twentieth century with the Egyptian Muslim Brotherhood (al-Ikhwan al-Muslimun) and the Jama'at-e Islami of Pakistan. Subsequently, it took root in other regions of the Islamic world, notably North Africa, Greater Syria, and the Malay Archipelago. Despite recent predictions of their demise in the face of militant and of purely missionary forms of Islamic activism, political Islamist movements like the Muslim Brotherhood remain vital forces in the political and cultural affairs of many Muslim countries.

The Founding of the Muslim Brotherhood

- *Document:* Excerpts from the memoir of Hasan al-Banna, founder of the Muslim Brotherhood. Translated from the Arabic by John Calvert.
- *Date:* Al-Banna's memoirs were published in 1950, one year after his death. The excerpts deal with events in the 1920s that led to al-Banna's founding of the Muslim Brotherhood in 1928.
- *Where:* Cairo and Isma'iliyya, Egypt.
- *Significance:* Hasan al-Banna's memoir is the primary source for the origins and early history of Egypt's Muslim Brotherhood, the first Islamist movement in the Arab world.

DOCUMENT

The Wave of Atheism and Debauchery in Egypt

After the First World War and during my stay in Cairo, a tide of atheism and lewdness overtook Egypt. In the name of individual and intellectual freedom, it devastated religion and morality. Nothing could stop this storm. Circumstances made it still more dangerous.

Mustafa Kemal brought about a revolution in Turkey by abolishing the Caliphate. He separated the state from religion. These changes were brought about in a country that only recently had been the site of the Commander of the Faithful on behalf of the Muslim World. The actions wrought by the Turkish government brought tremendous changes in all spheres of life. The Egyptian university was taken over by the government and many colleges were brought under its direct control. Now, a novel concept of research and university life had emerged. The essence of the new concept was that a university could not become such until it revolted against religion and waged a war against Islam and its social traditions. Hence the university adopted western materialistic thought and culture and its teachers and students relieved themselves of all moral restraints.

During this period the foundations of the Democratic Party were laid. But it died before its birth. The aim of the party had been to propagate democracy and free thinking. In truth, it aimed to spread dissolution and libertinism.

A so-called Theosophical Academy was established at Al Manakh Street, under the direction of a group of theosophists. In this academy lectures were arranged that attacked the ancient faiths and encouraged the advent of a new religion. The speakers consisted of individuals from the Muslim, Jewish, and Christian traditions. They spoke of the theosophical concept from various perspectives.

A large number of books and magazines were issued on the subject. These writings aimed to weaken the Islamic thinking of the people and divert them toward theosophy, so they would enjoy real freedom, according to those writers.

At the same time, "saloons" were opened in some of the major buildings in Cairo. These saloons propagated the same ideas and tried to mislead the youth especially.

The Reaction

There was a powerful reaction among those who were concerned with these issues, as for example, the Azhar and other Islamic centers and institutions. But the people were divided into two groups. There was a group of sophisticated young people who were very much influenced by modern ideas, and others who were ignorant and unable to think for themselves, being deprived of proper leadership. I was very much pained to see this state of affairs in the country. I saw the social life of the dear Egyptian people oscillating between precious Islam, which was native to Egypt and which Egyptians had defended and lived with over fourteen centuries, and this harsh Western invasion, which was armed with all of the destructive influences of money, wealth, prestige, ostentation, power, and the means of propaganda.

I could relieve my grief through discussions with the students and my sincere friends of al-Azhar, Dar al-'Ulum and other educational institutions ...

My visit to the Salafiyya library also provided me some relief. In those days it was situated near the Court of Appeal ...

A Positive Approach

But those efforts were not sufficient to deal with the dangerous situation. I was studying and surveying both camps. The camp of atheism and Westernism was getting stronger and stronger, whereas the Islamic camp was growing weaker and smaller by the day. This situation increased my anxiety and grief. I remember that I passed half the month of Ramadan restless and without sleep. Hence I determined to take some positive steps and I said to myself, "Why should I not throw this responsibility on Muslim leaders? I should tell them to rise up, united, and thwart the evil designs of the atheists. If these gentlemen agree with my view, all well and good, otherwise I shall have to find some other ways and means." I determined that I must actively take up the matter.

Reflections on Isma'iliyya

Isma'iliyya created very strange feelings in my heart. The British Cantonment in its Western sector caste its influence over the city and generated a feeling of sadness in every respectable and dignified nationalist. It made him reflect on the occupation and the disasters it brought on Egypt, on how it deprived the Muslims of their chance to acquire higher education and material benefits. It also reminded him how the occupation had become an obstacle to Egypt's progress, hindering the unity and fraternity among Muslims for over sixty years.

The beautiful, grand building of the officers of the Suez Canal Company still stands. Egyptians work in the offices and are treated like slaves. Foreigners, however, are accorded full respect and given the status of officers and rulers. The Office has sole monopoly over the affairs of the people. The supply of water, health care, sanitation and other affairs, which are usually managed by the councilors, have been taken over by the Company. No one can enter or leave the city without the Company's permission.

The foreigners' cantonment is comprised of beautiful bungalows and buildings. Opposite the cantonment are the narrow and dark dwellings of the Arab laborers. All of the sign boards on the roads are written in European languages. Even the name "Mosque Street" [in Arabic] is written "Rue de le Mosque." European names are popularized and given permanent status by means of these signs.

All these factors were constantly at work on my heart. The effect of these factors impressed themselves upon me as I pondered them in the dense gardens or at the shore of Lake Tamish, or amid the woods at the edge of the desert. Undoubtedly, the environment of Isma'iliyya created a very deep impression on me and steeled my determination to impart on my career as a missionary.

The Muslim Brothers

As far as I remember it was the month of Dhu al-Qi'ada, 1347, March 1928 when six friends—Hafiz 'Abd al-Hamid, Ahmad al-Hasri, Fu'ad Ibrahim, 'Abd al-Rahman Hasab Allah, Ismail 'Izz, and Zaki al-Maghribi—came to see me. These men were greatly influenced by the lectures and sermons that I delivered in Isma'iliyya. They began to discuss the means of preaching Islam. Their faces shone with determination. Their eyes were bright ad their voices powerful. They said:

> "We have heard your speech, pondered it with heart and soul and have been extraordinarily impressed by it. But we do not know what to do practically. We are disgusted with the present way of life; it is a life of humiliation and captivity. You see that the Arabs and Muslims have no dignified place in this country. They are no more than servants belonging to the foreigners. We have nothing to offer except the blood running in our veins, our lives, our faith, our honor, and these coins that we cut from our family expenses. You know better than we do how best to serve Islam, the Muslim *umma*, and our country. We have come to you to present to you whatever we possess so that we can feel relieved of our duties towards God. It is for you to be responsible before God and to guide us. This group, which has determined to serve the cause of Islam and the Muslims, does so simply to earn the pleasure of God and nothing else. Such a group deserves success, however meager may be its resources and number of followers."

The sincere utterances of these men impressed me very much. I could not escape the responsibility that they threw onto me. But it was the same responsibility for which I had struggled. And I responded in an emotional voice, "May God thank you and bless you all for your good intentions. May God help us to do good deeds, to earn His pleasure and serve the cause of the Muslim *umma*. Our duty is to try to work hard and leave the result to God. Let us swear before God that we shall be the soldiers of Islam. In the fulfillment of his mission lay the prosperity of our nation."

Consequently, the oath of allegiance was taken by all of us. We determined on solemn oath that we should live as brothers, work for the glory of Islam, and launch jihad for it.

One of the friends got up and asked, "What shall we call ourselves? Shall we go by the name of any society or club or religious sect or association? Thus would we attain a formal identity."

I replied, "We shall not be any of them. It is better to be distant from showiness and traditionalism. The basis of our unity should be our ideology, our moral thinking and particular way of implementing it. We are united to serve the cause of Islam. Therefore, we are brothers and shall be known as the Muslim Brotherhood (al-Ikhwan al-Muslimun)."

It came suddenly and became an example. Therefore, with the cooperation of these six men, the Muslim Brotherhood came into existence. Its emergence was sudden and simple and its aims and objectives were those defined above.

School for Moral Training

After that, we had to sketch out our programs and select a place for holding our meetings. We finally agreed to rent a room in the library of Shaykh Al Sharif at Faruq Street for sixty Qirsh a month ... We decided to name the place "The Moral Training School." The syllabus included Islamic studies with emphasis on the recitation of the Qur'an in accordance with the rules prescribed for it. It was decided that each brother should attempt to memorize some of the Qur'an and their commentaries. The brothers should also be taught hadith [traditions of the Prophet]. They should memorize hadith on a regular basis and learn their meanings. They should also be taught the correct doctrine, worship, the intricacies of Islamic legislation, and the correct pattern of behavior in Islamic society. They should study Islamic history and the biographies of the Prophet and his early followers. All of this was to be done in a simplified manner that focused on the practical and spiritual aspects of Islam. In addition, the school was to train able brothers in public speaking and preaching by learning relevant extracts of prose and poetry. By way of practical training they were to speak in front of one another and later speak to larger groups. The initial group at the school numbered seventy.

SOURCE: Hasan al-Banna, *Mudhakkirat al-Da'wa wa al-Da'iya* (Cairo: Dar al-Tawzi' wa al-Nashr al-Islamiyya, 1986 [1947]), 53–55; 75–77.

CONTEXT AND ANALYSIS

Hasan al-Banna was born in 1906 in the village of Mahmudiyya in Egypt's lush Nile Delta. His father was the prayer leader and teacher for the local mosque, and from him Hasan gained a deep appreciation for Islam's moral foundations. Hasan al-Banna's burgeoning religiosity found an outlet in the Hasafiyya Sufi order, whose "dhikrs," devotional exercises for "remembering" the divine reality, he joined. At the same time, he read the works of the medieval theologian and Sufi Abu Hamid al-Ghazali. In 1923 his father enrolled him in Cairo's Dar al-'Ulum, the Teachers' Training School. The college's semi-traditional curriculum, which combined modern subjects with courses in Islamic studies, provided al-Banna with a soft landing in the modernizing life of the capital.

Traditional society at that time had long been undermined by both internal and external forces. Although Great Britain had granted Egypt its independence in 1922, British officials continued to interfere in the country's internal affairs and shape its relations with other nations. Egypt's semi-independent status rankled al-Banna, whose patriotism had earlier been awakened by the anti-British demonstrations that rocked Egypt in 1919. Equally, if not more, disturbing to al-Banna was the wave of secularization and Westernization that was overtaking Egypt, which created confusion and self-doubt among large numbers of the Egyptian population. During the 1920s and 1930s Egypt's political and cultural institutions were dominated by a wealthy and arrogant ruling class. Some of these had been disciples of the Egyptian Islamic modernist Muhammad 'Abduh but took his reforming impetus in a westernizing, rather than an Islamic, direction. As al-Banna notes in the above selection, Western cultural values were evident in the literary fashions of the day but also in the proliferation of nightclubs and drinking establishments. Additionally, they were evident in the Egyptian University founded in 1908. In al-Banna's characterization, the university was a purveyor of "atheistic" liberal thought. Symptomatic of these trends was Mustafa Kemal Ataturk's secular revolution in the new republic of Turkey. In 1924 Mustafa Kemal abolished the universal caliphate. For al-Banna and other Muslims, it came as a shock that for the first time in history, Muslims were without a Caliph, the temporal successor of the Prophet Muhammad. In al-Banna's view, the currents of "atheism" and "debauchery" afoot in Egypt and elsewhere undermined the Islamic identity of Muslims by sapping the religious foundation of their moral strength.

Nowhere was the imprint of western power and culture more evident than in Isma'iliyya, a small city on Lake Timsah in the Suez Canal Zone, where al-Banna was recruited to teach Arabic after graduating from Dar al-'Ulum in 1927. As he settled into his rented quarters, Al-Banna took note of the luxurious homes of the European Suez Canal Company employees and compared them with the "miserable dwellings" of the Egyptian workers. Such was the degree of foreign influence in the city that even the street signs were printed in European languages, not in the Arabic language native to Egypt. Just beyond the city were the military bases of the British, a visible and humbling reminder of Egypt's subordination to a foreign power. Al -Banna decried the presence in Egypt of Christian and Bahai missionaries. He was also perturbed by the prevalence in Egypt of theosophy, a mystical philosophy founded by the Russian Madam Blavatsky in 1873. Among the prominent Egyptians who frequented the society in Cairo were the politicians 'Abd al-Khaleq Thawrat Pasha and Lutfi Bey al-Sayyid.

In the passage, al-Banna expresses disillusionment at the muted response of the religious scholars of the Azhar, the great mosque-university of Cairo, to the threat hanging over Islam. In his view, the clerical establishment was doing little to protect Egypt from the onslaught of Westernization. On the other hand, he expresses deep respect for the simple faith of the common people. In an effort to reach to the grassroots and spur them to action, al-Banna began to preach Islam in Isma'ilyya's coffeehouses, rather than the mosque, the traditional site of Islamic preaching. As the excerpt indicates, six of those who were influenced by al-Banna approached him in March 1928, asking him to be their leader, and he agreed. It is not clear how the Society of the Muslim Brothers was organized during the first months of its existence. What is clear is that al-Banna was initially concerned with the moral upbringing of his followers. Adopting the common language of the people, al-Banna encouraged them in the moral ethos of brotherhood, sacrifice, and selfless duty to Islam.

Goals and Strategies of the Muslim Brotherhood

- **Document**: Selection from "Between Yesterday and Today," a tract by Hasan al-Banna, founder and Supreme Guide of Egypt's Muslim Brotherhood.
- **Date**: Late 1930s (precise date uncertain).
- **Where**: Cairo, Egypt.
- **Significance**: The tract is a concise exposition of the mission, ideology, and program of the Muslim Brotherhood written shortly before the outbreak of World War II. The tract expounds general principles that remain cornerstones of political Islamist thought up to the present.

DOCUMENT

Our Mission Is One of Reawakening and Deliverance

(a) A Weighty Heritage: So, Brethren, did God will that we inherit this heritage weighty with consequence, that the light of your mission glow amidst this darkness, and that God prepare you to exalt His word and reveal His sacred Law and reestablish His state: "God will surely aid one who helps Him. God is Mighty, Glorious!" [Q.22: 40].

(b) Our General Aims: What do we want, Brethren? Do we want to hoard up wealth, which is an evanescent shadow? Or do we want an abundance of fame, which is a transient accident? Or do we want dominion over the earth?—"The earth is God's: He gives to inherit it those whom He will of His servants" [Q.7: 128]—even as we read the Speech of God (Blessed and Almighty is He!): "That is the Abode of the Hereafter which we assign to those who do not want exaltation in the earth, nor any corruption. The final consequence is to the pious" [Q.28: 83]. May God witness that we do not want any of these, that our work is not toward these ends, and that our mission is not on their behalf. Rather always bear in mind that you have two fundamental goals:

(1) That the Islamic fatherland be freed from all foreign domination, for this is a natural right belonging to every human being, which only the unjust oppressor or the conquering exploiter will deny.

(2) That a free Islamic state may arise in this free fatherland, acting according to the precepts of Islam, applying its social regulations, proclaiming its sound principles, and broadcasting its sage mission to all mankind. For as long as this state does not emerge, the Muslims in their totality are committing sin, and are responsible before God the Lofty, the Great, for their failure to establish it and for their slackness in creating it. In these bewildering circumstances, it is counter to humanity that a state should arise, extolling an ideology of injustice and proclaiming a propaganda of oppression, while there should be no one among all mankind working for the advent of a state founded on truth, justice, and peace. We want to realize these two goals in the Nile Valley and the Arab domain, and in every land which God has made fortunate through the Islamic creed: a religion, a nationality, and a creed uniting all Muslims.

(c) Our Special Aims: Following these two aims, we have some special aims without the realization of which our society cannot become completely Islamic. Brethren, recall that more than 60 percent of the Egyptians live at a subhuman level, that they get enough to eat only through the most arduous toil, and that Egypt is threatened by murderous famines and exposed to many economic problems of which only God can know the outcome. Recall too that there are more than 320 foreign companies in Egypt, monopolizing all public utilities and all important facilities in every part of the country; that the wheels of commerce, industry, and all economic institutions are in the hands of profiteering foreigners; and that our wealth in land is being transferred with lightning speed from the possession of our compatriots to that of these others. Recall also that Egypt, out of the entire civilized world, is the most subject to diseases, plagues, and illnesses; that over 90 percent of the Egyptian people are threatened by physical infirmity, the loss of some sensory perception, and a variety of sicknesses and ailments; and that Egypt is still backward; with no more than one-fifth of the population possessing any education, and of these more than 100,000 have never gone farther than the elementary school level. Recall that crime has doubled in Egypt, and that it is increasing at an alarming rate to the point that the prisons are putting out more graduates than schools; that up to the present time Egypt has been unable to outfit a single army division with its full complement of *matériel*; and that these symptoms and phenomena may be observed in any Islamic country. Among your aims are to work for the reform of education; to war against poverty, ignorance, disease, and crime; and to create an exemplary society which will deserve to be associated with the Islamic Sacred Law.

(d) Our General Means of Procedure: How will we arrive at these goals? Speeches, pronouncements, letters, lessons, lectures, diagnosis of the ailment and prescription of the medicine—all these by themselves are useless and will never realize a single aim, nor will they advance a single agent of our mission to any one of his goals. Nevertheless, missions do have certain means of procedure that they must adopt and according to which they must operate. The general procedural means used by all missions are invariable and unchanging, and they are limited to the three following matters:

(1) Deep faith.
(2) Precise organization.
(3) Uninterrupted work.

These are your general procedural measures, Brethren, so believe in your ideology, form your ranks about it, work on its behalf and stand unwaveringly by it.

(e) Additional Procedures: Besides these general procedures, there may be additional ones, which must be adopted and strictly adhered to. There are negative and positive ones, some of which accord with people's customary behavior, differ from it, and contradict it; there are mild ones and rigorous ones, and we must train ourselves to put up with all of these and to be prepared to resort to any of them in order to guarantee success. We may be asked to go against entrenched habits and usages, and to rebel against regulations and situations that people take for granted and are familiar with. But then in its deeper essence, our mission is actually a rebellion against accepted usage and a change in habits and situations. Are you then prepared for this, Brethren?

(f) Some Discouragement: Many people will say: What do these tracts mean? Of what use can they be for building an *umma* and rebuilding a society burdened with these chronic problems and sunk in such a welter of corruption? How will you manage the economy on a non-profit basis? How will you act on the woman question? How will you obtain your rights without the use of force? Know, Brethren, that Satan slips his whispered suggestions into the aspirations of every reformer, but that God cancels out what Satan whispers; then God decrees his miracles, for God is Knowing, Wise. Remind all of these people that history, in telling us of past and contemporary nations, also gives us admonitions and lessons. And a nation that is determined to live cannot die.

(g) Obstacles in Our Path: I would like to avow to you frankly that your mission is still unknown to many people, and that on the day they find out about it and grasp its import and its aims, you will encounter violent antagonisms and sharp hostility. You will find many hardships ahead of you, and many obstacles will rise up before you. Only at that time will you have begun to tread the path of those who come with a mission. At the present time you are still unknown, and you are still smoothing the way for your mission and getting yourselves ready for the necessary struggle and campaign—the ignorance of the people as to what constitutes true Islam will stand as an obstacle in your way, and you will find among the clerical classes and the religious establishment those who will regard your understanding of Islam as outlandish, and censure your campaign on that account. Chiefs, leaders, and men of rank and authority will hate you, all governments will rise as one against you, and every government will try to set limits on your activities and to put impediments in your way. The spoliators will use every pretext to oppose you, and to extinguish the light of your mission. For that end they will invoke the aid of weak governments and a weak morality, and of the hands stretched out to them in beggary and toward you in malignity and hostility. (They will all stir up around your mission the dust of suspicion and unjust accusations, and they will try to endow it with every possible defect and to display it before the people in the most repugnant possible guise, relying on their power and authority and fortified by their wealth and influence. "They desire to extinguish God's light with their mouths, but God will perfect His light though the unbelievers be averse to it" [Q.61: 68].) Without a doubt, you will then experience trials and tribulations, you will be imprisoned, arrested, transported, and persecuted, and your goods will be confiscated, your employments suspended, and your homes searched. This period of trial may last a long time: "Do men imagine that they will be left to say: 'We believe,' and that they will not be put to the test?" [Q.29: 2]. But God has promised you afterwards the triumph of those who have striven and the reward of those who work for the good: "O ye who believe, shall I show you a commerce that will save you from a painful chastisement? ... Then we sustained those who believed against their enemy, and they became victorious" [Q.61: 10 and 14]. Are you resolved to be God's helpers? [....]

An Exhortation

Muslim Brethren, listen!

Through these words I wished to present your ideology to your close scrutiny, for it is possible that critical times await us, and that communication between me and you will be cut off for a while so that I may not be able to speak or write to you. Therefore, I advise you to ponder these words carefully, to learn them by heart if you can, and to give them your whole-hearted acceptance. For behind every word lie manifold meanings.

Brethren, you are not a benevolent organization, nor a political party, nor a local association with strictly limited aims. Rather you are a new spirit making its way into the heart of this nation and revivifying it through the Qur'an; a new light dawning and scattering the darkness of materialism through the knowledge of God; a resounding voice rising and echoing the message of the Apostle (May God bless and save him!). It is simply the truth, and no exaggeration that you know that you are bearing the burden after the rest of mankind has shunted it off. If someone should ask you: To what end is your appeal made? say: We are calling you to Islam, which was brought by Mohammad (May God bless and save him!):

government is part of it, and freedom is one of its religious duties. If someone should say to you: This is politics! say: This is Islam, and we do not recognize such divisions. If someone should say to you: You are agents of revolution! say: We are agents of the truth and of peace in which we believe and which we exalt. If you rise up against us and offer hindrance to our message, God has given us permission to defend ourselves, and you will be unjust rebels. If someone should say to you: You are asking for the help of individuals and associations! say: "We believe in God alone, and reject that which you were associating with Him." And if they persist in their hostility, say: "Peace be unto you! We have no desire for the ignorant" [Q.28: 55].

Duties

Brethren,

We believe in God, exult in the knowledge of Him, rely upon Him and lean upon Him. Fear no one but Him, stand in awe of no other than Him. Perform His commandments and shun what He has forbidden.

Model yourselves on the virtues and cleave to the perfections. Be strong in your morality and mighty through the might which God has given to the believers, and through the nobility of the sincerely pious.

Apply yourselves to the Qur'an, and study it together assiduously, and devote yourselves to the Pure Life of the Prophet, taking counsel from it. Be active workers rather than wranglers, for when God bestows His guidance on a people He inspires them to work. And people do not go astray after receiving guidance, except when disputation becomes the vogue among them.

Love one another, and hold fast zealously to your union, for this is the secret of your strength and the buttress of your success. Stand fast until God judges justly between you and your people, for He is the best of Judges.

Listen, and obey your leaders both in duress and comfort, in good times and bad, for this is the token of your conviction and the bond of solidarity among you. Finally, look forward to God's aid and His support. The occasion will come, without a doubt: "And then the believers will rejoice in God's aid. He aids whom he will, and He is the Mighty, the Merciful" [Q.30:4].

May God grant us and you success in what He loves and approves, and may he conduct us and you along the paths of the good who are rightly guided; may He give us to live the life of the glorious and fortunate, and give us to die the death of the martyrs who have striven in jihad. For He is the best of Masters, and the best of Defenders.

SOURCE: *Five Tracts of Hasan al-Banna (1906–1949): A Selection from the Majmu'at Rasa'il al-Imam al-Shahid Hasan al-Banna*, translated and annotated by Charles Wendell (Berkeley: University of California Press, 1978), 31–37. Copyright © University of California Press. Reprinted with permission. Original Arabic source: *Majmu'at Rasail al-Imam al-Shahid Hasan al-Banna* (Cairo: Dar al-Kutub, n.d.).

IN HISTORY

Hasan al-Banna's "Letter to a Muslim Student" Abroad (1935)

"Dearest brother, what Allah has made *Haram* (unlawful) for us, those people consider it as *Halal* (lawful) for them. Hence, when they commit a *Haram* (unlawful) act, they will neither feel ashamed nor will they refrain from perpetuating it. You should neither agree with their whims nor mix with them in their sins. Otherwise, you will not be relieved from having to answer before Allah (swt) and it will not hold as an excuse on the Day of Judgment.

Do not take their girls for company, and do not let there develop between you and them, any special friendship or any emotional relationship. If this kind of socializing is a sin for other than you, then it is a sin twice as great for you—and you know well the meaning of this.

Although you are known to us as one that is trustworthy and decent, I have mentioned this to you, to caution you against the downfalls of sins so that your feet may never slip. And in your chastity let there be content and in your dignity let there be adequacy.

As for alcohol, do not approach it. And do not use the climate as an excuse, because when Allah made it *Haram* (unlawful), He had full knowledge about all types of climate but did not exclude one country from another from this prohibition. Allah (swt) made it forbidden with neither doubt nor exception."

SOURCE: Imam Hasan al-Banna, *Letter to a Muslim Student* (Leicester, UK: The Islamic Foundation, 1995), 24.

CONTEXT AND ANALYSIS

In 1932 Hasan al-Banna moved the Muslim Brotherhood's headquarters from Isma'iliyya to Cairo. In order to attract people into the movement he resorted to "methods of propaganda" that included "publications, journals, newspapers, articles, plays, film, radio broadcasting," all of which, in al-Banna's words, "have made it easy to influence the minds of mankind, women as well as men, in their homes, places of business, factories and fields." Al-Banna established Rover Scouts for the country's young Muslim males so as to instill in them the "ethos of *futuwwa* (noble manliness, chivalry, bravery, courage, and perseverance)." By the mid-1940s the Muslim Brotherhood was reputed to have half a million members and supporters throughout Egypt. Most Muslim Brothers were *effendis*, members of the modernizing middle class who were employed as civil servants and teachers and wore the tarbush (fez) and European-style trousers and jackets.

Organizationally, the Brotherhood was in the late 1930s and 1940s close to the conservative, populist, and secular nationalist groups that then operated in Egypt, including the proto-fascistic Young Egypt and the more respectable Wafd Party. Like these other groups, it had a hierarchical command structure capable of mobilizing the street against political opponents. Unlike other political groups, however, al-Banna understood that a long period of preparation was necessary before political power could be attained. He believed that ideological "acquaintance" and organizational" "formation" should precede the "execution" of the Brotherhood's reformist vision.

The Brotherhood's political involvements reflected its overall gradualist approach. Although al-Banna denied the legitimacy of individual nation-states for compromising the unity of the *umma*, he was nevertheless always prepared to work though the established channels of the state. Beginning in 1933 he directed a number of "messages" (*rasa'il*) to the Palace, the most notable being a 1936 missive to the recently crowned King Faruq, enjoining him to stand behind the Brotherhood's reformist program. By pulling the Palace into its orbit, the Brotherhood hoped to supplant the British as the power behind the throne. For its part, the Palace tended to encourage the Brotherhood's forays into street politics, viewing the movement as a valuable counterweight to the anti-monarchical ambitions of the Wafd. The Brotherhood also attempted to enhance its influence through the electoral process. In the campaign leading up to the 1941 elections, al-Banna ran for a seat in the district of Isma'iliyya but was persuaded by the Prime Minister Mustafa Nahhas to withdraw in return for specific social reforms, including the prohibition of alcohol and prostitution. Brotherhood candidates also participated in the 1945 elections but lost in an electoral process believed to have been the most obviously dishonest held in Egypt. The inability of the Muslim Brotherhood to gain political influence through legal channels contributed to the turn taken by some of its members in the mid- and late-1940s to the tactics of assassination and terrorism. In 1949, Egyptian political police assassinated al-Banna in retaliation for the earlier killing of Egypt's Prime Minister, Nuqrashi Pasha, by the Brotherhood's secret militant wing.

In the selection above, Hasan al-Banna spells out his basic philosophy. His audience in the document is the rank and file of the growing movement, which was at the time of writing only beginning to make its mark ("at the present time you are still unknown"). He urges the Brothers to be steadfast in their devotion to the cause and to prepare for persecution and resistance from the Westernized sectors of Egyptian society. Al-Banna is explicit as to his goals: Egypt's liberation from foreign rule and the creation in Egypt of a polity based upon scriptural principles. Notice that al-Banna does not define the Muslim Brotherhood as a "political party," or "local association," or as a charitable organization. Rather, he says, the Brotherhood transcends the limited aims and factional disputes of the other politically-oriented organizations as a unifying spirit of community rebirth. In formulating his ideas, al-Banna was eager to engage in a new and fresh understanding of the Qur'an and the hadith of the Prophet that was relevant to the creation of a just public order in the contemporary age. Such an approach was in line with that of Islamic modernists like Muhammad 'Abduh.

However, al-Banna differed from the Islamic modernists in his emphasis on jihad, struggle, and work. In the words of Richard Mitchell whose work on the Muslim Brotherhood remains authoritative, this "preference for 'deed' over 'idea' was demonstrated in preference for the word 'programme' (*minhaj*) as against 'ideology' (*fikra*) to describe what the Society believed" (Mitchell, *The Society of the Muslim Brothers*, 326).

FURTHER READINGS

Commins, David. "Hasan al-Banna (1906–1949)," in Ali Rahnema (ed.), *Pioneers of Islamic Revival* (London: Zed Press, 1994).

Harris, Christina Phelps. *Nationalism and Revolution in Egypt: The Role of the Muslim Brotherhood* (Stanford, CA: Hoover Institute on War, Revolution, and Peace, 1964).

Heyworth-Dunne, J. *Religious and Political Trends in Modern Egypt* (Washington, DC: Author, 1950).

Husayni, I. M. *The Moslem Brethren: The Greatest of Modern Islamic Movements*, trans. J. F. Brown and J. Racy (Beirut: Khayat's College Book Cooperative, 1956).

Lia, Brynjar. *The Society of the Muslim Brothers in Egypt: The Rise of an Islamic Movement, 1928–1942* (Reading, UK: Ithaca, 1998).

Mitchell, Richard P. *The Society of the Muslim Brothers* (New York: Oxford University Press, 1993 [1969]).

The Need for Islamic Leadership

- *Document*: Selection from Sayyid Abu A'la Maududi's *The Islamic Movement: Dynamics of Values, Power and Change*, edited by Khurram Murad.
- *Date*: The original text was delivered on April 21, 1945 at the First All India Conference of the Jama'at-e Islami.
- *Where*: Pathankot, Punjab, India.
- *Significance*: The document, originally written in Urdu by one of the most important pioneers of Islamism, addresses the importance of Islamic leadership, the moral nature of power, and the link between faith and organized struggle (jihad).

DOCUMENT

Power and Society

It is not difficult to see, even with little insight, that the factors which determine human advance or decline depend largely on the nature and role of those who exercise control over the sources of power and direct the affairs of society.

To take an example: a train will move in the direction the driver intends it to go. The passengers are in his hands. They will have to go in whatever direction the train goes. If they want to go in some other direction, they will have to change either the train or the driver. In the same way, human civilization travels in the same direction determined by the people who control the centers of power.

It is clear that mankind can hardly resist moving along the road shown by those who lead, if only by virtue of the fact that leaders control all resources, hold the reins of power and possess the means of shaping and molding minds and behavior. They have the power to influence individuals as well as social systems and moral values.

If power and leadership are vested in God-fearing people, society moves along the right line, and even the wicked have to follow certain rules. Good flourishes, and evils, if not altogether eradicated, are contained.

Conversely, if leadership is in the hands of those who have turned away from God, the lifestyle of that society drifts towards rebellion against God, towards man's exploitation by man and towards moral degeneration and cultural pollution. This, in turn, leads to a general corruption of ideas, affecting the arts and sciences, politics and social economy, culture, ethics and behavior, law and justice.

In such circumstances, evil flourishes and good is starved of the conditions it needs to take root and grow. And the virtuous find themselves swimming against the tide of an evil societal system. All their energies go into resistance rather than, as they would want, into the positive creation of a new order of society. Consider an individual in a crowd. He needs no effort to move along with it, but should he decide to move against it, he can hardly walk even a few steps; more likely the crowd would push him much further in the opposite direction.

These are not just theoretical generalizations. History bears them out. In our own country, attitudes, values and standards of behavior have changed radically over the last century. Everything is in flux and the question is: What, in the last analysis, is the origin of this transformation? The answer, surely, is leadership.

An objective appraisal of this period of our history shows that everything began to change with the change of leadership. The powers that came to rule over this country have succeeded in transforming both individual and society according to their own wishes. Is it not a fact that even the descendants of the very persons who yesterday led the resistance against those powers are today adrift in the current of the times and that the change that had overtaken the rest of the society has now penetrated even into their homes? Is it not a fact that among the descendants of the most pious and revered religious leaders have appeared those who even doubt the existence of God, of revelation and of prophethood? Changes in leadership and society have metamorphosed the entire lifestyle of a people.

In view of this evidence, it is difficult to accept that the decisive factor in human affairs is leadership—that is, who controls the sources and organs of power in a society?

This is not peculiar to the present; it has always been so. "The people follow the ways of their rulers" is a very old saying. That is why, according to Hadith, the responsibility for the advance or decline of a people rests on their learned men and rulers.

The Main Objective of Islam

Islam desires, above all, that people should commit themselves entirely to God's Truth and that they should serve and worship only God. Similarly, it desires that the law of God should become the law by which people lead their lives. It demands, too, that injustice be eradicated, that those evils be wiped out which incur God's anger and that those virtues and social values be fostered which are liked by God.

These aims cannot be realized so long as power and leadership in society are in the hands of disbelieving rulers gone astray, and the followers of Islam confine themselves to worship rites, that too depending on the often arbitrary patronage and support of those very rulers. Only when power in society is in the hands of the Believers and the righteous, can the objectives of Islam be realized. It is therefore the primary duty of all those who aspire to please God to launch an organized struggle, sparing neither life nor property, for this purpose. The importance of securing power for the righteous is so fundamental that, neglecting this struggle, one has no means left to please God.

Consider, why the Qur'an and the Hadith put so much emphasis on the necessity to establish a community (Jama'at) based on submission to the Divine will, on the duty to hear and obey—so much so that, if anyone rebels against such a community, it is incumbent on all Muslims to fight him even though he may profess belief in the unity of God and perform Prayers and observe Fasts.

The reason is that the establishment or preservation of a system of life based on Divine Guidance—the ultimate purpose of Islam—requires the good to possess collective organizational power; anyone who threatens to weaken that collectivity is guilty of a crime so serious that it cannot be expiated by the performance of Prayers nor the profession of God's unity.

Again, consider why it is that such importance is given to Jihad that the Qur'an condemns as hypocrites those who evade it? Jihad is but another name for the attempt to establish the divine order; the Qur'an therefore declares it to be a touchstone of belief. In other words, people who have faith in their hearts will neither succumb to domination by an evil system, nor begrudge giving their wealth and even their lives in the struggle to establish Islam. Those who show weakness in such situations cast doubt on the reality of their faith.

This is not meant to give a complete exposition of this matter, but what I have explained should be adequate to demonstrate that, from the standpoint of Islam, establishment of the leadership of the good is of central and fundamental importance. Those who profess faith in this religion cannot fulfill their duty merely by trying to pattern their lives on outward appearances. The nature of their faith requires them to concentrate all their efforts upon wresting leadership from unbelieving and corrupt men in order to entrust it to the righteous, and upon establishing and maintaining the way of life that has been ordained for the conduct of the world according to the will of God.

Because this end is unattainable without the highest degree of collective effort, there must exist a God-fearing community devoted to the sole purpose of establishing and maintaining the sovereignty of God on earth.

Even if there were only one man of faith on earth, it would not be right for him, on the plea of being isolated and powerless, to resign himself to the system of evil. Nor would it be right for him to search for legal excuses in the Shari'a (Islamic code of life) to try to justify an isolated, truncated religious existence under the domination of *Kufr* (disbelief in God).

On the contrary, the only right course for him would lie in calling all servants of God to the way of God.

If no one should respond to his call, it is nevertheless a hundred thousand times better than that he pursues the straight path and continues to call the people to God than that he succumbs to the promptings of evil, plays to the tunes of misguided persons and follows the ways of God's rebels. And, even if a few respond, he should immediately launch a movement to achieve the objective I have mentioned.

This, friends, is the conclusion of whatever little knowledge I have and whatever understanding of the Qur'an and Hadith I have attained. This is the main demand that the Qur'an makes upon you. This has been the life mission of all the prophets. I am open to be convinced against this, but only in the light of the Book of God and the Sunna of His Messenger.

SOURCE: Sayyid Abu A'la Maududi, *The Islamic Movement: Dynamics of Values, Power and Change*, ed. Khurram Murad (London: The Islamic Foundation, KUBE Publishing, 1984), 77–81. Courtesy of KUBE Publishing, Ltd. The original Urdu: *Tehrik Islami Ki Akhlaq Bunyadain*.

CONTEXT AND ANALYSIS

Maulana Sayyid 'Abu A'la Maududi (1903–1979) was born into an old notable family of Delhi, which had been associated with the Mughal court and later served the Nizams of Hyderabad. Growing up, Maududi shared the distress of many of his coreligionists at the decline of Muslim fortunes over the Indian Subcontinent that followed the suppression of the Great Mutiny in 1857. In the Muslim perspective, British rule in India had not only ended Muslim supremacy, it also created the opportunity for the Hindu majority of the country to assert its influence over civil and even political affairs. Maududi understood that unless Muslims responded effectively to the growing Hindu challenge, Muslims would be relegated to a position of inferiority in the independent Indian state for which both Hindus and Muslims at the time were struggling. Over the 1920s and 1930s, Maududi employed his talents as a journalist to urge Muslims to strengthen their community by returning to the pristine faith of the Prophet and the early generations of Muslims. He said Muslims must remove the cultural accretions that had crept into Islam as a result of the Muslims' close proximity with Hindus over the centuries. Equally, Muslims must free their souls from the damaging effects of Western materialism. Maududi's aim was to restore Islam as the politically and culturally dominant civilization on the Subcontinent.

Toward this goal, in 1941 he founded an organization called Jama'at-e Islami, which he conceived as the vanguard of the Islamic movement in India. Maududi was elected its first leader. Following the example of the Prophet, the Jama'at-e Islami withdrew from the larger society, lest the purity of its message be corrupted, and set up its base at the small city of Pathankot in the West Punjab.

The agenda of the Jama'at-e Islami was similar to that of the slightly older Muslim Brotherhood in Egypt, except that rather than draw its support from the masses, the Jama'at intentionally targeted the educated middle and upper classes of Muslim Indian society. Initially, Maududi argued against the creation of a geographically separate Muslim state in India. In Maududi's view, such a state, although created for Muslims, would necessarily bear the secular imprint of its Muslim League sponsors. Moreover, such a state would nullify the dream of Islamic Empire by severely circumscribing the territory of Muslims. However, after Pakistan was created in 1947, Maududi reconciled himself to the fact of its existence. Henceforth, he redirected the energies of the Jama'at-e Islami toward the islamization of the new state, which, as he had predicated, the Muslim League determined should be secular, rather than Islamic in nature. This he did peacefully by participating in Pakistan's political system. Over the course of his career, Maududi decried the tactics of radical opposition and militancy adopted by some other Islamist groups.

In his books and pamphlets, numbering over one hundred, including a six-volume commentary on the Qur'an, Maududi laid out an elaborate ideological vision. He argued that Islam was as much an ideology as a religion and that the main division in the world was between Islam and disbelief (*kufr*). He criticized capitalism for its secularism and association with Western imperialism, and communism and socialism for their atheism and their worship of society over God. In the above selection, Maududi emphasizes the importance of sound, Islamic leadership in taking over the institutions of the state and in Islamizing the society. What is important, in Maududi's view, is that virtuous, effective Muslim leaders—namely, leaders of the Jama'at-e Islami—be in charge. Only then would the socioeconomic maladies and identity crisis affecting the country be cured and the Muslims of the Subcontinent become empowered in relation to the British and the Hindu majority population. Some scholars have pointed to the influence of the totalitarian movements in Italy, the Soviet Union, and Germany on Maududi's concept of "revolution from above."

Maududi's writings became available in Arabic translation in the 1950s. They exercised an important influence on Sayyid Qutb (1906–1966), the chief theoretician of Egypt's Muslim Brotherhood in the years following Hasan al-Banna's assassination.

IN HISTORY

Abul Hasan Ali Nadwi (India): "Universal Sway of Materialism"

"It is a tragic fact of modern life that there exists no community worth the name in Europe, Asia, Africa, or America genuinely opposed to the pagan philosophy of materialism. The nations like the Germans in Europe or the Japanese or Indians in Asia, are all becoming increasingly convinced of the merits of materialism. The ideological differences that one encounters in the modern world are merely the off-shoots of an all-out struggle for political supremacy. They have no relation to moral or spiritual convictions. It is simply too much for the pride of a powerful nation that another should be in command of the international scene. No nation feels less inclined to address itself to the moral regeneration of humanity should the opportunity ever come its way....

What is to be regretted is that the traditional enemy of Paganism, the Muslim, too, has become its ally and is serving as its devoted camp-follower in many parts of the world. What better proof of the universal triumph of Paganism can there be that Muslims should regard those countries as their friends and well-wishers who are the leaders of the Pagan movement in the present age? The modern Muslim has totally given up the idea of leadership; he has lost faith in himself."

SOURCE: Abul Hasan Ali Nadwi, *Islam and the World* (Lucknow: Academy of Islamic Research and Publications, 1967 [1959]), 182–83.

FURTHER READINGS

Adams, Charles J. "Maududi and the Islamic State," in John L. Esposito (ed.), *Voices of Resurgent Islam* (New York: Oxford University Press, 1983), 99–103.

Ahmad, Mumtaz. "Islamic Fundamentalism in South Asia: The Jamaat-i-Islami and the Tablighi Jamaat," in Martin Marty and Scott Appleby (eds.), *Fundamentalisms Observed* (Chicago: University of Chicago Press, 1991), 457–530.

Ahmed, Rafiuddin. "Redefining Muslim Identity in South Asia: The Transformation of Jama 'at-i Islami," in Martin Marty and Scott Appleby (eds.), *Accounting for Fundamentalisms: The Dynamic Character of Movements* (Chicago: University of Chicago Press, 1994), 669–705.

Hasan, Masudul. *Sayyid Abul A'ala Maududi and His Thought* (Lahore: Islamic Publications, 1984).

McDonough, Sheila. *Muslim Ethics and Modernity: A Comparative Study of the Ethical Thought of Sayyid Ahmad Khan and Mawlana Maududi* (Waterloo, Canada: Wilfred Laurier University Press, 1984).

Nasr, Seyyed Vali Reza. *The Vanguard of the Islamic Revolution: The Jama'at-i Islami of Pakistan* (Berkeley: University of California Press, 1994).

Nasr, Sayyed Vali Reza. *Maududi and the Making of Islamic Revivalism* (New York: Oxford University Press, 1996).

The Primacy of the Shari'a

- **Document**: Interview with 'Umar al-Talmisani, third Supreme Guide of Egypt's Muslim Brotherhood (1973–1986). Translated from the Arabic by Mohammed Zakaria.
- **Date**: mid-1980s.
- **Where**: Cairo, Egypt.
- **Significance**: Al-Talmisani's interview reflects the thinking of the reconstituted Muslim Brotherhood in the 1980s, when it assumed an increasingly important and visible role in Egypt's social and political life. The interview draws attention to the Muslim Brotherhood's strong affirmation that Islam is a comprehensive ideology and system defined in adherence to Islamic law (Shari'a).

DOCUMENT

In your opinion, how important and necessary is it to apply Islamic Shari'a in Egypt?

When you understand that the Muslim considers his religion to be his constitution, and the Qur'an the source that determines the philosophy of his existence, sketching out his relationship with God, his inner self, his family, his nation, and the world—after you know these things you will realize that the absence of Islamic Shari'a is the source of the problem, rather than its cause. When we ask the state to apply Shari'a, we mean that it should be applied completely, not only the mandated punishments. Although these punishments are important, they are only part of Islam. We demand rather that Islam should dominate all the aspects of our lives and that people should commit themselves to Islam not only in the courts but in their thoughts, on the street, in schools, and in their houses. Because Islam—as I said—is a way of living that should direct each Muslim if he wants to correct his path in life.

[....]

Do you agree with the methods of other Islamic groups? What is your method in reforming the Egyptian society?

All Islamic individuals and groups agree on one main goal: Making Islamic rules and values dominant in our society. On our side we ask God to help us and other groups achieve this purpose. It is not a shame on us or them to disagree in the ways we should carry this mission—this is beyond doubt. As you know, there are no Islamic groups in the strictly legal sense. They are not officially recognized and protected by the state. All the differences among the groups that flow to the surface stem from the lack of freedom for people to form groups and parties that may function in an official, public, and organized way. We, the Muslim Brotherhood, have asked for the right to be granted this right. We have even filed a case before the high administrative court that our movement be restored. We have been persecuted for more than three decades.

Egypt is currently facing many problems: economic, political, and social. Do you think that under these conditions Egypt ought to implement Islamic Shari'a now?

I am afraid that your question is premised on the false notion that the Islamic Shari'a primarily concerns itself with punishments. If you understand Islam in its broad context, if you learn about specific Islamic stipulations that govern societies, you will become aware that Islam is a cure for the aforementioned problems. For this reason, Islam needs to be dominant. The Application of Islamic rules will release all of the creative energies in the minds and the hearts of the people, so that society may be reformed and its problems fixed. If the Islamic Shar'ia were combined with doctrinal sincerity in the hearts of the people, the result would be an honest society, one in which an adulterer would go to the Prophet to ask him to apply the Islamic ruling on adultery, which requires the death of the adulterous party.

Observe the extent of the bond between Islamic laws and the Islamic creed. This is how to construct a society in which a criminal is not afraid of God's judgment, but rather goes freely to the ruler so that he may be purified of his crime. At the same time, the governor will find himself bound to apply God's rule, which determines the degree of his authority, so he cannot spy on his people and know their secrets and degrade them even if they are guilty....

Look at how Islam is able to shape its people so that obedience to the law becomes an act of worship, and how it informs the ruler's conscience so that he and other authorities bow their heads to justice, freedom, and dignity on behalf of the people. All of these outcomes are the result of applying Islam.

I believe that it is the role of the Muslim Brotherhood to establish Islamic consciousness in the society.

If you believe that Egypt is not ready for a full application for Islamic Shari'a in the way other Islamic groups are demanding, what is your working plan and how do you intend to carry your vision as an Islamic organization?

Applying Islamic Shari'a in its broad context is something upon which no one disagrees. Egypt and other Islamic countries are capable of applying Islamic Shari'a instantly. In fact, Muslims are asking their governments to do precisely that. If you think that we cannot cut off the hand of a thief due to current economic conditions that have produced large numbers of poor people, you should know that this is a wrong view of point, because provisions for not cutting the hand of a thief are also provided by the Shari'a.

As for the Muslim Brotherhood's plans if it were to regain fully the influence we once had, know that it aims to put forward the same plan that it has had since it was established fifty-five years ago: The effort to raise Muslims who love their religion, bind themselves to its values, and spread mercy and goodness whenever they might be.

You saw Sudan's previous president al-Numayri attempt to impose Shari'a in Sudan, an experiment that looks as though it failed. What can Egypt learn from this experiment?

First, it must be understood that al-Numayri failed the people of Sudan, not because he applied Shari'a, but because of the corruption that surrounded his regime. The people of

Sudan still want to apply Shari'a. Second, the dominance of Islam and its rules and values is not established by merely setting Islamic punishment laws; Islam is bigger than that, as I mentioned previously. Third, the best person to apply Islamic Shari'a, is a governor bound by conscience and family to Islam. Fourth, you cannot use the Shari'a in order to pressure Muslims or to fool them, or else you will face the same fate as al-Numayri.

As for our national brothers, the Coptic Christians, I am sure—and I believe that many of them would also agree—that applying Islamic Shari'a would not harm them in any way, although it might increase the distance between us. It is a fact that our religion states that we should show love and passion for them. As the Qur'an states: "… and you will find nearest in love to the believers those who say, 'we are Christians.' Because among these (people) are men devoted to learning and men who have given up the world, and they are not haughty."

In your view, what does the imposition of Islamic Shari'a mean, and how would it variously affect Egypt?

Achieving the dominance of Islamic laws and rules in Egypt will restore the spirit of the Egyptian society. It is the starting point to solve all of the problems that Egypt is facing on a solid and correct basis. We do realize that there are internal and external forces that are against the call to Islam, due to fear of the justice of Islam, or to ignorance of the nature of Islamic message, or to historic hatred towards the faith. It is our hope that there are no conspiracies to deform or redirect the correct application of the Shari'a. For I say: you cannot deform the Shari'a, for it is stable in the hearts and minds of Muslims. Anyone who seeks such a thing will lose personally and will lose the respect of the nation.

How will the relations between Egypt and Israel be affected by the application of the Shari'a? Will you consider breaking the peace treaty between the two countries?

The relationship between Egypt and Israel following the peace treaty is conditioned by decades of war, hatred, and hostility that come from the Israeli side. Israel has attacked the Palestinian people, Syrian and Lebanese lands, and also Egyptian territory. It goes against both reason and any concept of right, even from a nationalist perspective, that we should establish a bond with them.

If we decided to look at the situation from the Islamic point of view, we see that Islam has set general laws concerning international relations. Islam granted Jews an opening to Muslim minds and hearts. For God says: "Allah does not forbid you to act justly and kindly with those (for friendship) who do not fight with you regarding (your) faith (of Islam), and do not drive you out of your homes. Verily, Allah loves those who practice quality and justice. Allah only forbids you, those (for friendship) who fight against you regarding (your) faith (of Islam), and driving you out, from turning to them (for friendship and protection). It is those who turn towards them that do wrong." So God does not ban us from showing love and compassion to Jews if they do not fight us in our religion and if they do not eject us out of our homes. But if they do these things, how can one show them any goodness? It is ironic that if you defend yourself against them, you are considered to be against peace! American politicians helped the Jews to eject us from our lands and interfere with our sacred holy places. What do you expect of us? Most Arab leaders view America as the only power able to broker peace. Americans should review their actions according to the Qur'anic verses I have just presented.

I hope that America, Europe, East, and West will learn how Muslims think, and then they might have different solutions on how to stop wars.

SOURCE: Rifa'at Sayyid Ahmad (ed.), *The Militant Prophet: The Rejectionists*, vol. 1 [in Arabic] (London: Ri'ad al-Ra'is Books, 1991), 199–202.

CONTEXT AND ANALYSIS

Always existing on the fringes of legality, Egypt's Muslim Brotherhood has experienced periods of tolerance interspersed with episodic persecutions at the hands of the state. The most severe and damaging of these persecutions occurred in 1954 and again in 1965 when members were subjected to massive arrests for alleged conspiracies against the secular government of Egyptian president Jamal 'Abd al-Nasser. However, Anwar Sadat, who succeeded 'Abd al-Nasser to the presidency in 1970, set free many of the Brothers from jail and allowed them once again to present their views publicly, although the Muslim Brotherhood remained a banned organization. Sadat's decision to release the Brothers was tied to his plan to reverse the course of 'Abd al-Nasser's revolution. In particular, he aimed to salvage Egypt's failing economy by opening the country to outside capitalist investment, and by putting an end to its on-going and expensive war with Israel. In allowing the Islamists to reorganize, Sadat hoped that they might be a counterweight to the still-strong Nasserists and socialists who resisted the about-face of the Egyptian Revolution. Scholars often refer to the reconstituted movement as the "neo-Muslim Brotherhood."

Although a majority of the Brothers welcomed the breathing space provided by the regime, some were not satisfied. They pointed to Sadat's refusal to make the Qur'an the principle source of Egyptian law, the inequities of his economic policies, and his 1977 peace treaty with Israel. Hardened by their experience in prison, and influenced by the radical Islamist ideas of Sayyid Qutb, they turned to militancy. In 1981 a group calling itself "Islamic Jihad" assassinated Sadat during the regime's commemoration of Egypt's semi-successful war against Israel in 1973.

However, the majority of Muslim Brothers eschewed violence and continued the tactics of advocacy and preaching practiced by Hasan al-Banna. Since the early 1970s, the leadership of the reconstituted Brotherhood was made up of men from the first generation of Islamists. Among them was 'Umar al-Talmisani (1904–1986), a former bureaucrat in Egypt's Finance Ministry who was elevated to the post of Supreme Guide in 1973. Buoyed by the current of religiosity sweeping Egypt in the 1970s and 1980s, the Brotherhood under al-Talmisani's leadership published magazines, including the influential journal al-Da'wa (The Call) and organized social services and Islamic schools. Through these services, the Brotherhood hoped to win the hearts and minds of the people. The Brotherhood's strategy of moderation and gradualism continued into the era of Husni Mubarak, Anwar Sadat's successor to the presidency. Banned from contesting elections outright, al-Talmisani's Brotherhood created alliances with legal political parties in 1984 and in 1987, and by means of those parties was able to become the largest single opposition group in the Egyptian parliament. During al-Talmisani's tenure as Supreme Guide, the Brotherhood worked to improve its relations with the Copts, Egypt's indigenous Christian population. The Brotherhood's nonviolent methods gained it relative peace. While the Mubarak regime came down hard on the militants, it allowed the movement considerable room to maneuver within the context of society, if not the state.

Originally the Muslim Brothers favored a rigid interpretation of the Shari'a, which followed in strict fashion the teachings of the *Salaf*, the exemplary first generations of Muslims. By the 1980s, however, many Muslim Brothers were insisting that Islamic law be adapted in a more liberal manner to the needs of contemporary society. As the passage above indicates, 'Umar al-Talmisani believed that such a body of law, adopted in its entirety, would guarantee fair economic practice, integrity in public affairs, and a foreign policy for Egypt that prioritized the interests of the worldwide community of Muslims. Note that al-Talmisani was against Egypt's normalization of relations with Israel. In fact, during the 1978 peace talks between Egypt and Israel, al-Talmisani used the pages of *al-Da'wa* to argue that Israel was part of *Dar al-Harb*, "the domain of war," and thus a deserving target of jihad.

In the passage, al-Talmisani makes reference to Sudan, where President Ja'far Numayri began a program of immediate and strict implementation of Islamic law in 1983. Many

Sudanese Islamic leaders criticized the program for selectively focusing on ordinances and punishments rather than implement the Shari'a as a whole. Al-Talmisani shared the concern of these critics.

The Muslim Brotherhood continues to exert a powerful influence among the disaffected, modern-educated middle class of Egypt and the other Arabic-speaking countries in which branches of the movement are present, such as Jordan.

FURTHER READINGS

Ajami, Fouad. *The Arab Predicament* (Cambridge: Cambridge University Press, 1999 [1981]).

Auda, Gehad. "The 'Normalization' of the Islamic Movement in Egypt from the 1970s to the Early 1990s," in Martin E. Marty and R. Scott Appleby (eds.), *Accounting for Fundamentalisms: The Dynamic Character of Movements* (Chicago: University of Chicago Press, 1994), 374–412.

Baker, Raymond. *Islam without Fear: Egypt and the New Islamists* (Cambridge, MA: Harvard University Press, 2003).

Kepel, Gilles. *Muslim Extremism in Egypt: The Prophet and the Pharaoh*, trans. Jon Rothschild (Berkeley: University of California Press, 1982).

Rosefsky, Carrie. *Mobilizing Islam: Religion, Activism, and Political Change in Egypt* (New York: Columbia University Press, 2002).

Sullivan, Dennis J., and Sana Abed-Kotob. *Islam in Contemporary Egypt: Civil Society vs. the State* (Boulder, CO: Lynne Rienner, 1999).

Voll, John O. "Fundamentalism in the Sunni Arab World: Egypt and the Sudan," in Martin E. Marty and R. Scott Appleby (eds.), *Fundamentalisms Observed* (Chicago: University of Chicago Press, 1991), 345–402.

Warburg, Gabriel R. and Uri M. Kupferschmidt (eds.), *Islam, Nationalism, and Radicalism in Egypt and the Sudan* (New York: Praeger, 1983).

From Arabism to Islamism

- *Document:* "From the Village to Zeitouna," the partial autobiography of Rashid al-Ghannushi, Islamist intellectual and leader of Tunisia's Islamic Tendency Movement (ITM).
- *Date:* Late 1980s (date uncertain).
- *Where:* Tunis, Tunisia.
- *Significance:* Rashid al-Ghannushi traces his transition from secular Arab nationalism to Islamism, a journey undertaken by a number of Arab intellectuals in the 1970s and 1980s.

DOCUMENT

Nasserism

Intellectually, I grew up as a Nasserist. Throughout much of the fifties and the sixties, Nasserism was the fashion that attracted my generation of Arabized Tunisians, and for good reasons. Soon after the independence of Tunisia, a conflict raged between the Arabists, who sought to preserve Tunisia's Arab identity and bolster its ties with its Arab brethren, and the Westernizers, who believed progress was possible only if Tunisia emulated and strengthened its ties with the West. Nasserism, which evolved in Egypt in 1952 and promised to achieve Arab unity and liberate Palestine, gave the Arabist trend in Tunisia an ideology and a moral support. The Arabists boasted that population-wise Egypt was the largest country in the Arab world and that it was, by virtue of its rich culture and "undeniable contribution throughout the history of Islam to the unity and strength of the *umma,*" the established leader of the Arab-Islamic trend. Hence, the Arabists were not viewed favorably by the authorities in Tunisia. In fact the bitter conflict between Bourguiba and Nasser was, at least partly, due to the fact that the former felt threatened in his own country by the support accorded to the latter by the Arabists in Tunisia. Following my graduation from high school, I discovered that like many Tunisians with an Arab education I stood no chance of entering a local university. French was the language of tuition in all local universities, and for a student to secure a place he or she would have had to come from a high school of French-language medium education. Graduates of Al-Zaytouna were in effect ostracized and those of them who were ambitious had no option but to leave home for one of the Arab countries in the Mashriq (East) in pursuit of further education.

I had only one option; to take up a teaching job at a primary school, which I did for two years. But I felt this was much less than I had hoped to achieve. After all, both of my older brothers had accomplished more; the eldest was a judge and the second eldest was a lawyer. Furthermore, I had always dreamed of going to the Mashriq, which constituted a spiritual refuge for the Tunisian Arabists in the face of the scorching wind that blew from the West and accomplished its objectives after independence through the instating of Bourguiba and his Francophone elite.

I increasingly loathed life in Tunisia and kept looking for an opportunity to leave the country. Since I arrived in the capital, I had been unhappy and restless. The events of the Algerian revolution between 1959 and 1962 had filled my mind and heart with detestation for colonialism and equally for the post-independence authority perceived as a continuation of the French rule.

In Egypt

In 1964, I enrolled with the Faculty of Agriculture at Cairo University. My choice of agriculture was motivated by the desire to acquire knowledge in this branch of science in order to alleviate the hardship endured by my family and fellow villagers whose agricultural methods were still primitive and laborious. I studied agriculture for three months prior to being forced to quit. The regimes in Cairo and Tunis had been engaged in talks aimed at improving relations. Eventually, the talks resulted in reconciling the differences between Nasser and Bourguiba. Upon the request of the Tunisian embassy in Cairo, the Egyptian authorities moved to expel from the country our group whom the Tunisian government referred to as 'the fugitives.' The incident was the first to shake my preconceived ideas about Nasserism as a pan-Arab unionist and anti-colonial movement and marked the beginning of my disenchantment with Arabism.

I thought of escaping to Albania. Perhaps I was influenced by the Arabic transmission of radio Tirana. Its anti-imperialist rhetoric might have impressed me as did before the anti-imperialist rhetoric of Nasserism. Just before reserving a seat on a plane bound for Tirana, I met at the ticketing office a compatriot student, who advised me not to go to Albania because 'it was a closed country.' He explained how bad the situation in that totalitarian state was and convinced me to change my destination. He encouraged me to go to Syria instead, and told me there were many friends there who could help. He also told me that in Syria I could still pursue my education and accomplish my ambition without having to throw myself into the unknown.

In Syria

Once in Syria, I decided to study philosophy instead of agriculture. In the sixties Syria was passing through a crisis. It was overwhelmed by the effects of ending its 31 months of unity with Egypt. I was not impressed by the Ba'th party. Still seemingly influenced by my former Nasserist background, and in spite of showing signs of disenchantment earlier in Egypt, I identified with the Syrian Nasserists, who campaigned for restoring unity between Egypt and Syria. During the period I spent in Damascus from 1964 to 1968, the Ba'th rule had still been in its early stage; it had not yet taken full control. Syria was still in the 'liberal age' in the sense that a reasonable margin of freedom, that was to be lost in later years, still existed. Although the country had no parliament at the time, the state had still not imposed itself completely on society. The Syrians utilized rather well the margin of freedom available to them. Students demonstrated, engaged in open debates and even clashed on campus over ideological or political differences.

Intellectual Debates

At Damascus University, I found myself in the midst of a raging intellectual battle. The nationalist trend was the most prominent. Conflict existed between the Nasserists and the Ba'thists. In the meantime, a conflict had been going on between the secularists and the Islamists. The Islamic trend had been making use of the mosque on campus, and was thus considered advantaged. The mosque played a major role; it acted as a center for the distribution of Islamic booklets and leaflets. The *khatib* (mosque orator) was professor Adib Salih, a prominent Islamic intellectual, a leading member of the Ikhwan (Muslim Brotherhood) in Syria and a senior Shari'a College lecturer at the University of Damascus. At the time he had been publishing a monthly periodical called *al-Hadara al-Islamiya* (Islamic Civilization). I was so impressed by this prestigious publication which remains unmatched by any other Islamic publication I had ever come across.

A strong debate had been taking place within the student community over the Israeli occupation of Palestine and over its ramifications. The debate focused mainly on how the Arabs could best resist the Zionist project. The Islamists insisted that the liberation of Palestine would only occur when Islam is adopted as a way of life, and therefore participating in an effort undertaken by an un-Islamic regime would be unthinkable. They questioned in particular the legitimacy of jihad under the leadership of the Ba'th Party. I felt inclined to disagree with them and considered their argument to be futile. As the prospect of war loomed in the summer of 1967, I joined demonstrations organized by the nationalists to demand the training and arming of students in order to defend Jerusalem, which was soon lost to the Israelis. The humiliating defeat of the Arabs in the six-day war of June 1967 was another tremor that shook the foundations of my Arabist leaning.

The attitude toward the West was another important topic of debate. The secularists considered Western progress, whether in the natural or social sciences, the ultimate accomplishment of humanity. They looked up to the West as a model. The Islamists on the other hand sought to highlight the imperfections of the Western civilization exposing its ills and prognosticating its downfall.

The Islamists would employ in criticizing the West some Western writings such as the work of Alexis Carrel, *Man: the Unknown*, the work of Oswald Spengler, *Decline of the West*, and the works of Toynbee, whose critique of the Western civilization impressed them most. The Islamists would in particular seek the authority of Western writings that predicted the collapse of the Western civilization to challenge the proponents of secularism within the nationalist trend. They used to refer to the writings of some dissident Communists, such as those of Arthur Koestler (1905–1983), the Hungarian-born British author and journalist. His book *The God that Failed*, which was first published in English in 1950 documenting his experience, disillusionment and eventually breaking with Communism, was translated into Arabic and published under the title of al-Sanam Allathi Hawa, meaning 'the idol that fell down.' The writings of Milovan Djilas, especially his book *The New Order*, were popular too. The Yugoslav politician was a lifelong friend of Tito and rose to a high position in the Yugoslav Government as a result of his wartime exploits as a partisan. However, he was discredited and imprisoned as a result of his outspoken criticism of the Communist system as practiced in Yugoslavia.

The Conversion

I remained loyal to Nasserism up to the second year of my stay in Damascus. The writings of Sati' al-Husri (1879–1968) was the Arabists' source of inspiration and were studied thoroughly by new recruits. Such writings did not provide me with any significant knowledge or with a supply of ammunition useful in the conflict that raged within university debate circles between Islamic and nationalist trends. I felt ill equipped in the fierce discussions I used to have with the members of the Islamic trend. I came to the conclusion that apart from language and history, Arab nationalism was nothing but a set of slogans and passions. The difference between one nationalist party and the other was simply the order in which these slogans were listed. While some chanted freedom-unity-socialism, others chanted socialism-freedom-unity. Let alone the fact that no clear definitions of such concepts were ever given and that no one bothered to investigate their philosophical origins or discuss the proposed strategies for their materialization. In this regard, my disenchantment with Arab nationalism may be attributed to the impression left on me by my Maghreb culture in which the terms 'Arab' and 'Muslim' were interchangeable, synonymous to be precise. My Syrian experience led me to believe that in the Middle East the concept of Arabism was often opposed to Islam. I had never felt or ever thought, by virtue of my Maghreb upbringing, that Arabism meant anything other than Islam. However, my presence within the nationalist movement exposed me to a position that clashed with religion. There was an alienation of religion from every activity within the party. I was shocked to discover that the dream I lived for, the dream of Arab nationalism, was an illusion.

I started searching for a camp that can accommodate both my Arabism and Islamic faith. My tour in search of an alternative to nationalism provided me with an opportunity to meet and learn from several prominent Islamic thinkers in the Syrian arena. Adib Salih, Shaykh al-Buti and Wahba al-Zuhayli were all lecturers at the Shari'ah College at Damascus University. Although I was not registered with the College, I developed an interest in attending, whenever I could, the lectures of these three scholars. I also made the acquaintance of Jawdat Sa'id who had been a member of the Ikhwan in Syria and was an outspoken critic of the political situation both in Syria and in the Arab region and then embraced Bennabi's rationalism.

The night of the 15th of June 1966 has been a turning point and a landmark in my life. That was the night I embraced the true Islam. That very night I shed two things off me: secular nationalism and traditional Islam. That night I embraced what I believed was the original Islam, Islam as revealed and not as shaped or distorted by history and tradition. That was the night I was overwhelmed by an immense surge of faith, love and admiration for this religion to which I pledged my life. On that night I was reborn, my heart was filled with the light of God, and my mind with the determination to review and reflect on all that which I had previously conceived.

I was invited by more than one organization, including the Ikhwan, to join in but I refrained. I thought that since I intended to return home, and not knowing what kind of Islamic activity I would find there upon returning, I deemed it inappropriate to commit myself and return to my country with an organizational affiliation. Nevertheless, I had acquainted himself with all sorts of trends, the Ikhwan, the Sufi orders, Hizb-ut-Tahrir Al-Islami and the Salafiyah.

SOURCE: http://www.ghannouchi.net/autobiography.htm

CONTEXT AND ANALYSIS

Islamist thinkers and activists were not, for the most part, born into Islamism. Rather, Islamism was a position that they adopted in response to circumstances and in contradistinction to the prevailing political ideologies of the day. A good many Islamists began their political careers in the 1950s and 1960s as Arab nationalists, attracted to the dream of Arab empowerment and unity preached by Jamal 'Abd al-Nasser in Egypt and by the Ba'thist ideologues in Syria and Iraq. Only after Arab nationalism faltered in the late 1960s and 1970s did these idealistic young men begin to gravitate to the "Islamic alternative." Yet their essential purpose remained constant. Despite the new appeal of scriptural authority, their primary concern remained to enhance the identity of the national community against the different and competing *alter ego* of the West. Arab nationalism had accomplished this purpose by reference to the linguistic,

---

IN HISTORY

Abdessalam Yassine, Founder of Morocco's Justice and Spirituality Movement

"Any action depends upon knowledge, and the success of any project is contingent upon a clear and comprehensive vision. That is even truer when such project aims to get our *umma* [the Muslim community worldwide] out of its backwardness-at once intellectual, moral, military, and as a civilization-in order to become a strong, united nation capable of fulfilling the mission that God assigned to it.

The coordination of the will and the intellect to implement a plan of action that seeks to fulfill the Promise of God [the advent of the second global Caliphate] and that follows the way drawn by the Qurān and the *sunna* is epitomized in a Qurānic word, *al-Minhāj* [the Method], that some call: program of education.

By speaking of the Method we think of how to enable our underdeveloped *umma* to recover and earn back its dignity. That can only be achieved through the education of a believing generation capable of building a distinguished Muslim civilization that defends the Divine Truth and that transmits the heavenly Message to mankind.

The Method that promises to re-establish the Caliphate as a system of government, according to the authentic *hadith* reported by Muslim and Imam Ahmad, is the only way that enables the Muslims to find the real meaning of the Message which they should personify and then transmit by exemplary conduct to the world at large. That will begin by educating the *mumin*, forming a community of *mumins*-the core of an Islamic society that will progressively supplant the society of *fitna* [secular disorder] in order to eventually establish the Islamic State."

SOURCE: http://www.yassine.net/en/Default.aspx?article=method_EN&m=1&sm=10

---

cultural, and ethnic identities of the Arabs. Now, they put forward Islam as the determining factor of individual and community identity. In so doing, they asserted that part of themselves, inherited from past generations, which allowed them to challenge the dominant order with dignity and conviction.

An example of an individual who turned from Arabism to Islamism is the Egyptian writer-jurist Tariq al-Bishri who presented his new thinking in the introduction to the third edition of his book, *The Political Movement in Egypt*. Whereas previously al-Bishri had distinguished the "endogenous" and the "exogenous" (i.e., the Arab World and the West), he now compared the "inherited" (Islamic culture) with the "imported" (Western cultural influences). Another example is Adel Husayn, the late Secretary of the Egyptian Labor Party whose newspaper *al-Sha'b* spoke for the Muslim Brotherhood. Eschewing the Marxist tinged nationalism that had marked him since his youth, Husyan came to regard Islamism as the new anti-imperialist creed in Egypt and the wider Islamic World.

The passage above presents the ideological journey of Rashid Ghannushi (b. 1941) the leader of Tunisia's Islamic Tendency Movement (ITM). As al-Ghannushi attests, Arab nationalism held for him and other Arabic-speaking youth the promise of upward mobility. There were few opportunities in Tunisia whose elite culture was francophone and which, under President Bourguiba, held apart from the other Arab countries. It was, he writes, only natural that he should have desired to travel to the Arab East whose culture had not been transformed by the West to the same degree as that of Tunisia and other North African states. Yet like so many of his generation he came to blame 'Abd al-Nasser and Arab nationalism generally for the humiliating defeat inflicted on the Arabs by Israel in 1967. The ideology of the Muslim Brotherhood provided him with a template with which to understand the deep connection between Islam and his ethno-linguistic identity.

Armed with this new Islamist understanding, al-Ghannushi traveled to France in 1968 where he studied philosophy at the Sorbonne. That same year he witnessed the uprising of French students against the European social and political order in the streets of Paris. The fiery denunciations by the students had the effect of further diminishing the stature of Western civilization in his view. In the above passage al-Ghannushi makes note of the fact that Islamists had a long been influenced by works of Western self-criticism, such as Alexis Carrel's *Man the Unknown*, in making their case against the West.

FURTHER READINGS

Burgat, Francois. *The Islamic Movement in North Africa*, trans. William Dowell. Middle East Monograph Series (Austin: Center for Middle Eastern Studies, University of Texas Press, 1997).

Davis, Joyce. *Between Jihad and Salaam* (New York: Palgrave Macmillan, 1997), chapter 5.

Dunn, Michael Collins. "The Al-Nahda Movement in Tunisia: From Renaissance to Revolution," in John Ruedy (ed.), *Islamism and Secularism in North Africa* (New York: St. Martin's Press, 1994).

Esposito, John, and John Obert Voll. *Makers of Contemporary Islam* (Oxford: Oxford University Press, 2001), chapter 5.

Esposito, John, and John Voll. "Rashid Ghannoushi: Activist in Exile," in *Makers of Contemporary Islam* (New York: Oxford University Press, 2001), 91–117.

Hermassi, Abdelbaki. "The Rise and Fall of the Islamist Movement in Tunisia," in Laura Guazzone (ed.), *The Islamist Dilemma: The Political Role of Islamist Movements in the Contemporary Arab World* (Reading, UK: Ithaca Press, 1995).

International Crisis Group. "Islamism in North Africa I: The Legacies of History," *Middle East/North Africa Briefing*, 12 (April 20, 2004).

Tamimi, Azzam S. *Rachid Ghannuchi: A Democrat within Islam* (Oxford: Oxford University Press, 2001).

2

ISLAMISM, DEMOCRACY, AND THE LIMITS OF FREEDOM

The Islamist group Hamas (the Islamic Resistance Movement) celebrates their victory over the ruling Fatah party in Palestinian legislative elections during a press conference in Gaza City, January 26, 2006. While some Islamist organizations see democratic elections simply as a means of gaining power, others emphasize Islam's compatibility with democracy. (AP photo/Alexandra Boulat/ VIII. Courtesy of AP Images.)

INTRODUCTION

Islamists generally oppose the separation of politics from religion. For many Islamists, freedom is inconceivable beyond the realm of religion. According to this way of thinking, democracy and Islam are incompatible because the former allows freedom of conscience whereas Islam does not. Islamists view Islam as a holistic order that does not permit beliefs and practices that would lead to divisions within the Muslim community. Yet there are indications that Islamists, like thinkers and activists working within the Judeo-Christian tradition, are capable of considerable ideological flexibility. Drawing upon the Islamic-sanctioned practices of *ijtihad* (independent reasoning) and *tajdid* (renewal), a number of contemporary Islamist writers evince a sincere desire to promote the values of political participation and pluralism. Building on the well-established Qur'anic principles of *shura* (consultation), they rescue Islamism from charges of despotism by stating the necessity of rulers consulting with the representatives of the people on points of Shari'a legislation and governing on the basis of community consensus (*ijma'*). The underlying conception is in all cases similar: The ruler, whether he is called *imam* (leader), president, or caliph, is the elected agent and representative of the Muslim community who is entrusted with executing God's law.

In a number of countries, parties representing Islamist movements have made attempts to run for political office, and in a number of cases the state has allowed them to do so. The success of these parties in the electoral arena has been varied. In Turkey the Islamist Justice and Development Party (*Adalet ve Kalkinma Partisi*, or AKP) captured a majority of parliamentary seats in Turkey's national elections in 2002—a political feat that had not been achieved by any party in the previous fifteen years. However, in Morocco and Pakistan Islamist parties have scored only limited successes. In the previous chapter we noted that members of the Muslim Brotherhood attempted to gain influence in Egypt's parliament beginning in the 1980s.

Despite these inroads, Islamist democracy remains a shaky proposition. In many cases Islamist democrats fail to define explicitly the specific nature and degree of popular participation in government. Nor do they always make clear whether secular parties should be allowed to contest elections. They can be vague, too, about the rights of religious minorities, such as Christians, Jews, and Hindus, in an Islamic state. It is a subject of dispute whether this new discourse on Islamist democracy conflicts with underlying principles central within Western democracy. Nevertheless, Islamist democrats do represent a trend in the Middle East and elsewhere in the Muslim world that points potentially to a distinctively Islamic path to a pluralist democratic society.

Hard-line Islamists vociferously deny that Islam is compatibile with democracy, holding that sovereignty (*hakimiyya*) rests with God who alone made the law and defined what is permitted and forbidden. According to Islamists of this sort, democracy ("the rule of the people") is a foreign practice associated with Western imperialist nations and thus is without roots in Islam. "Islamist democrats" are often vague on their views regarding free speech, free association, freedom of conscience, and equality between men and women; Islamists opposed to democracy explicitly reject these values. In their view, freedom of expression and the equality of all citizens are impossible in a "true" Islamic state. True liberation, they say, is only possible in the strict and exclusive application of the Shari'a, which frees man from vices, releases him from servitude to other humans, and arranges society in ways that are beneficial to all. The documents that follow reflect the divergent views of Islamists on the issue of pluralism and democracy.

"Impious Democratic Dogma"

- **Document:** The full text of an article by Ali Benhadj, co-founder in 1989 of Algeria's Islamic Salvation Front (FIS); entitled "A Severe Blow Leveled at Democratic Dogma;" published in the Islamist journal *al-Munqidh* (*The Savior*). Translated from the French by David Vanderboegh.
- **Date:** 1990.
- **Where:** Algiers, Algeria.
- **Significance:** Ali Benhadj represented the relatively hard-line, Salafist wing of Algeria's Islamic Salvation Party. In the document, Benhadj puts forward one Islamist view of Western-style democracy—condemning it as an innovation that diminishes the integrity and purpose of the Shari'a.

DOCUMENT

Democracy Puts Impiety and Faith at the Same Level

The democratic idea is among the number of unlucky intellectual innovations that obsesses the conscience of people. They flatter it from morning until night, forgetting that it is a matter of a mortal poison whose foundation is ungodly. That is why I resolved to take up the pen, to bring attention to what this word, imported from the world of the infidels, hides in corrupt beliefs and licentious conceptions, which strikes Islam in the most profound way and distills their false ideas within Muslim youth in particular and people in general....

Democracy is a Greek word, unknown in the language of the blessed century. It means "government of the people" or "power of the people"; it appeared in the eighth century B.C. in Sparta and not until the sixth century B.C. in Athens, which was however the city of philosophers and thinkers like Plato. It is therefore a word born on impious ground, of corruption and tyranny.

Those who study western political thought understand that the word democracy is not defined with precision: the conception of it held by capitalism and by communism differ entirely and, at the very heart of the capitalist world, it varies from one country to another; this is also the case for the communist world. As for us in the Islamic states, the conflict has become unbearable, to the point that one sees states claiming to be pioneers of the democratic experience and imposing policies of iron and fire on the people, as Yusuf al-Qaradawi showed in his book *The Imported Solutions* (1971, p. 50).

We must however ask ourselves: what does democratic liberalism mean? It is a matter of an expression of European origin, which we must study within the context of that unique culture, without losing sight of the fact that the ideological contents that are attributed to it contradict themselves greatly, rendering a precise definition difficult.

Let's talk about democracy: it is difficult to find a sociopolitical ideology in the twentieth century—liberalism, socialism, communism, even fascism and Nazism—that does not claim to incarnate authentic democracy and does not denounce the falsehoods of their competitors.… In this confusion, one cannot discern any call to moral and spiritual criteria, because each claims to jealously defend the freedom, equality, and dignity of humans; neither is there any call to positive social criteria, because each school puts forward a criterion that justifies its practice. Thus, western democratic intellectuals put the emphasis on policy and characterize democracy by political freedom, while Marxists emphasize economics and insist on social and economic liberty. As for the Chinese, they practice a synthesis between the two in the name of "new democracy." The Asian and African revolutionaries, finally, reject the aforementioned in the name of "democratic dictatorship."

Brothers in Islam, know that we all refuse impious democratic dogma, without the least weakness, and this for numerous reasons that would be too long to enumerate here, but of which I am going to extract the primary ones, while asking for God's support …

One must stop not at the word, but at the philosophy that bears it and which is an autonomous philosophy. The fundamental questions that men have always asked themselves are: from whence do we come, where are we going, and why? To these eternal questions, Islam in particular—and the revealed religions before their alteration—have brought forth very clear answers.

To the first question, the answer is: from God, who created men and all things. The scholars of the west have understood this very well. According to the French philosopher Bergson, "there have been and there are human groups devoid of science, techniques, and philosophy, but never of religions." In *History of Religions*, Ernest Renan affirms that if one can make everything that one loves disappear, such as intellectual, scientific, and industrial activity, one will never be able to abolish religious feeling. There will even remain the eloquent proof of the erroneous character of materialism, which wants to close human thought within the narrow limits of profane thought.

Liberty, a Masonic Slogan to Corrupt the World

For Anwar al-Jundi, in *Contemporary Research on Islam*, the word freedom is understood in an antagonistic fashion in liberal thought, in existentialism and in Marxism. Behind these three western ideologies, which appeal for total freedom, dangerous motives are hidden; the most serious of which is the victory of materialism and of Marxism, and licentious and atheist propaganda. All of this responds to the objectives contained in the *Protocols of the Elders of Zion*. According to the terms of the first protocol, "we were the first to call to the peoples in the name of *liberty, equality, brotherhood*." These words have not ceased being endlessly repeated up to today by parakeets; they have corrupted the world as they have corrupted the true freedoms of the individual.

The word liberty sets human groups against all authority, up to the *Sunna* of God. That is why, to the extent that we are able, we will erase this vocabulary, because it inspires the idea of brute force, which renders the population avid for blood like animals. The word freedom is among the number of Masonic and Jewish poisons, destined to corrupt the world on a grand scale. For us on the contrary, in Islam, freedom is connected to the Shari'a and not to the law, or, as they say, by the concern not to harm others. On the one hand, in fact, law is changing and on the other, freedom becomes an illusion: it is hindered by the state, by law and by the freedom of others, since there is not a man who does not want to reduce others to his mercy. As Jean-Jacques Rousseau says in the *Social Contract*, every man must cede a part of his freedom to the representatives charged with protecting the freedom of individuals, and that is how the Constitution was born. Are not the most fundamental democratic freedoms the freedoms of belief, of the person, of expression, and of property? Now these four freedoms are rendered sacred all together in Islam while they are divisible in the decadent conception of the west. It is forbidden for the Muslim to change religion: "He who changes religion, kill him," said the Prophet. One applies to him the punishment of the apostate. Freedom of expression does not permit the Muslim to blaspheme, to contest his religion or to revolt against its norms. He must not consume alcohol or have illicit sexual relations, under penalty of seeing applied to himself, publicly and without pity, the punishments foreseen for these transgressions.... A woman exposes herself to punishment if she goes out lightly dressed or in make-up. The Muslim must also limit himself to the foods that are permitted to him....

The freedom to acquire goods is also linked to the Shari'a. One cannot enrich oneself thanks to usury interest or by profiting from a monopoly situation, by engaging in the commerce of alcohol, or by opening a house of ill repute.

Non-regimented Freedom Is Anarchy, Decadence, and License

Taking into consideration what has just been said about freedom in Islam, we consider that absolute freedom, in the way in which it is understood in democracy, contradicts the condition of being submissive to God. According to Dr. Yusuf al-Qaradawi: "The Constitution must affirm the right of the individual—man or citizen—to freedom. Men are born free and they do not have to submit themselves to other men. To abandon oneself to one's passions, to follow one's most base instincts, that is bestiality, not freedom; to doubt, to allow oneself to be seduced by confused ideas and to follow seditions, that is anarchy. By freedom of man or of the citizen, we understand only this: ridding ourselves of all despotic authority on thought, conscience, and action, whether it comes from a tyrant, a shaman, a feudalist, or an arrogant capitalist."

Impious democracy considers that man constructs his destiny independently of his creator. The immoral expression "Render unto Caesar that which is Caesar's and unto God that which is God's" is at the origin of the principle of separation of religion and the state, philosophical foundation of democracy.

Dr. 'Uthmân Khalîl, one of its propagandists in the Arab and Muslim world, writes in his book *Islamic Democracy* (p. 64): "Modern democracy has nothing to do with the religious objection posed to the separation of religion and of the State." Secularization is, in fact, the hard core of democracy, and the best definition of it was given in the debates of the French parliament on the Constitution of 1946: "Secularism is the neutrality of the State with regard to religion." ... Which in fact amounts to the dispersion of the community. The Jews understood very well the interest of religion for the maintenance of unity of the community, as Yusuf al-Hajj, former mason who has broken with the vow, explained very well when he unmasked free masonry in his book *The Temple of Solomon*: "The great rabbi Emmanuel Rabinovitch pronounced, before the Council of Great Rabbis held in Budapest the twelfth of January 1952, a speech in which he said: 'We do not want to see any religion other than ours survive on the surface of the Earth, because the permanence of several religions would be a permanent danger to our sovereignty.'"

We also know what the claims of the wealthy Jews, Haïm Nahol and Lord Cardon, representatives of the Allies, were in order to hinder the independence of Turkey: (1) The Turks must abolish the Caliphate; (2) Turkey must be a secular state.

In fact, the apostles of secularism apply, consciously or not, the world policy of the Jews. They do not care about their appurtenance to Islam, and work in Muslim countries in general and Algeria in particular. I have written elsewhere that the separation of religion and the state is very exactly tantamount to the pretensions of the Jews and the Christians to cut the life of religion, which God has formally condemned.

Democracy means that sovereignty belongs to the people and that the community is the source of authority. In his book *Principles of Constitutional Law*, Dr. Sayyid Sabri writes (p. 52): According to article 6 of the Declaration of the Rights of 1789, the law is the expression of the will of the nation," which means that law is made by man. If I believe the press, the President of the Republic declared to the newspaper *Al-Sharq al-Awsat*: "There are of course alternatives, but I consider the Algerian people to be sovereign. If they want to construct socialism, let them elect representatives, and if a majority manifests itself, let them form a government to apply that policy. It works in the same way if they want to opt for communism or for the application of the Shari'a. They are free to opt for whatever they desire, through the path of democracy. I will never be disposed to impose socialism, communism, or the application of the Shari'a, through decree or by virtue of an article of the Constitution; which means that I will not decide in the place of the Algerian people."

Do you not see, Brother Muslim, the danger of such statements that put profane doctrines and divine Law on an equal footing? And where is this taking place? In a State where the people are Muslim, whose men and women are fighting to uplift the word of God and put down that of the impious! The Chief of State must repent for such remarks, which strike directly at our faith, and this even more so in that he just attended the sermon of the festival of sacrifice, in which the President of the Superior Islamic Council was calling secular parties to repent publicly on television screens.

The idea of the sovereignty of the people contradicts fundamentally a number of verses of the Qur'an, which address the sovereignty of God.... These Qur'anic texts establish that the people have no power to legislate and that any government that does not respect the sovereignty of God is satanic and must not be obeyed.... It is for this reason that Ja'far al-Sâdiq said: "When a people submit themselves to God, pray, make legal alms, fast during the sacred month and go on pilgrimages, then contest a *hadîth* of the Prophet, they are impious." Ibn 'Arabi wrote in *Ahkâm al-Qur'ân*, I-456: "He who contests a decision of the Prophet is an infidel." And Ibn al-Qayyim, in *A'lâm al-muwaqqi'în*, I-49/50: "He who governs without bearing in mind what the Prophet has prescribed is an idolater." The idolater is one who transgresses the limits of submission that are imposed on him, and those peoples who submit themselves to that which neither God nor his Prophet have prescribed are idolaters.

The great exegete Ibn Akbar wrote in his commentary, II-76: "He who does not obey the word of God is worthy of blame ..., in the manner of what the men of the *Jâhiliyya* were doing...." And Sayyid Qutb: "There is only one order, which is the order of Islam; all other regimes are only *Jâhiliyya*. There is only one Shari'a, which is the *Shari'a* of God, all others are only fantasy."

> In Islam, the sovereignty of divine Law;
> in democracy, the sovereignty of the people,
> the rabble, and charlatans

That which is forbidden is forbidden, even if the order were to come from all the Parliaments of the Earth. The people have only the right to choose the supreme Muslim who governs according to the Shar'ia.

According to the Pr** Anwar al-Jundi, author of the book *The Poisons of Orientalism and the Orientalists in Islamic Sciences* (p. 84): "Islamic political thought differs essentially from western thought when it comes to the very conception of politics. The principle of the sovereignty of the nation is one of the major constitutional principles of western democracy." This while taking into consideration moreover the divergence of opinions as to the origins of sovereignty: with an individual, a class, a group, or a community.

Muhammad Qutb writes in *Jâhiliyya of the Twentieth Century* (p. 123): "The 'will of the people' is the most advanced degree of the new *Jâhiliyya*. The 'will of idolatry' is the true face of this new *Jâhiliyya*. Historically, the *Jâhiliyya* is defined as being the government of the possessing class, exercised in its interest to the detriment of the other classes...." As Muhammad al-Mubârak says in *The Regime of Islam* (p. 31): "The powers that be and the people are both bound by the norms contained in the Qur'an and in the *Sunna*, neither of the two has the capacity to legislate by itself.... In the case of a conflict between the governing powers and the people, one refers to the Shari'a."

We see that power in Islam differs from absolute power which used to prevail in ancient oriental and western nations and which prevails today in the democratic regime, as in single-party modern regimes, in which an individual or a party is the absolute reference of legislation. In these regimes, man is constrained to submit to a limitless authority, which is considered by Islam as contrary to the word of God.

The government is not qualified to modify the law.... There is only the *ijtihâd* and the exercise of personal opinion in the changes of law that do not impact the fundamental sources of the law. This right belongs neither to the government nor to the people, but to scholars who know the rules of interpretation (*ijtihâd*) as well as the temporal conditions in which the societies belonging to it live.

SOURCE: *Al-Munqidh*, 23 (1990), 87–103. French translation of the Arabic original in M. Al-Ahnaf, B. Bottiveau, and F. Fregosi, *L'Algerie par ses Islamistes* (Paris: Editions Karthala, 1991), 87–103.

CONTEXT AND ANALYSIS

Algeria stood out among Arab countries in the late 1980s and early 1990s in taking concrete steps toward the establishment of a liberal democracy. In a desperate attempt to shore up its legitimacy, the secular ruling FLN (National Liberation Front) arranged for Algeria's first national elections. The provision of a political opening was a gamble, but the regime assumed that the electorate would rally behind its newly founded liberalism, thus restoring its political fortunes. It therefore came as a shock to the FLN when the Islamist FIS (Front Islamique du Salut) handily won the initial round of municiple elections and appeared set to win the next national round of voting scheduled for 1992. In order to prevent the FIS from assuming power over the nation, the army intervened on January 11, 1992 to unseat President Chadli Benjadid and call off the electoral proceedings. Rather than experience a flowering of civil society, Algeria slipped into a civil war of exceptional savagery, which pitted a variety of armed Islamist groups, several of them spin-offs of the FIS, against the security forces of the state.

The Islamic Salvation Front was founded in Algiers on February 18, 1989 by Islamists who took advantage of the 1988 amendment to the Algerian constitution that allowed parties other than the FLN to organize politically. The precipitous decline of the Algerian economy in the 1980s, starting with the fall in oil prices in 1984, had not only politicized Algeria's restive youth and pious middle class but deepened Algeria's social, political, and cultural divides. Roiling with anger, many Algerians viewed FIS's program of social welfare, cultural authenticity, and autonomy from Western imperialism as a viable solution to the failure of Algeria's Europeanized elite to bring prosperity and dignity to the nation. Under the leadership of Abbassi Madani and Ali Benhadj, the FIS gained a large following. By 1990, the readership of its press organ, *al-Munqidh* (The Savior), numbered in the hundreds of thousands. Following its success in the municiple elections, FIS imposed its "moral revolution" by encouraging, and sometimes forcing, female municipal employees to wear the headscarf, and used its power to close liquor stores and video outlets.

Despite unanimity on many points, FIS's thinking was divided on others, including the issue of political pluralism, reflecting its status as a "front" or coalition. Abbassi Madani drew on his formal training as a religious scholar to argue for democracy within an Islamic context, even stating "We will make Algeria a Hyde Park not only for free expression but also for choice and behavior." On the other hand, the younger Ali Benhadj preached a more militant and uncompromising message. Addressing the masses of frustrated and deprived youth, he argued that FIS would participate in elections but only as a means of gaining power. Once the government was defeated at the polls, Benhadj aimed to dismantle the edifice of

IN HISTORY

"In Islam, Truth Comes from Allah"

Irfan Awwas chairs the Executive Committee of the Indonesian Council of Mujahidin (MMI). The organization follows the radical teachings of Abu Bakar Ba'asyir. Awwas makes the following arguments against democracy:

Firstly, democracy has driven out Allah SWT from national life. Allah's sovereignty has been replaced by the people's sovereignty. If the people hold sovereignty, then almost all of Islamic law is useless. Then people say, 'Don't bring Islamic law into national life,' and, 'Why must the state handle religion, it's a private matter?' Secondly, democracy states that truth lies with the majority. Whatever the majority says is correct. In Islam truth comes from Allah. Thirdly, democracy uses the principle of 'one man, one vote'. In democracy, a professor, a prostitute, a thief and a religious scholar all have the same say. In Islam, an educated Muslim has greater say than a layperson. [The scholar] Martin van Bruinessen asked me, 'What if the prostitute is clever?' But what does that matter if they have no morals? Finally, democracy says nothing of the hereafter, so people don't care about morals. In secular democracy, nudists are more valued than those wearing *jilbab* (Islamic headscarf). In France, people who wear *jilbab* are demeaned, while people are free to go nude in demonstrations. In all democratic countries, in the name of human rights people who drink, gamble or engage in prostitution have greater status than people who declare all of this forbidden. This is because democracy doesn't deal with judgment in the hereafter. In Islam, it's extremely important to build a virtuous life in this world and the hereafter.

SOURCE: Imam Subkahn, "Islam and Democracy Cannot Meet: Irfan Awwas Sets Out His Vision of Islamic Law in Indonesia," *Inside Indonesia*, July-September 2004. At: http://www.insideindonesia.org/

democracy and work to establish a "true" Islamic state, one which upholds the religious integrity of the society. As the document clearly indicates, Benhadj believed that the people have no right to legislate. The law is present in the form of the Shari'a and it is the duty of the ruler simply to implement and enforce it. Further, the right of interpreting the law does belong to the government or the people but to learned scholars. Drawing on the work of Muhammad Qutb, brother of the influential Egyptian Islamist Sayyid Qutb, Benhadj goes on to brand democracy as constitutive of *jahiliyya*, the barbarous ignorance of the divine mandate that is the special feature of the modern age. In the document, Benhadj lays the blame for the spread of materialist philosophies on "Masons and Jews," thus exhibiting a penchant for conspiracy theory and anti-semitic tropes.

In 1991, just prior to the FIS victory in the first round of elections, state authorities arrested Ali Benhadj and Abbassi Madani on charges of threatening state security. Benhadj spent the years of civil war in prison. He was released in 2003 but in 2005 was once again arrested, this time for praising the jihadist wing of the insurgency in Iraq. In March 2006 he was freed under Algeria's Charter for Peace and National Reconciliation, which seeks to heal the nation by offering amnesty to those who committed acts of violence on both sides of the conflict.

FURTHER READINGS

Burgat, Francois. *The Islamic Movement in North Africa*, translated by William Dowell. Middle East Monograph Series. (Austin: Center for Middle Eastern Studies, University of Texas Press, 1997).

Fuller, Graham E. *Algeria: The Next Fundamentalist State?* (Santa Monica, CA: Rand, 1996).

Malley, Robert. *The Call from Algeria: Third Worldism, Revolution, and the Turn to Islam* (Berkeley, CA: University of California Press, 1996).

Martínez, Luis. *The Algerian Civil War, 1990–1998*, with a preface by John P. Entelis; translated from the French by Jonathan Derrick (New York: Columbia University Press, in association with the Centre d'Etudes et de Recherches Internationales, Paris, 2000).

Roberts, Hugh. *Embattled Algeria, 1988–2002: Studies in a Broken Polity* (New York: Verso, 2003).

Ruedy, John, ed. *Islamism and Secularism in North Africa* (Washington, DC: Center for Contemporary Arab Studies, Georgetown University; New York: St. Martin's Press, 1994).

Willis, Michael. *The Islamist Challenge in Algeria: A Political History* (London: Ithaca Press, 1996).

Representative Government in Islam

- **Document:** Excerpt from an article entitled "The Islamic State," by Hasan al-Turabi, Sudan's most prominent Islamist thinker and activist.
- **Date:** 1983.
- **Where:** Khartoum, Sudan.
- **Significance:** In his article, Hasan al-Turabi puts forward a relatively liberal and inclusive interpretation of the Shari'a that stands in contrast to the view of Islam prpounded by radical Isalmist theocrats.

DOCUMENT

The freedom of the individual ultimately emanates from the doctrine of *tawhid* which requires a self-liberation of man from any worldly authority in order to serve God exclusively. Society, and particularly those in power, is inspired by the same principle and the collective endeavor is not one of hampering the liberty of the individual but of cooperation toward the maximum achievement of this ideal. To promote this cooperation, the freedom of one individual is related to that of the general group. The ultimate common aim of religious life unites the private and the social spheres; and the *shariah* provides an arbiter between social order and individual freedom.

I do not have to go into the various rights of man vis-a-vis the state or society in Islam. The individual has the right to his physical existence, general social well-being, reputation, peace, privacy, to education and a decent life. These are rights that the state ought to provide and guarantee for a better fulfillment of the religious ideals of life. Freedom of religion and of expression should also be guaranteed and encouraged. Thus, while a Muslim would not oppose the *shariah* because he believes in it, if he does not agree to a particular interpretation of the law, he is entitled to his view. Actually, these are not pure rights that the individual is free to exercise. He owes it to God and to his fellow Muslims to observe these as a social obligation as well. He should contribute to the political solidarity and well-being of the state. If government becomes so alien as to transcend the *shariah*, he has the right and obligation to revolt. This is the revolutionary element in Islam. A Muslim's ultimate obedience is to God alone.

What about representative institutions in an Islamic government? This depends on the particular historical circumstances. In the period of the Prophet all the functions of the state were exercised by him as teacher and sovereign. He wisely but informally consulted with his companions. Later this consultative process was almost developed into an indirect representative institution called *ahl al-Shura* or *majlis-i-shura* (consultative council). The breakdown of the early legitimate political order did not allow the procedures and institutions of *shura* to crystallize. Today this could very well be formulated through a parliament, a council or *majlis-i-shura*. People may directly, through referendum, exercise their *'ijma* consensus or otherwise delegate power to their deputies. There would, however, be certain rules regulating the qualifications of candidates and election campaigns for the choice of deputies or other officers of the state. In Islam, for example, no one is entitled to conduct a campaign for themselves directly or indirectly in the manner of Western electoral campaigns. The presentation of candidates would be entrusted to a neutral institution that would explain to the people the options offered in policies and personalities. Factors of relative wealth or access to the communications media are also not allowed to falsify the representative character of deputies. The prevailing criteria of political merit for the purposes of candidature for any political office revolves on moral integrity as well as other relevant considerations. All this would, no doubt, influence the form and spirit of accession to positions of power.

The other central institution in an Islamic government is that which provides both leadership and effective execution of the general will: Caliph, Commander of the Believers, President of the Republic, or Prime Minister. As noted earlier, the word "caliph" was not originally chosen for any specific reason except to denote succession and compliance with the prophetic example of leadership. Most modern and contemporary constitutional theory tends to vest political leadership in one individual and not in a collegiate body—a presidency rather than a council of ministers. But neither a president nor a prime minister can be very powerful and representative of the unity of political purpose so essential to an Islamic polity. Whatever form the executive may take, a leader is always subject both to the *shar'ia* and to the *ijma* formulated under it. He enjoys no special immunities and can, therefore, be prosecuted or sued for anything he does in his private or public life. This is a fundamental principle of Islamic constitutional law, ensuing from the supremacy of the *shari'a*. No rigid theory of separation of government functions can develop in a comprehensive, coherent system like the Islamic political order, except to provide some necessary checks and balances to safeguard liberty or justice. Besides those powers delegated by the *majlis-i-shura* or consultative council and subject to its control, the executive may derive powers both directly from the *shari'a* and *ijma*.

The judiciary, although appointed, as part of the administration, plays an extremely important role in an Islamic state because of the special legalistic nature of the political order which is organized in accordance with a strict hierarchy of norms. The *shari'a* is the highest revealed law followed by popular laws based on *ijma* and by executive orders and regulations. Because of this, judges, as the guardians of the *shari'a*, adjudicate in all matters of law. Early Muslims were very keen to provide judges with a generous income to protect them against temptation and to allow them a very large degree of autonomy with broad powers to administer justice. However, the legal systems of Islam did not know a lawyer's profession. The modern capitalist institution which requires the participation of solicitors and barristers in the administration of justice ultimately works in favor of the rich who can afford the expenses and the delays of justice in a system administered in this way. I realize as a lawyer, myself, that adjudication in a contemporary society is a very complicated, time-consuming process. Judges cannot listen to all the complaints and determine the issues. But such a difficulty was resolved in early Islam by the office of a counselor to the judge: an assistant who first heard the parties, ascertained the matters in issue, marshaled all the relevant evidence, and researched the law in preparation for a decision by the judge. In an Islamic state there would be a tendency to do away with or to minimize the role of the legal profession by establishing an extended system of legal counsel and assistance, especially for the poor.

As far as public law for the administration of an Islamic state or government is concerned, one can draw upon early Islamic history and tradition regarding service for forms of achieving the political ideals of Islam. But due to the transformation of public life in contemporary societies, the Muslim would also draw heavily on comparative constitutional history and practice. This has a legal basis in Islamic jurisprudence. Any form or procedures for the organization of public life that can be ultimately related to God and put to his service in furtherance of the aims of Islamic government can be adopted unless expressly excluded by the *shari'a*. Once so received, it is an integral part of Islam whatever its source may be. Through this process of Islamization, the Muslims were always very open to expansion and change. Thus, Muslims can incorporate any experience whatsoever if not contrary to their ideals. Muslims took most of their bureaucratic forms from Roman and Persian models. Now, much can be borrowed from contemporary sources, especially appreciated in the light of the *shari'a* values and norms, and integrated into the Islamic framework of government.

Finally, I come to the inter-state and inter-faith relations of the Muslim state. I have remained quiet about the status of non-Muslims because I did not want to complicate issues. The historical record of Muslims' treatment of Christians and Jews is quite good especially compared with the history of relations between different religions and religious denominations in the West. The first Islamic state established in Medina was not simply a state of Muslims; it had many Jews, and many non-Muslim Arabs. Therefore, the problem of non-Muslim minorities within a Muslim state is nothing new. Muslims do not like the term "minorities." They call them People of the Book (*ahl al-Kitab*), the *dhimmi*, or protected people. These non-Muslims have a guaranteed right to their religious conviction, to profess and defend their own convictions and even to criticize Islam and engage in a dialogue with Muslims. Non-Muslims also have the right to regulate their private life, education, and family life by adopting their own family laws. If there is any rule in the *shari'a* which they think religiously incompatible, they can be absolved from it. There can be a very large degree of legal and political decentralization under an Islamic government. The more important thing is that, morally, Muslims are bound to relate to non-Muslim minorities positively. It is more than a matter of tolerance and legal immunity. Muslims have a moral obligation to be fair and friendly in their person-to-person conduct toward non-Muslim citizens, and will be answerable to God for that. They must treat them with trust, beneficence, and equity. There may be a certain feeling of alienation because the public law generally will be Islamic law. However, the public law of Islam is one related rationally to justice and to the general good and even a non-Muslim may appreciate its wisdom and fairness. Christians in particular who now, at least, do not seem to have a public law, should not mind the application of Islamic law as long as it does not interfere with their religion. It is a moral based on values which are common and more akin to Christian values that any secular law—Caesar's law.

As to the inter-state or international relations of a Muslim state, we have noted earlier the limitations on state sovereignty imposed by the *Shari'a* in favor of nationals of other states. The sanctity of treaty obligations and the vocation to world peace, except in situations of aggression, provide a basis for the development of extensive international relations. The international practice of Muslim states in history is well known. What is not as well-known is its contribution to the development of modern international law.

In conclusion, it is important to note that an awareness of the general nature and features of the Islamic state is necessary for an understanding of modern Islam as a resurgent force seeking to make up for a failure to realize Islam fully. Muslims are presently focusing more on general ideals—ideals as standards for guiding their different attempts to implement Islam. Whatever diverse forms their practice assumes as these universal ideals come to be expressed in the light of differing circumstances of particular Muslim states, the clarity of the universal model is necessary on the one hand to guide Muslims toward a greater unity and on the other hand, to enable them to grasp both the general and the particular in Muslim life. Otherwise, they run the risk of discerning nothing beyond the confusion of a multiplicity of Islams, determined purely by historical factors.

SOURCE: Hasan al-Turabi, "The Islamic State," in John L. Esposito, ed., *Voices of Resurgent Islam* (New York and Oxford: Oxford University Press, 1983), 247–51. By permission of Oxford University Press, Inc.

CONTEXT AND ANALYSIS

In Sudan the driving force behind the Islamist movement was Hasan al-Turabi, a charismatic scholar who had earned higher academic degrees at the University of London and the Sorbonne in Paris in the 1950s. In the early 1960s Turabi joined and worked his way up to a leadership position in the Sudanese Muslim Brotherhood. When General Ja'far Numayri took power in a military coup in 1969, Turabi's Islamist party was dissolved and its members arrested; like similar groups of officers in Egypt and Libya, General Numayri wanted to establish a progressive, secular regime and viewed the Islamists as an impediment to this goal. However, beginning in 1977 Numayri reached out to the Islamists as a way to gain popular support and undercut the appeal of the leftist forces in the country. He released Turabi from prison and made him his attorney general. In September 1983 Numayri even went so far as to enforce the Shari'a throughout Sudan, including *hudud* punishments stipulated in the Qur'an, which call for the amputation of thieves' hands and the stoning of adulterers. The sudden imposition of this penal code on the population contributed to a popular nonviolent overthrow of Numayri in 1985, and the reinstatement of parliamentary rule, although Islamism in various forms maintained its grip among the pious middle class. In the 1986 elections, Turabi led a new faction of the Muslim Brotherhood, the National Islamic Front (NIF), to third place in the national assembly. These developments unfolded against the backdrop of war between the Muslim and Arab northern region of Sudan and secessionist forces representing the country's black-African and largely Christian and animist south.

In 1989, the National Islamic Front joined with General 'Umar Hasan al-Bashir to overthrow the elected government. From that time until 2001, Turabi was the power behind the regime. The NIF filled the bureaucracy with its own men and carried out purges and summary executions of political enemies. People were interrogated and tortured in "ghost houses." Political parties and movements, including other Islamic ones, were banned and press freedoms severely curtailed. Meanwhile, in the south, hundreds of thousands died as a result of war, which the NIF accelerated, and from accompanying famines.

Despite the brutality of the NIF regime, Turabi was keen to present Sudan as a burgeoning Islamic utopia. In 1991 he set up a regional umbrella for political Islamists, the Popular Arab Islamic Conference (PAIC), headquartered in Khartoum. It was formed with the initial aims of countering the Saudi-sponsored Organization of the Islamic Conference and opposing the American presence in the Gulf following the war with Iraq. Under Turabi's leadership, the Sudan government created an open-door policy for Arabs, including Turabi's Islamist associate Usama bin Laden, who made his base in Sudan in 1990–1996. In the end, there was no disguising the failure of the NIF-led regime to bring prosperity and dignity to the country. Fearing an anti-government backlash, General Bashir forced Turabi to step down as speaker of parliament and subjected him to house arrest until his release in 2005. Although General Bashir remained committed to Islamism, he subsequently adopted a more moderate and pragmatic approach to politics and economic issues.

The document above represents an extreme case of disjuncture between Islamist theory and practice. Turabi is well known throughout the Muslim world as the advocate of an accommodating, liberal expression of Islamism. Yet, although Turabi emphasizes *shura* (consultation) as the central and legitimizing concept of political rule, and advocates tolerance and respect for other religions, the reality of Sudan's political life under the National Islamic Front negated the positive and potentially progressive aspects of his Islamist discourse. Turabi's liberal Islamism, it would seem, is limited to the realm of rhetoric, although it is true that the problems facing Turabi and the NIF were significant, and prevented Turabi from fully implementing his vision. In addition to civil war, Sudan was saddled with economic sanctions imposed by members of the United Nations. Such problems required harsh and uncompromising measures if they were to be solved. Yet the heart of the problem for Islamists in power—or indeed for any ideological party—is the question of means and ends: how to attain a pure Islamic state without compromising the principles on which the vision is based.

FURTHER READINGS

El-Affendi, Abdelwahab. *Turabi's Revolution: Islam and Power in Sudan* (London: Grey Seal, 1991).

Esposito, John, and John Voll. "Hasan al-Turabi: The Mahdi-Lawyer," in *Makers of Contemporary Islam* (New York: Oxford University Press, 2001), 118–49.

Hamdi, Mohamed Elhacmi. *The Making of an Islamic Political Leader: Conversations with Hasan al-Turabi*, trans. Ashur A. Shamis (Boulder, CO: Westview Press, 1998).

Moussalli, Ahmad S. "Hasan al-Turabi's Islamist Discourse on Democracy and Shura," *Middle Eastern Studies* 30, no. 1 (January 1994), 52–63.

Moussalli, Ahmad S. *The Islamic Quest for Democracy, Pluralism, and Human Rights* (Gainesville: University Press of Florida, 2001).

Turabi, Hasan. *Islam, Democracy, the State, and the West: A Round Table with Dr. Hasan Turabi, May 10, 1992*, edited by Arthur L. Lowrie and transcribed by Maria Schone. WISE Monograph Series, no. 1 (Tampa, FL: World and Islam Studies Enterprise, 1993).

IN HISTORY

Indonesia's Prosperous Justice Party

The Prosperous Justice Party (Partai Keadilan Sejahtera), known as PKS, began as the little-known Justice Party in 1998 with students and urban intellectuals as its base. Under the leadership of Hidayat Nur, it has since grown to include three million members and in 2004 won city council elections in Jakarta and Banda Aceh. Some party members hope to secure the presidency in 2009 and make Indonesia more of an Islamic state. The founders of the PKS argue that democracy provides a way to establish an Islamic government and that there is no contradiction between Islam and democracy. The PKS sees itself as a "centrist Islamic Party" occupying the middle ground between radical Islamist groups and mainstream Muslim organizations. The party's motto, "clean and concerned," was put into action during its campaign to bring relief to Tsunami victims in 2005. In 2006 the party attempted to enact a wide-ranging anti-pornography bill. The PKS is now faced with the task of upholding its image as the party of moral reform while engaging in pragmatic politics.

SOURCES: Elizabeth Fuller Collins and Ihsan Ali Fauzi, "Islam and Democracy: The Successful New Party PKS Is a Moderate Alternative to Radical Islamism," *Inside Indonesia*, January–March 2005 at: http://www.insideindonesia.org/. PKS Web site: http://pk-sejahtera.org/2006/index.php

An Islamist View of the Media

- **Document:** Article published in the Islamist journal *al-Munqidh* ("The Savior"). Translated from the French by David Vanderboegh.
- **Date:** 1989.
- **Where:** Algiers, Algeria.
- **Significance:** The article expresses the common Islamist view that the news must be reported from a Qur'anic perspective and must advance the interests of Islam. In so doing, the article reflects many Islamists' distrust of the "liberal" media.

DOCUMENT

I. Islamic News and Current Challenges

The colonial States realized very early the importance of news and its role in the service of their expansionist goals. Therefore they created news monopolies of a great scope, dividing the world, from the beginning of the century, into zones of influence of information thus distributed:

1. The German agency Wolf established a news monopoly in Germany, Austria-Hungary, and Scandinavia.
2. The agency Reuters monopolized news in Great-Britain, in its colonies and in the Far-East.
3. The French agency Havas exercises its monopoly in France, the French colonies, and in Latin America.

The Jews have, in their turn, grasped the importance of news in the preparation of minds to receive ideas and opinions; to orient or mystify public opinion. This is what pushed them to put their hands on the majority of newspapers and magazines throughout the world, in addition to the great publishing houses, printers, and control of the great companies of cinematographic production, television stations and radios. All of that in the framework of their general plan traced out in the *Protocols of the Elders of Zion*....

For Muslim countries, and Arabs in particular, news still suffers from technical and intellectual dependence, and the crisis of civil defeatism. The cause of this is that it is the Christians of the East who established the first basis of Arab news (Khalil al-Khuri; Al-Bustani, etc.). Things become clearer when we know that the first two newspapers to have appeared in the Arab countries were of French origin and language. These are the *Décade égyptienne* and the *Courrier d'Egypte* created at the time of Bonaparte's expedition in Egypt (1798–1801).

Still in Egypt, we find the oldest and greatest newspapers: *Al-Ahram, Al-Hilal, Al-Muqattam*, which were created by Maronite Christians, who chose Egypt instead of Lebanon, for the place it occupies in the heart of the Muslim world.[1]

These newspapers "have contributed in spreading the roots of nationalism in the place of Islam,"[2] and in spreading secular thought in the hearts of Muslims, with the help of evangelical missions and the states that support them.

News in the Arab world today does not differ much from what it was yesterday. And if previously hegemony belonged to the Christians who wanted to separate the Arabs from Turkey and abolish the Muslim Caliphate, news in our day obeys more than one tendency. The doors have been opened wide to the communists, leftists, nationalists, and the secularists, so that they publish their "mystifications and everything that fights Islam and mocks Muslims,"[3] without taking into account the feelings and beliefs of the *Umma*. All of that, and even more things, are taking place while committed Islamic news is nearly absent from the scene, due to the humiliation and the marginalization that it encounters and the intellectual terrorism coming from the authorities and ideologies, official or not. If one considers Islamic news in this context, it isn't surprising to find only a few persons demonstrating assiduousness and endurance "in order to defend the truth in an arena where magician's tricks are multiplying."[4]

Islamic news needs an independent and distinct framework, which is directly inspired by the Islamic method, because there are people who believe, from a narrow conception of Islam, that this news is only "exhortation and reminder." They wanted the mass of Muslims to adhere to an Islam that cannot go beyond the threshold of the Mosques, while Islamic news consists in fact of "considering all affairs of life from an Islamic vision and position."[5] It is news that resembles no other. As Muhammad Qutb [brother of Sayyid] wrote: "The Islamic press, in a Muslim country, has a way of presenting the news that makes the reader feel that he is a Muslim—even if he can't do anything—and that he has a vision of things that resembles no other. He can be dissatisfied with things that satisfy others, and be content with things that afflict them ... he can also share things with others, but from his own viewpoint."[6]

We must also define the framework within which Islamic news moves, whether it be in the presentation of facts, the analysis of events, or the confrontation of problems. Within all of that, Islamic news must respect the defined framework. And so that there will be no misunderstandings, we say that the Islamic framework in all aspects of life—including news—is the Book of Allah and the *Sunna* of his Prophet, and their understanding in the manner of the pious ancestors.

Islamic news is a news of predication and not a news of propaganda. The call to the establishment of the Law of Allah is a noble objective, and for its accomplishment we make use of noble means. Islamic news is a news of education and formation, not a news of commerce and interests. It does not encumber minds with nonsense and mystifications—as the mass-media does today—but chooses that which can be useful to people in this world and in the hereafter.

The Islamic analysis of events and facts obeys neither passions nor whims; ... its slogan is "to speak the truth before an unjust power;"[7] "Not obedience to the creature in disobedience to God"; and its method is that word of God: "Oh you who believe: if a perverse man comes to bring you a piece of news, be careful! Because if by inadvertence, you were to bring harm to a people, you would have to repent for that which you would have done" (Qur'an, XLIX-6).

Today, as the first Islamic newspaper appears in our country, after a long absence, and taking into account the situation lived by our people and the transformations experienced by our society, Islamic news must confront many challenges on several fronts.

- Islamic news in Algeria must work to form the Islamic base in the heart of the popular masses through uninterrupted orientation and global education in order that Muslims renew their ties to the principles of their religion; and that the barriers that prevent them from grasping the truth of their faith and applying the law of their God are broken.
- It must also confront foreign ideas and imported ideologies, and reveal their fraud and mystification that leads the masses astray from the teaching of their creator and makes them adhere to positive laws incapable of leading humanity to happiness; and whose facts have proven to be bankrupt.
- Islamic news must finally confront the political, economic, social, and cultural problems that afflict our people, among them: unemployment, debt and inflation ... social and bureaucratic ills; the cultural and civilizational invasion and its repercussions for our society. We do not deny that the resolution of these problems is not easy, but wise and balanced analysis of these questions and the unveiling of their causes are likely to reduce their gravity, even if they do not manage to resolve them all at once.

Such an undertaking requires enormous means that Islamic news does not yet possess in our country. This incites [us] to rapidly resolve this situation, by finding competent and specialized officials, and the material and technical means necessary.... This task must be the work of all Muslims, especially if we know that the present-day imported ones are supported by regimes and organizations, and that Islam suffers alone, orphaned and foreign among its own.

NOTES

1. Muhammad Qutb: *Wâqi' una al-Mu'àsir*, 239–40.
2. Fouad Rifà'i: *Al-Nufud al-Yahudi*, 15.
3. Ibid.
4. Muhammad al-Ghazali: introduction to the book *Ta'mmulât fi masirat al amal ad-islami* by Umar Abid Taha.
5. M. Qutb: op. cit., 242.
6. M. Qutb: op. cit., 241.
7. Authentic Hadith (see *al-Jami al-Saghir*, n. 1111).

SOURCE: *Al-Munqidh*, #3 (1990), 87–103. French translation of the Arabic original in M. Al-Ahnaf, B. Bottiveau, and F. Fregosi, *L'Algerie par ses Islamistes* (Paris: Editions Karthala, 1991).

CONTEXT AND ANALYSIS

The secular orientation of the news media has long been a thorny issue among Islamists. The first newspapers in the Muslim world were established in the late eighteenth and early nineteenth centuries by modernizing reformers and political elites within the context of European imperial conquest. In Egypt, the lead in news reporting was taken by Arabic-speaking Christians from Syria. The British facilitated the appearance of newspapers in Bengal and Madras and the Dutch were instrumental in the founding of news media in the East Indies. In most cases, these early newspapers ignored conservative Muslim views in favor of a vision that preferred secular Western-style modernity.

The secular trend in news reporting continued, but in a new way, under the nationalist and socialist regimes that took power in many parts of the Muslim World in the 1950s and 1960s. In Egypt, Syria, Iraq, Algeria, and Indonesia, new revolutionary governments nationalized the press and used it as a vehicle of state propaganda. For the most part, the populations of these countries were provided only the news that their governments were willing to allow. Afraid of ideological challengers to their rule, the regimes monitored, censored, and controlled all forms of dissident political expression, including the many Islamist periodicals and newspapers that sprang up in the middle decades of the twentieth century. Relegated to the margins of political life, Islamists resented the state-controlled media, which propagated nationalist ideologies that elevated the secular rulers of the Muslim world above God.

State censorship was particularly acute in Algeria, where the secular and left-leaning National Liberation Front (FLN) had held sway since coming to power in the early 1960s. However, in response to country-wide anti-regime riots in 1988, the FLN eased its censorship laws and allowed the publication of a variety of politically-oriented newspapers and periodicals. By 1990 the Algerian press had developed into one of the freest in the Arab world. Among the journals that took advantage of the opening were *Furqan* (The Qur'an) and *al-Munqidh* (The Savior), the official press organs of The Islamic Salvation Front (FIS). Yet, the progress that had been made in press freedoms was reversed in 1992 when Algeria's new military government decided to reinstate censorship over the media as part of its crackdown on the various components of Algeria's Islamist movement, including FIS. The government shut down both *Furqan* and *al-Munqidh* on account of what officials termed the journals' inflammatory articles against the state. Over the ensuing decade, freedom of expression continued to be restricted in Algeria, as the secular state continued to silence the privately owned press.

The above article from *al-Munqidh* illustrates the authoritarian discourse of Algeria's FIS (Islamic Salvation Front), which constituted an uncompromising, Islamicized version of the secular nationalism of the National Liberation Front. According to the article's anonymous author, "Islamic news" constitutes the unique "truth" and for that reason ought to prevail over news reported from a secular perspective. It is an essential component in the Islamic movement's effort to dismantle the hegemonic ideologies of the West and its representatives in the Muslim world. The article does not specify explicitly whether or not in an "Islamic system" FIS authorities would allow the public to hear and read secular viewpoints. However, the article's confrontational and monistic world view does not suggest openness or pluralism.

FURTHER READINGS

Abootalibi, Ali. "Islam and Democracy," in Barry Rubin (ed.), *Revolutionaries and Reformers: Contemporary Islamist Movements in the Middle East* (Albany, NY: SUNY Press, 2003).

Abou El Fadl, Khaled. "Islam and the Challenge of Deomocracy," *Boston Review* (April/May 2003). Online at: http://bostonreview.net/BR28.2/abou.html.

Al-Ahnaf, M., B. Botiveau, and F. Fregosi. *L'Algerie par ses islamistes* (Paris: Karthala, 1991).

Feldman, Noah. *After Jihad: America and the Struggle for Islamic Democracy* (New York: Farrar, Straus and Giroux, 2003).

Kramer, Gudrun. "Islamist Notions of Democracy," *Middle East Research and Information Project (MERIP)*, 23, no. 183 (July–August 1993), 2–8.

Miles, Hugh. *Al Jazeera: The Inside Story of the Arab News Channel That Is Challenging the West* (New York: Grove Press, 2005).

Poole, Elizabeth, and John E. Richardson. *Muslims and the News Media* (London: I. B. Tauris, 2006).

Robinson, Glenn E. "Can Islamists Be Democrats? The Case of Jordan," *Middle East Journal*, 51, no. 3 (Summer 1997).

3

WOMEN AND FAMILY IN ISLAMIST DISCOURSES

Indonesian Muslim women shout slogans protesting the participation of an Indonesian woman in the Miss Universe contest held in Thailand, during a demonstration outside an office of Indonesian cosmetic company Mustika Ratu, one of the sponsors for Indonesian participation in Jakarta, Indonesia, May 20, 2005. Islamist leaders and many government officials in Indonesia, the world's most populous Muslim nation, say women in swimsuits are offensive and violate religious tenets requiring them to dress modestly. (AP photo/Tatan Syuflana. Courtesy of AP Images.)

INTRODUCTION

Family life holds an important place in the cultural traditions of Islam. This importance is reflected in the centrality of family law in the Shari'a. For much of Islam's history, the legal basis of Muslim family life remained more or less constant. However, in the twentieth century new discourses emerged that challenged traditional Islamic understandings of family life and of women's role in society, especially regarding marriage, divorce, and succession. In response to economic forces and cultural developments stemming from Europe, many Muslims, particularly among the socioeconomic elite, began to question the system of conjugality and reproduction sanctioned by Shari'a formulations. They adopted, in various ways and to different degrees, Western-inspired patterns of family organization. In many cases the state took the lead in this development but individual reformers were also important. In the Arabic-speaking world, figures such as Huda Sharawi, Nazira Zayn al-Din, Malak Hifni Nasif, and Fatima Mernissi stand out.

Islamists have responded to these transformations in Muslim family life, often vociferously. In their view, the social, cultural, and economic changes marking the Muslim world have had negative effects on the structure and function of the family unit, which they consider to be the backbone of a viable Islamic society. They see the danger to family organization as relating, in the first instance, to the entry in many Muslim-majority countries of women into the workplace and the concomitant decline of male authority in the home, trends that became especially strong in the decades following World War II. At the same time, Islamists are aggrieved at support of ostensibly Muslim governments for the "alleged" legal emancipation of women, including granting women the right to vote and hold public office, in addition to limited rights to initiate divorce. Although many Muslim women take pride in the fact that they now perform jobs and enter professions once reserved for men, for most Islamists female employment and legal emancipation are dangerous trends that lead to the dissolution of traditional gender roles associated with the extended family.

This threat, coupled with the more general desire to distance Islamic culture from the colonizing Western "other," has prompted Islamists to provide Islamic direction to the contemporary family structure. The struggle is intense, especially in so far as family law is the only feature of the Shari'a surviving in anything like full measure. However, it is not for the Islamists a simple matter of returning to earlier forms of cultural practice. The socioeconomic circumstances of modernity require that they address the issue of family life within the contexts of female employment and the withering of domestic patriarchal authority. In so doing, Islamists provide the modern, nuclear middle-class family with Islamic content in the definition of the private roles of men and women. They explicitly conceive the family as the moral center of Muslim collective life. In the Islamist view, the family is the most significant manifestation of Islam's exceptional nature.

Given this purpose, it is perhaps natural that the Islamists should provide detailed instructions of the ethical precepts that the members of the Muslim family are to observe. Following the methodology of classical Islamic jurisprudence, Islamists propagate a system of classification that pronounces on all forms of behavioral and cultural activity as either *haram* (disallowed) or *halal* (allowed). These directives tend overwhelmingly to focus on issues related to the body, sexuality, reproduction, and legitimate authority within the household. They resonate among the ranks of the pious middle classes, many of whom are only one generation removed from the old Muslim traditions of the countryside. The harsh and uncompromising nature of many of the Islamists' pronouncements suggests that they function as boundary mechanisms, which mark off "true" Muslim believers from the Westernized political culture of the political and economic elite. In their appeal to the Qur'an and the Prophetic *sunna*, Islamists are able to provide their quest for empowerment with a "cultural affect" grounded in the validating sentiment of Islamic identity. While most Islamists recognize the utility of Western organizational and technical expertise viewed as value neutral, they are insistent that the inner domain of culture, especially as it relates to the intimate realm of home and family, remain wed to what they perceive as Islamic norms.

"When Islam Prohibits Something, It Closes All the Avenues of Approach to It"

- **Document:** Excerpt from Yusuf al-Qaradawi's book, *The Lawful and the Prohibited in Islam (Al-Hala wal Haram Fil Islam)*.
- **Date:** Early 1990s.
- **Where:** Qatar/Egypt.
- **Significance:** Yusuf al-Qaradawi attempts to stem moral dissolution in the Islamic world by providing a legalistic guide to appropriate behavior between the sexes. His book illustrates the Islamist view that the building of a virtuous society and state begins at home.

DOCUMENT

The Physical Appetites

Allah Subhanahu wa Ta'ala created man as His vicegerent on earth in order that he might populate and rule it. Obviously this purpose cannot be realized unless the human species perpetuates itself, living, thriving, cultivating, manufacturing, building, and worshipping its Creator. Accordingly, the Creator has placed certain appetites and impulses in man so that he is impelled toward the various activities which guarantee the survival of the species.

Among the appetites which an individual must satisfy for his personal survival is that of food and drink. The sexual appetite, however, is for the purpose of the survival of the species. Sex is a strong driving force in the human being which demands satisfaction and fulfillment. Human beings have responded to the demands of the sexual appetite in three different ways:

1. One way is to satisfy ones sexual need freely with whomever is available and whenever one pleases, without any restraints of religion, morality, or custom. This is the position of the advocates of free sex, for they do not believe in any religion. This philosophy reduces the human being to the status of an animal, and, if practiced universally, would result in the destruction of the family structure and of all society as we know it.

2. The second approach is to suppress, and try to annihilate, the sexual drive; this approach is advocated by ascetic religions and other-worldly philosophies, approaches which lead toward monasticism and an escape from the world. Such advocacy of suppression of a natural appetite, or rather annihilation of its functioning, is contrary to Allah's plan and purpose, and is in conflict with the course of the natural order which requires the use of this appetite for the continuity of life.

3. The third approach is to regulate the satisfaction of this urge, allowing it to operate within certain limits, neither suppressing nor giving it free rein. This is the stand of the revealed religions, which have instituted marriage and have prohibited fornication and adultery. In particular, Islam duly recognizes the role of the sexual drive, facilitates its satisfaction through lawful marriage, and just as it strictly prohibits sex outside of marriage and even what is conducive to it; it also prohibits celibacy and the shunning of women.

This is the just and intermediate position. If marriage were not permitted, the sexual instinct would not play its role in the continuation of the human species; while if fornication and adultery were not prohibited, the foundation of the family would be eroded. Unquestionably, it is only in the shade of a stable family that mercy, love, affection, and the capacity to sacrifice for others develop in a human being, emotions without which a cohesive society cannot come into being. Thus, if there had been no family system, there would have been no society through which mankind would be able to progress toward perfection.

The Prohibition of Approaching Zina

It is not surprising that all the revealed religions (According to the Qur'an there has been only one true, authentic faith, Al-Islam. Islam means the attainment of peace through conscientious and loving submission to the Will and Guidance of Allah. This was the mission of all Prophets and Messengers in human history. It is the same fundamental faith which was revealed to Moses, Jesus, and Muhammad (peace be upon them). The original revelations given to Moses and Jesus are no longer available in their complete, original and unadulterated form. The Qur'an is the only divine revelation which was meticulously preserved in its complete, original, and unadulterated form. As such, it is to be used as the criterion to judge the authenticity of the present forms of previous revelations.) have prohibited fornication and adultery (zina) and have fought against these crimes against society. Islam, the last of the divinely revealed religions, is very strict in prohibiting zina, for it leads to confusion of lineage, child abuse, the breaking-up of families, bitterness in relationships, the spread of veneral diseases, and a general laxity in morals; moreover, it opens the door to a flood of lusts and self-gratifications. Assuredly, the command of Allah Ta'ala, "And do not come near zina; indeed, it is an abomination and an evil way" (17:32), is just and true.

As we know, when Islam prohibits something, it closes all the avenues of approach to it. This is achieved by prohibiting every step and every means leading to the haram. Accordingly, whatever excites passions, opens ways for illicit sexual relations between a man and a woman, and promotes indecency and obscenity, is haram.

Khulwah

Islam prohibits khulwah (Privacy or khulwah denotes a man and woman's being alone together in a place in which there is no fear of intrusion by anyone else, so that an opportunity exists for sexual intimacy such as touching, kissing, embracing or even for intercourse.) between a man and a woman who are outside the degree of a mahrem relationship. (Mahrem denotes a relationship either by marriage or by close blood ties of such degree that marriage is permanently prohibited. With reference to a woman, a mahrem is either her husband or any male relative with whom marriage is permanently forbidden, such as her father, grandfather, son, brother, uncle or nephew. For the purposes of this discussion, all other relationships will be referred to as "non-mahrem." (Trans.) The reason for this is not a lack of trust in one or both of them; it is rather to protect them from wrong thoughts and sexual feelings which naturally arise within a man and a woman when they are alone together without the fear of intrusion by a third person. The Prophet (peace be on him) said: Whoever believes in Allah and the Last Day must never be in privacy with woman without there being a *mahrem* (of hers) with her, for otherwise Satan will be the third person (with them). (Reported by Ahmad on the authority of 'Amir ibn Rabi'ah.) Allah Ta'ala tells the Companions of the Prophet (peace be on him), "And when you ask them (the Prophet's wives) for anything, ask them from behind a curtain; that is purer for your hearts and for their hearts" (33:35).

In an explanation of this verse, Imam al-Qurtabi says, "This means such thoughts as occur to men regarding women and to women regarding men. This will remove any possibility of suspicion and accusation, and will protect (their) honor. This command implies that no one should trust himself to be in privacy with a non-mahrem woman; the avoidance of such situations is better for one's purity of heart, strength of soul, and perfection of chastity." (*Tafsir* of al-Qurtabi, vol. 14, p. 228.)

The Prophet (peace be on him) particularly warned women concerning *khulwah* with male in-laws such as the husband's brother or cousin, since people are quite negligent in this regard, sometimes with disastrous consequences. It is obvious that a relative has easier access than a stranger to a woman's quarters, something concerning which no one would question him. The same is true of the wife's non-mahrem relatives, and it is prohibited for any of them to be in *khulwah* with her. The Prophet (peace be on him) said: "'Beware of entering where women are.' A man from the Ansar asked, 'O Messenger of Allah, what about the in-law?' He replied, 'The in-law (Al-Nawawi) explains, "The in-law here means a relative of the husband other than his father and sons (who are *mahrem* to his wife), such as his brother, nephew, and cousins, etc., with whom marriage would be permissible for her, if she were to be divorced or widowed." Al-Mazari is of the opinion that it includes the husband's father as well.'" See *Fath al-Bari*, vol. 11, p. 344.) (Reported by al-Bukhari and Muslim.)

He meant that there are inherent dangers and even destruction in such privacy: religion is destroyed if they commit sin; the wife is ruined if her husband divorces her out of jealousy; and social relationships are torn apart if relatives become suspicious of each other.

The danger lies not merely in the possibility of sexual temptation. It is even greater in relation to the possibility [of] gossip about what is private and personal between the husband and wife by those who cannot keep secrets to themselves and relish talking about others; such talk has ruined many a marriage and destroyed many a home. In explaining the meaning of "The in-law is death," Ibn al-Atheer says, "It is an Arabic figure of speech like, 'The lion is death' or 'The king is fire,' which means that meeting a lion is similar to facing death and a confrontation with a king is like being in the fire. Thus privacy between an in-law and a woman is far more dangerous than in the case of a stranger because he might persuade her to do things against her husband's wishes, such as asking him for things he cannot afford, nagging him, and the like."

Looking with Desire at the Opposite Sex

What Islam prohibits in the sphere of sex includes looking at a member of the opposite sex with desire; for the eye is the key to the feelings, and the look is a messenger of desire, carrying the message of fornication or adultery. A poet of ancient times has said, "All affairs begin with the sight; The raging fire a spark can ignite," while a contemporary poet declares, "A look, then a smile, then a nod of the head, Then a talk, then a promise, then the warmth of a bed …"

This is why Allah Subhanahu wa Ta'ala has commanded the believing men and the believing women alike to lower their gaze together with His command to guard their sexual parts: "Tell the believing men that they should lower their gazes and guard their sexual organs; that is purer for them. Indeed, Allah is well-acquainted with what they do. And tell the believing women that they should lower their gazes and guard their sexual organs, and not display their adornment, except that which is apparent of it; and that they should draw their head-coverings over their bosoms, and not display their adornment except to their husbands or their fathers or their husbands' fathers, or their sons or their husbands' sons, or their brothers or their brothers' sons or their sisters' sons, or their women, or those whom their right hands possess, or male servants who lack sexual desire, or children who are not aware of women's nakedness; and that they should not strike their feet in order to make known what they hide of their adornment" (24:30-31).

Several divine injunctions are contained in these two verses. Two of them pertain to both men and women, namely, the lowering of the gaze and the guarding of the sexual organs, while the rest are addressed exclusively to women.

A difference is to be noted here between the expressions, "lower their gazes" and "guard their sexual organs," signifying that while the sexual organs must be totally guarded without any leeway, the lowering of the gaze is only partial, because necessity and the general interest of the people require that some looking at members of the opposite sex be allowed.

"Lowering the gazes" does not mean that in the presence of the opposite sex the eyes should be shut or that the head should be bowed toward the ground, since this would be impossible; in another place the Qur'an says, "Lower thy voice" (31:19), which does not mean sealing the lips. Here "lowering of the gazes" means to avert one's gaze from the faces of the passers-by and not to caress the attractive features of the members of the opposite sex with one's eyes. The Prophet (peace be on him) told 'All ibn Abu Talib, "Ali, do not let a second look follow the first. The first look is allowed to you but not the second."(Reported by Ahmad, Abu Daoud, and al-Tirmidhi.)

The Prophet (peace be on him) considered hungry and lustful looks at a person of the opposite sex as "the zina of the eye," according to his saying, "The eyes also commit zina, and their zina is the lustful look." (Reported by al-Bukhari and others.)

He termed the lustful look zina because it gives sexual pleasure and gratification in an unlawful way. This is also what Jesus (peace be on him) is reported to have said in the Gospel of Matthew: "You have heard that it was said, 'You shall not commit adultery'. But I say to you that everyone who so much as looks at woman with evil desire for her has already committed adultery with her in his heart" (Matt. 5:2728).

Indeed, such hungry and lustful looks are not merely a danger to chastity but they also result in agitation of the mind and disturbed thoughts. The poet says,

"If you let your looks go a-wandering, Many charming sights will make your heart pine.
The one you see cannot belong to you altogether, Nor will your heart remain content with the little you saw."

The Prohibition of Looking at the 'Awrah of Others

Looking at the 'awrah (Awrah (lit., that which is to he hidden) denotes those parts of the body which Islam requires to be covered in front of others whether of the same or the opposite sex (Trans.)) of another person must be avoided. The Prophet (peace be on him) forbade that any person should look at the 'awrah of another, whether of the same or the opposite sex, and whether with or without desire, saying, "A man should not look at the 'awrah of another man, nor a woman of a woman, nor should a man go under one cloth with another man, nor a woman with another woman." (Reported by Muslim, Abu Daoud, and al-Tirmidhi. Scholars have inferred from this that two men, or two women, should not lie under the same covering so that parts of their bodies touch.)

The 'awrah of a man referred to in this *hadith* is from his navel to his knee, although some scholars, such as Ibn Hazm and some Maliki jurists, do not include the knee. With respect to a man who is not her *mahrem*, a woman's 'awrah is her entire body excepting only her face and hands, while with respect to a *mahrem* such as her father or brother it is different. This we will discuss later.

What it is *haram* to look at is also of course *haram* to touch with the hands or with any other parts of the body.

What we have said concerning the prohibition of looking at or touching the parts of the body which must be covered becomes void in case of need or necessity such as first aid or medical treatment. At the same time, what we have said about the permissibility of looking becomes void in case of lust, as the ways leading to sin must be blocked.

SOURCE: Yusuf al-Qaradawi, *The Lawful and the Prohibited in Islam (Al-Hala wal Haram Fil Islam)*. Translated by Kamal El-Helbawy, M. Moinuddin Siddiqui, and Seyed Shukry (Plainfield, IN: American Trust Publications, 1994), 148–54.

CONTEXT AND ANALYSIS

Yusuf al-Qaradawi was born in 1928 in the Egyptian Delta province of Gharbiyya at a time when Egypt was attempting to gain its full independence from Great Britain. A combination of talent and ambition led him early in his life to the Azhar, the venerated mosque-university in Cairo, where he studied Islamic jurisprudence and doctrine. His studies at the Azhar were periodically interrupted by responsibilities that devolved upon him as a member of the Muslim Brotherhood. It was unusual for a scholar in training to be involved with what essentially was a lay movement. He supported his fellow Muslim Brothers in the anti-British Suez Canal Zone insurgency of 1952, for which he earned a prison sentence. Upon his release he continued his Islamist activities. His ideological position did not endear him to the 'Abd al-Nasser regime and in 1959 that regime banned him from preaching. A break came in 1962 when the Azhar sent him to the Gulf emirate of Qatar to aid the ruling Al Thani family establish an institute of religious studies.

Support from the Al Thani provided al-Qaradawi with security he had not known in Egypt. His practical approach to scripture established him as an Islamic thinker able to couch the learned discourse of the 'ulama in terms that were accessible to a global audience of Muslims. More recently, his broadcasts on the Qatar-based al-Jazeera TV, in addition to his much-visited Web site, have put him in the forefront of contemporary Muslim scholars who are attempting to craft an "enlightened jurisprudence" relevant to the requirements of modernity. If crafting opinions, al-Qaradawi does not confine himself to any one of the four recognized schools of Islamic law but rather makes judgments that appear to him prudent.

One of the chief themes in al-Qaradawi's writings is the danger posed to Muslim family life in the contemporary era by the proliferation of dissolute lifestyles and loose morals. According to al-Qaradawi, Muslims living in the hedonistic societies of the West are especially at risk. Al-Qaradawi makes the point that Muslims, wherever they live, must be aware of the limits that God has set for men and women in their family lives and in other aspects of social existence. These boundaries, he writes, are in people's best interests. Echoing generations of Muslim scholars, he explains that the sexual urge is a potentially destabilizing force in society. It is able to provoke even the most disciplined men to commit acts of fornication (*zina*), resulting in the confusion of lineages, bitterness in relationships, the spread of venereal disease, and the breakup of families. Although the Qur'an and the hadith regard sexual activity as one of the desirable pleasures of life, it must, he says, be regulated if the negative consequences of this tempestuous instinct are to be kept at bay.

IN HISTORY

Rashid al-Ghannushi on "The Female Sector" (1984)

The impact of this sector on the fate of societies is well known: It suffices to point out that at least half of society is female and the other half is brought up and educated among them.

We must grasp the utmost importance of this sector. Here the influence of the Islamists has been restricted for the same reason: a lack of awareness and insensitivity toward the oppression, degradation, abasement, restrictions of their horizons and roles in the life of society that women have endured during the long centuries of decline. Women's personality was obliterated and she was transformed into an object of pleasure—in the name of religion!—until the Western invasion came to sweep away our values in its destructive currents and brought with it the illusory values of freedom and equality.

It was only natural for women to be influenced by the enticements if the West, because she was already suffering under the yoke of oppressive, false Islam, sustained by the silence of the "men of religion"....

For women, there was no path to freedom or self-determination except through a revolt against Islam and its mores and the imitation of the West— until the Islamist movement...

The real issue is ... Westernization and the oppression and enslavement of mankind as a whole, the denial of the right to decide one's own destiny and the transformation of mankind into an object, a thing....

What the Muslim woman needs now is a liberation movement to restore her to herself and to her innate nature as a guardian of the heritage of mankind and a companion of man in the jihad to liberate herself and him from the forces of exploitation and oppression in the world and to liberate herself from all control and submission except to God...

SOURCE: Rashid al-Ghannoushi, "Deficiencies in the Islamic Movement," translated by Linda G. Jones, *Middle East Report* (July-August 1988), 23–24.

The legitimate outlet provided by marriage is the most obvious solution to this quandary, but al-Qaradawi also prescribes other, complementary forms of external moral enforcement. With an eye on the young people of Islam's crowded and modernizing cities, al-Qaradawi underlines Islam's prohibition of unmarried men and women meeting alone, unless they are relatives. For, according to a well-documented hadith, "Satan will be the third party with them." Similarly, he emphasizes the Qur'anic injunction (Qur'an 24:30-31) that "believing men and women" should lower their gazes when addressing individuals of the opposite sex, since the eyes are capable of committing fornication. As regards women's dress, he follows the standard Islamic injunction that all of a woman's body should be covered save the face and hands. Men, too, must dress modestly and must certainly cover the areas extending from their navel to their knees. Al-Qaradawi lays much of the blame for the alleged loose morals of many contemporary Muslim women on the weakness of their husbands who are either unable or unwilling to control them.

Al-Qaradawi states boldly that in his scholarly works he does not adopt the apologetic stance common among some Muslims, whereby elements of Islam are emphasized that bear close resemblance to the liberal ethos of Europe while those that do not are either ignored or explained away. As he states, "I cannot compromise my religion by taking the West as my god after accepting Allah as the Lord, Islam as the religion, and Muhammad (peace be on him) as the Messenger."

FURTHER READINGS

Ayubi, Nazih. *Political Islam: Religion and Politics in the Arab World* (London and New York: Routledge, 1991).

Fernea, Elizabeth, ed. *Women and the Family in the Middle East: New Voices of Change* (Austin, TX: University of Texas Press, 1985).

Ismail, Salwa. "Confronting the Other: Identity, Culture, Politics, and Conservative Islamism in Egypt," *International Journal of Middle East Studies*, 30 (1998), 199–225.

Karram, Azza M. *Women, Islamism, and the State: Contemporary Feminisms in Egypt* (London: MacMillan, 1998).

Rugh, Andrea B. "Reshaping Family Relations in Egypt," in Scott Appleby and Martin Marty, eds., *Fundamentalisms and Society: Reclaiming the Sciences, the Family and Education* (Chicago: University of Chicago Press, 1993), 151–80.

"Woman Has Been Guaranteed Complete Equality with Man"

- **Document:** Excerpt from Sayyid Qutb's book *Social Justice in Islam.*
- **Date:** 1949.
- **Where:** Cairo, Egypt.
- **Significance:** Sayyid Qutb adopts an apologetic tone in this defense of women's role in an Islamic society. The selection is from Qutb's first true Islamist work. He would go on to become Islamism's most influential ideologue. We will meet him again in this book.

DOCUMENT

As between the two sexes, woman has been guaranteed complete equality with man in respect to sexual difference as such and to human rights, and precedence of one sex over the other is established only in some specific situations connected with natural and recognized capacities, skills or responsibilities, which do not affect the essential nature of the human situation of the two sexes. Wherever these capacities, skills and responsibilities are equal, the sexes are equal, and wherever they differ in some way there is a corresponding difference between the two sexes.

In religious and spiritual matters they are equal. "And whosoever does deeds of righteousness, whether male or female, believing—they shall enter Paradise, and not be wronged a single date-spot" (translator's note: Surat al-Nisa' [4], 124). "And whosoever does a righteous deed, whether male or female, believing, We shall assuredly give him to live a goodly life; and We shall recompense them their wage, according to the best of what they did" (translator's note: Sural al-Nahl [16], 97). "And their Lord answers them: 'I waste not the labor of any that labors among you, whether male or female—the one of you is as the other'" (translator's note: Surat al-'Imran [3], 195).

In matters of economic and financial competency they are also equal. "To the men a share of what parents and kinsmen leave, and to the women a share of what parents and kinsmen leave" (translator's note: Surat al-Nisa' [4], 7), "To the men a share from what they earned, and to the women a share from what they have earned" (translator's note: Surat al-Nisa' [4], 32).

As for the fact that a man receives a larger share of an inheritance than a woman, the reason is the responsibilities that he bears in life. When he marries a woman he has the obligation of supporting her and supporting their children, as well as the other aspects of maintaining the family; also, payment of bloodwit and other legal compensation is his responsibility alone. It is right that he should have a double share for this reason alone. If a woman marries her livelihood is guaranteed by the support her husband provides, and if she remains single or is widowed it is guaranteed by what she inherits or by the support of her male relatives. The point here is that a difference in responsibilities requires a difference in inheritance.

As for the fact that men are managers of women's affairs (*qawwam 'alayha*): "Men are the managers of the affairs of women for that God has preferred in bounty one of them over another, and for what they have expended of their property" (translator's note: Surat al-Nisa' [4], 34). The preference is based on natural capacities and skills and the flexibility with which the authority for management is specified. Because a man is free of the obligations of motherhood he confronts the affairs of society over a longer period of time and all his mental faculties fit him for this, while the obligations of motherhood restrict the woman for most of her days and develop her emotional and passionate side. By the same token, it is a man's reflective and deliberative side that develops. So, if he is made the manager of women's affairs it is because of his natural capacity and skill for this task, in addition to the expenses he is obligated to, and the financial aspect is closely linked to this management authority. Thus he has a right corresponding to his duties, and in the end it works out to an equality of rights and duties in the broader perspective of the relations between the sexes and of life as a whole.

....

There may also appear to be discrimination in the matter of giving evidence: "And call in to witness two witnesses, men; or if the two be not men, then one man and two women, such witnesses as you approve of, that if one of the two women errs, the other will remind her" (translator's note: Surat al-Baqarah [2], 282). But the verse itself explains the reason. By the nature of the tasks of motherhood, the woman develops her emotional and passionate side, while the man develops his reflective and deliberative side, as we have seen. So if she forgets or is carried away by her feelings, the other woman will remind her. So it is a question of the practical circumstances of life, not a question of preferring one sex as such over the other or an absence of equality.

Islam has taken into account what assures the woman of her religious and economic equality and provided guarantees arising from the fact that she can be married only with her permission and acceptance and without any compulsion or having her wishes ignored. "Do not marry a mature woman until you consult her or a virgin until you ask her permission, and her permission is silence." Also the *mar*: "Give them their wages apportionate" (translator's note: Surat al-Nisa' [4], 24). And their other marital rights, whether as wives or as divorcees: "retain them honorably or set them free honorably; do not retain them by force, to transgress" (translator's note: Surat al-Baqarah [2], 231). "Consort with them honorably" (translator's note: Sural al-Nisa' [4], 19).

We must remember that Islam guarantees women all these rights and ample assurances in a spirit of pure respect and honor, unsullied by economic or materialistic considerations. It has fought the idea that a woman is a burden better done away with as an infant, and thus has fought unrelentingly the custom of burying girl babies alive which was practiced in some of the Arab tribes. It has dealt with this custom in the same spirit of pure respect and honor with which it has looked upon all humans, and so has forbidden it just as it has forbidden killing in general, making no exception. "Slay not the soul that God has forbidden, except by right" (translator's note: Surat al-An'am [6], 151). And it has specifically forbidden the killing of children and the only children that were killed were the females: "And slay not your children for fear of poverty: We will provide for you and them" (translator's note: Surat al-Isra' [17], 31). And it stresses the sustenance of children in this verse because they were the cause of fear and poverty and in order to give their parents confidence in God's sustenance, but its assurance is for the children before the parents. Then it mobilizes the feelings of justice and mercy when it says concerning the day of resurrection: "When the buried infant shall be asked for what sin she was slain" (translator's note: Surat al-Takwir [81], 8–9); thus it makes it the occasion of a prominent and searching question on that fearful day.

Thus, when Islam granted women their spiritual and material rights, it was looking upon them as humans and acting in accordance with its view of human unity: "It is He who created you out of one living soul, and made of its spouse that it might rest in her" (translator's note: Surat al-A'raf [7], 189). It wanted to raise them to the status of being an equal half of the one "soul."

We must remember this about Islam, and then we must also remember that the freedom that the materialistic West has granted to women does not arise from this honorable source nor were its motives the innocent motives of Islam.

It is well that we not forget history, and not be charmed by the deceptive tinsel of modern life. It is well to remember that the West made women leave the home to work because the men there shirked their responsibility to support their families, and made their women pay the price of their chastity and their honor. Only thus were women driven to work.

It is well for us to remember that when women went out to work, the materialistic West took advantage of their need and exploited the increased supply to lower their wages, and that employers used cheap woman's labor to replace the workers who were beginning to raise their heads and demand a decent wage.

When women demanded equality there, this meant first and foremost equality of pay, so they could eat and live! When they could not get this equality, they demanded the right to vote so as to have an effective voice. Then they demanded the right to enter the parliaments so as to have a positive voice in establishing that equality! This is because the laws that governed society were made by men alone and are not—as in Islam—the laws (shar') of God, which strike a just balance between His servants, men, and women.

It is well for us to remember that France continued until the time of the Fourth Republic after the last war without granting women the right to control their own property—a right which Islam does grant—without the permission of a guardian, while it does grant them the right to be unchaste, openly or secretly. This last right is the only right Islam forbids to women! It likewise forbids it to men, out of consideration for human honor and feelings and to raise the level of sexual relations above that of mere physical relations outside the bonds of home or family.

When we see the materialistic West prefer women to men today in some occupations, especially in shops, embassies, consulates, and the news media, such as newspapers and the like, we must not ignore the detestable and unsavory significance of this preference. It means being on the slave block in an atmosphere dense with opium! It is the exploitation of the sexual feelings in the souls of the customers, for the shop owner, like the state which appoints women to embassies and consulates and the transport companies that hire hostesses, like the newspaper editor who sends women to collect rumors and news, each of these knows what a woman can do, knows how she achieves her success in these areas, and knows what she sacrifices to achieve that success! And even if she herself does not sacrifice anything—an unlikely supposition—he knows that hungry passions and treacherous eyes flicker about her body and take in her words, and he exploits this hunger for material gain and petty success, because honorable human values are far, far from him.

As for communism, it makes broad claims concerning the equality of men and women and the destruction of the chains that bind women, arguing that equality means equality of work and pay, and that when work and pay are equal women will be liberated and will have the same right to uninhibited activity as men do. For the matter in communist thinking does not go beyond economics, so that all human motives and all humane ideas are implicit in that one element out of all the elements of life.

The bare truth is that men shirk their duty to provide for women and compel them to do men's work in a male environment in order to live. Communism, therefore, is the natural completion of the materialistic Western spirit which lacks the spiritual values in human life.

We must remember all this before our eyes are deceived by the false glitter, for Islam gave women rights fourteen centuries ago that Western "civilization" has not given them to this day. Islam gave them—in the case of need—the right to work and the right to earn, but it also preserved for them the right to be provided for within the family, because it considers life more that the body or possessions and its aims are higher than mere food and drink. Also, it looks at life from many angles and sees different tasks for different individuals, but tasks that are mutually supporting and complementary. In this way it sees the task of the man and the task of the woman, and it obligates each of them to do his task first, so that life may develop and progress. It ordains for each of them the rights that guarantee the achievement of this general human goal.

SOURCE: William E. Shepard, *Sayyid Qutb and Islamic Activism: A Translation and Critical Analysis of Social Justice in Islam* (Leiden, New York, Koln: E. J. Brill, 1996), 61–66. Reprinted with permission of BRILL.

CONTEXT AND ANALYSIS

Sayyid Qutb (1906–1966) is Islamism's most influential ideologue, surpassing even Hasan al-Banna and Abu A'la Maududi in overall significance to the development of the Islamist movement. His most well-known work was *Ma'alim al-Tariq* (1964), translated as *Milestones*, an excerpt of which is provided in this volume (Chapter 6). He came to Islamic activism relatively late, however.

Qutb was born into a relatively prosperous family in the Upper Egyptian village of Musha. Following World War I he went to Cairo to further his education. For the first half of his adult life Qutb was a fairly prominent member of the secular intellectual elite that flourished during the period of the monarchy (1922–1953) and included such figures as Taha Husayn and Naguib Mahfouz. Qutb was a poet and literary critic, as well as a writer on educational and social matters. He was inspired by the example of 'Abbas Mahmud al-'Aqqad, a journalist, man of letters, and one of the leading secular intellectuals of the time. After the end of the Second World War, Qutb and many others in his circle began to speak out forcefully against Zionism and the continuing European imperialism, and the political corruption, social stress, and economic inequality that would soon bring about the collapse of Egypt's Old Regime. In early 1948 he began to express his nationalist sentiments by drawing heavily on the Qur'an whose contents he fashioned into a theological argument that addressed the issues of the day. In the absence of an explanation from Qutb himself, it is difficult to account for his move toward a political, as opposed to a purely cultural, understanding of the role of Islam in society. Probably, Qutb adopted the Islamist approach to find a comprehensive ideological solution to Egypt's faltering political and economic order.

Qutb's first major Islamist work was *Al-'Adala al-Ijtima'iyya fi al-Islam* (*Social Justice in Islam*), published in 1949 just after the Egyptian government sent him to the United States on an educational mission. As its title suggests, the book focuses on Islam's role in fostering mutually beneficial relations among the various sectors of the population, including the family, the cornerstone of society responsible for the nurturing its values and morals.

In drawing attention to male-female relationships, Qutb responded to the far reaching social changes that were affecting Egypt and other countries of the Muslim world at the time. Growing numbers of girls and women benefited from expanding opportunities in all levels of education and entered the workforce as clerks and factory hands. The example of pioneering, Western-influenced feminists, such as Huda Sharawi, encouraged many women to challenge the gender roles accorded by the traditional patriarchy.

Having grown up in a traditional village that was affected only minimally by these developments, Qutb was unprepared for the more open and diverse gender relationships that were taking root in society. Although he declares that he did not want to see women revert to their former condition of seclusion, which he considered to be out-of-date and socially debilitative, he made it clear that he was uncomfortable with their current level of freedom. In Sayyid Qutb's estimation, the health and balance of Egyptian society was contingent on the strict maintenance of functionally differentiated social roles for men and women. A woman's job is in the home and the family; she is the nurturer, responsible for raising the children, and is the source of love and kindness for her husband whose God-given duty is to maintain the family financially. Unchecked, women's sexuality has the power to entice men and upset the social order. To follow uncritically the Western example is to open the door to moral degeneracy. Qutb says that the only reason that women in the West work is because men ceased to support them. Moreover, the West capitalizes on women's place in the public sphere by turning them into sex objects. As opposed to the West, Islam respects the dignity of women.

Qutb paid a personal price for the transformation of middle-class Cairo society. Unwilling to choose a bride from among the "dishonorable" women he was in contact with in the workplace, and unable for lack of family connections to meet a woman of sufficient "moral purity," Qutb reconciled himself to a life of bachelorhood, something unusual in Egyptian society.

FURTHER READINGS

Binder, Leonard. *Islamic Liberalism* (Chicago: University of Chicago Press, 1988), chapter 5.

Calvert, John. "'The World Is an Undutiful Boy!': Sayyid Qutb's American Experience," *Islam and Christian-Muslim Relations*, 11, no. 1 (2000), 87–103.

Khatab, Sayed. *The Political Thought of Sayyid Qutb: The Theory of Jahiliyya* (New York: Routledge, 2006).

Musallam, Adnan. *From Secularism to Jihad: Sayyid Qutb and the Foundations of Radical Islam* (Westport, CT: Praeger/Greenwood, 2005).

Shehadah, Lamia Rustam. "Women in the Discourse of Sayyid Qutb," *Arab Studies Quarterly* (Summer 2000).

IN HISTORY

"Slaves of Desire"

Sayyid Qutb visited the United States between November 1948 and August 1950. He recorded his impressions of America in a number of letters and periodical articles, which he composed during and immediately after his American sojourn. In his American writings, Qutb aimed to distinguish the values of Egypt and other Muslim countries from what he perceived to be American materialism and degeneracy.

Nature has given this country wealth of every kind. There are all sorts of natural wonders and beautiful faces and bodies. But, like the beasts in the jungle, no one feels this beauty. A girl suddenly appears as a magical genie or runaway nymph. And when she comes closer you can feel the crude instinct devoid of all radiance, and you can smell the burning body, not the sweet smelling fragrance or perfume. Then she becomes flesh, mere flesh, mouth-watering flesh, in any case, just flesh.

I watched the movies that depict this jungle life, and I observed the life of the American people. Every time I see men chasing women, and women chasing men, in couples and groups, I shut my eyes for a moment, and all I see is a huge thunderous jungle in which males and females run after one another. Oh, those starved looks, those feverish bodies, that animal joy. Everything here is like a jungle, only with the crowded factories, businesses, schools, and bars. This is the only noticeable difference. The most beautiful body resembles the body of an animal, and the most beautiful eyes are those of desire and hunger! There is nothing that distinguishes between what is human and what is animal.

When a person spends all his or her life in exhausting labor directed toward the "dollar," and when all there is to life is money, then there is no place for passion of affection. What is left, other than bodily love?

Source: "An Islamist's View of America," translated by John Calvert, in Vincent Burns and Kate Dempsey Peterson, *Terrorism: A Documentary and Reference Guide* (Westport, CT: Greenwood Press, 2005), 73–74.

"Muslim Sister … Show Your Pride!"

- *Document:* Selections of statements issued by Hamas during the first Intifadha (Palestinian uprising). Translated by Mohammed Zakaria and John Calvert.
- *Date:* 1988.
- *Where:* The Occupied Palestinian Territories (West Bank and Gaza).
- *Significance:* For Hamas Islamists, the *hijab* [Islamic dress] represents a rejection of imported and imposed modernity. Within the context of occupation, it is also a symbol of defiance.

DOCUMENT

The Muslim woman has a role no less important than that of the Muslim man in the battle of liberation. She is the maker of men. Her role in guiding and educating the new generation is great, and it is understood by the enemy. The enemy believes that if it is able to influence her life, far from Islam, they will have won the battle. That is why you find the enemy making constant attempts to undermine her social role by means of disinformation campaigns, films, and school curricula, using for this purpose Zionist-inspired lackeys who belong to organizations that take various names and shapes, such as Freemasons, Rotary Clubs, espionage groups and others, which are nothing less than agents of subversion and sabotage. These organizations have ample resources that enable them to fulfill their purpose of achieving Zionist aims and deepening the concepts that serve the enemy. These organizations operate in the absence of Islam and its estrangement among their societies. The Islamic peoples must confront the conspiracies of these saboteurs. The day Islam is in control of guiding the affairs of life, these organizations, hostile to humanity and Islam, will be obliterated.

The Woman, whether she is a mother or sister, plays a most important role in the home of the fighting family, looking after its members and rearing the children, imbuing them with moral values and thoughts derived from Islam. She has the responsibility of teaching them to perform the religious duties in preparation for [the] fighting role that awaits them. That is why it is necessary to pay great attention to the educational curriculum in the schools, which educates Muslim girls, so that they should grow up to be good mothers, aware of their role in the battle of liberation.

The Muslim woman must have sufficient knowledge and understanding of the duties and performance of housekeeping because economy and the avoidance of waste are necessary in the difficult conditions surrounding us. She should understand the fact that the money available to her is as blood, which should never flow except through the veins so that children and grown-ups can continue to live.

> "Verily, the Muslims of either sex, and the true believers of either sex, and the devout men, and the devout women, and the men of veracity, and the women of veracity, and the patient men, and the patient women, and the humble men, and the humble women, and the alms-givers of either sex who remember Allah frequently; for them hath Allah prepared forgiveness and a great reward." (Qur'an, 33:35).

Muslim sister ... who shows pride before the world in being a Muslim ... Islam, the only system that liberated women from their cages ... this system that set women free to build, rise up, learn, teach, and erect the banner of righteousness ... this system that guaranteed women the right of decent living after having been buried in the dirt, and the rights in inheritance.

O daughter of great Islam: Islam did well by you when you were a child.... Islam did well by you as a woman. The Prophet said: "Believers with the most complete belief are those with the best morals, and the best among you is he who treats his women best." And Islam did well by you as a mother, since it considers heaven to be underneath your feet.

O sister ... Our hope. God called his prophet from above the seven levels of heaven to tell you to keep your purity so you would remain a protected gem not exposed except to your husband. This gem is not a cheap kind of good, not a body exposed to anyone, or an instrument to destroy the soundness of societies. Therefore, God directed you to cover yourself with a veil....

Let it be known to you, my dear sister: that your veil is a cover and it is proof of your purity, civility, modernity, and rationalism. It is not as the enemies of Islam claim, that it reduces your freedom. For God distinguished humans from animals by having them wear clothes. And if nudity was a sign of civilization, nude animals would be more civilized than humans, and women in the forests of Africa should be considered more civilized than the women of Europe and the United States.

SOURCE: *Wathaiq Haraka al-Muqawama al-Islamiyya "Hamas": Min Wathaiq al-Intifadha al-Mubaraka* (*Documents of the Islamic Resistance Movement "Hamas": Documents of the Blessed Uprising* (Gaza: Palestine: Hamas Media Office, 1991), 206–11.

CONTEXT AND ANALYSIS

Palestinian women played important public roles during the first Intifadha (uprising) against Israel's occupation of the West Bank and Gaza Strip, which erupted at the end of 1987, as their husbands and sons were killed, injured, or arrested. They joined in collective action to boycott Israel. To sustain the uprising, they planted "victory gardens" and raised chickens and goats. Women's organizations were divided into factions: Fatah, the Communist party, the Democratic Front for the Liberation of Palestine (DFLP), and the Popular Front (PFLP) each had its own women's wing. However, Hamas, the Palestinian offshoot of the Muslim Brotherhood that came into being during the uprising, was not part of the Intifadha's "unified leadership." Hamas women stayed at home.

Yet, as the passage above attests, the limitations placed by Hamas on women were not imposed out of malice. The male author(s) of the above document express deep respect for women as the foundation of the family and the larger society. They charge women with the

IN HISTORY

Fatiha Hakiki Talahite: "*Hijab* Is a Woman's Affirmation That They Submit to God"

On an individual level ... wearing the *hijab* [Islamic dress] is not necessarily the sign of regression that it might appear to be at first glance ... You could say that the *hijab* is a woman's affirmation that they submit to God before they submit to man. Here, submission to man means submission to a social order in which man has the dominant role.... Of course, she is not going as far as to question her submission to man since religion has preordained it. But to claim her first direct submission to God, with reference to man, can be interpreted as an affirmation of the self, the start of the emergence of women as individuals, in a society where even the male individual is still in its infancy.

SOURCE: Francois Burgat, Face to Face with Political Islam (London: I.B. Tauris, 2003), 149.

important responsibility of "manufacturing men," not creating governments. Generally speaking, the women of Hamas acquiesced to the patriarchal structures imposed by the Hamas leadership, belying the image in the West of women as victims of Islamism.

Yet paradoxically, Hamas' struggle to build an Islamic society at the expense of the Israeli occupation encourages women to transgress social norms that Islamism supposedly upholds. The women of Hamas say that a woman's proper place is in the home, but like their male counterparts they are eager to participate in the realization of Hamas' ideological vision. Of special interest to Hamas women were the organization's welfare programs, which filled the gaps left by the failure of the secular authorities to provide adequate services in health and education. Slowly, Hamas' male leadership came around to recognizing the utility of women's participation in this public realm: In a gender-segregated community, effective welfare provision would be impossible without the contribution of a women's wing, which has access to other women and to private homes.

A similar paradox is to be found in the life of Zaynab al-Ghazali, an Egyptian who was the most famous female Islamist until her death in 2005. Al-Ghazali was highly independent by any standards. Despite not being a formal member of the Muslim Brotherhood, she became an important figure in the movement. Her first marriage broke down and she told her second husband that she would initiate divorce if he protested her political involvements. Yet in her advice to other women, she opined that married women should remain in the home and obey their husbands.

More recently, the role of Hamas women in the larger society has expanded to an even greater extent. During recent elections in the Palestinian Territories, Palestinians elected Hamas women to 6 of the party's 74 seats in parliament—giving the women of the radical group, guided in all ways by their understanding of Islam, a new and unaccustomed public role.

For many Islamist women, the struggle to build what they regard as a truly Islamic society provides a reason for entering public life. While some maintain that such a society will retain a place for women in the public realm, others imply that women will then return full-time to the home. It is hard to imagine that these restless, energetic women will be happy if limited to the home.

FURTHER READINGS

Fisher, Ian. "Women, Secret Hamas Strength, Win Votes at Polls and New Role," *New York Times* (February 3, 2006).

Hammami, Rema. "From Immodesty to Collaboration: Hamas, the Women's Movement, and National Identity in the Intifada," in Joel Beinin and Joe Stork (eds.), *Political Islam: Essays from Middle East Report* (Berkeley: University of California Press, 1997).

Joseph, Suad, and Susan Slymovics, eds. *Women and Power in the Middle East* (Philadelphia: University of Pennsylvania Press, 2000).

Meyer, Tamar. *Women and the Israeli Occupation: The Politics of Change* (New York: Routledge, 1994).

Mishal, S., and A. Selah. *The Palestinian Hamas: Vision, Violence, and Coexistence* (New York: Columbia University Press, 2000).

Sabbagh, Suha, ed. *Palestinian Women of the West Bank and Gaza* (Bloomington: Indiana University Press, 1998).

The Need for *Ijtihad*

- *Document:* Nadia Yassine.
- *Date:* December 12, 2005.
- *Where:* Barcelona, Spain, and Morocco.
- *Significance:* In her writings and public speeches, Nadia Yassine calls on Muslim women to challenge, within an Islamic context, patriarchal readings of the Qur'an.

DOCUMENT

Islam has honored women, Islam has granted rights to women, Islam has protected women; that is the same old song that each man and woman hear when they happen to ask questions on the status of women in the Muslim world.

We do not have enough time to delve into details and enumerate the real differences that may exist between one woman and another in the reality of a world that is so large, so stratified and so diverse as the Muslim world. The daily life of a Tuareg woman undoubtedly has almost nothing in common with that of a woman from the Lebanese upper class except that they share the same faith. There are certainly huge differences if we broach every single case apart; however, the fact is that there is well and truly a certain specificity of the status of women in the Islamic world. Such specificity is reflected in traditions, mentalities, curricula; worse still, it finds expression in laws and statistics which, it is time we admitted it, side with a variety of discourses that Muslims have hitherto refuted and denied.

Yes, the Muslim woman is oppressed in the name of Islam. Sure, she is treated like a child in the name of Islam. Yes, she is repudiated and cast away in the street in the name of Islam; she is marginalized in the name of Islam. Yes, she is excised in the name of Islam.

Questioning

More and more, an essential question is being asked: do the original texts, which are the Qur'an and the Sunna (The Prophet's Tradition), support the disparagement of women?

Or is it actually our estrangement from these sources that has made people ascribe such obvious underestimation of women to Islam?

Soon as we rid ourselves of the ideological straitjackets made by centuries of accumulated and heterogeneous jurisprudence and we go straightforward to the sources and the teachings the Prophet of Islam, it becomes clear to us that the dynamic inherent to his teachings has been slowly but surely eclipsed.

We easily find out that we have estranged ourselves from the spirit of the Islamic laws. That is due to several causes that are inevitably and intrinsically linked but that we may bring out and caricature out of illustrative concern as follows:

1. The political break represented by the Umayyad coup d'état inhibited the dynamic of liberation established by the teachings of the Messenger.

2. The splits occasioned by the political break weakened even more such dynamic, wasted the lifeblood of the umma (the Islamic community) and relegated to the background any exhaustive reflection on a privileged status that was newly gained by women in the time of the Prophet Muhammad.

3. Ijtihad, this living and anti-stagnation force in constant search of the best and most adequate of solutions to safeguard the spirit of the law, transformed progressively into a struggle against stopgaps, and then declined altogether and faded away to leave room for taqleed "conformist literalism." From the light of necessary ijtihad we passed to an endless and inevitable night of intellectual and spiritual ossification for which the women pay dearly the price. Instead of enjoying the rights granted by the original texts, they found themselves prisoners of a certain jurisprudence based on "sad ad-darâi'" (which we may translate literally as "stopgap" jurisprudence).

4. The resurgence of certain tribal practices disguised, knowingly or unknowingly, by certain jurisprudence in order to grant them legitimacy.

5. The spread of Islam brought about two major phenomena that are intrinsically linked:
   — It delayed the dynamic initiated by the Qur'an regarding the abolition of slavery.
   — That exacerbated the propensity to confine Muslim women in order to underline their distinction from female slaves and servants: locking up women to better protect them. Such was the motto.

Plan of Action

The reality is surely very complicated; so are the solutions that we may suggest in order to draw on the sources in an appropriate manner. The fact is that such effort needs to be concentrated on three dimensions:

— Recharging our spiritual batteries by means of the heart: the spiritual field and the intuitive knowledge are essential elements that will enable us to draw on texts that were revealed mainly to remind us of the spiritual dimension of Islam and the practice of such spirituality.

— Renewing our rational capabilities through acquiring theological instruments. In other words, infusing life into ijtihad, "which I may define as an effort of exhaustive reflection," and exerting every possible effort so that more women take part in its process. Making of the effort of reflection [is] an undertaking inspired by collective effort and group work. To a complicated world the solutions to be found cannot be the fruit of the work of one individual.

— Transcending our political legacy. The effort of reflection can only be done in societies that are really democratized, that is, societies that have ridded themselves of these coercive regimes that are behind the very alienation of the women and men of those societies.

The work to be done is then a work of education coupled with a work at the political level. However, we must count on the long term and especially ensure that our action does not come within the tradition of classical Western feminism that has an inevitable materialist vocation. It is not a matter of taking reprisals against a male chauvinist society. It is a matter of achieving a certain complementarity wherein women and men are equal partners in a society that is more equitable and, therefore, more human and spiritual: a society of good sense and confidence.

Promoting western-style feminism amounts to taking the wrong historical path and choosing the wrong points of references. That will amount particularly to disrupting violently the course of an age-old history, to generating more acts of resistance and to exacerbating still more paradoxes.

Knowing the provisions that our sacred texts have really prescribed concerning the rights of women is something that is required; yet attempting to put them in force right now, overnight and in one stroke, amounts to committing a social suicide or making a systemic condemnation of society.

SOURCE: http://nadiayassine.net/en/page/10191.htm

This paper was presented to the First International Congress on Islamic Feminism, Barcelona, October 27–29, 2005.

CONTEXT AND ANALYSIS

Nadia Yassine is the daughter of Shaykh 'Abd al-Salam Yassine, the leader and chief ideologue of Morocco's banned but tolerated Islamist organization "Justice and Charity." The group campaigns peacefully for the creation of an Islamic state, and derives its power and popularity from helping the poor through a network of charities across the country. Like her father, Nadia Yassine believes that Muslims are living in a critical period of their history. Concerned about the roots of decline and decadence in the contemporary Muslim world, she enjoins Muslims openly to embrace self-criticism. Only when Muslims take an honest look at their present shortcomings will Islam again rise as a unified power capable of leading humankind.

Yassine is part of a new breed of Islamist activist—western-educated but not westernized—who believes that women's position in society has been undermined by the patriarchal biases that dominate both traditional Islamic and Islamist discourses. Throughout history, she writes, it has been men who have crafted Shari'a. Islamic jurisprudence, *fiqh*, consolidated in its classical form in the ninth century, was itself heavily influenced by the patriarchal thinking and behaviors of the day. The *hadith*, the reported, but not always authentic, sayings and deeds of the Prophet Muhammad, have also been often used to shore up patriarchal ideas and practices. Sometimes the *hadiths* are of questionable provenance or reliability, and sometimes they are used out of context.

As a result of this patriarchal-oriented jurisprudence, men have come to dominate women in the same way that Muslim kings and dictators have ruled over their populations since medieval times. According to Yassine, it is time that Muslim women challenge patriarchal readings of the Qur'an, especially in the realm of Muslim personal law. Only then will they be able to reclaim Islam's original vision, which provides women with dignity and rights. Muslim women must bypass previous interpretations of the law and go straight to the Qur'an and the authentic hadith in order to recuperate Islam's original message. Muslims, including women, must revive the practice of *ijtihad*, the individual effort to understand scripture within the context of the current period. Searching the Qur'an Yassine finds nothing that

IN HISTORY

Nadia Yassine: "Liberated, Responsible Women"

The Message fashioned a generation of women among whom Aisha (God bless her) is the symbol par excellence, a generation of responsible and free women. Islam educated magnificent women who knew their rights as well as their obligations, and who perfectly understood their roles in establishing that society of confidence. With admirable force, they took hold of God's gift to them of their humanity, at last recognized, and their dignity.

We thus had such figureheads as Um Haram. This great lady of Islam, were we to cite her alone, did not content herself with entering the public arena as a full believer responsible, just like any other Muslim, man or woman, for the life of the community: She even requested the Prophet (grace and peace be upon him) to beseech God so that she might die with a group to whom he predicated martyrdom in distant lands. The Messenger (grace and peace be upon him) found it natural to answer her request. Dozens of examples of female disciples of the Prophet can be mentioned.

SOURCE: Nadia Yassine, translated by Farouk Bouasse, *Full Sails Ahead* (Iowa City, IA: Justice and Spirituality Publishing, 2006), 211.

prohibits a woman from divorcing her husband, something that traditional formulations of the Shari'a have disallowed. But she admits that on certain issues scripture places clear limits as to what can be accomplished. The Qur'an is clear cut on the issue of polygamy; no Muslim can change the text. Given her denunciation of mainstream Islamist positions, it is not surprising that hard-line Islamists in Morocco and elsewhere condemn her campaign for women's rights within the framework of Islam as excessively liberal and even blasphemous.

But this does not mean that Nadia Yassine supports Western feminist positions. In 2002 Nadia Yassine joined with Muslim traditionalists in opposing the King to reform Morocco's Personal Status Code, the Moudawana, a mixture of custom and Islamic law, which among other functions governs the relationship between a husband and wife. Although Yassine agreed with the reformers that the Moudawana is hugely disadvantageous to women, denying them many rights and making them almost entirely subject to their husband's control, she was opposed to the western orientation of the reforms. Yes, she said, the Personal Status Code did need reform, but not in ways that would impose a foreign agenda on the Moroccan people. According to Nadia Yassine, any changes to the social law should be made within a Muslim context. Until that occurred, she was prepared to march with Muslim conservatives in opposition to the proposed changes. The campaign against the reforms has, in the short term at least, succeeded in delaying the implementation of new law. King Mohammed was obliged to set up a commission to re-evaluate the proposals.

Nadia Yassine believes that the success of women's efforts to restore their rights is tied to the more encompassing effort among Muslims to inculcate attitudes of freedom at the political level. Like some of the Islamists we have examined, she believes that Islam upholds free inquiry and participatory government. The attainment of Muslim women's rights depends to a large extent on the eradication of dictatorship and religiously sanctioned kingship in the Muslim world.

FURTHER READINGS

Ahmed, Leila. *Women and Gender in Islam: Historical Roots of a Modern Debate* (New Haven, CT: Yale University Press, 1992).

Burgat, Francois. *Face to Face with Political Islam* (London: I. B. Tauris, 2005), chapter 11.

Cooke, Miriam. *Women Claim Islam* (London: Routledge, 2000).

Huband, Mark. *Warriors of the Prophet* (Boulder, CO: Westview Press, 1998), chapter 5.

Maddy-Weitzman, Bruce. "Islamism, Moroccan-Style: The Ideas of Sheikh Yassine," *Middle East Quarterly* (Winter 2003). Online at: http://www.meforum.org/article/519.

Yassin, Nadia. *Full Sails Ahead*, translated by Farouk Bouasse (Iowa City, IA: Justice and Spirituality Publishing, 2006). Also see Nadia Yassine's Web site: http://www.nadia yassine.net.

4

SOCIAL AND ECONOMIC JUSTICE

Egyptians stand at a bus stop in Cairo, Egypt in front of an Arabic Muslim Brotherhood slogan "Islam is the Solution," November 8, 2005. The Muslim Brotherhood has been banned in Egypt for decades. Some Egyptians, especially in poor areas, believe the Muslim Brotherhood tackles the problems of daily life ignored by a government they see as aloof, corrupt, and inefficient. (AP photo/Amir Nabil. Courtesy of AP Images.)

INTRODUCTION

Islamists proclaim that Islam is a comprehensive ideological system that covers all domains of human existence, including economics. Islamists claim that the Qur'an and the Prophet's *Sunna*, the latter documented in the hadith, contain solutions, rendered either explicitly or by way of analogy, to economic problems of every kind. Generally speaking, Islamists believe that economic endeavors must build on the Qur'anic ideals of social justice, self-sacrifice, brotherhood, and harmony. Whereas in earlier Islamic discourses the term *justice* ("adl") referred primarily to the attainment of moral and religious perfection under the guardianship of a virtuous prince, with the Islamists it came also to include the collective ideals of social responsibility and solidarity. Whether Islamists admitted it or not, the new emphasis on socio-economic issues was in large part influenced by the critique proffered by European socialist groups in the middle decades of the twentieth century. By implementing Qur'an-inspired economic solutions, Islamists sought to establish Islam's dominance over an area of endeavor in which Muslims had come to rely on the West's expert knowledge.

Islamists understand the major cause of the Muslim world's economic backwardness to be its moral decline. In the Islamist perspective, the high point of Islamic morality was reached during the time of the Rightly Guided Caliphs (A.D. 632–661). Not surprisingly, for Islamists, during that period Islamdom flourished materially, as well as spiritually. However, over succeeding centuries Islam was compromised by corrupt rulers and by the introduction into the faith of extraneous influences. But it was only in the past two centuries, under the impact of the political power and cultural influence of the West, that the trend of decline reached a crisis point. According to Islamists, the cultural subjugation of Muslims by the West has led to the weakening of solidarity among Muslims. Instead of working toward the common good, Muslims are mired in abject materialism and selfish individualism. In order to reverse the trend of economic stagnation and community decline, market behavior and social relations must be governed by norms found in the Qur'an and prophetic traditions. While some Islamists are content to correct bad behavior by focusing on the conversion of hearts and minds, others "favor supplementing norm-guided self-regulation by state-enforced controls."

For Islamists, the most important vehicle for the establishment of social and economic justice is the institution of *zakat*. Derived from *zaka* (thrive, increase, be pure in heart, righteous, good), *zakat* is obligatory alms giving for all adult males who possess a modicum of personal wealth. By tradition, *zakat* is levied on between 2.5 percent and 20 percent of an individual's liquid assets, depending on conditions and the source of income, and is paid during the fasting month of Ramadan. The proceeds of *zakat* are distributed to specific categories of impoverished and disadvantaged individuals, although many Islamist groups also use the proceeds to fund their activities. As Sayyid Qutb wrote in his book *Social Justice in Islam*, "The whole Islamic *umma* is one body and feels as one body; whatever happens to one of its members, the remainder of the members are also affected." *Zakat* became one of the five pillars of Islam following the Prophet Muhammad's flight to Medina in 622. In the modern era *zakat* has been mostly a voluntary affair. As the readings below indicate, many Islamists want *zakat* to be administered by the state.

Mutual Responsibility

- *Document:* Selection from *Ishtirakiyyat al-Islam* (*The Socialism of Islam*), by Shaykh Mustafa al-Siba'i.
- *Date:* 1960.
- *Where:* Damascus, Syria.
- *Significance:* Responding to Socialist ideology, which was dominant in the Arab world in the decades following World War II, Mustafa Siba'i details how Islam provides the foundation for a caring and organically whole society.

DOCUMENT

People, in the society in which they live, need each other in all phases of life. As a whole, they make up a coherent force which comes to perfection or completion only through the strength of each individual and his happiness, just as an army's strength is not completely fulfilled unless each individual in it is strong physically and morally. A strong society depends on the degree of the strength of the individuals and a happy society depends on the degree of the happiness of each individual.

The world in modern times has become aware of this fact and has begun to call for *al-takaful al-ijtima'i* (mutual or joint responsibility) among the individuals of the society, and to limit the concept of *al-takaful al-ijtima'i* to fulfilling the demands of deprived groups in terms of food, clothing, housing and the like. But Islam recognized this fourteen centuries ago. After legislating for each citizen the Five Rights, without which human dignity and happiness could not be fulfilled, it [Islam] looked at those whose circumstances prevented their enjoyment of [the Five Rights] and held society responsible for making them possible. This is the source of the idea of *al-takaful al-ijtima'i* in Islamic socialism.

When Islam in its socialism calls for *al-takaful al-ijtima'i,* it does not mean simply food, housing or clothing needs, but rather it broadens the concept to include the five rights about which we spoke. Thus, its idea of *al-takaful al-ijtima'i* has come to include all material and moral aspects of life.

The Principle of *al-Takaful al-Ijtima'i* in Islam

Islam's declaration of the principle of *al-takaful al-ijtima'i* is manifested in many texts in the Qur'an and the Sunnah. We take two quotations from the book of God Almighty and three from the Hadith of the Prophet of God.

From the Glorious Qur'an: "The believers are brethren." To declare "brotherhood" among the individuals of any society necessitates *al-takaful* (mutual responsibility) among them, not only in eating, drinking and bodily needs but also in every other necessity of life. Could you ever see a brother who cares only to feed his hungry brother? Doesn't he also care for his brother's life, freedom, education, dignity, and social status? Don't you see him unhappy because of his brother's unhappiness even if such a brother is one of those who feed and clothe [others]? Don't you find him anxious about his present and future, even if such a brother is established and settled down?

To acknowledge brotherhood between two [persons] is an acknowledgement of *al-takaful* (mutual responsibility) and *tadamun* (solidarity) between them in sentiments and feelings, in demands and needs, and in status and dignity. This is the truth of *al-takaful al-ijtima'i* in Islamic socialism.

The Qur'an has also mentioned, "And help one another in righteousness and piety; and help not one another in sin and aggression." Such cooperation is al-*takaful* and solidarity (*tadamun*) in the realization of something. This verse demands *takaful* in order to be righteous and pious. But what is righteousness and what is piety in Islam? We do not want to conclude from the Qur'anic texts that its true meaning can be arrived at only by learned men who have thorough knowledge of the secrets of Islamic law (*shari'ah*) and who are acquainted with its foundations and principles. But we do want to know the meaning of righteousness and piety from the clear, frank texts of the Qur'an. What do they mean in the Qur'an?

1. Righteousness in the Qur'an has the meaning of maintaining good relationships, good social associations, good morals and avoiding mischievous and tyrannical behavior. About this the Almighty said, "(He) hath made me kind to my mother, and not over-bearing or miserable."

2. It also has the meaning of spending and sacrifice for the sake of God. Righteousness is the wholesome path of truth, goodness and usefulness. Concerning this He, the Almighty said, "By no means shall ye attain righteousness unless ye give (freely) of that which ye love."

3. Righteousness has the meaning of worship in terms of prayer and almsgiving (*zakat*). In this He, the Almighty, said after he ordered the children of Israel to perform prayer and pay the *zakat*, "Do ye enjoin right conduct on the people, and forget (to practice it) yourselves, and yet ye study the scripture? Will ye not understand?"

4. It has the meaning of a group of psychological, dogmatic and moral virtues. In this He, the Almighty, said, "It is not righteousness that you turn your faces towards East or West, but it is righteousness to believe in God and the last day, and the angels, and the Book, and the messengers; to spend of your substance, out of love for Him, for your kin, for orphans, for the needy, for the wayfarer, for those who ask, and for the ransom of slaves; to be steadfast in prayer, and practice regular charity; to fulfill the contracts which ye have made; and to be firm and patient in pain (or suffering) and adversity, and throughout all periods of panic. Such are the people of truth, the God-fearing."

As for defining the meaning of piety, it has been mentioned clearly and frankly in many verses of the glorious Qur'an.

1. It means a group of psychological, dogmatic and moral virtues as mentioned in paragraph four which defines the meaning of righteousness. He, the Almightly, says, "This

is the Book; in it is guidance sure, without doubt, to those who fear God, who believe in the Unseen, are steadfast in prayer, and spend out of what we have provided for them."

2. It means also the glorification of God's rules and laws: "And whoever holds in honor the symbols of God (in the sacrifice of animals), such (honor) should come truly from piety of heart."

3. It means forgiveness and tolerance: "And remission is the nearest to righteousness."

4. It means justice and avoidance of oppression: "Be just; that is next to piety."

5. It means the opposite of wickedness and immorality: "And its [the soul's] enlightenment as to its wrong and its right."

6. It means faithfulness and truth: "And he who brings the truth and he who confirms (and supports) it—such are the men who do right."

7. It means the fulfillment of promise: "So fulfill your engagements with them to the end of their term: for God loveth the righteous."

8. It means the fight for God (al-jihad) with money and self: "To fight with their goods and persons and God knoweth well those who do their duty."

9. It means the absence of tyranny and corruption on earth: "That home of the hereafter, we shall give to those who intend not high-handedness or mischief on earth. And the end is (best) for the righteous."

10. It means the fear of God and the penitence of the heart: "And the garden will be brought nigh to the righteous—no more a thing distant. (A voice will say): This is what was promised for you—for everyone who turned (to God) in sincere repentance, who kept (His law), who feared (God) most gracious unseen, and brought a heart turned in devotion (to Him)."

11. It means undertaking the affairs of the deprived and the needy and giving them their right which God has legislated to them in His religion: "As to the righteous they will be in the midst of gardens and springs, taking joy in the things which their Lord gives them, because, before then, they lived a good life. They were in the habit of sleeping but little by night, and in the hours of early dawn they (were found) praying for forgiveness; and in their wealth and possessions (was remembered) the right of the (needy), him who asked, and him who (for some reason) was prevented (from asking)."

12. It means the desertion of oppressors, and not trusting or relying upon them: "It is only wrongdoers (that stand as) protectors, one to another: but God is the protector of the righteous."

[The principle of al-takaful al-ijtima'i is manifested] in the true Hadith: "You see the believers in their friendly relations with each other, in their kindness to each other, and their love for each other, for if one member of a body complains, the other members stay up all night with a fever." This is a text on takaful (mutual responsibility) in society and the responsibility of its members towards the suffering of an individual, which does not need more discussion or explanation.

In the true Hadith it is also written: "The believer to his fellow believer is like the parts of a structure which are supported by each other." The Prophet joined [folded] his hands to assure the meaning, "to support each other." This, too, does not need to be discussed to show its bearing on the principle of al-takaful al-ijtima'i. In explaining this Hadith al-Munawi said, "That is because the strongest among them constitute a pillar and the weakest among them lean on that strong pillar. If the strong support the weak, they become stronger from within." He also reports, "It has become difficult for each one to attain for himself the minimum of what he needs except though the help of others. For example, it would be difficult to check on the amount of labor involved in making a piece of bread, such as planting [the seed], sending it to the mill and baking it, as well as manufacturing the machinery [used for baking]. Therefore, it has been said that man is civilized by nature and cannot live in isolation from the group."

Perhaps the most definitive statement in the Hadith regarding the establishment of the bases of *al-takaful al-ijtima'i* is the Prophet's saying, "None of you can be a believer unless he would love for his brother what he loves for himself."

Does man love only bread, meat, clothing and shoes for himself? Does he not also value life, dignity, freedom, education and whatever brings happiness in life?

SOURCE: Sami A. Hanna and George H. Gardner, *Arab Socialism: A Documentary Survey* (Salt Lake City, UT: University of Utah Press, 1969), 149–53. Reprinted with permission.

CONTEXT AND ANALYSIS

Mustafa al-Siba'i belonged to the generation of Islamist thinkers and activists that included Hasan al-Banna, Sayyid Qutb, and Abu A'la Maududi. Born in 1910 in Homs, Syria, Shaykh Mustafa journeyed to Cairo, Egypt where he obtained from the prestigious al-Azhar University the *alimiyya* degree, which provided him the credentials of an Islamic scholar. In Egypt Shaykh al-Siba'i was influenced by the ideas of Hasan al-Banna and on his return to Damascus was instrumental in founding a group called *Shabab Muhammad*, "Young Men of Muhammad." In the mid-1940s al-Siba'i linked his group to the Egyptian Muslim Brotherhood. Unlike Egypt's Muslim Brotherhood, which was mostly middle class, the Syrian version was closely aligned with wealthy Sunni landowners and merchants; most of these lived in Hama and Aleppo. This ultra-conservative alliance was cemented by overlapping socioeconomic and sectarian fault lines, as the political forces that challenged Syria's political establishment included Christian, Druze, and Alawite minorities (10 percent, 3 percent, and 12 percent of the Syrian population, respectively). The Muslim Brotherhood and its allies among the Sunni merchant and landowning classes were marginalized when the Alawite dominated Ba'ath Party came to power in Syria in the 1960s.

Shaykh Mustafa al-Siba'i was an active participant in his country's political life, using Syria's newly independent political institutions to advance an Islamist agenda. In 1947 he was elected deputy from Homs in Syria's parliament and in 1949 became a member of the parliament's constitutional committee. That same year he founded the Islamic Socialist Front, which functioned as the political wing of Syria's Muslim Brotherhood. A staunch opponent of the state of Israel, Shaykh al-Siba'i called on Syria's government to establish close relations with the Soviet Union to counterbalance the West's support for the Jewish State.

His book, *Ishtirakiyyat al-Islam* (*The Socialism of Islam*), from which the above selection is taken, reflects his ongoing concern for the Islamic roots of social justice. Central to Shaykh al-Siba'i's argument is the Islamic principle of "mutual social responsibility," which balances the ideal of individual responsibility against that of individual freedom. In the Arab world, the principle of mutual social responsibility was pioneered in Egypt in the late 1940s at a time when conventional leftist forces were challenging mainstream nationalism in terms that emphasized the inseparability of economic and political forms of liberation. All of the contending forces among the Egyptian opposition were affected by the persuasive logic of the leftist critique, including the Muslim Brothers. Fearful of losing out to the Communists and Socialists for influence in the textile union, the Brotherhood devoted attention to workers' issues, introducing social welfare schemes into its activities. In 1949, Sayyid Qutb provided a theoretical framework for economic concerns in his book *Social Justice in Islam*. Qutb and other Egyptian Brotherhood writers saw the problem of economic injustice as issuing from the alien, non-Islamic values that had infiltrated Egypt on the heels of imperialism.

Shaykh al-Siba'i's *The Socialism of Islam* owes much to the Egyptian-Islamist critique of Western capitalism. Following his Egyptian mentors, he proffers a holistic solution to society's ills. People, he explains need each other in all phases of life. As individuals they are powerless and vulnerable. But gathered together they make up a coherent force. Just as an army's strength is not completely fulfilled unless each individual in it is strong physically and morally, so too society comes to perfection or completion only through the strength of each individual and his happiness. A society is strong only in as far as the individual is strong, and is happy only in as far as each individual is happy.

Shaykh Mustafa al-Siba'i makes the important point that the concept of mutual responsibility includes more than physical well-being, it also covers the moral aspects of life. Further, the concept did not arise out of class warfare or out of a desire to control the wealth of the rich. Rather, it emerges organically as a value that is inherent to Islam.

FURTHER READINGS

Enayat, Hamid. *Modern Islamic Political Thought* (Austin: University of Texas Press, 1982), 152.

Ismael, Tareq. *The Arab Left* (Syracuse, NY: Syracuse University Press, 1976).

Tripp, Charles. *Islam and the Moral Economy: The Challenge of Capitalism* (New York: Cambridge University Press, 2006).

Voll, John O. "Fundamentalism in the Sunni Arab World: Egypt and the Sudan," in Martin E. Marty and Scott Appleby (eds.), *Fundamentalisms Observed* (Chicago: University of Chicago Press, 1995).

IN HISTORY

Khurshid Ahmad: The Moral Foundations of Socioeconomic Development

Khurshid Ahmad (b. 1934) is a former professor of economics with close ties to Pakistan's Jama'at-e Islami. In the following passages he puts Islam forward as a third way of economic development that takes the whole person into consideration:

But here we must reject the archetypes of capitalism and socialism. Both are exploitative and unjust and fail to treat man as man, as god's vicegerent (*khalifa*) on earth. Both have been unable to meet in their own realms the basic economic, social, political and moral challenges of our time and the real needs of a humane society and a just economy. Both are irrelevant to our situation, not merely because of the differences in ideological and moral attitudes and in socio-political frameworks, but also for a host of more mundane and economic reasons, like differences in relative resource bases, changed international economic situations, bench-mark differences in the levels of the respective economies, socioeconomic costs of development, and above all, for the fundamental fact that the crucial development strategy of both the systems—industrialization primarily through maximization of investible surplus—is not suited to the conditions of the Muslim world and the demands of the Islamic social ideals.

Islam is deeply concerned with the problem of economic development, but treats this as an important part of a wider problem, that of total human development. The primary function of Islam is to guide human development on correct lines and in the right direction. It deals with all aspects of economic development but always in the framework of total human development and never in a form divorced from this perspective. That is why the focus, even the economic sector, is on human development, with the result that economic development remains an integrated and integrated element of moral and socioeconomic development in human society.

SOURCE: Khurshid Ahmad, *The Challenge of Islam*, ed. Altaf Gauhar (London: Islamic Council of Europe, 1978), 341–45.

Our Economy

- *Document:* Selection from *Iqtisaduna* (*Our Economy*) by Muhammad Baqir al-Sadr.
- *Date:* 1960.
- *Where:* Najaf, Iraq.
- *Significance:* Muhammad Baqir al-Sadr, in one of the most complete Islamist works on the economic system to date, explicates the ethical underpinnings of Islamic economic theory and practice.

DOCUMENT

Islamic Morals and Values Are Different

There is in fact an Islamic morality alive to one degree or other in the Islamic world, and there is a morality of European economy which accompanied modern Western civilization and wove for it its general spirit and prepared the way for its success on the economic level. The two moralities differ substantially in their orientation, their point of view and their value systems. To the extent that the morality of modern Western man is sound for European economic systems, the morality of man in the Islamic world is compatible with it. This morality has deep roots which cannot be extirpated by merely diluting the religious creed.

Planning—any planning for the battle against backwardness—must necessarily take into account the resistance of nature in the country for which the plan is intended, the degree to which it will resist operations of production. So too, account must be taken of the resistance of the human element and the extent to which it is in harmony with this or that plan.

European man looks always to earth, not to heaven. Even Christianity, the religion in which European man believed for hundreds of years, was not able to overcome his earthly tendency. Rather than the Christian raising his view to heaven, he was able to bring the God of Christianity down to earth and incarnate him in an earthly being.

The attempts to tie man's lineage to groups of animals and to explain humanity as an objective adaptation to the land and environment in which he lives, or the scientific attempts to explain the whole human edifice on the basis of productive forces which represent the earth and the potential within it, these attempts are nothing other than endeavors to bring God down to earth. This is their psychological signification. They are all morally tied to that deep-seated view of the soul of European man towards the earth, even though their style and scientific or mythical character may differ.

This view towards the earth allowed European man to give values to matter, resources and property which harmonize with his basic orientation.

The values rooted in European man over the ages expressed themselves in schools (*madhahib*) of sensual delight and pragmatism which inundated moral philosophical thinking in Europe. These schools, in as much as they were the product of European thought, registered great success in Europe. They had psychological significance and meaning for the general temper of the European soul.

FREEDOM IS MATERIALISTIC ABERRATION

In the same way, European man's cutting of the true tie with his God and his looking to earth instead of to heaven snatched from his mind any true notion of a lofty presence on high or of limits imposed from outside the circle of his own self. This prepared him psychologically and noetically to believe in his right to liberty and to submerge himself in a flood of feelings of independence and individualism …

Freedom played a principle role in European economy and the operation of development was able to use to advantage the deep-rooted feelings of European man concerning freedom, independence and individualism for the success of free economy; it was a means in accord with the deep-rooted tendencies in the souls and minds of European peoples …

We all know that the deep sentiment of freedom provided a basic condition without which many of the activities in the process of development would never have taken place—that condition was the absence of any feeling of moral responsibility.

Freedom itself was an instrument to open up European man to the concept of struggle because it set every man loose from all limits save that of the presence of the other person opposite him. Every individual, by his existence, formed a limit to the liberty of the other person. Thus the notion of struggle grew in the mind of European man, and this notion expressed itself on the philosophical level, as we saw, in the other basic thoughts which went to make up the mixture of modern Western civilization. This notion of struggle expressed itself in scientific and philosophical ideas on the inevitability of class struggle within society or on dialectical movement and the explanation of the universe on the basis of thesis, antithesis and the synthesis arising out of the struggle between two contradictories. All these tendencies which bear a scientific or philosophical stamp are before all else an expression of the general psychological state and the vehement feelings of the man of modern civilization concerning struggle.

Struggle had a great effect in orienting modern European economy and the operations of development which accompanied it. This was so whether it took the individualist form and expressed itself in fierce unlimited competition between personal capitalist institutions and projects under a free economy, developing all resources through competition and struggle for existence, or whether it took the class form and expressed itself in revolutionary groups which took over key positions of production in the country and moved all potential to the benefit of economic development.

This is the morality of European economy and on these grounds this economy was able to set itself in motion, achieve growth and register huge gains.

Eastern Man Is Oriented to the Invisible

This morality differs from that which the *umma* in the Islamic world lives as a result of its religious history. Eastern man, brought up on the heavenly missions which lived in his lands, extensively educated in religion by Islam, naturally looks to heaven before he looks to earth.

He accepts the invisible world before the world of matter and sense. His deep infatuation with the invisible world expresses itself on the level of thought in the life of Muslims by the orientation of thought in the Islamic world towards the intellectual spheres of human knowledge rather than those tied to sense reality.

This profound other-worldliness in the character of Muslim man limits the seductive force of matter for him and its capacity to impress him. This fact explains why man in the Islamic world, when he is deprived of moral motives for interacting with matter and finds no enticement to exploit it, tends to take a negative attitude towards it—an attitude which takes the form of asceticism at times, temperance at others or even laziness at others.

This other-worldliness has trained him to feelings of an unseen supervision which may express itself in the pious Muslim's consciousness of his clear responsibility before God Almighty, or in the mind of another Muslim as a well defined and directed conscience. In any case, it keeps man in the Islamic world far from sensing personal freedom and moral freedom in the way modern man does.

... And to the Community

This internal limitation felt by Muslim man has its moral base in the interests of the community in which he lives; consequently he feels a profound tie with the group to which he is related. There is harmony between him and the community, not struggle, the notion which dominates modern European thought. This notion of community reinforces the world framework of the mission of Islam for the Muslim and charges this mission with the responsibility of assuring its presence in the world and its extension in time and place....

If we look on this morality which man in the Islamic world lives as a truth represented in the being of the *umma*, we can put it to good use in the economic program within the Islamic world by placing that program in a framework which marches with that morality so that it may become a force of impulsion and movement just like the morality of modern European economic programs was a great factor in the success of those programs because of the harmony between the two.

The regard of man in the Islamic world towards heaven before earth could lead to a negative attitude to earth, its resources and goods—asceticism, moderation and laziness—if earth is separated from heaven. If, however, earth is clothed in the framework of heaven and action with nature is given the quality of duty and worship, then this otherworldly view is transformed for the Muslim man into active energy and impulsive force to participate to the greatest degree possible in raising the economic level. Instead of the coldness towards earth which the negative Muslim feels today, or the psychological anxiety which the active Muslim who follows the styles of free economy or socialism feels for the most part, even though he is a watered down Muslim, there will be generated a full harmony between the psychology of the man of the Islamic world and his anticipated positive role in the process of development.

The concept of internal limits and other-worldly supervision which prevents man in the Islamic world from living according to the European notion of freedom can help to avoid, to a great degree, the difficulties which spring from free economy and hinder economic development by providing moral justification for general planning.

Group ties and sensibilities can share in mobilizing the energies of the Islamic *umma* for the battle against backwardness if the battle is waged under a slogan which coincides with those sensibilities, such as jihad for preserving the essence and existence of the *umma*. This is what the Qur'an does when it says: Make ready for them all that you can (Sura viii, 60). The order is to prepare all forces including the economic which are represented by the level of production as part of the battle of the *umma* and its jihad to preserve its existence and sovereignty.

This brings out the importance of the Islamic economy as an economic program capable of using to advantage the morality of man in the Islamic world and transforming it into a great impulsive and constructive energy for operations of development and for success in sound planning for economic life.

When we adopt the Islamic system we will profit from this morality and be able to mobilize it in the battle against backwardness, contrary to what would happen if we adopted the programs in economy which are psychologically and historically rooted in the ground of another morality.

Stewardship

Some European thinkers have begun to realize this truth and to take note of it, acknowledging that their programs do not accord with the nature of the Islamic world.... I would like to expand on this on another occasion, for now suffice it to say that the orientation of man in the Islamic world towards heaven does not in its authentic sense mean that man submits to fate and relies on the conditions, opportunities and feelings of complete incompetence concerning creativity and invention ... rather this orientation of Muslim man is a true expression of the principle of stewardship of man on earth. By his very nature he inclines to see his position on earth as an expression of his stewardship to God. I know of no concept richer than this for affirming the capacity of man and his energies; it makes him the absolute master of the universe. And I know of no concept further removed from surrender and fate than the concept of stewardship to God because stewardship gets to the bottom of the sense of responsibility concerning what one is made steward of. There is no responsibility without liberty and a sense of choice and an ability to master circumstances. Otherwise, what stewardship would this be if man was bound or remotely controlled? For this reason, we say that clothing the earth in the framework of heaven releases the energies of Muslim man and stirs up his potential, whereas cutting earth off from heaven annuls the sense of stewardship and fixes the view of Muslim man on earth in a negative way....

One Foundation for All—Islam

In addition to all that precedes, we would like to remark that taking Islam as the basis for general organization allows us to set up all of our life, both spiritual and social aspects, on one foundation because Islam extends to both, whereas many of the social programs other than Islam are limited to the social and economic relations in the life of man and his ideals. If we take our general program for life from human sources instead of the Islamic system, we leave the organization of the spiritual side unsatisfied. There is no sound source for the organization of our spiritual life except Islam. There is no way but to establish both sides, spiritual and social, on the foundation peculiar to Islam. Moreover, the two sides are not isolated from one another but interact to a great degree. The interaction makes it more sound and harmonious to set up the two on one base given the unmistakable inter-connection of spiritual social activities in the life of man.

SOURCE: Preface to second printing of M.B. Al-Sadr, *Iqtisaduna*, Dar al-Fikr, Beirut, 1974. Translated by John J. Donohue in John J. Donohue and John L. Esposito, *Islam in Transition: Muslim Perspectives*, 2nd ed. (New York and Oxford: Oxford University Press, 2007), 254–59. By permission of Oxford University Press, Inc.

Original complete translation by Tehran World Services, 1981.

CONTEXT AND ANALYSIS

Muhammad Baqir al-Sadr was born in 1935 in Kazimiyya, West Baghdad, to a family famous in the Shi'i world for its learning. In 1945 the family moved to Najaf where Baqir al-Sadr spent the rest of his life. Al-Sadr's mastery of Islamic jurisprudence at Najaf's seminaries eventually earned him the title of Ayatollah, a high-ranking title given to major Shi'i clerics. In 1958 Iraq's constitutional monarchy fell to officers within Iraq's armed forces under

IN HISTORY

Muhammad Baqir al-Sadr and the Da'wa Party

Muhammad Baqir al-Sadr was the driving force behind the creation of the Da'wa Party, launched in the late 1950s in the holy city of Najaf in Iraq. Organized into secret cells, the party's objective was to preserve Shi'i identity against the influence of Western ideologies, which in 1950s and 1960s Iraq chiefly meant Communism. Al-Sadr's writings on philosophical, social, and economic topics provided the party with its ideology. From being a traditionalist, al-Sadr sought the renewal of Shi'i Islam in the modern period through the reform of Islamic institutions. Over the 1970s Baqir al-Sadr and the Da'wa Party protested Saddam Husayn's suppression of the Shi'i population. Inspired by the Islamic Revolution in neighboring Iran, some members of al-Da'wa turned to violence. In response, Saddam hanged Muhammad Baqir al-Sadr and his sister Fatima in 1980. The executions diminished the party's standing in Iraq. However, remnants of the party found a safe haven in Iran. Unlike Iran's Ayatollahs, the Da'wa Party does not subscribe to the doctrine of clerical rule over the state (*Wilayat al-Faqih*). Hojjatoleslam Muqtada al-Sadr, the fiery cleric who opposes the U.S. presence in Iraq, is the son-in-law of Muhammad Baqir al-Sadr.

the command of 'Abd al-Karim Qasim. Qasim was a secularist who curried the support of Iraq's substantial Communist movement. Afraid that Iraq's new rulers would further marginalize the Shi'i clerical establishment, and fearing a Communist takeover of the state, Baqir al-Sadr was instrumental in forming the Shi'i-dominated Islamic Da'wa Party whose goal was to combat secularism and Communism in Iraq. The Da'wa organized dedicated Muslim believers with the goal of seizing power and establishing an Islamic state.

In addition, al-Sadr began to write *Iqtisaduna* ("Our Economy"), a multivolume work that was published in 1961 when he was in his thirties. By that time al-Sadr was one of the leading scholars in the religious school of Najaf with a distinguished reputation in jurisprudence. The book is a significant contribution to the concept of an Islamic economic system distinct from the dominant Capitalist and Socialist systems. It takes aim, in particular, at Communism, which al-Sadr feared would spread beyond its established base to the general population of Shi'is, among whom the appeal of social justice and revolutionary ideas was strong. According to al-Sadr, Marxism is concerned solely with production and distribution. In theory and practice it ignores the spiritual dimensions of life. Capitalists and workers, says, al-Sadr, are not simply units in an economic system, but human beings with moral responsibilities. It is true that humans are often motivated by the desire to command resources, but for Marxists this is an end while for Muslims it is only the means to a more encompassing fulfillment, one that is defined by spiritual value. In al-Sadr's view, power over resources provides men the ability to carry out God's ordinances and to create a just society. His discourse on Islamic economics was enormously influential, especially among Shi'i Muslims, inspiring activists such as Abol Hasan Bani Sadr who was to become the first President of the Islamic Republic of Iran. Baqir al-Sadr perhaps did more than any other Islamist writer in demonstrating to Muslims that Islam possessed a superior and unique understanding of social and economic issues.

Muhammad Baqir al-Sadr did much to empower the majority Shi'i population of Iraq against Communists and the Sunni-dominated secular establishment. He was the driving force behind the "Shi'i Rennaisance" that took root in Iraq in the 1960s. However, after coming to power in 1968, the Ba'th Party initiated a crackdown on Shi'i assertiveness. The Ba'thists targeted the Islamic Da'wa Party, arresting and imprisoning many of its members. In 1975, the Ba'thists forbade Iraq's Shi'is to carry out the annual procession from Najaf to Karbala, one of the most important events in the Shi'i calendar. In 1977, al-Sadr was sentenced to life in prison following uprisings in Najaf, but was released two years later due to his immense popularity. Upon his release, however, he was put under house arrest. In 1980, after writing in the defense of Khomeini and the Islamic Revolution, al-Sadr was once again imprisoned, tortured, and executed by the regime of Saddam Husayn. His sister, Amina Sadr bint al-Huda, was also imprisoned, tortured, and executed. It is worthwhile to mention that al-Sadr's and Khomeini's visions of an Islamic Republic differed sharply in certain respects. While Khomeini argued the power of the state should rest with the religious scholars, al-Da'wa supported the notion of power resting with the community.

FURTHER READINGS

Aziz, T. M. "The Role of Muhammad Baqir al-Sadr in Shi'i Political Activism in Iraq from 1958–1980," *International Journal of Middle East Studies*, 25 (1993), 209–19.

Batatu, Hanna. "Iraq's Underground Shi'a Movements: Characteristics, Causes, and Prospects," *Middle East Journal*, 35, no. 4 (1981), 578–94.

Mallat, Chibli. *The Renewal of Islamic Law: Muhammad Baqer al-Sadr, Najaf, and the Shi'i International* (Cambridge: Cambridge University Press, 1993).

Walbridge, John. "Muhammad Baqir al-Sadr: The Search for New Foundations," in Elizabeth Walbridge (ed.), *The Most Learned of the Shi'a: The Institution of the Marja Taqlid* (New York: Oxford University Press, 2001).

Wilson, Rodney. "The Contribution of Muhammad Baqir al-Sadr to Contemporary Islamic Economic Thought," *Journal of Islamic Studies*, 9, no. 1 (1998), 46–59.

"The Goal of Islam
Is to Eliminate Misery"

- **Document:** Selections from, *Islam between East and West*, by the late president of Bosnia, Alija Izetbegovic.
- **Date:** 1984.
- **Where:** Sarajevo, Bosnia-Herzegovina.
- **Significance:** In this wide-ranging book, Izetbegovic explicates Islam's comprehensive nature. In contrast to Western philosophies, it exalts the spirit without denigrating the body. Izetbegovic wrote the book on the eve of Yugoslavia's break-up and the commencement of the war in Bosnia.

DOCUMENT

Socialism, as a practical and social consequence of materialism, does not deal with man but rather with the organization of the life of the social animal. Man is primarily a spiritual and not a biological or social factor, and could originate only by the act of divine creation. Thus, if there were no God, there could be no man, and if there were no man, there would be no culture, only the needs and their satisfaction—that is, only civilization. Atheism accepts science and progress; yet in its essence, it implies the negation of man and by the same token a refutation of humanism, freedom, and human rights. Behind the contradiction between culture and civilization stands in fact the basic contrast between conscience/mind and being/nature, or on the practical plane, between religion and science....

Is man able to overcome this contradiction, this either or between heaven and earth, or is he condemned forever to this stretching between the two? Is there a way by which science can serve religion, hygiene, piety, progress, and humanism? Could the utopia of civitas be inhabited with human beings instead of anonymous and faceless individuals and have the features of "God's kingdom" on earth?

... The answer is yes, in Islam. Islam is not only a religion or way of life but primarily the principle of the organization of the universe. Islam existed before man and it is, as the Qur'an explicitly states, a principle by which man was created. Hence, one finds an inherent harmony between man and Islam or ... the "manlikeness" of Islam. In the same way as man is a unity of spirit and body, Islam is a unity of religion and social order, and just as the body in prayer (*salah*) can follow the movement of the soul, the social order can serve the ideals of religion and ethics. This unity, foreign both to Christianity and materialism, is basic and the "most Islamic" characteristic of Islam.....

The metamorphosis of religion in Islam is ... clearly evident in the example of *zakah*. In the early period of Islam (the Mekkan period), *zakah* was voluntary giving to the poor, a kind of alms. When the Medinian community was established—(the historical moment at which a purely spiritual community was turned into a state), Muhammad began to treat *zakah* as a legal obligation, a tax to be paid by the rich to the poor—as far as we know, the first tax in history. By adding a component of force to the Christian institution of alms, Islam created *zakah*, "the obligatory charity" as Risler named it. The same logic which had turned prayer into *salah* now turned alms into *zakah*, and in the final result, religion into Islam.

With the proclamation of *zakah*, Islam began to take on the contours of a social movement. It no longer functioned only as a religion. *Zakah* only took on its true weight with the formation of the Medinian political community. A certain indication of this character of *zakah* is the fact that it is mentioned in the Qur'an eight times in the Mekkan suras, and twenty-two times in the Medinian *suras*.

Zakah is a response to a phenomenon which by itself is not one-sided. Misery is not only a social issue. Its cause is not only the privation but also the evil in human souls. Deprivation is its external side, and sin is its internal side. How else can we explain the existence of misery in human societies? In the second half of the twentieth century, one-third of mankind is chronically undernourished. Is that owing to a lack of goods or to a lack of feelings? Every solution to the problem of misery must include the confession of guilt and, in addition, must serve as penitence. Every social solution must include a human solution. It should not only change economic relations but also the relations between man and man. It should bring about the just distribution of goods as well as proper upbringing, love, and sympathy.

Poverty is a problem, but it is also a sin. It is not solved only through a shift of the ownership of goods but also through personal striving, aim, and good will. Nothing would be done in the true sense of the word if the ownership of this world's goods changed, but hatred, exploitation, and subjugation remain in man's soul. This is the reason for the failure of Christian religious revolts and socialist revolutions. "For two thousand years, the sum of evil in the world has not lessened. Not a single empire, divine or revolutionary, has attained its end" (Albert Camus, *l'Homme revolte* (Paris: Gallimard, 1951). Religious revolts were too religious and social revolutions too social. Religion felt that it would be more religious if it rejected politics and violence, while socialism held as its main duty to convince its adepts that violence is the only way, whereas charity is just a deception. Man needs a religion which is politics and politics which are ethics, or charity which can become a social obligation, a tax. Thus we come to the definition of *zakah*.

People are mirrored in *zakah*. It depends on them whether it will be a tax or a voluntary giving from man to man. *Zakah* is a great river of goods flowing from heart to heart, from man to man. *Zakah* eliminates poverty among the poor and indifference among the rich. It reduces material differences between people and brings them closer to each other.

The goal of Islam is not to eliminate riches but to eliminate misery. What is misery? It is a shortage of the things which are indispensable for a normal life, having less than the necessary minimum for life, being below "the minimum living standard." The "minimum living standard" is a natural and historical category and represents the sum of goods that is necessary for a man and his family to satisfy their physical and social needs. It follows that society is not bound to reduce everyone to the same level, but first of all to give every man the said minimum standard. Islamic social measures are limited to the elimination of misery and do not extend to the equalization of property, the moral and economic justification of which is dubious.

Theological considerations concerning *zakah* are usually limited to how much of what to give. Except for the institution of *zakah*, the very principle of solidarity is more important than percentages and figures. The principle according to which the higher part of society is obliged to financially help the poorer part is of crucial importance. Doubtless, one day when the true Islamic order is established, it will strive to fulfill the very intention of this principle, whether income level and population statistics are overstepped or not. Also, the goal of this principle will be attained only when the richer part of society will give to the poorer part according to the needs of the latter. Since *zakah* is the right of the poor, it will be, if necessary, provided by force.

According to some authors, there are eighty-two places in the Qur'an where the obligation or suggestion of giving is mentioned. Due to this persistent Islamic teaching on giving, a quiet revolution took place in Muslim societies through the institution of *waqf*. *Waqf*, by its widespread character and importance, has no parallel in non-Islamic societies. There is almost no Muslim country where big properties have not been given as *waqf* to serve the common welfare. *Waqf* is not mentioned in the Qur'an, but it did not appear by chance. It emerged as the result of a spirit of mutual assistance and as a consequence of *zakah*'s educational function. This humane practice offers the hope that certain important social goals can be attained without violence. The *waqf* or material goods in the service of ethical aims prove that great changes can be brought about in the field of economics without the intervention of material interest. In this regard, *waqf* is the opposite of the so-called "natural laws of economics." It is an anomaly from the viewpoint of political economy, but with its duality ("economic category with a soul") it is a typical Islamic practice.

SOURCE: 'Alija 'Ali Izetbegovic, *Islam between East and West* (Indianapolis, IN: American Trust Publications, 1984), xviii–xix; 205–208.

CONTEXT AND ANALYSIS

Alija Izetbegovic was born in 1925 in Bosanski, Samac, Bosnia-Herzegovina into a well-to-do family. In 1928 the family moved to multi-ethnic Sarajevo, a city where Bosnian Muslims, mostly Slavic converts to Islam, lived in relative harmony with their Serbian and Croatian neighbors. At the age of sixteen, while a student at the city's German Gymnasium, he founded the Muslim Youth Society of Bosnia, which he modeled on Egypt's Muslim Brotherhood. He went on to study agriculture. But his true passion remained the empowerment of Muslims in the Balkans. His involvement with a journal called *Mujahid* ("Fighter for the Faith") attracted the attention of Yugoslavia's Communist authorities and he was sentenced to three years in prison. After his release he became a lawyer and used his legal skills to defend fellow Muslims in the courts. In 1970 he issued a strongly worded tractate called "The Islamic Declaration," which called on Muslims to create an Islamic state, thereby taking control of their destiny, although he made no specific reference to Bosnia. In a controversial passage, he declared that "there can be no coexistence between the Islamic faith and non-Islamic social and political institutions." This work contributed to his portrayal by the Yugoslav state as a radical Islamist.

Izetbegovic's major intellectual accomplishment was his *Islam between East and West*, published in 1980. In stark contrast to the strident tone of his "Islamic Declaration," it is a learned work full of comparative references to Western philosophy. In the book, Izetbegovic made the point that unlike Christianity, which focuses on the salvation of the individual, Islam enchants all aspects of life with divine meaning. According to Izetbegovic, Islam's encompassing nature is expressed in the Five Pillars of the Faith. The passage above focuses on the social and spiritual aspects of *Zakat*, but Izetbegovic also discusses the "dual nature" of *salah* (prayer), Islam's second pillar, which "is not only a gathering of people for a common prayer but also for personal immediate contacts, and as such, it is in direct opposition to negative individualism and separation." In common with other Islamist theorists, Izetbegovic emphasizes Islam's strong social justice message.

Islam between East and West is clearly not the narrow work of a religious fundamentalist. Evidently, Izetbegovic's views on the role of Islam in state and society had mellowed since the "Islamic Declaration" was issued. Yet, the book's message of Islamic revival earned him another prison sentence, which he served until his release in 1988 when the Yugoslav State began to falter. Taking advantage of the Yugoslav Communist Party's loss of authority, Izetbegovic was instrumental in forming a new political movement, the Party of Democratic Action (SDA), which looked to the interests of Bosnia-Herzegovina's Muslim population. Increasingly, the party adopted Islamic symbols and insignia. When Yugoslavia finally collapsed in 1990, Izetbegovic fulfilled the wishes of the majority of Muslims in declaring Bosnia-Herzegovina an independent republic. The Serbian population of Bosnia, led by Radovan Karadizc, reacted to Muslim assertiveness by seizing territory in Bosnia-Herzegovina and driving more than 2.5 million Muslims from their homes. In the course of fighting, perhaps 350,000 Bosnian Muslims were killed. During the war Izetbegovic lived precariously in a besieged Sarajevo.

Izetbegovic died of natural causes in 2003. However, debate still rages in both political and scholarly circles as to the nature of his Islamism. Did he, as many Serbs attest, push for the creation of a theocratic Islamic state in the Balkans? Or was his Islamism primarily theoretical and not meant to be applied to the situation in Bosnia? Any answer to this question must contend with Izetbegovic's own contradictory statements on the issue. What is clear is that most Bosnian Muslims were uncomfortable with Izetbegovic's public identification of Bosnian national identity with Islam. By and large, Bosnian Muslims were decidedly secular and regarded Islam in terms of collective heritage, not as a system of laws governing society.

IN HISTORY

Zakat

"As interpreted by contemporary Islamic economics, *zakat* is a voluntary tax on wealth (i.e., productive assets) administered through the mosques, which generates a welfare fund to pay for various charitable and social projects (such as health care, education, and disaster relief). Islamic economists, who tend to be critical of the post-colonial secular states ruling in Muslim countries today, favor substituting this private, mosque-controlled network of benevolent societies for the inefficiently run, overly bureaucratic welfare-state institutions of their respective governments."

SOURCE: Karen Pfeifer, "Is There an Islamic Economics?" Joel Beinin and Joe Stork, eds., *Political Islam: Essays from Middle East Report* (Berkeley, CA: University of California Press, 1997), 158.

FURTHER READINGS

Izetbegovic, Alija. *Izetbegovic of Bosnia and Herzegovina: Notes from Prison, 1983–1988* (Westport, CT: Praeger/Greenwood, 2001).

Pinson, Mark, ed. *The Muslims of Bosnia-Herzegovina: Their Historic Development from the Middle Ages to the Dissolution of Yugoslavia* (Cambridge, MA: Harvard University Press, 1994).

Sells, Michael Anthony. *The Bridge Betrayed: Religion and Genocide in Bosnia* (Berkeley: University of California Press, 1998).

Takeyh, Ray, and Nikolas K. Gvosdev. *The Receding Shadow of the Prophet: The Rise and Fall of Radical Political Islam* (Westport, CT: Praeger, 2004), chapter 5.

"Islam Distinguishes between the Property of the State and Collective Property"

- **Document:** Article from Algerian periodical *al-Munqidh,* by 'Ali Ibn al-Shukri. Translated from the French version of the original Arabic by David Vanderboegh.
- **Date:** 1991.
- **Where:** Algeria.
- **Significance:** Reacting to the Algeria's large state sector, the author argues for a community-centered concept of property.

DOCUMENT

Islam treats the principal of property according to a method that is radically different from that used by capitalism and Marxism (historical materialism). This divergence is a result of the economic and social philosophies that found the various economic schools. Capitalism and Marxism assimilate the resources and the means of production; that is, on the one hand, nature, which is the fundamental source of production, and on the other hand, tools and work, both of which constitute the means of production. It is thanks to the latter that a great part of natural resources unfit for direct use are transformed into usable merchandise in order to satisfy individual and collective needs. On the basis of this assimilation, the principle of property was uniformly applied to the resources and the means. Capitalism institutes the principle of private property and individual economic freedom as the basis of the economic activity of the society: The individual is free to appropriate the natural resources and the means of production that he can appropriate for himself, and this aptitude for acquisition depends on the abilities and personal conditions of each one, which determine the opportunities for his economic activity, of his possibilities of appropriation and of the nature of the latter. As for Marxism, it envisages property from the point of view of historic materialism or the historical period to which the development of production corresponds: the property of resources and means of production is linked in an historical or transitory fashion to the evolution of social production. For Marxism, for example, the stage of agrarian society assumes feudal property, that of industrial society, capitalist property; then at the industrially advanced stage, property is transferred to the working class: that is, according to the Marxist theory of production, the current state of industrial society. The Socialist state is considered as representing the interests of the working class and holds the ensemble of resources and means of production.

Property of the State and Collective Property

The Islamic economy distinguishes itself from Capitalism and Marxism by separating the resources and the means of production, and in that way, it diverges on the principle of property. We will limit ourselves in this article to briefly explaining the Islamic concept of non-private property, which is the property of the state, and collective property. By property of the state, we mean the appropriation by the one who, in the Islamic state, holds authority (wâli al-'amr) over capital, which allows him to act in the interests of those over which he has been charged and undertake the public responsibilities that fall upon him. It follows that he uses these goods to protect the interests of the community or to preserve its internal equilibrium; the state appropriates mines, for example. As for collective property, we mean the appropriation of certain goods by the community and by the society understood as a whole. Collective property results from concrete social relationships between the individuals of that society, conceived as constitutive units of the social structure; the collective needs generated by that social structure making necessary the collective or social property of goods, in such a way as to satisfy these needs and to prevent an individual or a group from privately appropriating these goods thereby depriving others of their benefit. As examples of this type of property, one can cite waterways and seas, as well as the waters, fishes and other resources that they contain. The meaning of this collective property is to maintain the capital in the state, but it differs from the state property already mentioned. In fact, the latter (an integral part of collective property) is limited to possession of the control of the capital in the state, in conformance with the Shari'a, and allowing the protection of the rights of the community and social equilibrium, without affecting a total control of capital in order to guarantee public property, which is the right of the people to enjoy goods.... Collective property concerns the different types of wealth that are subject to it and the resources and means of production susceptible to privatizing appropriation, state or public; the latter comprised of four elements: the earth, raw materials contained in the soil, natural waters, and finally the remaining natural wealth spread throughout this ground, such as fish or birds.

Important Differences

It is important here to clearly distinguish the meaning and the contours of the property of the state and those of collective property. From the point of view of the Shari'a as with positive law, three things differentiate the two types of property:

1. The investment of goods belonging to the collective must take place in order to satisfy the interests and the needs of the community as a whole, and not those of a clan or a particular group, unless they are organically linked with those of the community. It follows that the freedom that the state or the government has at its disposal to use public goods is determined and limited to an investment profitable to the collective, such as the creation of hospitals, schools, roads, and other things; whereas that state or that governing body has the greatest freedom to invest goods that belong to the state in its own right, without the existence of a collective right to extract a profit from them. It is understood that the state spends these goods in the interest of the collective and in order to guarantee social equilibrium. It results from this conception that the powers that be use these goods belonging to the state conformingly to what they believe useful to the collective and to social equilibrium, or to both at the same time. It is up to them to distribute the goods to a group or to a single

individual when they are in need of them, as well as to all of those placed under their authority.

2. No individual may appropriate privately collective goods, in whole or in part, regardless of the effort that he expends in the service of these goods. In the same manner, and from this point of view, neither the state nor the powers that be are authorized to transfer the ownership of collective goods to one or more individuals, while they may do it when it is a matter of goods possessed by the state in its own right.

3. The role of the state as to collective goods is to protect them loyally from the risk of a bad usage by individuals, susceptible of creating harm to the community, its interests, and its capacity to make use of these goods. It is not for the state to sell, loan, or give collective goods to anyone, be it an individual, an institution, or a group.

On the other hand, the governing body may act as it pleases to sell, give, or place as collateral goods belonging to the state "if it judges it proper" for the interest of the state, public utility and social equilibrium. We understand therefore the concepts of state property and collective property according to the spirit of the Islamic economy, which differs by definition from capitalism and Marxism from the point of view of the content and the judicial capacity acknowledged to the state and to the holder of authority, by the Shari'a and positive law, to use this right.

SOURCE: Ali Ibn al-Shukri. "Contrary to Capitalist and Marxist Regimes: Islam Distinguishes between the property of the State and Collective Property," *al-Munqidh* no. 28, in M. Al-Ahnaf, B. Bottiveau, and F. Fregosi, *L'Algerie par ses Islamistes* (Paris: Editions Karthala, 1991).

Translated from the French version of the original Arabic by David Vanderboegh.

CONTEXT AND ANALYSIS

Many observers of Islamism take the surface aspects of the phenomenon for its essence. Is Islamism primarily a reaction to poverty, economic malaise, and dysfunction, as some observers would have it? Or is it a discourse born of a more wide-ranging impulse, one anchored in the inspirational force of political myth?

A number of documents in this collection suggest that the core concepts of Islamist dissent constitute a myth—Islam's rebirth as a vital force in world affairs, to be attained by confrontation with the West and its allies in the Muslim world. Composed of images and notions that speak to the humiliation, despair, and alienation felt by many Muslims, as well as to their hope for the future, the myth addresses the fundamental malaise of modern Islam, the sense that "something has gone wrong with Islamic history." Not only does the myth function to mobilize activists in support of Islamic resurgence, it can also provide the necessary justification for acts of terror.

We use the term "*myth*" not in the common meaning of an unfounded or false notion, but in the sense of a body of beliefs that express the fundamental, largely unconscious or assumed political and cultural values of a society—in short, as a dramatic expression of ideology. The galvanizing power of myth has made it a prominent feature of dissident movements that stand in opposition to a dominant order. Given the distinctive antiestablishment orientation of Islamist discourse, that too is enmeshed in myth, authorizing opposition to the status quo with reference to emotionally charged symbols that connect Muslims to paradigmatic moments of their past.

Much like European fascism, Islamism makes the revolutionary process central to its concerns at the expense of a fully thought-out final stage when its enemies have been defeated and new institutions created. Nevertheless, a number of Islamists have made attempts to envision precisely what a "proper" Islamic state should look like, not least in the realm of economic development. The reading above, taken from an Algerian Islamist periodical just prior to the military intervention, maps out the rough contours of an Islamist economic policy. The main constituents of the Islamic Salvation Front (FIS) were small merchants, civil servants, and first-generation university graduates. These sectors of the population were victims of the economic restructuring forced on Algeria in the late 1980s as oil revenues fell. Their members suffered from unemployment, falling wages, and the lack of adequate housing and education opportunities. The loss of social status by these groups fueled, but did not create the demand for a new identity defined in terms of Islam. As in the other cases examined in this chapter, Islamist economics is primarily about identity and asserting the primacy of Islam, and only secondarily an instrument of economic change. In this sense, the "mythic" dimension of Islamism is primary.

But what also demands notice is the content of the Islamic economic solution proffered in the article. Clearly, it was shaped by the conceptual framework of the secular nationalist regime that FIS sought to replace, namely, the provision of a strong hand to look after the economic interests of the people. As in other cases of Islamist "planning," oppositional Islamism targeted the existing order and in the process absorbed many of its structural features.

FURTHER READINGS

Burgat, Francois. *Face to Face with Political Islam* (London: I. B. Tauris, 2003), 21–23.

Kuran, Timur. *Islam and Mammon: The Economic Predicaments of Islamism* (Princeton, NJ: Princeton University Press, 2004).

Pfeifer, Karen. "Is There an Islamic Economics?" in Joel Beinin and Joe Stork (eds.), *Political Islam: Essays from Middle East Report* (Berkeley: University of California Press, 1997), 154–65.

5

THE IRANIAN REVOLUTION

Shi'i Muslim cleric Ayatollah Ruhollah Khomeini, center, waves to followers as he appears on the balcony of his headquarters in Tehran, Iran, on February 2, 1979, the second day of his return from exile. Thousands jammed surrounding streets to get a view of the Ayatollah. The Iranian Revolution is one of the great revolutions in world history. (AP photo/Campion. Courtesy of AP Images.)

INTRODUCTION

Islamism's greatest political success was, of course, the Iranian Revolution of 1978–1979. In ousting the Shah from power, the revolution transformed Iran's political, economic, and social structures, and replaced secular laws with Shari'a. It severely diminished Western cultural influences in the country and excised Iran from America's geostrategic orbit. Although the revolution took place in an overwhelmingly Shi'i country and was led by Shi'i clerics, chief among them the Ayatollah Khomeini, it served as a source of inspiration for Islamists in Sunni Muslim countries. However, the rulers of Middle Eastern states did not share the elation the revolution generated among large sectors of the region's population. Viewing Khomieni's rise to power as a threat to the political status quo, Saudi Arabia and Iraq, in particular, attempted in the 1980s and 1990s to contain and even destroy the revolution.

The Iranian Revolution emerged in response to the flawed policies of the Pahlavi Shah, Mohammed Reza. Although Iran possessed considerable oil wealth, the revenues were spread unevenly among the population, with the result that during the 1960s and 1970s the gap between the rich, represented by the aristocratic and big business classes, and the poor increased. The Shah severely circumscribed the range of legitimate political expression and imprisoned and even tortured political dissidents. In addition, the Shah followed his father's lead in imposing Western, secular culture on Iran's population, many of whom were traditional and religiously conservative.

By the 1970s two streams of opposition had emerged. One segment of the dissenting population was represented by the modernizing middle class, people who had received modern educations, either in Iran or abroad, and were integrated into the modern sectors of the country's economy. These people resented the Shah's dictatorship and the political elite's monopoly of wealth. They looked back with nostalgia to the National Front of Iranian Prime Minister Mohammed Mossadegh in the early 1950s. Although the modernizing middle class had no desire to revert to traditional lifestyles, its members were uncomfortable with the current level of westernization, which they believed compromised the Islamic elements of the national identity. By and large, the leaders of this branch of the opposition were led and inspired by laymen, such as Jalal Al-e Ahmed (1923–1969), Mehdi Bazargan (1907–1995), and 'Ali Shariati (1933–1977) who put forward modern and flexible interpretations of the Qur'an and traditions.

The second, and in the end most consequential stream of political dissent was represented by an alliance of clerics, bazaar merchants, and lower classes. These social sectors shared the grievances of the modernizing middle class, but they did not equate social justice with democracy and were even more anti-western in their attitudes than those who looked to Shariati. The Ayatollah Ruhollah Khomeini (1902–1989) emerged as the leader of these traditional elements of the population. While some clergy simply urged the restoration of Iran's constitution and the reduction of the Shah's power, Khomeini advocated the overthrow of the monarchy and its replacement by an Islamic state ruled by senior clerics. When the revolution broke out in 1978, Khomeini emerged as the unifying symbol of both streams of opposition, and when the Shah stepped down in January 1979, it was Khomeini who assumed power. In the brief struggle between Khomeinists and Islamist-leftists that followed, it was Khomeini's forces that prevailed.

A quarter-century after the momentous events of 1979, Iran's population is divided between those who want to maintain the original revolutionary policies of Khomeini and sectors that are pushing for reform of the Islamic republic, including the implementation of more liberal policies.

"The *Shahid* Is Always Alive and Present"

- *Document:* Selections from Iranian ideologue 'Ali Shariati's "Jihad and Shahadat."
- *Date:* Early 1970s.
- *Where:* Tehran, Iran.
- *Significance:* Shariati evokes the mobilizing symbol of Imam Husayn's martyrdom at Karbala. Shariati's understanding of martyrdom would become increasingly common in Islamist circles, both Shi'i and Sunni.

DOCUMENT

A Discussion of *Shahid*

"Martyr" is a noun meaning "the one who dies for God and faith." Thus a martyr is, in any case, the one who dies. The only difference between his death and that of others is to be seen in the "cause." He dies for the cause of God, whereas the cause of the death of another may be cancer. Otherwise, the essence of the phenomenon in both cases, that is to say, death, is one and the same. As far as death is concerned it makes no difference whether the person is killed for God, for passion, or in an accident. In this sense, Christ and those killed for Christianity are "martyrs." In other words, they were "mortals," because, in Christendom the term "martyr" refers to the person who has died [as such].

But a *shahid* is always alive and present. He is not absent. Thus the two terms, "shahid" and "martyr" are antonyms of each other. As it was said, the meaning of *shahid* (pl. *shuhada*), whether national or religious, in Eastern religions or otherwise, embodies the connotation of sacredness. This is right. There is no doubt that in every religion, school of thought, and national or religious attitude, *shahid* is sacred. [This is true], even though the school of thought in question may not be religious, but materialistic. The attitude and feeling toward the *shahid* embodies a metaphysical sacredness. In my opinion, the question from whence the sacredness of a *shahid* comes needs hair-splitting scientific analysis. Even in religions and schools of thought in which there is no belief in sacredness and the sacred, there is however belief concerning the sanctity of a *shahid*. This status originates in the particular relation of a *shahid* to his school.

In other words he develops a spring of value and sanctity. It is because, at any rate, the relationship of an individual with his belief is a sacred relationship. The same relation develops between a *shahid* and his faith. In the same way, yet indirectly, the same relationship develops between an adherent to a belief and its *shuhada*. Thus the origin of the sanctity of a *shahid* is the feeling of sacredness that all people have toward their school of thought, nationality, and religion.

....

A *Shahid* is the one who negates his whole existence for the sacred ideal in which we all believe. It is natural then that all the sacredness of that ideal and goal transports itself to his existence. True, that his existence has suddenly become non-existent, but he has absorbed the whole value of the idea for which he has negated himself. No wonder then, that he, in the mind of the people, becomes sacredness itself. In this way, man becomes absolute man, because he is no longer a person, an individual. He is "thought." He had been an individual who sacrificed himself for "thought." Now he is "thought" itself. For this reason, we do not recognize Husayn as a particular person who is the son of Ali. Husayn is a name for Islam, justice, *imamat*, and divine unity. We do not praise him as an individual in order to evaluate him and rank him among shuhada. This issue is not relevant. When we speak of Husayn, we do not mean Husayn as a person. Husayn was that individual who negated himself with absolute sincerity, with the utmost magnificence within human power, for an absolute and sacred value. From him remains nothing but a name. His content is no longer an individual, but is a thought. He has transformed himself into the very school [for which he has negated himself].

An individual who becomes a *shahid* for the sake of a nation, and thus obtains sacredness, earns this status. In the opinion of the ones who do not recognize a nation as the sum of individuals, but recognize it as a collective spirit above the individuals, a *shahid* is a spiritual crystallization of that collective spirit which they call "nation." Likewise, when an individual sacrifices himself for the sake of knowledge, he is no longer an individual. He becomes knowledge itself. He becomes the *shahid* of knowledge. We praise liberty through an individual who has given himself to liberty; we do not praise "him" because he was a good person. This is not of course in contradiction with the fact that, from God's perspective, he is still an individual, and in the hereafter, he will have a separate destiny and account. But in the society, and by the criterion of our school, we do not praise him as an individual; we praise the thought, the sacred. At this point, the meaning of the word "shahid" is all the more clear. When the belief in a sacred school of thought is gradually eroding, is about to vanish or be forgotten in a new generation due to a conspiracy, suddenly an individual, by negating himself, reestablishes it. In other words, he calls it back again to the scene of the world. By sacrificing his existence, he affirms the thitherto vanishing existence of that ideal. For this reason, he is *shahid* (witness, present) and *mashhud* (visible). He is always in front of us. The thought also obtains presence and permanence through him. It becomes revived and obtains a soul again.

We have two kinds of *shahid*, one symbolized by Hamzah, the master of martyrs, and the other symbolized by Husayn. There is much difference between Hamzah and Husayn. Hamzah is a *mujahid* and a hero who goes (into battle) to achieve victory and defeat the enemy. Instead, he is defeated, is killed, and thus becomes a *shahid*. But this represents an individual *shahadat*. His name is registered at the top of the list of those who died for the cause of their belief.

Husayn, on the other hand, is a different type. He does not go (into battle with the intention of) succeeding in killing the enemy and winning victory. Neither is he accidentally killed by a terroristic act of someone such as Wahshi. This is not the case. Husayn, while he could stay at home and continue to live, rebels and consciously welcomes death. Precisely at this moment he chooses self-negation. He takes this dangerous route, placing himself in the battlefield, in front of the contemplators of the world and in front of time, so that [the consequence of] his act might be widely spread and the cause for which he gives his life might be realized sooner. Husayn chooses *shahadat* as an end or as a means for the affirmation of what is being negated and mutilated by the political apparatus.

....

Shahadat has such a unique radiance; it creates light and heat in the world and in the cold and dark hearts. In the paralyzed wills and thought, immersed in stagnation and darkness, and in the memories which have forgotten all the truths and reminiscences, it creates movement, vision, and hope and provides will, mission, and commitment. The thought, "Nothing can be done," changes into, "Something can be done," or even, "Something must be done." Such death brings about the death of the enemy at the hands of the ones who are educated by the blood of a *shahid*. By shedding his own blood, the *shahid* is not in the position to cause the fall of the enemy, [for he can't do so]. He wants to humiliate the enemy, and he does so. By his death, he does not choose to flee the hard and uncomfortable environment. He does not choose shame. Instead of a negative flight, he commits a positive attack. By his death, he condemns the oppressor and provides commitment for the oppressed. He exposes aggression and revives what has hitherto been negated. He reminds the people of what has already been forgotten. In the icy hearts of a people, he bestows the blood of life, resurrection, and movement. For those who have become accustomed to captivity and thus think of captivity as a permanent state, the blood of a *shahid* is a rescue vessel. For the eyes which can no longer read the truth and cannot see the face of the truth in the darkness of despotism and *istihmar* (stupification), all they see being nothing but pollution, the blood of the *shahid* is a candle light which gives vision and [serves as] the radiant light of guidance for the misguided who wander amidst the homeless caravan, on mountains, in deserts, along by-ways, and in ditches.

SOURCE: Mehdi Abedi and Gary Legenhausen, eds., *Jihad and Shahadat: Struggle and Martyrdom in Islam. Essays and Addresses by Ayatollah Mahmud Taleqani, Ayatollah Murtada Mutahhari, and Ali Shariati* (Houston, TX: Institute for Research and Islamic Studies, 1986).

CONTEXT AND ANALYSIS

The Iranian philosopher, lecturer, romantic, and poet 'Ali Shariati was born in 1933 into a religious family in a village near the northeastern city of Mashhad. He studied in Paris where he was influenced by Algerian rebels, and by the example of Che Guevara and the writings of Frantz Fanon. He earned his doctorate at the Sorbonne in 1965. Back in Iran, he lectured to students at a meeting hall outside of Tehran called the Husainiyeh Ershad. In his lectures, he railed against the injustice of the Pahlavi Shah's dictatorship, including its brutal suppression of open political discourse, and the political quietism of the Islamic scholars. In his critique of the politico-religious order, he combined Marxist-inspired revolutionary ideology with symbols taken from Iran's Shi'i heritage. Tapes of his lectures spread across the country, mostly among literate young men.

Mohammed Reza Shah responded to Shariati's dissident attitude by imprisoning him in 1973 and closing down the Ershad. Upon his release he was exiled to Iran's eastern Khurasan Province. Later, he made his way to London where in 1977 he died mysteriously, giving rise to rumors that he had been murdered at the hands of SAVAK, the Shah's political police.

The most potent Shi'i symbol adopted by 'Ali Shariati was the martyrdom of Husayn, the third Imam in the line of 'Ali (the Prophet's cousin) and Fatima (daughter of the Prophet). Imam Husayn was killed in 680 at Karbala in present-day Iraq, by the Sunni Umayyads of Damascus, whom the Shi'i supporters of Ali's family regarded as usurpers and tyrants. In the Shi'i view, the Imams, the descendants of Ali and Fatima, were the legitimate religio-political rulers of Islam. Traditionally, Shi'i Muslims commemorated Husayn's death by participating in mourning rituals that included self-flagellation, weeping, and enactments of the tragedy at Karbala—all designed to allow worshipers vicariously to participate in the Imam's passion. Shariati emphasized Husayn's dissenting role, presenting him as a revolutionary determined to overthrow the unjust political order of the Umayyads. Taking cues from

IN HISTORY

Dr. 'Ali Shariati: "Man and Islam"

As a nation and a society possesses economic resources, rich in energy, but worthless when raw, it also possesses vast cultural and spiritual resources that have accumulated throughout history. An inept and incompetent nation will sit upon such rich treasures which are capable of making people comfortable, nevertheless its people will remain ignorant, stagnant and deprived. At the present time we know of large nations in Asia and Africa that own vast and rich cultural resources, but they are being stereotyped as backward, ignorant and spiritually and morally bankrupt. There is a correspondence between the cultural and economic resources of a nation. In short, a generation looking for a way to solve its economic and cultural-spiritual problems and to transform its society into a progressive and creative one, must possess a historical and cultural awareness as well as technical-scientific know-how. This does not mean it should merely emulate another progressive society. Rather, it must possess an independent experience, and original principles and virtues, with a new mission in moving towards its goals.

SOURCE: http://www.shariati.com/

Husayn's example, Shariati told his Iranian audience that they must defeat the tyranny of their own day. Yazid, the Sunni Caliph, had a direct analogue in the Pahlavi Shah. Each exploited the people for his own selfish ends. Under Shariati's influence, the traditional mourning processions of Ashura turned into politically-charged marches. In crafting an "Islamic theology of liberation," Shariati hoped to prod Iran's clergy out of their political quietism. Traditionally the Shi'i clergy was prepared to put up with illegitimate, even tyrannical rulers until the Twelfth Imam arrived to spread justice on earth (see the next reading on the Twelfth Imam). At the same time, he aimed to provide Iranians with a culturally authentic ideology that could compete with imported, Western sociological and philosophical theories. Not surprisingly, Shariati's negative attitude toward the clerical establishment earned him the rebuke of senior religious scholars, who in any case were distrustful of his reinterpretation of Shi'i doctrine in a way that was inspired by Marxism and the issues of the Third World.

Shariati's discourse on "martyrdom" is rooted in the Qur'an and the hadith, both of which define the *shahid* as a person who is deserving of heavenly reward on account of dying while fighting for the faith. According to these sources, the *shahid* goes straight to Heaven where he is alive with God, enjoying the fruits of paradise (Q 2:154). However, the Qur'an cautions against sacrificing oneself on the battlefield unless such an action results in a positive outcome. According to Shariati, Husayn's sacrifice at Karbala was an example of just such a positive result. In confronting a numerically superior enemy, Husayn manifestly stood for justice against the forces of iniquity, and in so doing inspired future generations of Muslims to do the same. Although "martyrdom" remained an ideal among both Shi'i and Sunni Muslims over the medieval and early modern eras, it was only within the context of the Iranian Revolution that it gained prominence in the modern period. Here the writings of Shariati and other Islamist thinkers and activists had their effect. During the culmination of the Iranian Revolution in December 1978, tens of thousands of protesters took to the streets wearing white shrouds of martyrdom signifying their willingness to emulate the example of Imam Husayn. Iranian troops evoked the ideal of martyrdom in their attacks against the army of Saddam Husayn during the 1980–1988 Iran-Iraq War. During the later stages of the conflict in Lebanon in the 1980s, the Shi'is of that country launched "sacrificial" attacks against first the Americans and then the Israelis, which induced those powers to pull out of Lebanon.

FURTHER READINGS

Abidi, A. H. H. "Shariati's Social Thought," in Nikkie Keddie (ed.), *Religion and Politics in Iran: Shi'ism from Quietism to Revolution* (New Haven, CT: Yale University Press, 1983), 124–44.

Abrahamian, Evrand. *The Iranian Mojahidin* (New Haven, CT: Yale University Press, 1992).

Aghaie, Kamran Scot. *The Martyrs of Karbala: Shi'i Symbols and Rituals in Modern Iran* (Seattle: University of Washington Press, 2004).

Boroujerdi, Mehrzad. *Iranian Intellectuals and the West: The Tormented Triumph of Nativism* (Syracuse, NY: Syracuse University Press, 1996).

Chehabi, Houchang. *Iranian Politics and Religious Modernism: The Liberation Movement of Iran under the Shah and Khomeini* (London: I. B. Tauris, 1990).

Rahnama, Ali. *An Islamic Utopian: A Political Biography of Ali Shariati* (London: I. B. Tauris, 2000).

Sachedina, Abdulaziz. "Ali Shariati: Ideologue of the Iranian Revolution," in John L. Esposito (ed.), *Voices of Resurgent Islam* (New York: Oxford University Press, 1983), 191–214.

Sachedina, Abdulaziz A., and Hamid Enayat. "Martyrdom," in Seyyed Vali Reza and Hamid Dabashi (eds.), *Expectation of the Millennium: Shi'ism in History* (Albany, NY: SUNY Press, 1989), 44–57.

"The Awaited Savior"

- **Document:** Extracts from "The Awaited Savior" by Ayatollah Baqir al-Sadr and Ayatollah Murtada Mutahhari.
- **Date:** Late 1960s.
- **Where:** Iran/Iraq.
- **Significance:** The document, by one of Iran's most respected clerics, illustrates how the Twelver Shi'i doctrine of Messianic fulfillment (i.e., the coming of the Mahdi) was harnessed for the purposes of the Iranian Revolution.

DOCUMENT

A figure more legendary than that of the Mahdi, the Awaited Savior, has not been seen in the history of mankind. The threads of the world events have woven many a fine design in human life but the pattern of the Mahdi stands high above every other pattern. He has been the vision of the visionaries in history. He has been the dream of all the dreamers of the world. For the ultimate salvation of mankind he is the Pole Star of hope on which the gaze of humanity is fixed.

The Qur'anic prophecy of the inevitable victory of Islam will be realized following the advent of the Mahdi who will fight the wrong, remedy the evils and establish a world order based on the Islamic teachings of justice and virtue. Thereafter there will be only one religion and one government in the world.

It may be mentioned here that the movement for the establishment of a world government is already afoot and this point is engaging the attention of many prominent intellectuals. The setting up of the United Nations is a step in this very direction. In spite of the growing consciousness of its desirability, the unification of the world is still a distant dream. The vested interests and the mutual rivalries of the regimes in the various countries and the mutual animosities of the divergent blocs constitute a big hurdle in the way of its materialization. Hence, its consummation cannot be expected to come off automatically. It will need the active struggle of a world reformer in the person of Mahdi. Anyhow, a start has been made and the things are gradually turning out exactly as predicted by Islam fourteen centuries ago.

The belief in an expected reformer and a savior of humanity is not peculiar to the Shi'a School of Islam. It is common not only to all the Muslim sects, but is also shared by all the great religions such as Christianity, Judaism, Buddhism and Zoroastrianism.

In this quest for the truth about the Mahdi there is no distinction of any caste, creed, or country. The quest is universal, exactly in the same way as the Mahdi himself is universal. He stands resplendent high above the narrow walls in which humanity is cut up and divided. He belongs to everybody. For all that and much more, what exactly is the Mahdi? Surely that is the big question which the thinking people all over the world would like to ask.

It is only Islam that has given this concrete shape to an abstract idea. The Mahdi is not to be born in the distant future. He is already living amongst us and shares our joys and sorrows: His appearance will mean not only the materialization of an Islamic aspiration, but will also be the realization of a hope cherished by the entire humanity.

Prof. Henry Corbin of Sorbonne University says:

> To my mind the Shi'ite is the only sect which has preserved and perpetuated the link of Divine guidance between man and God through its belief in the Imamate. According to the Jews the Prophethood, a real link between man and God, came to an end with Moses. They do not believe in the Prophethood of Jesus and Muhammad. The Christians, too, do not go beyond Jesus. The Sunnite sect has also stopped at the Prophet Muhammad and believes that the link between man and God has been severed with the end of the Prophethood.

It is only the Twelver Shi'a that believe that the link still exists through the Mahdi and will continue to exist forever.

It is hardly necessary to give an explanation as to why the Mahdi disappeared immediately after assuming the Imamate. Let it suffice to say that Allah in His Divine Wisdom ordained so.

In the meantime it is the duty of all the Muslims, especially the Shi'a, to strive steadfastly for the creation of the proper atmosphere and the right climate for the establishment of a world order based on justice, virtue and piety. They should not only mould their individual lives according to the teachings and high ideals of Islam, but they should also bend their efforts to set up the Islamic order on the collective and communal level. They should devote themselves to the service of the faith and be prepared to receive the Awaited Savior. That is what was meant by the Imams when they exhorted the Muslims to keep on waiting for the Mahdi.

....

To hope for the appearance and revolution of the Mahdi is an inspiring Islamic social idea. Besides being a repose of trust in the future, it is an appropriate mirror in which the nature of the Islamic aspirations of mankind can be seen.

This prophecy comprises many elements, some of them philosophical, others cultural, political, economic or social and still others human or physio-human.

It is not possible in this short article to discuss the subject in detail nor to quote extensively from the holy Qur'an and the Sunna, but, in order to make the nature of "The Big Expectation" clear, we propose briefly to throw some light on its salient features. They are as below:

Optimism about the Future of Humanity

There are divergent views about the future. There are some who believe that adversity, distress, disorder and mischief are the lot of humanity and on that account life has no value. In the eyes of such people the most judicious action would be to put an end to life.

Some others think that human life has already been thrown into disarray. They believe that, following the marvelous technological progress and the accumulation of huge stockpiles of the means of mass destruction, mankind has reached a stage where its final annihilation is Imminent.

The English philosopher, Bertrand Russell, says in his book, "New Hopes" that there are people, including Einstein, who see the possibility of man having completed his span of life and think that with his wonderful scientific skill he may, in a few years, succeed in completely exterminating himself.

According to this theory there is a great possibility of the total extinction of the human race just when it is on the threshold of attaining maturity. If we rely on perceptible evidence only, such a possibility cannot be ruled out.

According to a third theory distress and disorder are not a part of human nature. Nor will the tragedy of collective suicide ever take place. In fact, a very happy and bright future awaits humanity. A great man will appear who will uproot all corruption and mischief. This is a religiously inspired theory and it is in this context that Islam gives the glad tidings of Mahdi's revolution. Its salient features will be:

- Final victory of righteousness, virtue, peace, justice, freedom and truth over the forces of egoism, subjugation, tyranny, deceit and fraud.
- Establishment of a world government (one government in the whole world).
- Reclamation and rehabilitation of the whole earth so that no area remains waste.
- Attainment of full sagacity by mankind, adherence to ideology and emancipation from animal impulses and undue social restrictions.
- Maximum utilization of the gifts of the earth.
- Equal distribution of wealth and property among all human beings.
- Complete eradication of all vices like adultery, fornication, usury, use of intoxicants, treachery, theft and homicide and total disappearance of abnormal complexes, malice and ill-will.
- Eradication of war and restoration of peace, friendship, co operation and benevolence.
- Complete coherence between man and nature.

All these points require detailed discussion and analysis but here the idea is just to acquaint the readers with the nature of the Islamic tidings and aspirations.

Big Expectations

It simply means hoping and aspiring for the materialization of the order (referred to above) which the Divine Will has destined for the world. Now let us turn back to the point that the expectation is of two kinds. One kind is constructive and dynamic, which is an act of virtue, and the other is destructive and paralyzing which is a sort of licentiousness. We have already mentioned that these two kinds of expectations are the outcome of two divergent notions of the great appearance of the promised Mahdi. These two notions have sprung from the two approaches to the nature of historical development. Now let us explain further the two kinds of expectations.

Destructive Expectation

The concept which some people have of the rising of the Mahdi and the revolution which he will bring about is only of an explosive nature. These people believe that the appearance of the Mahdi depends solely upon the spread of injustice, discrimination, frustration and disasters. They are of the opinion that, immediately prior to the appearance of the Mahdi, the forces of evil will gain a complete hold and not a single good man will be left in the world. They look forward to an explosion, following which the divine forces will redeem the truth but not the supporters of truth, for they would not be existing. On this basis they would condemn every reform and regard every sin, every excess and every injustice as valid and proper, because, according to their idea, corruption and tyranny bring the explosion nearer and pave the way for the eventual betterment of a permanent nature. They believe in the maxim that ends justify the means and as such unlawful means become lawful if the objective is desirable. That is how deadly sins besides giving pleasures are supposed to help in bringing about the final sacred-revolution. The following lines most appropriately apply to their case:

> "Win the heart of your beloved even by deceit and treachery. Commit a sin if you are unable to perform a good deed."

Such people naturally dislike the reformers and all those who enjoin good and forbid evil, because they think that their action is delaying the appearance of the promised Mahdi. They, even if they do not commit the sins themselves, at least appreciate the reprehensible activities of the sinners who, according to them, are preparing the ground for the appearance of the Mahdi.

This sort of notion may be called semi-dialectic, because it regards corruption and distress as a prelude to the sacred explosion. The dialectic thinking also opposes partial reforms and allows the creation of unrest, but it has some merit, because it does so with a view to making the split wider and the fight hotter, whereas the supporters of this outrageous notion simply allow corruption and disorder and then do nothing except to sit back and hope for the desired result to follow automatically. It need not be added that this sort of notion of the appearance of the promised Mahdi is against the tenets of Islam and must be regarded as a sort of licentiousness.

Constructive Expectation

All the verses of the holy Qur'an, which form the basis of the concept of the Mahdi and all the traditions cited in support thereof go against the above notion. What is inferred from the holy Qur'an is that the appearance of the Mahdi is a link in the series of fights between the righteous and the wicked and the Mahdi is the symbol of the final and complete victory of the righteous and the faithful. The holy Qur'an says:

> Allah has promised the righteously striving believers to appoint them as His deputies on earth, as He had appointed those who lived before. He will make the religion that He has chosen for them to stand supreme. He will replace their fear with peace and security. They will worship their Lord without fear and will not submit to anyone other than Him and will associate nothing with His worship and obedience. (Surat al-Nur, 24:55)

The appearance of the Mahdi is Allah's favor for the oppressed and the weak and is a means of their coming to power and gaining the promised Divine succession in the whole world. The holy Qur'an says:

> We have decided to grant favor to the suppressed ones by appointing them leaders and heirs of the earth. (Surat al-Qasas, 28:5)

The appearance of the Mahdi means the realization of the promise Allah made to the righteous in His sacred Book.

> Verily We have written in the Psalms after the Torah had been revealed: My righteous servants shall inherit the earth. (Surat al-Anbia, 21:105)

The well-known saying of the holy Prophet that Allah will fill the earth with justice after its having been filled with injustice and tyranny testifies to the fact that at the time of the appearance of the Mahdi there will exist two classes. One will consist of the oppressors and the other, howsoever small, of the oppressed who are subjected to injustice and tyranny.

Shaykh Saduq [tenth c. Shi'i scholar] narrates on the authority of Imam Ja'far ibn Muhammad al Sadiq [the sixth Imam] that the Mahdi would appear only when the virtuous would become the most virtuous and the wicked the most wicked. From this also it is evident that both the virtuous and the wicked will be in existence.

Islamic traditions make mention of a group of people who will come forward and join Imam Mahdi immediately on his appearance. From this again it is evident that the virtuous will not be completely wiped out and though their number may be insignificant, yet they will be best in the quality of faith and comparable to the companions of Imam Husayn ibn Ali.

According to Islamic traditions the rising of the Mahdi will be preceded by other risings of the virtuous. What has been mentioned as the Yamani's rising is an instance.

In some Islamic traditions a mention has been made of a government of the righteous people which will continue to exist till the rising of the Mahdi (May Allah hasten his solace) and, as we know, some Shi'ah *ulama*, who held good opinions about some of their contemporary Shi'a governments, considered it probable that it would be those very governments which would last till the rising of the Mahdi.

It is gathered from the various Qur'anic verses and traditions taken together that rising of the promised Mahdi will be the last one of the chain of the battles which has taken place between truth and falsehood since the creation of the world.

The promised Mahdi will realize the ideal of all the prophets, saints and fighters in the path of truth.

SOURCE: Ayatollah Baqir al-Sadr and Ayatollah Muratda Mutahhari, *The Awaited Savior*, (Karachi: Islamic Seminary Publications, n.d.). Accessed at: http://onlinebooks.library.upenn. edu/webbin/book/lookupname?key=Mutahhari%2C%20Murtaza

---

CONTEXT AND ANALYSIS

In the 1970s the Ayatollah Baqir al-Sadr cooperated with Iran's Ayatollah Murtada Mutahhari in composing an essay on another primary symbol of Shi'i Islam that was adopted for revolutionary purposes—that of the Twelfth Imam, Muhammad al-Mahdi.

Ayatollah Murtada Mutahhari was a significant figure in the movement that brought the Islamic Republic of Iran into being. He was born in 1920 and educated at the Madrasas (Islamic schools) at Mashhad, site of the tomb-shrine of the Eighth Imam, 'Ali al-Rida, and Qum, which in the 1940s was establishing itself as the center of Islamic studies in Iran. At Qum, he studied under Ayatollahs Burujerdi, Khomeini, and Tabataba'i, three of the most distinguished scholars in the Shi'i world at that time. But his criticism of the Shah and the conservative ways of most scholars earned him the rebuke of the Grand Ayatollah Burujerdi who was against confrontation with the regime and a defender of "dry scholasticism." Mutahhari therefore relocated to Tehran where in 1952 he assumed teaching duties at Tehran University. Around this time he became friendly with the Fida'yan-e Islami, the militant Islamist organization founded in Iran by Nawwab Safavi, a relationship that bespeaks his increasingly dissident frame of mind. In 1963 he was arrested during the confrontation against the regime led by the Ayatollah Khomeini and briefly imprisoned. He remained in touch with Khomeini during the latter's years of exile and in 1978 was appointed by him as head of the Council of the Islamic Revolution, set up in late 1978 to coordinate the revolution and to study what form of government should be adopted following the departure of the Shah. At the same time, he opposed groups and individuals among the opposition that were leftist or that blended Marxist analysis into their discourses. To this extent, he opposed 'Ali Shariati. On May 1, 1979, a member of the anti-clerical Muslim leftist organization, Furqan, assassinated the Ayatollah Mutahhari. Mutahhari therefore did not live to see the consolidation of Iran's Islamic Revolution. Yet his influence is present in the Islamic Republic's constitution and political structure. Today he is regarded as a martyr of the revolution.

The above essay treats the topic of the Twelfth Imam—the Mahdi. In Shi'i doctrine, the institution of the Imamate ensured the continuity of divine inspiration. As the designated successors of the Prophet Muhammad, the Imams' existence was "proof" that God's grace toward the Shi'i community was on-going. Shi'i Muslims believe that in the year 874 God concealed the Twelfth Imam in order to protect him from his Sunni Muslim enemies. Accordingly, the Twelfth Imam is invisible, even to believers. He will, however, return one day to earth as the Mahdi—the "Guided One." Hailing from the House of the Prophet, he will restore justice and equity to the world when it is filled with evil and oppression. He will wreak vengeance against the illegitimate usurpers of religio-political authority and expand his just rule throughout the world through jihad. Following his victory, the material world will terminate. The Day of Judgment will commence and the virtuous will be rewarded with Paradise and the evil condemned to everlasting Hell Fire. This millennial scenario, elaborated and embellished over centuries in a vast body of apocalyptic literature, has much in common with Messianic traditions in other faiths, notably Judaism and Christianity. It is especially apparent among members of religious communities that are routinely oppressed or marginalized, as has been the historical experience of the Shi'is throughout the Middle East.

In the document, Mutahhari and al-Sadr challenge the traditional Shi'i doctrine, which holds that until the Mahdi returns to bring relief from oppression,

IN HISTORY

Ayatollah Murtada Mutahhari: "Peace Is Not Submission"

…We cannot say that because we are the advocates of peace, we are opposed to war. Such a thing would mean that we are advocates of misery; advocates of surrender. Make no mistake, peace and surrender are as different from one another as chalk and cheese. The meaning of peace is honorable coexistence with others, but surrender is not honorable coexistence; it is coexistence that on one side is absolutely dishonorable. In fact, it is coexistence that is absolutely dishonorable on both sides. On one side the dishonor is aggression, and on the other side, it is the dishonor of surrender in the face of zulm [tyranny], in face of injustice and oppression.

So this fallacy must be eradicated, and a person who declares himself opposed to war, saying that war is totally bad—be it injustice or be it defense and resistance in the face of injustice—has made a great mistake. War that means aggression must be fully condemned while war that means standing up (qiyam) in the face of transgression is to be commended and necessary for human existence.

The Qur'an also indicates this matter, in fact it illuminates it. It says:

'And if God did not prevent mankind, some with others, the earth would be full of corruption' (2:251).

And elsewhere it tells us:

'If God did not prevent people, some with some (others) then truly the cloisters and churches and synagogues and mosques—in which is oft brought to mind the Name of God—would have been destroyed' (22:4).

SOURCE: Ayatollah Motteza Mutahhari. *Jihad: The Holy War of Islam and its Legitimacy in the Qur'an* (Tehran: Islamic Propagation Society, n.d.).

believers should take no action except vigilance and, if the situation required it, dissimulate true beliefs in the face of danger. In Mutahhari's and al-Sadr's view, rather than passively awaiting the Imam Mahdi's return, Muslims should actively and persistently challenge the iniquitous order, because the Mahdi's appearance on earth is tied to the struggle of the virtuous against the wicked. Mutahhari's discourse on the Mahdi dovetails with the effort of the Khomeini-led clergy to encourage religious scholars to assume a politically active role among the disaffected Shi'i population. This activist approach was relatively novel. Traditionally, Shi'i religious scholars seldom challenged the state beyond occasional rebukes of its conduct.

FURTHER READINGS

Dabashi, Hamid. *Theology of Discontent: The Ideological Foundation of the Islamic Revolution in Iran* (New Brunswick, NJ: Transaction Books, 2006), chapter 3.

Davari, Mahmood. *The Political Thought of Ayatollah Murtaza Mutahhari: An Iranian Theoretician of the Islamic State* (London: Routledge, 2005).

Furnish, Timothy. *Holiest Wars: Islamic Mahdis, Their Jihads, and Osama Bin Laden* (Westport, CT: Praeger/Greenwood, 2005).

Nasr, Seyyed Hossein, Hamid Dabashi, and Seyyed Vali Reza Nasr, eds. *Expectation of the Millennium: Shi'ism in History* (Albany, NY: SUNY Press, 1989).

Sachedina, Abdulaziz A. *Islamic Messianism: The Idea of the Mahdi in Twelver Shi'ism* (Albany, NY: SUNY Press, 1981).

Tabataba'i, Allamah, Jassim M. Hussaini, and Abdulaziz A. Sachedina. "Messianism and the Mahdi," in Seyyed Vali Reza and Hamid Dabashi (eds.), *Expectation of the Millennium: Shi'ism in History* (Albany, NY: SUNY Press, 1989), 8–43.

"Laws and Social Institutions Require the Existence of an Executor"

- *Document:* Selections from a compendium of thirteen speeches entitled "Islamic Government" (*Hukumat-i Islami*) by Imam Sayyid Ruhollah al-Musavi al-Khomeini.
- *Date:* January 21 to February 8, 1970.
- *Where:* Najaf, Iraq.
- *Significance:* Here Khomeini explicates the innovative theory that men of religion, because of their knowledge of Shari'a, should manage the affairs of state.

DOCUMENT

A body of laws alone is not sufficient for a society to be reformed. In order for law to ensure the reform and happiness of man, there must be an executive power and an executor. For this reason, God Almighty, in addition to revealing a body of law (i.e., the ordinances of the shari'ah), has laid down a particular form of government together with executive and administrative institution.

The Most Noble Messenger (s) headed the executive and administrative institutions of Muslim society. In addition to conveying the revelation and expounding and interpreting the articles of faith and the ordinances and institutions of Islam, he undertook the implementation of law and the establishment of the ordinances of Islam, thereby, bringing into being the Islamic state. He did not content himself with the promulgation of law; rather, he implemented it at the same time, cutting off hands and administering lashings, and stonings. After the Most Noble Messenger (s), his successor had the same duty and function. When the Prophet (s) appointed a successor, it was not only for the purpose of expounding articles of faith and law; it was for the implementation of law and the execution of God's ordinances. It was this function—the execution of law and the establishment of Islamic institutions—that made the appointment of a successor such an important matter that the Prophet (s) would have failed to fulfill his mission if he had neglected it. For after the Prophet (s), the Muslims still needed someone to execute laws and establish the institution of Islam in society, so that they might attain happiness in this world and the hereafter.

By their nature, in fact, laws and social institutions require the existence of an executor. It has always and everywhere been the case that legislation alone has little benefit: legislation by itself cannot assure the well-being of man. After the establishment of legislation, an executive power must come into being, a power that implements the laws and the verdicts given by the courts, thus allowing people to benefit from the laws and the just sentences the courts deliver. Islam has therefore established an executive power in the same way that it has brought laws into being. The person who holds this executive power is known as the *valī-yi amr....*

Islamic government does not correspond to any of the existing forms of government. For example, it is not a tyranny, where the head of state can deal arbitrarily with the property and lives of the people, making use of them as he wills, putting to death anyone he wishes, and enriching anyone he wishes by granting landed estates and distributing the property and holdings of the people. The Most Noble Messenger (s), the Commander of the Faithful ('a), and the other caliphs did not have such powers. Islamic government is neither tyrannical nor absolute, but constitutional. It is not constitutional in the current sense of the word, i.e., based on the approval of laws in accordance with the opinion of the majority. It is constitutional in the sense that the rulers are subject to a certain set of conditions in governing and administering the country, conditions that are set forth in the Noble Qur'an and the Sunnah of the Most Noble Messenger (s). It is the laws and ordinances of Islam comprising this set of conditions that must be observed and practiced. Islamic government may therefore be defined as the rule of divine law over men.

The fundamental difference between Islamic government, on the one hand, and constitutional monarchies and republics, on the other, is this: whereas the representatives of the people or the monarch in such regimes engage in legislation, in Islam the legislative power and competence to establish laws belongs exclusively to God Almighty. The Sacred Legislator of Islam is the sole legislative power. No one has the right to legislate and no law may be executed except the law of the Divine Legislator. It is for this reason that in an Islamic government, a simple planning body takes the place of the legislative assembly that is one of the three branches of government. This body draws up programs for the different ministries in the light of the ordinances of Islam and thereby determines how public services are to be provided across the country....

Thus, the view of the Shī'ah concerning government and the nature of the persons who should assume rule was clear from the time following the death of the Prophet (s) down to the beginning of the Occultation. It is specified that the ruler should be foremost in knowledge of the laws and ordinances of Islam, and just in their implementation. Now that we are in the time of the Occultation of the Imām ('a), it is still necessary that the ordinances of Islam relating to government be preserved and maintained, and that anarchy be prevented. Therefore, the establishment of government is still a necessity.

Reason also dictates that we establish a government in order to be able to ward off aggression and to defend the honor of the Muslims in case of attack. The *sharī'ah*, for its part, instructs us to be constantly ready to defend ourselves against those who wish to attack us. Government, with its judicial and executive organs, is also necessary to prevent individuals from encroaching on each other's rights. None of these purposes can be fulfilled by themselves; it is necessary for a government to be established. Since the establishment of a government and the administration of society necessitate, in turn, a budget and taxation, the Sacred Legislator has specified the nature of the budget and the taxes that are to be levied, such as *kharāj, khums, zakāt*, and so forth.

Now that no particular individual has been appointed by God, Exalted and Almighty, to assume the function of government in the time of Occultation, what must be done? Are we to abandon Islam? Do we no longer need it? Was Islam valid for only two hundred years? Or is it that Islam has clarified our duties in other respects but not with respect to government?

Not to have an Islamic government means leaving our boundaries unguarded. Can we afford to sit nonchalantly on our hands while our enemies do whatever they want? Even if we do put our signatures to what they do as an endorsement, still are failing to make an effective response. Is that the way it should be? Or is it rather that government is necessary, and that the function of government that existed from the beginning of Islam down to the time of the Twelfth Imām ('a) is still enjoined upon us by God after the Occultation even though He has appointed no particular individuals to the function?

The two qualities of knowledge of the law and justice are present in countless *fuqahā* [jurists] of the present age. If they come together, they could establish a government of universal justice in the world.

If a worthy individual possessing these two qualities arises and establishes a government, he will possess the same authority as the Most Noble Messenger ('a) in the administration of society, and it will be the duty of all people to obey him.

The idea that the governmental power of the Most Noble Messenger (s) were greater than those of the Commander of the Faithful ('a), or that those of the Commander of the Faithful ('a) were greater than those of the *faqīh*, is false and erroneous. Naturally, the virtues of the Most Noble Messenger (s) were greater than those of the rest of mankind, and after him, the Commander of the Faithful was the most virtuous person in the world. But superiority with respect to spiritual virtues does not confer increased governmental powers. God has conferred upon government in the present age the same powers and authority that were held by the Most Noble Messenger and the Imāms ('a), with respect to equipping and mobilizing armies, appointing governors and officials, and levying taxes and expending them for the welfare of the Muslims. Now, however, it is no longer a question of a particular person; government devolves instead upon one who possesses the qualities of knowledge and justice.

When we say that after the Occultation, the just *faqīh* [jurist] has the same authority that the Most Noble Messenger and the Imāms ('a) had, do not imagine that the status of the *faqīh* is identical to that of the Imāms and the Prophet ('a). For here we are not speaking of status, but rather of function. By "authority" we mean government, the administration of the country, and the implementation of the sacred laws of the *sharī'ah*. These constitute a serious, difficult duty but do not earn anyone extraordinary status or raise him above the level of common humanity. In other words, authority here has the meaning of government, administration, and execution of law; contrary to what many people believe, it is not a privilege, but a grave responsibility. The governance of the *faqīh* is a rational and extrinsic matter; it exists only as a type of appointment, like the appointment of a guardian for a minor. With respect to duty and position, there is indeed no difference between the guardian of a nation and the guardian of a minor. It is as if the Imām were to appoint someone to the guardianship of a minor, to the governorship of a province, or to some other post. In cases like these, it is not reasonable that there would be a difference between the Prophet and the Imāms ('a), on the one hand, and the just *faqīh*, on the other....

Now that this much has been demonstrated, it is necessary that the *fuqahā* proceed, collectively or individually, to establish a government in order to implement the laws of Islam and protect its territory. If this task falls within the capabilities of a single person, he has personally incumbent upon him the duty to fulfill it; otherwise, it is a duty that devolves upon the *fuqahā* as a whole. Even if it is impossible to fulfill the task, the authority vested in the *fuqahā* is not voided, because it has been vested in them by God. If they can, they must collect taxes, such as *zakāt*, *khums*, and *kharāj*, spend them for the welfare of the Muslims, and also enact the penalties of the law. The fact that we are presently unable to establish a complete and comprehensive form of government does not mean that we should sit idle. Instead, we should perform, to whatever extent we can, the tasks that are needed by the Muslims and that pertain to the functions an Islamic government must assume....

Since Islamic government is a government of law, those acquainted with the law, or more precisely, with religion—i.e., the *fuqahā*—must supervise its functioning. It is they who supervise all executive and administrative affairs of the country, together with all planning.

The *fuqahā* are the trustees who implement the divine ordinances in levying taxes, guarding the frontiers, and executing the penal provisions of the law. They must not allow the laws of Islam to remain in abeyance, or their operation to be effected by either defect or excess. If a *faqīh* wishes to punish an adulterer, he must give him one hundred lashes in the presence of the people, in the exact manner that has been specified. He does not have the right to inflict one additional lash, to curse the offender, to slap him, or to imprison him for a single day. Similarly, when it comes to the levying of taxes, he must act in accordance with the criteria and the laws of Islam; he does not have the right to tax even a *shāh* in excess of what the law provides. He must not let disorder enter the affairs of the public treasury or even so much as a *shāhi* be lost. If a *faqīh* acts in contradiction to the criteria of Islam (God forbid!), then he will automatically be dismissed from his post, since he will have forfeited his quality of trustee....

Law is actually the ruler; the security for all is guaranteed by law, and law is their refuge. Muslims and the people in general are free within the limits laid down by the law; when they are acting in accordance with the provisions of the law, no one has the right to tell them, "Sit here," or "Go there." An Islamic government does not resemble states where the people are deprived of all security and everyone sits at home trembling for fear of a sudden raid or attack by the agents of the state. It was that way under Mu'āwiyah and similar rulers: people had no security, and they were killed or banished, or imprisoned for lengthy periods, on the strength of an accusation or a mere suspicion, because the government was not Islamic. When an Islamic government is established, all will live with complete security under the protection of the law, and no ruler will have the right to take any step contrary to the provisions and laws of the immaculate *sharī'ah*.

The meaning of "trustee," then, is that the *fuqahā* execute as a trust all the affairs for which Islam has legislated—not that they simply offer legal judgments on given questions. Was that the function of the Imām ('a)? Did he merely expound the law? Was it the function of the prophets ('a) from whom the *fuqahā* have inherited it as a trust? To offer judgment on a question of law or to expound the laws in general is, of course, one of the dimensions of *fiqh*. But Islam regards law as a tool, not as an end in itself. Law is a tool and an instrument for the establishment of justice in society, a means for man's intellectual and moral reform and his purification. Law exists to be implemented for the sake of establishing a just society that will morally and spiritually nourish refined human beings. The most significant duty of the prophets ('a) was the implementation of divine ordinances, and this necessarily involved supervision and rule.

SOURCE: Ayatollah Ruhollah Khomeini, "Islamic Government," in *Islam and Revolution: Writings and Declarations of Imam Khomeini*, translated and annotated by Hamid Algar (Berkeley, CA: Mizan Press, 1981), 40–41; 55–56; 61–63; 79–80.

CONTEXT AND ANALYSIS

Until the September 11 attacks on the United States, no other figure in the Islamic world figured as large in the collective American consciousness as the Ayatollah Khomeini. Ruhullah Ibn Mustafa Musawi Khomeini was born near Isfahan in 1902. He studied under revered Ayatollah Hair-Yazdi at Qum and by 1937 had amassed sufficient credentials to take up teaching. He specialized in theology (*kalam*), ethics (*akhlaq*), and philosophy, and had a particular interest in mysticism (*irfan*). In 1944 he published his first major work, *Discovery of Secrets* (*Kashf al-Asrar*), which proffered a critique of materialism and condemned the secular-oriented regime of Reza Shah. Following the lead of earlier clerical critics of the monarchy, he also argued that government should be limited by the provisions of the Shari'a under the guidance of Ayatollahs, but he still allowed the legitimacy of temporal authorities provided that they ruled justly.

During the 1940s and 1950s Khomeini remained out of the political limelight in deference to the nonpolitical stance of Grand Ayatollah Burujerdi, whose views as leading cleric carried weight. However, following the Grand Ayatollah's death in 1962, Khomeini began openly to preach against the Pahlavi monarchy. In 1963 he led a demonstration of seminary students during which he drew parallels between the Umayyad "tyrant" Yazid and the Shah. The following year he was arrested for protesting the Shah's plan to grant American personnel in Iran diplomatic immunity. Forced into exile by the regime, he went initially to Turkey but in 1965 moved to Najaf, Iraq where he taught jurisprudence at the Shaykh Murtaza Ansari *madrasa*. At the *madrasa*, he delivered lectures between January 21 and February 8, 1970 that were published the following year in a book entitled *"Islamic Government"* (*Hukumat-i Islami*).

Following other ideologues of Islamic resurgence, he argued that Islam was not simply an ethical system but had all the necessary laws and principles to guide Muslims in the economic and administrative realms. He stated further that, although there is no specific provision in the Qur'an or the hadith for designating a ruler during the absence of the Twelfth Imam, social order is necessary if the Shari'a is to be enforced. And, according to Khomeini, the persons most fitted for this role are the top-ranking experts in religious jurisprudence, the ayatollahs, who alone have sufficient knowledge of the Shari'a. Khomeini states that the jurist (or jurists—Khomeini is not explicit in the work whether the "government of the jurist" should reside in one person or a collective body) is not equal to the Twelfth Imam in station, yet has the authority to carry out his functions as both religious guide and political ruler in his absence.

Khomeini's theory of the Government of the Islamic Jurist is novel within the context of the Shi'i intellectual tradition. Although the nineteenth-century Shi'i scholar, Mulla Ahmad Naraqi (d. 1829), held a similar view regarding the political prerogatives of the *'ulama*, he did not make it the central point in his writings the way that Khomeini did. Until Khomeini, Shi'i religious scholars in Iran and elsewhere held fast to the traditional notion that they should simply guide Kings in their behavior and policy making. Khomeini, on the other hand, argued that the most prominent jurist (or

IN HISTORY

What Is an "Ayatollah"?

There is no formal hierarchy among the *'ulama* in Shi'i Islam. Rather, the situation has been described as a "hierarchy of deference" (Momen, 204). The most revered clerics are given the title "marja-e taqlid," "source of imitation," so called because they provide religious guidance to Shi'i Muslims; every Shi'i Muslim must follow the teachings and advice of a living marja. In providing such guidance, the marja-e taqlid represents the authority of the Twelfth Imam in his absence. In the twentieth century, the title "ayatollah" (literally, "sign of God") became customary for designating a marja-e taqlid. The title "hojjatoleslam" ("Authority on Islam") has come to be used for aspiring Ayatollahs. At any given time, there is only a handful of ayatollahs available to dispense wisdom.

The route to becoming an ayatollah is long and difficult. Clerics must prove their wisdom over years of studying, teaching, writing, and preaching, slowly gathering the respect of senior clerics and ordinary believers. Normally, an aspirant to the position will study theology, jurisprudence, ethics, and philosophy at a seminary in one of the Shi'i shrine towns, such as Najaf in Iraq or Qom in Iran. Soon, he will begin delivering his own lectures and offering his own edicts from the sources of Islamic law. He starts to write important juristic books and students travel from afar to partake of his wisdom. Once the cleric has gathered a large number of followers and gained the respect of established teachers, he is considered an ayatollah.

See Moojan Momen. *An Introduction to Shi'i Islam* (New Haven, CT: Yale University Press, 1985), and Linda S. Walbridge, *The Most Learned of the Shi'a: The Institution of the Marja-i Taqlid* (Oxford, UK: Oxford University Press, 2001).

jurists) should supplant the monarch and govern in his place. He wrote that those scholars who acquiesced to the unjust rule of the Shah were enemies of Islam. Quite clearly, in his book Khomeini was laying the theoretical foundations for the theocratic order that he and his mostly-clerical associates would eventually impose on the Iranian state.

From his exile in Iraq, Khomeini kept close watch on developments in Iran. His ideas concerning Islamic government were widely circulated among the pious middle class of the country. As demonstrations against the regime picked up, the Shah convinced the Iraqi government to expel Khomeini from Iraq. Khomeini left and ended up in France. He returned in triumph to Iran on January 31, 1979, shortly after the Shah had been forced to abandon the country as the result of the growing strength of the revolutionary movement. Soon after, Khomeini agreed to his elevation to the position of top jurist, the position that he had theorized about in his 1971 book. He spent the duration of his life in a closely guarded compound in Tehran, where he exercised complete power as the representative of the Hidden Imam.

FURTHER READINGS

Abrahamian, Evrand. *Iran between Two Revolutions* (Princeton, NJ: Princeton University Press, 1992).

Arjomand, Said Amir. *The Turban for the Crown: The Islamic Revolution in Iran* (New York: Oxford University Press, 1989).

Bakhash, Shaul. The *Reign of the Ayatollahs: Iran and the Islamic Revolution* (New York: Basic Books, 1990).

Brumberg, Daniel. *Reinventing Khomeini: The Struggle for Reform in Islam* (Chicago: University of Chicago Press, 2001).

Dabashi, Hamid. *Theology of Discontent: The Ideological Foundation of the Islamic Revolution in Iran* (New Brunswick, NJ: Transaction Books, 2006).

Fisher, Michael M. J. "Imam Khomeini: Four Levels of Understanding," in John L. Esposito (ed.), *Voices of Resurgent Islam* (New York: Oxford University Press, 1983), 150–74.

Hiro, Dilip. *The Iranian Labyrinth: Journeys through Theocratic Iran and Its Furies* (New York: Nation Books, 2005).

Khomeini, Ruhollah. *Islam and Revolution: Writings and Declarations of Imam Khomeini.* Translated and annotated by Hamid Algar (Berkeley, CA: Mizan Press, 1981).

Moin, Baqer. *Khomeini: Life of the Ayatollah* (London: I. B. Tauris, 1999).

Mottahedeh, Roy. *The Mantle of the Prophet: Religion and Politics in Iran* (New York: Simon and Schuster, 1985).

"Dialogue of Civilizations"

- **Document:** Address by H.E. Mohammed Khatami, President of the Islamic Republic of Iran.
- **When:** September 5, 2000.
- **Where:** United Nations, New York.
- **Significance:** President Mohammed Khatami's speech to the United Nations represents the reformist impetus present in Iranian society after the death of the Ayatollah Khomeini.

DOCUMENT

The following is an Address by H.E. Mr. Mohammed Khatami, President of the Islamic Republic of Iran.

President Khatami (*interpreted from Farsi*): The General Assembly of the United Nations has only recently endorsed the proposal of the Islamic Republic of Iran for dialogue among civilizations and cultures. Still this proposal is daily attracting increasing support from numerous academic institutions and political organizations. In order to comprehend the grounds for this encouraging reception it is imperative to take into account the prevailing situation in our world and to ponder the reasons for widespread discontent with it. It is, of course, only natural for justice-seeking and altruistic human beings to feel discontented with the status quo. The political aspects of dialogue among civilizations have already been touched upon in various settings. Today in this esteemed gathering allow me instead to begin with certain historical, theoretical, and, for the most part, nonpolitical grounds for the call to a dialogue among civilizations.

One reason, which I can only briefly touch upon today, is the exceptional geographical location of Iran, a situation connecting various cultural and civilizational domains of Asia to Europe. This remarkable situation has placed Iran on a route of political hurricanes as well as pleasant breezes, of cultural exchange and also venues for international trade.

One of the unintended if only natural consequences of this strategic geographical location has been the fostering of a certain cultural sense which has formed a primary attribute of the Persian soul in the course of its historical evolution. Should we try to view this primary attribute from the vantage point of social psychology and then attempt to scrutinize the constituent elements of the Persian or Iranian spirit, we would recognize a remarkable and exceptional capacity, a capacity that we could refer to as its capacity to integrate. This capacity to integrate involves reflective contemplation of the methods and achievements of various cultures and civilizations in order to augment and enrich one's cultural repertoire. The spiritual wisdom of Sohrevardi [twelfth century Iranian philosopher and sufi], which elegantly synthesizes and integrates ancient Persian wisdom, Greek rationalism, and Islamic intuitive knowledge, presents us with a brilliantly exceptional example of the Persian capacity to integrate.

We should also note that Persian thought and culture owes an immense debt to Islam as one of its primary springs of efflorescence. Islam embodies a universal wisdom. Each and every human individual, living in each and every corner of time and place, is potentially included in the purview of Islam. The Islamic emphasis on essential human equality and its disdain for such elements as birth and blood, conquered the hearts of those yearning for justice and freedom. The prominent position, on the other hand, accorded to rational thought in Islam, and the rejection of an allegedly strict separation between human thought and divine revelation, also helped Islam to overcome dualism in both latent and manifest forms.

Islamic civilization is indeed one of only a few world civilizations to have become consolidated and to have taken shape around a sacred text, in this case the noble Koran. The essential unity of the Islamic civilization stems from the unique call that reached all Islamic peoples and nations. Its plurality derives from the diversity of responses evoked after Islam reached various nations.

What we ought to consider in earnest today is the emergence of a global culture. Global culture cannot and ought not to overlook characteristics and requirements of native local cultures with the aim of imposing itself upon them. Cultures and civilizations that have naturally evolved among various nations in the course of history are constituted from elements that have gradually adapted to collective souls and to historical and traditional characteristics. As such, these elements cohere with each other and consolidate within an appropriate network of relationships. In spite of all constitutive plurality and diversity, a unique and harmonious form can be abstracted from the collection.

In order to provide natural unity and harmony in form and content for global culture and to prevent anarchy and chaos, all concerned parties should engage in a dialogue in which they can exchange knowledge, experience, and understanding in diverse areas of culture and civilization. Today it is impossible to bar ideas from freely traveling between cultures and civilizations in disparate parts of the world. However, in the absence of dialogue among thinkers, scholars, intellectuals, and artists from various cultures and civilizations, the danger of cultural homelessness seems imminent. Such a state of cultural homelessness would deprive people of solace both in their own culture and in the vast open horizon of global culture.

The notion and proposal of dialogue among civilizations undoubtedly raises numerous theoretical questions. I do not mean to belittle such intellectual and academic undertakings. Rather, I want to stress that in formulating this proposal the Government of Iran has attempted to present an alternative paradigm for international relationships. This should become clearer when we take comparative notice of already existing and prevailing paradigms that underlie international relations today. It is incumbent upon us to radically examine the prevalent master paradigm and to expound the grounds for replacing it with a new one.

In order to call on the governments and peoples of the world to follow the new paradigm of dialogue among cultures and civilizations, we ought to learn from the world's past experience, especially from the tremendous human catastrophes that took place in the twentieth century. We ought to critically examine the prevalent master paradigm in international relations based on the discourse of power and the glorification of might.

From an ethical perspective, the paradigm of dialogue among civilizations requires that we give up the will for power and instead appeal to the will for empathy and compassion. Without the will for empathy, compassion, and understanding there would be no hope for the prevalence of order in our world.

There are two ways to realize dialogue among civilizations. First, actual instances of the interaction and interpenetration of cultures and civilizations with each other, resulting from a variety of factors, present one mode in which this dialogue takes place. This mode of interaction is clearly involuntary and optional and occurs in an unpremeditated fashion, driven primarily by vagaries of social events, geographical situation, and historical contingency.

Second, alternatively, dialogue among civilizations could also mean a deliberate dialogue among representative members of various civilizations such as scholars, artists and philosophers from disparate civilizational domains. In this latter sense, dialogue entails a deliberate act based upon premeditated indulgence and does not rise and fall at the mercy of historical and geographical contingency.

Even though human beings inevitably inhabit a certain historical horizon, we could still aim at meta-historical discourse. Indeed, a meta-historical discussion of eternal human questions such as the ultimate meaning of life and death or goodness and evil ought to substantiate and enlighten any dialogue on political and social issues. Without a discussion of fundamentals, and by simply confining attention to superficial issues, dialogue would not get us far from where we currently stand. When superficial issues masquerade as real, urgent, and essential, and where no agreement, or at least mutual understanding, obtains among parties to dialogue concerning what is truly fundamental, in all likelihood misunderstanding and confusion will proliferate instead of any sense of empathy and compassion.

The movement of ideas and cultural interaction and interpenetration recur in human history as naturally and persistently as the emigration of birds in nature. Translation and interpretation have always proved to be one of the prime venues for the movement of ideas. The subtlety lies in cases where the language under translation or interpretation sounds the same as the one we use today, whereas the world, or universe of discourse to which the two languages belong, has changed over time. Particular difficulty arises when one of the parties to the dialogue attempts to communicate with another by employing a basically secularist language in an essentially sacred and spiritual discourse. By secularism here I mean the general rejection of any intuitive spiritual experience and any faith in the unseen. The true essence of humanity is more inclusive than language, and this more encompassing nature of the existential essence of humanity makes it meaningful to hope for fruitful dialogue.

It now appears that the Cartesian-Faustian narrative of Western civilization should give way and begin to listen to other narratives proposed by other human cultural domains. Today the unstoppable destruction of nature stemming from the ill-founded preconceptions of recent centuries threatens human livelihood. Should there be no other philosophical, social, political, and human grounds necessitating dialogue but this pitiable relationship between humans and nature, then all selflessly peace-seeking intellectuals should endeavor to promote dialogue as urgently as they can.

Another goal of dialogue among cultures and civilizations is to recognize and to understand not only the cultures and civilizations of others, but also one's own. One ought to take a step away from oneself in order to get an enhanced perspective on oneself. Seeing in essence requires taking distance in perspective, and distance provides the grounds for immersion into another existential dimension.

In dialogue among cultures and civilizations, great artists should undoubtedly get due recognition together with philosophers, scholars, and theologians. For artists do not see the sea, mountain, and forest as mere mines and sources of energy, oil, and fuel. For the artist the sea embodies the waving music of a heavenly dance, the mountain is not just a mass of dirt and boulders, and the forest is not merely an inanimate collection of timber to cut and use. A world so thoroughly controlled by political, military, and economic conditions today inevitably begets the ultimate devastation of the environment and the eradication of all spiritual, artistic, and intuitive havens. To alleviate this crisis we need the magical touch and spell of the enchanted artist and the inspired poet to rescue life at least part of it from the iron clasp of death and to make possible the continuation of life. Poets and artists engage in dialogue within and through the sacred language of spirit and morality. That language has remained safe from the poisonous winds of time.

So far as the present relationship between man and nature is concerned, we live in tragic times. The sense of solitude and monologue and the anxiety rooted within this situation embody this tragic world. Our call to dialogue aims at soothing this sense of tragedy. In addition to poetic and artistic experience, mysticism also provides us with a graceful, profound, and universal language for dialogue. Mystical experience, constituted of the revelation and countenance of the sacred in the heart and soul of the mystic, opens new existential pathways on to the human spirit. A study of mystical achievements of various nations reveals to us the deepest layers of their life experience in the most universal sense. The unified mystical meaning and content across cultures and the linguistic parallelism among mystics, despite vast cultural, historical and geographical distances, is indeed perplexing. The proposal for a dialogue among civilizations builds upon the study of cultural geography of various fields of civilization. Yet the unique and irreplaceable role of governments should never be overlooked in this process.

In the absence of governmental commitment to their affirmative vote to the resolution on dialogue among civilizations, we cannot maintain high hopes for the political consequences of this proposal. Member States of the United Nations should endeavor to remove barriers from the way of dialogue among cultures and civilizations and should abide by the basic precondition of dialogue. This fundamental principle rejects any imposition and builds upon the premise that all parties to dialogue stand on essentially equal footing.

The symbolic representation of Themis, goddess of divine law and justice, has already gained virtually global acceptance as its statue appears on judiciary courts in many nations. It is now time to ask Themis to remove her blindfold. Let us ask her to set aside the lofty scale that currently weighs political and economic might as the sole measure. Instead, she should call all parties to an open discussion in various domains of thought, culture, and civilization. She ought to look observantly at the evidence with open eyes and, by freeing herself from any prior obligations, she should then finally charge citizens of the world with the task of making political, economic, and cultural decisions.

The escalating development of information technologies will continue to penetrate deeper layers of our lives far beyond the realm of social relationships and will form common underlying interconnections between disparate cultural and geographical regions. The science of semiotics provides us with tools to excavate such common underlying links and would form the common language we need for any dialogue. We should listen in earnest to what other cultures offer, lest by relying on profound human experiences we can seek new ways for human life.

Dialogue is not easy. It is even more difficult to prepare and open up vistas upon one's inner existence to others. A belief in dialogue paves the way for vivacious hope: the hope of living in a world permeated by virtue, humility, and love, and not merely by the reign of economic indices and destructive weapons. Should the spirit of dialogue prevail, humanity, culture, and civilization should prevail. We should all have faith in this triumph and we should all hope that all citizens of the world will be prepared to listen to the divine call:

"So Announce the Good News to My Servants ? Those who listen to the Word,
And follow The best (meaning) in it." (*The Holy Koran, XXXIX:17–18*)

Let us hope that enmity and oppression will end and that the clamor of love for truth, justice, and human dignity will prevail. Let us hope that all human beings will sing along with Hafez of Shiraz, that divinely inspired spirit, that:

"No ineffable clamor reverberates in the grand heavenly dome more sweetly than the sound of love."

I take this opportunity as the representative of one of the most ancient human civilizations to present to the Secretary-General of the United Nations, as a token of friendship, one of the most ancient artifacts found in the world.

SOURCE: Round Table: Dialogue among Civilizations, United Nations, New York, September 5, 2000. Provisional verbatim transcription available at: http://www.unesco.org/dialogue 2001/en/khatami.htm. Reproduced by permission of UNESCO.

CONTEXT AND ANALYSIS

During the first decade of the Islamic Revolution, the Iranian people rallied around the Ayatollah Khomeini. To be sure, the revolution had alienated many Iranians. Dissatisfied with the rule of the Ayatollah these Iranians fled the country or else joined militant, anti-regime organizations such as the Mujahidin-e Khalq. But by and large, the 1980s were marked by the solidarity of Iranians with the new, revolutionary Islamic Republic.

The people were generally satisfied with Iran's new government. The constitution provided for a parliament (*majlis*) and an elected president. All laws proposed by the parliament had to be approved by a twelve-member Council of Guardians whose members made sure that they were compatible with Islam. In addition, the council supervised parliamentary elections and vetted candidates. Standing over both the parliament and the council was the Supreme Leader (i.e., Khomeini, and after his death in 1989, Ayatollah Khamene'i) who crafted the country's foreign policy and possessed veto power over all legislation.

One reason for the support of the Iranian people for the Islamic regime was the war with Iraq. In 1980 the president of Iraq, Saddam Husayn, invaded Iran in order to elevate Iraq to a dominant position in the Gulf and to neutralize the possibility of the Iranian Revolution influencing Iraq's majority-Shi'i population. Saddam Husayn believed that it would be an easy matter to defeat the nascent Islamic Republic. After all, in 1980 the Islamic Republic had yet to reconstitute fully Iran's military forces. Instead, the war had the effect of uniting Iran's people against a common enemy, thereby strengthening, rather than weakening, Iran's new order.

However, by the 1990s approval for clerical rule began to wane, for a number of reasons. First, the end of the war with Iraq ended the need to stand in absolute solidarity with the government. Second, Iran's economy began to stall as a result of a bloated state sector, resource mismanagement, and corruption. Third, a demographic boom resulted in a new generation of Iranians who could not find jobs. Many of these young Iranians were not old enough to have remembered the tyranny of the Shah. Therefore they were more willing than their parents to question the foundations of the new order. Taken together, these factors gave rise to a reform movement spearheaded by dissident clerics, such as Ayatollah Ali Montazeri and Hojjat-i Islam Mohsen Khadivar, and lay intellectuals such as Abdol Karim Soroush, which called for political liberalization and, in some cases, an explicit rejection of clerical rule.

In 1997 and again in 2001 the reformist surge was strong enough to elect Mohammed Khatami, a top-ranking cleric, to the presidency. Khatami was, and remains, a strong supporter of the Iranian Revolution. Yet he shared many of the reformers concerns. Despite being blocked at almost every turn by conservative hard-liners in the government, he succeeded in loosening restrictions on the freedom of speech and broadening democracy by allowing elections for local councils. Emboldened by Khatami's challenge to the conservative establishment, student organizations at Iran's universities emerged that pushed for greater political openness.

One of Khatami's goals was to improve relations with the West, including the United States, which had been damaged by the revolution. As part of this effort, he introduced the theory of "Dialogue among Civilizations." After introducing the concept of his theory at several international societies, the United Nations proclaimed the year 2001 as its Year of Dialogue among Civilizations, thus recognizing Khatami's initiative. Countering U.S. scholar Samuel Huntington's influential theory of the "Clash of Civilizations," Khatami argued for mutual understanding and respect among states and civilizations, and called for the entry of moral considerations into politics. Although the countries of the European Union responded favorably to his call, in part seeing in it commercial opportunities, the United States turned its back on Khatami and Iran. Some American policy analysts regard the rebuff of Khatami's overture as a lost opportunity to improve relations between the two countries, especially in light of the subsequent consolidation in Iran of hard-line positions. It is to those hard-line positions that we now turn.

"The People of the Region Are Becoming Increasingly Angry"

- *Document:* Iranian President Ahmadinejad's Letter to President Bush.
- *When:* May 8, 2006.
- *Where:* Tehran, Iran.
- *Significance:* President Ahmadinejad's letter presents a hard-line Iranian view within the context of rising tensions between the United States and its allies and the Islamic Republic of Iran.

DOCUMENT

Mr. George Bush, president of the United States of America

For some time now, I have been thinking, how one can justify the undeniable contradictions that exist in the international arena—which are being constantly debated, especially in political forums and amongst university students. Many questions remain unanswered. Those have prompted me to discuss some of the contradictions and questions, in the hopes that it might bring about an opportunity to redress them.

Can one be a follower of Jesus Christ (Peace Be Upon Him), the great Messenger of God,

Feel obliged to respect human rights,

Present liberalism as a civilization model,

Announce one's opposition to the proliferation of nuclear weapons and WMDs,

Make "War on Terror" his slogan,

And finally, work towards the establishment of an unified international community—a community which Christ and the virtuous of the Earth will one day govern,

But at the same time, have countries attacked. The lives, reputations and possessions of people destroyed and on the slight chance of the presence of a few criminals in a village, city, or convoy for example, the entire village, city or convoy set ablaze.

Or because of the possibility of the existence of WMDs in one country, it is occupied, around 100,000 people killed, its water sources, agriculture and industry destroyed, close to 180,000 foreign troops put on the ground, sanctity of private homes of citizens broken, and the country pushed back perhaps 50 years. At what price? Hundreds of billions of dollars spent from the treasury of one country and certain other countries and tens of thousands of young men and women—as occupation troops—put in harm's way, taken away from family and loved ones, their hands stained with the blood of others, subjected to so much psychological pressure that everyday some commit suicide and those returning home suffer depression, become sickly and grapple with all sorts of ailments; while some are killed and their bodies handed to their families.

On the pretext of the existence of WMDs, this great tragedy came to engulf both the peoples of the occupied and the occupying country. Later it was revealed that no WMDs existed to begin with.

Of course, Saddam was a murderous dictator. But the war was not waged to topple him, the announced goal of the war was to find and destroy weapons of mass destruction. He was toppled along the way towards another goal; nevertheless the people of the region are happy about it. I point out that throughout the many years of the imposed war on Iran Saddam was supported by the West.

Mr. President, You might know that I am a teacher. My students ask me how can these actions be reconciled with the values outlined at the beginning of this letter and duty to the tradition of Jesus Christ (Peace Be Upon Him), the Messenger of peace and forgiveness?

There are prisoners in Guantanamo Bay that have not been tried, have no legal representation, their families cannot see them and are obviously kept in a strange land outside their own country. There is no international monitoring of their conditions and fate. No one knows whether they are prisoners, POWs, accused or criminals.

European investigators have confirmed the existence of secret prisons in Europe too. I could not correlate the abduction of a person, and him or her being kept in secret prisons, with the provisions of any judicial system. For that matter, I fail to understand how such actions correspond to the values outlined in the beginning of this letter, i.e., the teachings of Jesus Christ (Peace Be Upon Him), human rights and liberal values.

Young people, university students, and ordinary people have many questions about the phenomenon of Israel. I am sure you are familiar with some of them.

Throughout history, many countries have been occupied, but I think the establishment of a new country with a new people, is a new phenomenon that is exclusive to our times.

Students are saying that 60 years ago such a country did not exist. They show old documents and globes and say try as we have, we have not been able to find a country named Israel.

I tell them to study the history of WWI and II. One of my students told me that during WWII, which more than tens of millions of people perished in, news about the war, was quickly disseminated by the warring parties. Each touted their victories and the most recent battlefront defeat of the other party. After the war they claimed that six million Jews had been killed. Six million people that were surely related to at least two million families. Again let us assume that these events are true. Does that logically translate into the establishment of the state of Israel in the Middle East or support for such a state? How can this phenomenon be rationalized or explained?

Mr. President, I am sure you know how—and at what cost—Israel was established:

— Many thousands were killed in the process.
— Millions of indigenous people were made refugees.
— Hundreds of thousands of hectares of farmland, olive plantations, towns and villages were destroyed.

This tragedy is not exclusive to the time of establishment; unfortunately it has been ongoing for 60 years now.

A regime has been established which does not show mercy even to kids, destroys houses while the occupants are still in them, announces beforehand its list and plans to assassinate Palestinian figures, and keeps thousands of Palestinians in prison. Such a phenomenon is unique—or at the very least extremely rare—in recent memory.

Another big question asked by the people is "why is this regime being supported?"

Is support for this regime in line with the teachings of Jesus Christ (Peace Be Upon Him) or Moses (Peace Be Upon Him) or liberal values?

Or are we to understand that allowing the original inhabitants of these lands—inside and outside Palestine—whether they are Christian, Muslim or Jew, to determine their fate, runs contrary to principles of democracy, human rights and the teachings of prophets? If not, why is there so much opposition to a referendum?

The newly elected Palestinian administration recently took office. All independent observers have confirmed that this government represents the electorate. Unbelievingly, they have put the elected government under pressure and have advised it to recognize the Israeli regime, abandon the struggle and follow the programs of the previous government.

If the current Palestinian government had run on the above platform, would the Palestinian people have voted for it? Again, can such position taken in opposition to the Palestinian government be reconciled with the values outlined earlier? The people are, also asking "why are all UNSC resolutions in condemnation of Israel vetoed?"

Mr. President, As you are well aware, I live amongst the people and am in constant contact with them—many people from around the Middle East manage to contact me as well. They do not have faith in their dubious policies either. There is evidence that the people of the region are becoming increasingly angry with such policies.

It is not my intention to pose too many questions, but I need to refer to other points as well.

Why is it that any technological and scientific achievement reached in the Middle East region is translated into and portrayed as a threat to the Zionist regime? Is not scientific R&D one of the basic rights of nations?

You are familiar with history. Aside from the Middle Ages, in what other point in history has scientific and technical progress been a crime? Can the possibility of scientific achievements being utilized for military purposes be reason enough to oppose science and technology altogether? If such a supposition is true, then all scientific disciplines, including physics, chemistry, mathematics, medicine, engineering, etc, must be opposed.

Lies were told in the Iraqi matter. What was the result? I have no doubt that telling lies is reprehensible in any culture, and you do not like to be lied to.

Again, do such actions correspond to the teachings of Christ and the tenets of human rights? ...

The brave and faithful people of Iran too have many questions and grievances, including: the coup d'etat of 1953 and the subsequent toppling of the legal government of the day, opposition to the Islamic revolution, transformation of an Embassy into a headquarters supporting the activities of those opposing the Islamic Republic (many thousands of pages of documents corroborate this claim), support for Saddam in the war waged against Iran, the shooting down of the Iranian passenger plane, freezing the assets of the Iranian nation, increasing threats, anger and displeasure vis-a-vis the scientific and nuclear progress of the Iranian nation (just when all Iranians are jubilant and celebrating their country's progress), and many other grievances that I will not refer to in this letter....

Mr. President, It is not my intention to distress anyone.

If Prophets Abraham, Isaac, Jacob, Ishmael, Joseph, or Jesus Christ (Peace Be Upon Him) were with us today, how would they have judged such behavior? Will we be given a role to play in the promised world, where justice will become universal and Jesus Christ (Peace Be Upon Him) will be present? Will they even accept us?

My basic question is this: Is there no better way to interact with the rest of the world? Today there are hundreds of millions of Christians, hundreds of millions of Muslims and millions of people who follow the teachings of Moses (Peace Be Upon Him). All divine religions share and respect one word and that is "monotheism" or belief in a single God and no other in the world....

Mr. President,

According to divine verses, we have all been called upon to worship one God and follow the teachings of divine Prophets.

To worship a God which is above all powers in the world and can do all He pleases." "The Lord which knows that which is hidden and visible, the past and the future, knows what goes on in the Hearts of His servants and records their deeds....

We believe a return to the teachings of the divine prophets is the only road leading to salvation and have been told that Your Excellency follows the teachings of Jesus (Peace Be Upon Him) and believes in the divine promise of the rule of the righteous on Earth.

We also believe that Jesus Christ (Peace Be Upon Him) was one of the great prophets of the Almighty. He has been repeatedly praised in the Koran. Jesus (Peace Be Upon Him) has been quoted in Koran as well: (19.36) And surely Allah is my Lord and your Lord, therefore serve Him; this is the right path....

Divine prophets have promised:

The day will come when all humans will congregate before the court of the Almighty, so that their deeds are examined, The good will be directed towards Heaven and evildoers will meet divine retribution. I trust both of us believe in such a day, but it will not be easy to calculate the actions of rulers, because we must be answerable to our nation and all others whose lives have been directly or indirectly affected by our actions....

Mr. President, History tells us that repressive and cruel governments do not survive. God has entrusted the fate of men to them. The Almighty has not left the universe and humanity to their own devices. Many things have happened contrary to the wishes and plans of governments. These tell us that there is a higher power at work and all events are determined by Him.

Can one deny the signs of change in the world today?

The Structure of the Government of the Islamic Republic of Iran

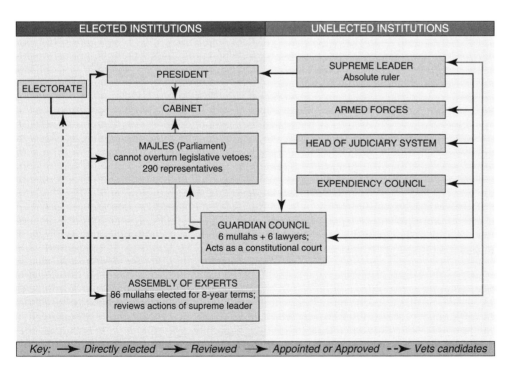

SOURCE: http://upload.wikimedia.org/wikipedia/commons/9/94/Schema_gvt_iran_en.png

Is the situation of the world today comparable to that of 10 years ago? Changes happen fast and come at a furious pace.

The people of the world are not happy with the status quo and pay little heed to the promises and comments made by a number of influential world leaders. Many people around the world feel insecure and oppose the spreading of insecurity and war and do not approve of and accept dubious policies.

The people are protesting the increasing gap between the haves and the have-nots and the rich and poor countries.

The people are disgusted with increasing corruption.

The people of many countries are angry about the attacks on their cultural foundations and the disintegration of families. They are equally dismayed with the fading of care and compassion. The people of the world have no faith in international organizations, because their rights are not advocated by these organizations.

Liberalism and Western-style democracy have not been able to help realize the ideals of humanity. Today these two concepts have failed. Those with insight can already hear the sounds of the shattering and fall of the ideology and thoughts of the Liberal democratic systems.

We increasingly see that people around the world are flocking towards a main focal point—that is the Almighty God. Undoubtedly through faith in God and the teachings of the prophets, the people will conquer their problems. My question for you is: "Do you not want to join them?"

Mr. President, Whether we like it or not, the world is gravitating towards faith in the Almighty and justice and the will of God will prevail over all things.

SOURCE: http://www.washingtonpost.com/wp-dyn/content/article/2006/05/09/AR20060509 00878.html

---

CONTEXT AND ANALYSIS

President Khatami and the reformers he represented were defeated in Iran's 2005 presidential election by Mahmud Ahmadinejad who received 62 percent of the popular vote, nearly twice as much as his competitor, ex-president Akbar Hashemi Rafsanjani. Prior to becoming president he was mayor of Tehran. As a student he was politically active in the revolution of 1978–1979 and may have been directly involved in the 1979 takeover of the U.S. Embassy in Tehran by radical students. Ahmadinejad is a staunch critic of the Bush Administration and supports strengthened relations between Iran and Russia. He is a vocal supporter of Iran's nuclear program, emphasizing that building a nuclear bomb is not the policy of his government. The Iranian nuclear enrichment program, he says, is for peaceful purposes only. On several occasions he has publically condemned the state of Israel, even calling for it "to be wiped off the map," a statement that earned him international condemnation. In addition, he has referred to the Holocaust of the Jews during the Second World War as a "myth." However, for all of that, Ahmadinejad denies that he is an anti-Semite.

Although a religious conservative, Ahmadinejad is not a cleric. His lay status appears to play in his favor. As an anti-corruption candidate, he appealed to the Iranian electorate who were sick of the graft and corruption that had crept into Iranian politics during the presidencies of Khamene'i, Hashemi Rafsanjani, and even Mohammed Khatami. Ahmadinejad had support, in particular, from the traditional population of south Tehran and the smaller cities of the provinces who, although supportive of the revolution, felt that clerical rule had deprived them of the economic benefits which were supposed to accrue to them as the "wretched of the earth." In contrast to the "self-satisfied" clerics, Ahmadinejad projected the image of an honest and pious "son of the country" yet, as an engineer with a Ph.D., one who was fully tuned to the requirements of modernity. His strident demand to the world community that Iran be allowed to develop nuclear power has established him as a proud Islamo-nationalist who refuses to bow down to the great powers, the United States in particular. In this, he continues the aspirations of Iranians of past generations who similarly aimed to reestablish Iran as a great nation.

On May 8, 2006, Ahmadinejad sent a personal letter to U.S. President George Bush. The letter was the first official communication between the two countries since 1980. U.S. Secretary of State Condoleeza Rice dismissed the letter as a propaganda ploy and stated that it was devoid of substance. Yet the letter does accurately communicate various Iranian points of view. In the letter, reproduced above, Ahmadinejad attempts to soothe American fears about Iran's nuclear ambitions. In addition, he presents a list of Iranian grievances against U.S. administrations, past and present, including the CIA involvement in the ouster of Iran's populist Prime Minister Mohammed Mossadegh in 1953, and U.S. support for Saddam Husayn during the 1980–1988 Iran-Iraq War. He criticizes Bush for his invasions of Afghanistan and Iraq, and condemns U.S. treatment of Muslim prisoners at Guantanamo Bay, Cuba, and Abu Ghuraib, Iraq. America, he writes, must honor the prophets, including Moses and Jesus of Nazareth. The strength of the letter's religious message has led some observers to compare it to a traditional invitation to embrace Islam (da'wa), which Muslim leaders in the past addressed to Christians.

FURTHER READINGS

Abdo, Geneive, and Jonathan Lyons. *Answering Only to God: Faith and Freedom in Twenty-First-Century Iran* (New York: Henry Holt, 2003).

Ansari, Ali. *Confronting Iran: The Failure of American Foreign Policy and the Next Great Crisis in the Middle East* (New York: Basic Books, 2006).

Beeman, William. *The Great Satan vs. the Mad Mullahs* (Westport, CT: Praeger/Greenwood, 2005).

Clawson, Patrick, and Michael Rubin. *Eternal Iran* (New York: Palgrave/Macmillan, 2005).

Ehteshami, Anoushiravan. *After Khomeini: The Second Iranian Republic* (London: Routledge, 1995).

Menashri, David. *Post-Revolutionary Politics in Iran: Religion, Society, and Power* (London: Routledge, 2001).

Nafisi, Azar. *Reading Lolita in Tehran: A Memoir in Books* (New York: Random House, 2003).

Vahdat, Farzin. "Mohammad Khatami: The Philosopher President," *International Institute for the Study of Islam in the Modern World Review*, 18 (Autumn 2006), 21.

Wright, Robin. *The Last Great Revolution: Turmoil and Transformation in Iran* (New York: Alfred A. Knopf, 2000).

Zanganeh, Lila Azam, ed. *My Sister, Guard Your Veil, My Brother, Guard Your Eyes: Uncensored Iranian Voices* (Boston: Beacon Press, 2006).

6

THE NEAR ENEMY

Lt. Col. Khalid al-Islambuli shouts "the blood of a Muslim is not a sacrifice for Jews or Americans!" from the court cell at his trial for the assassination of President Anwar al-Sadat in Cairo, Egypt, March 6, 1982. Islambuli was sentenced to death for his role in the assassination. According to al-Islambuli and his colleagues, Egypt's Sadat regime constituted "the near enemy," as opposed to the "far away" enemies of Israel and the United States. (AP photo/Foley. Courtesy of AP Images.)

INTRODUCTION

Throughout the 1980s and the first half of the 1990s some Islamist groups turned to violence in the effort to establish theocratic states governed by Shari'a. The origins of Islamist "direct action" can be traced to the formation in the mid-1940s of a Secret Apparatus (*al-jihaz al-sirri*) within Egypt's Muslim Brotherhood. Operating without the official approval of Supreme Guide Hasan al-Banna, the apparatus assassinated leading political figures, including Egypt's Prime Minister, Nuqrashi Pasha. However, it was only after the consolidation of the Egyptian Free Officers' secular, revolutionary regime that a number of Islamist thinkers and organizations began consistently to regard the Islamist contest with the state as a zero sum game. For these radical Islamists, the gradualist politics of the Muslim Brotherhood and other mainstream movements appeared ineffectual against the power of the Arab nationalist governments, which were prepared to incarcerate and even torture fellow Muslims to preserve their authority.

Inspired both by the 1978–1979 Islamic Revolution in Iran and the radical doctrine of Egyptian Islamist Sayyid Qutb, the radical trend within Sunni Islamism gained momentum during the presidencies of 'Abd al-Nasser's successors, Anwar Sadat and Husni Mubarak. By the early 1990s radical Islamist violence had overtaken Algeria. A review of the documents, manifestos, and actions of these radical Islamist groups indicates their willingness to match the force of the state with tactics of sabotage and terrorism. The radical Islamists justified their use of violence against the regimes by emphasizing militant understandings of the jihad concept, and by portraying Muslim governments and the Muslims that supported them as traitorous. Over this period, concern mounted in the capitals of the Middle East and the West that Islamist regimes might emerge in the heart of the Arab world.

In the wake of 9/11, many in the West and the Islamic world have supposed that radical Islamists have always possessed an agenda of global conquest, and that their chief concerns have been the power and cultural influence of the United States. While it is true that Islamists of all varieties have long held a dim view of Western power, particularly as regards U.S. foreign policy, their primary efforts were directed at the secular local orders—what Islamist ideologues referred to as "the near enemy." The radicals' key goal was to capture the state and Islamize it—along with society—from the top down. They viewed the state as a strategic tool to restructure society and politics. Only once countries like Egypt and Algeria "returned to the Islamic fold," would they turn their attention to Islam's "far enemies," namely, America, Israel, and their Western allies. During the period of the insurgencies, radical Islamists attacked soft Western targets at home, for example, tourists in Egypt. However, these attacks were ways of diminishing the power of the "near enemy" by discouraging Westerners from spending the foreign hard currency on which the government depended. Only in the late 1990s did elements within the radical Islamist camp abandon the struggle against the political establishments in their home countries in favor of strikes against American and European targets.

The Modern *Jahiliyya*

- **Document:** Introduction to Sayyid Qutb's tractate, *Milestones*.
- **Date:** 1964.
- **Where:** Cairo, Egypt.
- **Significance:** Sayyid Qutb's call for committed Muslims to challenge the "corrupt" and ungodly regimes in the Middle East and elsewhere, would help direct succeeding generations of Islamists in a radical direction.

DOCUMENT

Mankind today is on the brink of a precipice, not because of the danger of complete annihilation which is hanging over its head—this being just a symptom and not the real disease—but because humanity is devoid of those vital values for its healthy development and real progress. Even Western scholars realize that their civilization is unable to present healthy values for the guidance of mankind and does not possess anything to satisfy its own conscience and justify its existence.

Democracy in the West has become sterile to such an extent that its intellectuals borrow from the systems of the Eastern bloc, especially in the economic sphere, under the name of socialism. It is the same with the Eastern bloc. Foremost among its social theories is Marxism, which in the beginning attracted a large number of people not only from the East but also from the West as a way of life based on a creed. But now Marxism stands intellectually defeated and it is not an exaggeration to say that in practice not a single nation in the world is truly Marxist.

Marxist theory conflicts with man's nature and its needs: it prospers only in a degenerate society or in a society which is tyrannized over a period and becomes docile and cowed as a result of it. But now, even under these extreme circumstances, its materialistic economic system is failing, although this was the only foundation on which its structure was based. The Soviet Union which has been the leader of the Communist countries in Europe and the Americas, is itself suffering from shortages of food. During the times of the Tsars, Russia used to produce surplus food, it now has to import food from abroad and has to sell its reserves of gold for this purpose. The main reason for this is the failure of the system of collective farming, or, one can say, the failure of a system which is against human nature.

It is essential for mankind to have new leadership! The leadership of mankind by the West is now on the decline, not because Western culture has become poor materially or because its economic and military power has become weak. The era of the Western system has come to an end primarily because it lost those life-giving values which enabled it to be the leader of mankind.

It is necessary for the new leadership to preserve and develop the material fruits of the creative genius of Europe, and also to provide mankind with the high ideals and values previously unknown in the West, that can restore harmony with human nature, in a positive, constructive, and practical way of life.

Islam is the only System which possesses these values and this way of life.

The era dominated by the resurgence of science has also come to an end. This period, which began with the Renaissance in the sixteenth century A.C. and reached its zenith in the eighteenth and nineteenth centuries, does not possess a spirit capable of reviving a dynamic civilization.

All nationalistic and chauvinistic ideologies that have appeared in modern times, and all the movements and theories derived from them, have also lost their vitality. In short, all man-made theories, both individualistic and collectivist, have proved to be failures.

At this crucial and bewildering juncture, the time for Islam and the Muslim community has arrived because it has the needed values. Islam does not stand in the way of material progress or prohibit material inventions. Indeed, it considers material prosperity and creativity to be an obligation given to man at the very beginning of time, when Allah granted him the vicegerency on earth. Islam regards initiative in multiplying the bounties of Allah on earth with the proper intent as worship of Allah and one of the purposes of man's creation.

And remember the time when your Sustainer said to the angels, "I will create a vicegerent on earth." I have only created jinns and men that they may serve me.

Thus the turn of the Muslim community has come to fulfill its divinely appointed task for mankind.

You are the best community raised for mankind, enjoining what is best and forbidding what is wrong, and you believe in Allah.

And thus have We made of you a community justly balanced, that you may be witnesses over the nations, and the messenger a witness over yourselves.

Islam cannot fulfill its role except by taking concrete form in a society, or more precisely, in a nation. Men do not listen, especially in this age, to an abstract theory which is not seen materialized in a living society. From this point of view, we can say that the Muslim community has been extinct for a few centuries, for this Muslim community does not denote the name of a land in which Islam resides, nor is it a people whose forefathers lived under the Islamic system at some earlier time. It is the name of a group of people whose manners, ideas and concepts, rules and regulations, values and criteria, are all derived from the Islamic source, so that the Muslims' way of life is an example to all mankind, just as the Messenger is an example to them: "And thus have we made of you a community justly balanced that you may be witnesses over the nations, and the Messenger a witness over yourselves."

Islam cannot fulfill its role except by providing the leadership for all of mankind, for which the Muslim community must be restored to its original form. That Muslim community is now buried under the debris of the man-made traditions of several generations and is crushed under the weight of those false laws and customs that are not even remotely related to the Islamic teachings. In spite of all this the modern Muslim world calls itself the "world of Islam." I am aware that between the attempt at "revival" and the attainment of "leadership" there is a great distance, as the Muslim community has long ago vanished from existence and the leadership of mankind has long since passed to other ideologies and other nations, other concepts and other systems. This was the era during which Europe's genius created its marvelous works in science, culture, law, and material production, due to which mankind has progressed to great heights of creativity and material comfort. It is not easy to find fault with the inventors of such marvelous things, especially since what we call the "world of Islam" is completely devoid of all this beauty.

But the growing bankruptcy of Western civilization makes it necessary to revive Islam. The distance between the revival of Islam and the attainment of world leadership may be vast, and there may be great difficulties on the way; but the first step must be taken towards this revival.

If we are to perform our task with insight and wisdom, we must first clearly know the nature of the qualities on the basis of which the Muslim community can fulfill its obligation as the leader of the world. This is essential so that we may not commit any blunders at the very first stage of its reconstruction and revival.

The Muslim community today is neither capable of nor is required to present before mankind great genius in material inventions, such as would make the world bow its head before its supremacy and thus reestablish once more its world leadership. Europe's creative mind is far ahead in this area, and for a few centuries to come we cannot expect to compete with Europe and attain supremacy over it in these fields.

Hence we must have some other quality, a quality that modern civilization does not possess.

But this does not mean that we should neglect material progress. We should also give our full attention and effort in this direction, not because at this stage it is an essential requirement for attaining the leadership of mankind, but because it is an essential condition for our very existence. Islam elevates man to the position of vicegerent of Allah on earth, and, under certain conditions, considers the responsibilities of this vicegerency as worship of Allah and the purpose of man's creation. The responsibility of this vicegerency includes the material progress that comes from multiplying the bounties of Allah.

To attain the leadership of mankind, we must have something to offer besides material progress, and this other quality can only be a faith and a way of life that both promotes the benefits of modern science and technology and fulfills basic human needs. The same effort that has produced material comfort and leisure should be exerted to design and apply technology in meeting the minimum needs of the poor. And then this faith and way of life must take concrete form in a human society—in other words, in a Muslim society.

If we look at the sources and foundations of modern modes of living, it becomes clear that the whole world is steeped in *jahiliyyah*, and all the marvelous material comforts and advanced inventions do not diminish its ignorance. This *jahiliyyah* is based on rebellion against the sovereignty of Allah on earth. It attempts to transfer to man one of the great attributes of Allah, namely, sovereignty, by making some men lords over others. It does so not in the simple and primitive ways of the ancient *jahiliyyah*, but in the more subtle form of claiming that the right to create values, to legislate rules of collective behavior, and to choose a way of life rests with men, without regard to what Allah has prescribed. The result of this rebellion against the authority of Allah is the oppression of His creatures. Thus the humiliation of the common man under the communist systems and the exploitation of individuals and nations due to the greed for wealth and imperialism under capitalist systems are but a corollary of the rebellion against the authority of Allah and the denial of the dignity of man bestowed upon him by Allah.

In this respect, Islam's way of life is unique, for in systems other than Islam, people worship others in one form or another. Only in the Islamic way of life do all men become free from the servitude of some men to others and devote themselves to the worship of Allah alone, deriving guidance from Him alone, and bowing before Him alone.

This dignity of man in submission to Allah is where the roads separate, and this is the new concept that we possess and can present to mankind. This concept and the way of life covering all the practical aspects of man's life is the vital message that mankind lacks. We call it the Islamic *din*. It is not a product of Western invention or of European genius, whether of "socialism" or "capitalism."

Without doubt, we are able to offer this *din* which is perfect to the highest degree, and which most of mankind still knows only dimly and is not capable of "producing." But as we have stated before, the beauty of this new system cannot be appreciated unless it takes a concrete form. It is essential that a community arrange its affairs according to it and show it to the world. In order to bring this about, we need to initiate the movement of Islamic revival in some Muslim country. Only such a revivalist movement will eventually—sooner or later—attain world leadership.

How to initiate the revival of Islam? A vanguard must set out with this determination and then keep going, marching through the vast ocean of *jahiliyyah* which encompassed the entire world. During its course, this vanguard, while distancing itself somewhat aloof from this all encompassing *jahiliyyah* should also retain contacts with it.

The Muslims in this vanguard must know the landmarks and the milestones on the road to this goal so that they would know the starting point as well as the nature, the responsibilities, and the ultimate purpose of this long journey. Not only this, but they ought to be aware of their position vis-à-vis this *jahiliyyah*, which has struck with others and when to separate from them; what characteristics and qualities they should cultivate; and with what characteristics and qualities the *jahiliyyah*, immediately surrounding them, is armed; how to address the people of *jahiliyyah* in the language of Islam; what topics and problems to discuss with them; and where and how to obtain guidance in all these matters.

The milestones will necessarily be determined in the light of the first source of this faith—the Noble Qur'an—and from its basic teachings. The milestones will reflect the concept that the Qur'an created in the minds of the first generation of Muslims, those whom Allah raised to fulfill His will, those who did change the course of human history in the direction ordained by Allah.

I have written Milestones for this vanguard, which I consider to be a waiting reality about to be materialized. Four chapters are taken from my commentary, *Fi Zilal al-Qur'an*, which I have changed here and there to suit the topic. This introduction and the other chapters I wrote at various times. In writing these chapters I have set down the deep truths that I grasped during my meditation over the way of life presented in the Noble Qur'an. These thoughts may appear random and disconnected, but one thing is common in them. These thoughts are milestones on the road, and it is the nature of signs along the road to be disconnected. Taken together, these writings are the first installment of a series, and with Allah's help I hope to write more on this topic. And Allah alone grants guidance.

SOURCE: Sayyid Qutb, *Milestones*, revised translation (Indianapolis, IN: American Trust Publications, 1990), 5–10.

CONTEXT AND ANALYSIS

Sayyid Qutb greeted the 1952 Free Officers coup in Egypt with guarded optimism. He knew that the military men came to power in the name of social justice and national independence. In 1953 he formalized his Islamist leanings by joining the Muslim Brotherhood. He was appointed head of its propaganda department and used his position to try to convince 'Abd al-Nasser and the officers to implement Islamic law in Egypt. But when it became clear to all that Nasser aimed to uphold the established secular orientation of Egyptian politics, Qutb and his fellow Muslim Brothers adopted a dissenting view toward the soldiers. Fearing an Islamist countercoup, Nasser moved against the Brothers in October 1954. Qutb was one of those caught in the dragnet. Tried by three partisan judges, including future president of Egypt, Anwar Sadat, he was convicted for plotting against the Nasser regime and sentenced to fifteen years imprisonment.

Torturers unleashed an orgy of violence against the imprisoned Muslim Brothers, including Sayyid Qutb. The torture wore Qutb down. Eventually, his jailors moved him to the prison hospital where he stayed for the next ten years, spending much of his time writing. Even before his imprisonment, he had begun a lucid, highly personal commentary called *Fi Zilal al-Qu'ran*

(*In the Shade of the Qur'an*). Some of the Brothers who were imprisoned with him staged a strike and refused to leave their cells. They were gunned down—twenty-three were killed and forty-six wounded.

The torture and the massacre of prisoners had a radicalizing effect on Qutb's ideas. Up to this point, he had believed that secularism simply created selfishness and social isolation. But the torture showed him that secular, materialist culture also unleashed the most brutal and barbarous aspects of human beings. Qutb began secretly to write of a disease that was spreading from the West throughout the World. He called it *jahiliyya*—ignorance of the divine mandate.

Historically, the word had been used by Muslims to describe the condition of barbarism that prevailed in the Arabian Peninsula prior to the advent of Islam. Following Maududi who earlier had come to a similar conclusion, Qutb removed *jahiliyya* from its original chronological framework and redefined it as a state of being, an existential condition, which was possible any time or place. In Qutb's view, all aspects of the contemporary era were *jahili*—society, manners, art, literature, law, including much of what passed as Islamic culture. Nowhere in the world did there exist a true Islamic society, one that recognized God's sovereignty.

According to Qutb, what made *jahiliyya* so terrifying and insidious was that people didn't realize that they were infected. They believed that they were free agents and that their politicians were taking them forward to a better world. But in fact, they were regressing to a state of barbarism.

To Qutb, this force of *jahiliyya* had now gone so deep into the minds of Muslims that a dramatic way had to be found to free them. In a series of letters that family and friends smuggled out, Qutb called on a revolutionary vanguard to rise up and overthrow the leaders who had allowed *jahiliyya* to infect their countries. Qutb did not mention Nasser, but he clearly had the Egyptian president in mind. Within the context of Islamic thought, this was a novel way of thinking. Historically, jurists had cautioned Muslims to obey their leaders, even if they were corrupt, to prevent war and disorder. Qutb's letters, some of which he took from his Qur'an commentary, were published in 1964 under the title *Ma'alim fi al-Tariq* ("*Milestones*," or "*Signposts on the Road*"). Its urgent call to action invites comparison with Lenin's "*What Is to Be Done.*" The book remains the principle manifesto of radical Islamism.

In 1964 the Egyptian authorities granted Qutb early release. But he was almost immediately implicated in another alleged conspiracy against the regime. The second trial of Sayyid Qutb, which included forty-two of

IN HISTORY

Amina Qutb: "Do You Envision Us Meeting?"

Poem by Amina Qutb, sister of Sayyid. The poem may be about her brother, Sayyid, or about her husband Muhammad Kamal al-Din Siniri who was also imprisoned by the 'Abd al-Nasser regime.

Do you envision us meeting, or has it already,
Taken place in the land of the mirage;
Then it withdrew and its shadow vanished,
And turned into torturous memories;
Thus asks my heart whenever,
The days grow long, after your absence;
When your shadow stares, smiling,
It is as if I am listening to the response;
Did we not walk upon Truth together,
So that Good can return to barren land;
So we walked along a thorny path,
Abandoning all our ambitions;
We buried our desires deep within ourselves,
And we strove on in contentment, expecting reward from Allah;
We had made a pact to walk together,
And then you hurried in responding and departing;
When a Benevolent Lord called me,
To a life amidst gardens and vast lands;
And towards a sublime meeting amidst divine favors,
With the Soldiers of Allah, joyful in companionship;
Presenting their souls and lives, a sacrifice,
Responding without slightest doubts;
So to renew your heart from its slumber,
An ever-lasting meeting in such a land;
Oh traveler, Forgiveness from my complaints,
Unto me is your ghost, to him a patient reproach;
I abandoned my heart to bleed heavily,
Lost in the night, in the depths of fog;
And if I traverse, confused and alone,
I'll interrupt the path, long it is in depression;
And if in the night, I find a gloomy sea,
Encountering in it waves of pain;
Ceasing in my nights, is the radiance of lightening,
And the brightness of stars have disappeared;
Despite this, I shall continue just as,
You used to find me, in the face of adversity;
I shall continue keeping my head raised, And won't,
Consent to weakness in speech, nor reply;
I shall be guided by the sweet-scented blood,
And light has illuminated the horizons of escape;
Do you envision us meeting, or has it already,
Taken place in the land of the mirage;
Then it withdrew and its shadow vanished,
And turned into torturous memories;
Thus asks my heart whenever,
The days grow long, after your absence;
When your shadow stares, smiling,
It is as if I am listening to the response; …

SOURCE: http://talk.islamicnetwork.com/archive/index.php/t-1474.html

his followers, began April 19, 1966. It did not take long for the court to sentence him and two others to death. Sayyid Qutb was hanged after dawn prayers on August 29, 1966.

FURTHER READINGS

Abu Rabi, Ibrahim. *Intellectual Origins of Islamic Resurgence in the Modern Arab World* (Albany, NY: SUNY Press, 1996).

Euben, Roxanne. *The Enemy in the Mirror: Islamic Fundamentalism and the Limits of Modern Rationalism* (Princeton, NJ: Princeton University Press, 1999).

Haddad, Yvonne. "Sayyid Qutb: Ideologue of Islamic Revival," in John L. Esposito (ed.), *Voices of Resurgent Islam* (New York: Oxford University Press, 1983), 67–98.

Kepel, Gilles. *Muslim Extremism in Egypt: The Prophet and the Pharaoh* (Berkeley: University of California Press, 1993).

Khatab, Sayed. *The Political Thought of Sayyid Qutb: The Theory of Jahiliyya* (New York: Routledge, 2006).

Moussalli, Ahmad. *Radical Islamic Fundamentalism: The Ideological and Political Discourse of Sayyid Qutb* (Beirut: American University of Beirut Press, 1992).

Musallam, Adnan. *From Secularism to Jihad: Sayyid Qutb and the Foundations of Radical Islamism* (Westport, CT: Praeger/Greenwood, 2005).

Shepard, William. "Sayyid Qutb's Doctrine of *Jahiliyya*," *International Journal of Middle East Studies*, 35 (2003), 521–45.

"What Immorality Could Allow This Kind of Behavior?"

- *Document:* Selections from Zainab al-Ghazali's memoir, *Return of the Pharaoh (Ayyam min Hayati)*.
- *Date:* 1972.
- *Where:* Cairo, Egypt.
- *Significance:* The passage illustrates in graphic terms the harsh treatment accorded Zainab al-Ghazali and other Islamists in 'Abd al-Nasser's prisons. In the case of Qutb and later of his followers in the 1970s, torture helped to radicalize their outlooks. There is some truth to the dictum that radical Islamism "was born in Nasser's prisons."

DOCUMENT

On my way to Room 24, accompanied by two men holding whips, I was deliberately taken past different places inside the prison such that I could see for myself the hideous things taking place there. Almost unable to believe my eyes and not wanting to accept such inhumanity, I silently watched as members of the Ikhwan [Muslim Brothers] were suspended in the air and their naked bodies ferociously flogged. Some were left to the mercy of savage dogs which tore at their bodies. Others, with their face to the wall awaited their turn. Worse still, I knew many of these pious believing youth personally. They were as dear to me as my own sons, and had attended study circles of Tafsir [interpretation of Qur'an] and Hadith in my home, in their own homes and at Ibn al-Aqram house.

One by one, these youth of Islam, sheikhs of Islam, were tortured, left standing with their face to the wall, and flogged ferociously. Some had blood running down their foreheads. Foreheads that did not bow to anyone except Allah. The light of Tawhid [God's Unity] shone from their raised faces, proud to belong to the cause of Allah.

One of them shouted to me: "Mother! May Allah make you firm!"

"Sons! It is a pledge of allegiance. Be patient Yasir's family, your reward is Paradise."

The man with me struck me so hard on my head that I felt my eyes and ear turning as if hit by an electrical force. And the light from inside the prison made me aware of the many, many more tortured bodies filling the place.—[Let it be] for the sake of Allah!

"Let it be for the sake of Allah!," I braved.

At that moment, a voice, as if coming from Paradise, could be heard saying: "O Allah! Hold their steps firm and protect them from the perverts. Had it not been for You, O lord!, we would not have been guided. Nor would we have prayed nor given anything in charity. So, please hold out steps firm in trial and in adversity."

The sound of flogging became louder and more intense, but the voice of *iman* [faith] was both stronger and clearer. Another voice rallied: "There is no god but Allah."

And, I again repeated: "Patience my sons, it is a pledge of allegiance. Patience, your reward is Paradise."

I was struck sharply on my back but I would not relent: "Allah is the Greatest, praise be to Allah. O Allah! Give us patience and contentment. Praise and thanks are due to You, O Allah! For the bounties of Islam, *Iman* and Jihad in Your way which You bestowed upon us."

The door to a dark room was opened, I was hurled inside, and the door crashed shut behind me.

Inside Room 24

"In the Name of Allah, peace be upon you," I repeated.

The next moment the door was locked and a bright light switched on. Now their purpose was revealed; the room was full of dogs! I could not count how many!

Scared, I closed my eyes and put my hands to my chest. Within seconds the snarling dogs were all over me, and I could feel their teeth tearing into every part of my body. Clenching my hands tight into my armpits, I began to recount the Names of Allah, beginning with "O Allah! O Allah! "The dogs were unrelenting, digging their teeth into my scalp, my shoulders, back, chest and wherever another had not already taken hold. I repeatedly invoked my Lord, calling: O Lord! Make me not distracted by anything except You. Let all my attention be for You Alone, You my Lord, the One, the Only, the Unique, the Eternal Absolute. Take me from the World of Forms. Distract me from all these phenomena. Let my whole attention be for You. Make me stand in Your Presence. Bestow on me Your Tranquility. Clothe me with the garments of Your Love. Provide me with death for Your Sake, loving for Your sake, contentment with You. O Lord! Hold the steps of the faithful firm."

I repeated this inwardly for what seemed like several hours until at last the door was opened, the dogs forced from my body and I was taken out.

I expected that my clothes would be thoroughly stained with blood, for I was sure the dogs had bitten every part of my body. But, incredulously, there was not a single blood-stain on my clothes, as if the dogs had been in my imagination only. May God be exalted! He is with me. I began questioning inwardly whether I deserved all these bounties and gifts from Allah. My warders could not believe it either. I glimpsed the sky outside filled with evening twilight, indicating sunset. I concluded that I must have been locked in with the dogs for more than three hours. Praise be to God for any adversity!

I was pushed, and staggered along for what seemed a long time. A door was opened, and I felt lost in the vast hall which it gave onto. I was led along another long corridor, past many closed doors. I noticed one of these doors slightly ajar, and giving out enough light to brighten the obscurity of the corridor. Through it I caught a glimpse of the illuminated face of Muhammad Rashad Mahna, once Egypt's Crown Prince. The Nasir regime believed that the *Ikhwan* would install him as Head of State if they took over power. Hence his arrest. Cell no. 3, next to Cell no. 2, was opened and I was hurled inside.

....

The Vision

I do not know how but I fell asleep while invoking Allah, and it was then that I experienced the first of four visions of the Prophet (peace be upon him) that I was to see during my stay in prison. There in front of me, praise be to Allah, was a vast desert and camels and hawdahs as if made of light. On each hawdah were four men, all with luminous faces. I found myself behind this huge train of camels in that vast, endless desert, and standing behind a great reverent man. This man was holding a halter which passed through the neck of each camel. I wondered silently: Could this man be the Prophet (peace be upon him)?

Silence has no safeguard with the Prophet, who replied: "Zainab! You are following in the footsteps of Muhammad, Allah's servant and Messenger."

"Am I, master! Following in the footsteps of Muhammad, Allah's Servant and Messenger?"

"You, Zainab Ghazali, are following in the footsteps of Muhammad, Allah's Servant and Messenger."

O my Beloved! Am I truly following in your footsteps?

"Zainab! You are on the right path. You are on the right path, Zainab! You are following in the footsteps of Muhammad, Allah's Servant and Messenger."

Twice more I repeated my question, receiving the same response from the Prophet.

I woke up feeling I owned the world. Astonished, I had forgotten my whereabouts and what I was facing. Nor did I feel any pain nor see the wooden post near the window. It seemed that I had been taken to another place whereof voices came from afar. Furthermore, I was also astonished for, although I am known as Zainab al-Ghazali, my recorded name at birth was Zainab Ghazali, and it was by this name that the Prophet had called me. Indeed, the vision had transported me beyond time and space. I did *tayammum* [the dry ablution using sand or dust, performed if no clean water is available] and began praying, thanking Allah for this gift. In one of my prostrations I found myself invoking: "Lord! By what means am I going to thank You? There is nothing I can thank You with except by renewing my allegiance to You. O Allah! I pledge allegiance to die for Your Sake. O Allah! I pledge allegiance to You that none should be tortured because of me. O Allah! Hold me firm in following the truth that You are pleased with, and confine me within the limits of right that pleases You!

Tranquility and peace of mind were mine.

I heard a commotion outside. The noise of countless lorries arriving filled with a new shift of butchers whilst others left, their duties for the time being completed. A new wave of torture would soon begin. I could hear Adhan of Fajr [call to the dawn prayer], and so made *tayammum* and prayed.

I remained in my cell for six consecutive days: from Friday 20th August to Thursday 26th August, 1965. My cell door, during these six days was never opened. I was given neither food, drink, allowed to go to the toilet nor any contact with the outside world, except my warder who, now and then, peeped through the small hole in my cell door. You can imagine, dear reader, how a person can live in such circumstances. For if one can do without food and drink, one cannot do without going to the toilet. Remember also, that all this took place during August! Would Judaism or even Paganism allow such treatment, let alone by people claiming to be Muslims? Could such things be possible?

O Allah! How often did these despotic dictators abuse human dignity and wash their hands of any and all religion and morals. For the oppressed, however, certainty in Allah, belief in truth and living guided by one's Lord produce strength capable of transcending such degradation. Therefore, dear reader, don't be amazed that I could live for six days without water, food, or going to the toilet. Indeed I was able to survive for those six days because of two things:

Firstly, it is Allah's favor on us that we believe in Him. Islam bestows us with a strength which helps us to surmount problems and difficulties. This is Allah's favor. *Iman* gives tremendous strength and energy for bearing hardships. A strength beyond that of those perverse despots who think it is they who truly rule. The believer lives in contact with Allah, independently of shape or form.

Secondly, it was that blessed vision which was like food or a tonic from Allah which enabled me to live in distraction from all that was happening around me. It was this which helped me endure, in submission and acceptance, this earthly hell.

On the morning of the seventh day, my guard brought some water, a quarter of bread stained with human excrement and a piece of yellow cheese. He threw these onto the floor, shouting: "B....! Since you are still alive, this is your food!"

I touched neither the bread nor the cheese, but I took of the water despite the filthy pot in which it was brought, blocking my nose to reduce the stench from the pot and saying: "In the Name of Allah with Whose name nothing can harm neither on earth or in heaven, and He is the All-Hearing, All-Knowing. O Allah! Let it be food, water, effort, learning, patience and submission."

I slowly drank the water. Then, just before sunset my warder entered my cell, hitting the walls and floor with his whip.

Get up B....! You can go to the toilet!, he yelled.

I tried to get up but quickly fell back from sheer exhaustion.

The warder pulled me up roughly by the arm and walked me there himself but, as I tried to close the toilet door, he shouted: "You're not allowed to close it!"

"Take me back to my cell then, I don't want anything."

"Get in B....! How should we watch over you!", he retorted savagely, his insolence matched only by his pleasure at my humiliation.

What immorality or what Jahiliyya could allow this kind of behavior?

SOURCE: Zainab al-Ghazali, *Return of the Pharaoh: Memoir in Nasir's Prison*, translated by Mokrane Guezzou (Leicester, UK: The Islamic Foundation, KUBE Publishing, 1994/1415 AH), 48–56. Courtesy of KUBE Publishing, Ltd.

CONTEXT AND ANALYSIS

One of those in contact with the imprisoned Sayyid Qutb was Zainab al-Ghazali (1917–2005) who is legendary in Islamist circles as a "soldier of God." In the 1920s she was a teenage disciple of Huda Sharawi, founder of the European-inspired Egyptian Feminist Union, but in 1935 took a different path and dedicated her life to Islam. A year later, al-Ghazali founded her own group, the Muslim Women's Association whose purpose was to help women study Islam and to engage in welfare activities. Hasan al-Banna, Supreme Guide of the Muslim Brotherhood, tried to persuade her to incorporate her group into his movement but she resisted, offering instead to cooperate with the Brothers. In keeping with the Islamist vision of women's role in society, al-Ghazali preached women's domesticity. She justified her activity in the public sphere by prioritizing women's responsibilities. In her view, during times of mission and struggle women who had fulfilled their domestic duties could, if they chose, devote their extra time and energy to the cause of forging an Islamic state. As Miriam Cooke writes, her "argument strongly suggests that public action represents the culmination of private activities. These are not separate realms but rather behaviors ranging across a continuous spectrum" (Cooke 2001, 91). Having divorced her first husband on account of his unwillingness to sanction her activism, she wrote in the contract of her second marriage the stipulation that she be allowed to carry on with her public work, a condition her second husband accepted.

Like many Islamists, Zainab al-Ghazali had originally supported 'Abd al-Nasser and the Free Officers, believing them to be sympathetic to the Islamist cause. However, when it became apparent that 'Abd al-Nasser had no intention of turning Egypt into an Islamic state and outlawed the Muslim Brotherhood, her admiration turned into hatred. She turned her energies to taking care of the families of Muslim Brothers who had been executed or imprisoned. In 1957 she met a young Muslim Brother who had escaped prison named 'Abd al-Fattah Isma'il. Together they set out to rebuild the Muslim Brotherhood from the ashes of its defeat.

By 1962 al-Ghazali, Isma'il, and others who joined them were in touch with Sayyid Qutb's sister Hamida, who gave them chapters from Qutb's work-in-progress, *Milestones*. Sayyid Qutb became the little group's spiritual leader. In the words of Emmanuel Sivan, *Milestone's* radical analysis of the 'Abd al-Nasser regime gave their "quest for revenge an edge it did not otherwise possess" (Sivan, *Radical Islam*, 26). In 1964 Qutb was released from prison on grounds of ill health, but the regime of Free Officers soon after implicated him in an alleged anti-government conspiracy. 'Abd al-Nasser claimed that the reborn Muslim Brotherhood aimed to assassinate high-ranking officials and destroy key communication and transportation facilities, and in the ensuing chaos, they planned to take over the government. By the end of August more than a thousand Islamists were behind bars. On April 3, 1966 charges were presented against Qutb and forty-three other Islamists, including Zainab al-Ghazali and Sayyid Qutb's sister Hamida and brother, Muhammad. In order to expedite proceedings, 'Abd al-Nasser promulgated what was known in Islamist circles as "Pharaoh's Law," emergency powers that gave the regime wide latitude in the arraignment and handling of suspects.

In *Return of the Pharaoh*, Zainab al-Ghazali recounts her six years in prison, first at Liman Tura, where Sayyid Qutb was also interned before his execution, and then at the women's prison at Qanatir. Yet, through all of this torment she was apparently able to protect her virtue, and her will was unbroken. After her release in 1970 by President Anwar al-Sadat, she returned to the world to minister to others. *Return of the Pharaoh* is an Islamist indictment of the nationalist governments that took root in Egypt and other Muslim countries in the 1950s and 1960s. For many Islamists, the treatment meted out to al-Ghazali and other prisoners provides Sayyid Qutb's theory of the modern *Jahilyya* with legitimacy.

FURTHER READINGS

Ahmed, Leila. *Women and Gender in Islam* (New Haven, CT: Yale University Press, 1992).

Cooke, Miriam. *Women Claim Islam: Creating Islamic Feminism through Literature* (New York: Routledge, 2001).

Hatem, Mervet. "Secularist and Islamist Discourse on Modernity in Egypt and the Evolution of the Postcolonial Nation-State," in Yvonne Haddad and John L. Esposito (eds.), *Islam, Gender, and Social Change* (Baltimore: Oxford University Press, 1998).

Hoffman, Valerie. "An Islamic Activist: Zaynab al-Ghazali," in Elizabeth W. Fernea (ed.), *Women and the Family in the Middle East: New Voices of Change* (Austin: University of Texas Press, 1985).

Karram, Azza M. *Women, Islamisms, and the State: Contemporary Feminisms in Egypt* (London: Macmillan, 1998).

The Neglected Duty

- **Document:** Selections from *Al-Farida al-Gha'iba* (*The Neglected Duty*), by 'Abd al-Salam Faraj.
- **Date:** 1981.
- **Where:** Cairo, Egypt.
- **Significance:** 'Abd al-Faraj, the author of *The Neglected Duty*, takes Qutb's theses to their logical conclusion: the state is *jahili* (ignorant of God's commands) and must be overthrown by jihad. The tract was used to justify the assassination of President Anwar al-Sadat. 'Abd al-Faraj writes that the "near enemy" must be confronted prior to taking on the "far away" enemy, i.e., Israel and the West.

DOCUMENT

In the Name of God the Most Compassionate

Preface

Glory to God. We Praise Him, we ask for His help, we ask Him to forgive us, we ask Him to give us guidance. We seek protection with God against the wickedness of our souls and against the evilness of our acts. If God sends someone on the right path, no one can send him astray. I acknowledge that there is no god but God alone, He has no associate, and I acknowledge that Muhammad is His Servant and His Apostle.

The most reliable Speech is the Book of God, and the best guidance is the guidance of Muhammad, may God's peace be upon him. The worst of all things are novelties, since every novelty is an innovation (*bid'a*) and every innovation is a deviation, and all deviation is from Hell.

Jihad (struggle) for God's cause, in spite of its extreme importance and its great significance for the future of this religion, has been neglected by the *'ulama* (leading Muslim scholars) of this age. They have feigned ignorance of it, but they know that it is the only way to the return and the establishment of the glory of Islam anew. Every Muslim preferred his own favorite ideas and philosophies above the Best Road, which God—Praised and Exalted He is—drew Himself (a road that leads back) to (a state of) Honor for His Servants.

There is no doubt that the idols of this world can only be made to disappear through the power of the sword. It is therefore that (the Apostle Muhammad)—God's peace be upon him—said: "I have been sent with the Sword at this Hour, so that God alone is worshipped, without associate to Him, He put my daily bread under the shadow of my lance, He brings lowness and smallness to those who disagree with what I command. Whosoever resembles a certain group of people will be counted as a member of that group." (This Tradition) is reported by Imam Ahmad (ibn Hanbal) on the authority of Ibn 'Umar.

Ibn Rajab says: The saying of (the Apostle Muhammad)—God's peace be upon him—"I have been sent with the Sword" means that God sent him to call with the sword for (acknowledgment of) God's unity after he had called (for this) with arguments. Whosoever did not comply (and accept) the unity (of God), (being called upon to do so) by (the text of) the Qur'an, by arguments and by proof, would then be called upon by the sword....

The Establishment of an Islamic State

This is a duty which is rejected by some Muslims and neglected by others although the proof for the obligatory character of the establishment of a state is clear, and made obvious by the (text of the) Book of God—Blessed and Supreme He is—for God—Glory to Him—says: "and that you must rule between them according to what God sent down," and He says: "Whosoever does not rule by what God sent down, those, they are unbelievers." He says—Glorious and Majestic He is—in (the first verse) of Sura 24, about the obligatory character of the precepts of Islam: "A Sura which we sent down and which we made obligatory." From this (verse) it follows that the establishment of the Rule of God over this earth (mentioned in verse 55 of this Sura) must be considered to be obligatory for the Muslims, for something without which something which is obligatory cannot be carried out becomes (itself) obligatory. If, moreover, (such a) state cannot be established without war, then this war is an obligation as well.

Muslims are agreed on the obligatory character of the establishment of an Islamic Caliphate. To announce a Caliphate must be based on the existence of a (territorial) nucleus (from which it can grow). This (nucleus) is the Islamic State. "Whosoever dies without having taken upon himself (the obligation of) a pledge of allegiance does not die as a Muslim." So it is obligatory for every Muslim to seriously strive for the return of the caliphate in order not to fall into the category of people (mentioned in the) Tradition (quoted in this paragraph). By "pledge of allegiance" (the text of the Tradition) means "allegiance to the Caliphate."

The House in Which We Live

Here a question appears: Do we live in an Islamic State? One of the characteristics of such a state is that it is ruled by the laws of Islam. The Imam Abu Hanifa gave as his opinion that the House of Islam changes into the House of Unbelief if three conditions are fulfilled simultaneously: 1. if it is ruled by other laws than those of Islam, 2. the disappearance of safety for the Muslim inhabitants, 3. its being adjacent or close ... and this (means) that the House (of Islam) is close to the House of Unbelief to such an extent that this is a source of danger to the Muslims and a cause for the disappearance of their safety.

The Imam Muhammad and the Imam Abu Yusuf, both (jurists) from the school of Abu Hanifa, gave as their opinion that a House must be categorized according to the laws by which it is ruled. If (a House) is ruled by the laws of Islam, then it is the House of Islam. If (a House) is ruled by the laws of Unbelief, it is the House of Unbelief. (This opinion can be found in a book entitled) Bada'i al-Sina'i, vol. 1....

The Ruler Who Rules by Other (Laws) Than (the Laws) Which God Sent Down

The Laws by which the Muslims are ruled today are the laws of Unbelief, they are actually codes of law that were made by infidels who then subjected the Muslims to these (codes) although God—Praised and Exalted He is—says in Sura 5 (of the Qur'an): "Whosoever does not rule (*yahkum*) by what God sent down, those are the Unbelievers (*kafirun*)." (This quotation is taken from Qur'an 5.44.) After the disappearance of the Caliphate definitely in the year 1924, and (after) the removal of the laws of Islam in their entirety, and (after) their substitution by laws that were imposed by infidels, the situation (of the Muslims) became identical to the situation of the Mongols, as the Qur'an commentary of Ibn Kathir corroborates (in its comment) on Qur'an 5.50: "Do they then desire the (mode) of judgment of the un-Islamic World (*Jahiliyya*)? But who is better than God (Himself) in judgment, to a people who are convinced?"

(In his comment on this verse) Ibn Kathir says: "God disapproves of whoever (firstly) rebels against God's laws, (laws) that are clear and precise (*muhkam*) and that contain everything which is good and that forbid everything that is bad, and (secondly) turns away (from these) laws in order to follow other (mere human) opinions, ideas and conventions, that were made by humans who had no recourse to the Law of God, like the erroneous and mistaken ideas and opinions which the people of the period before the Coming of Islam had created for themselves as laws which they used to live. Similarly, the Mongols rule themselves by royal decrees (*siyasat*) which were derived from their king Genghis Khan who made for them the *Yasiq*. (The Mongol word *yasiq*) is an expression (which designates) a book which contains (legal) rules which he (Genghis Khan) had derived from different systems of (revealed) law (*shari'a*, not only from Christianity and Judaism but also from the Islamic Community and others). It contains many legal rulings which he simply made up himself because he liked them. Yet it became a system of law that is applied and that they (the Mongols) prefer above the Rule by the Book of God and the example (*sunna*) of the Apostle of God—God's Peace be upon Him—Whosoever does so is an infidel (and not a Muslim) and he must be fought (*yajib qitaluhu*) until he returns to the Rule of God and His Apostle, and until he rules by no other law than God's law." (This quotation is taken from the Qur'an commentary by) Ibn Kathir, vol. 2, p. 67.

The Rulers of this age have rebelled against the religion of Islam in multiple ways to such a degree that there is little doubt as to (how to judge) people who follow the ways of these (Rulers). (To their many transgressions of the laws of Islam) one should, moreover, add the question of the (un-Islamic) laws (which they impose on their Muslim subjects)....

The Rulers of the Muslims Today Are in Apostasy from Islam

The Rulers of this age are in apostasy from Islam. They were raised at the tables of imperialism, be it Crusadersism, or Communism, or Zionism. They carry nothing from Islam but their names, even though they pray and fast and claim (*idda'a*) to be Muslim. It is a well-established rule of Islamic Law that the punishment of an apostate will be heavier than the punishment of someone who is by origin an infidel (and has never been a Muslim), and this in many respects. For instance, an apostate has to be killed even if he is unable to (carry arms and) go to war. Someone, however, who is by origin an infidel and who is unable to (carry arms and) go to war (against the Muslims) should not be killed, according to leading Muslim scholars like Abu Hanifa and Malik and Ahmad (ibn Hanbal). Hence, it is the view of the majority (of the jurists) that an apostate has to be killed, and this is in accordance with (the opinions held in) the Schools of Law of Malik, Al-Shafi'i and Ahmad (Ibn Hanbal). (Other examples of this difference are) that an apostate cannot inherit, cannot conclude a legally valid marriage, and to eat from the meat of animals which he slaughtered is forbidden. No such rules exist concerning someone who is by origin an infidel (and has never been a Muslim). When apostasy from a religion is worse than having always been an infidel, then apostasy from the prescripts (of a religion) is (also) worse than having always been an infidel. So, apostasy is worse than rebellion against the prescripts of a religion which comes from someone who has always been out-side (this religion)....

The Enemy Who Is Near and the Enemy Who Is Far

It is said that the battlefield of *jihad* today is the liberation of Jerusalem since it is (part of) the Holy Land. It is true that the liberation of the Holy Land is a religious command, obliga-tory for all Muslims, but the Apostle of God—May God's Peace be upon Him—described the believer as "sagacious and prudent" (*kayyis fatin*), and this means that a Muslim knows what is useful and what is harmful, and gives priority to radical definitive solutions. This is a point that makes the explanation of the following necessary:

First: To fight an enemy who is near is more important than to fight an enemy who is far.

Second: Muslim blood will be shed in order to realize this victory. Now it must be asked whether this victory will benefit the interests of an Islamic State? Or will this victory benefit the interests of Infidel Rule? It will mean the strengthening of a State which rebels against the Laws of God ... These Rulers will take advantage of the nationalist ideas of these Mus-lims in order to realize their un-Islamic aims, even though at the surface (these aims) look Islamic. Fighting has to be done (only) under the Banner of Islam and under Islamic Leader-ship. About this there is no difference of opinion.

Third: The basis of the existence of Imperialism in the Lands of Islam are (precisely) these Rulers. To begin by putting an end to imperialism is not a laudatory and not a useful act. It is only a waste of time. We must concentrate on our own Islamic situation: we have to establish the Rule of God's Religion in our own country first, and to make the Word of God supreme.... There is no doubt that the first battlefield for *jihad* is the extermination of these infidel leaders and to replace them by a complete Islamic Order. From here we should start.

The Answer to Those Who Say That in Islam Jihad Is Defensive Only

Concerning this question it is proper that we should refute those who say that jihad in Islam is defensive, and that Islam was not spread by the sword. This is a false view, which is (nevertheless) repeated by a great number of those who are prominent in the field of mission-ary activities. The right answer comes from the Apostle of God—God's Peace be upon Him—when he saw asked: "What is jihad for God's cause?" He then said: "Whosoever fights in order to make the Word of God supreme is someone who (really) fights for God's cause." To fight is, in Islam, to make supreme the Word of God in this world, whether it be by attacking or by defending....

Islam spread by the sword, and under the very eyes of these Leaders of Unbelief who con-ceal it from mankind. After the (removal of these leaders) nobody had an aversion to Islam....

It is obligatory for the Muslims to raise their swords under the very eyes of the Leaders who hide the Truth and spread falsehoods. If (the Muslims) do not do this, the Truth will not reach the hearts of Men....

SOURCE: Johannes J. G. Jansen, *The Neglected Duty: The Creed of Sadat's Assassins and Islamic Resurgence in the Middle East* (London: Macmillan Publishers, 1986), 160–61, 165–69, 192–93.

CONTEXT AND ANALYSIS

Sayyid Qutb's legacy was most pronounced in Egypt where his ideas were modified to accommodate the outlooks of several extremist organizations that emerged during the presidency of Anwar Sadat (1970–1981). Many, though not all, of the leading members of these organizations had been Muslim Brothers caught up in the police sweeps of 1954 and 1965. As was the case with Qutb, their incarcerations had given them opportunities to review the career of the Islamist movement in Egypt and to put forward solutions for its future success. In their view, the Brotherhood's strategy of gradualism and advocacy had failed. After their release in the 1970s, many of these Islamists joined with others of like mind in plotting an end to the Egyptian regime. Qutb's notions, with which they were familiar, functioned as catalysts for the conceptualization of their ideas. Yet they tended to interpret concepts such as *jihad* and *jahiliyya* in ways that suited their purposes.

The militants were egged on by the apparent failures of the Sadat presidency. Although Egypt's army had managed to cross into Israeli-occupied Sinai during the 1973 October War, Egypt did not score a victory, and the shame of 1967 still hung in the air. Moreover, the country's economy continued to stagnate. The government was widely seen as corrupt and many Egyptians, though certainly not all, resented Sadat's peace treaty with Israel. The secular nature of Egypt's laws was a particular grievance for the Islamist militants.

The Jihad Group, widely known as Egyptian Islamic Jihad, emerged in the late 1970s in a number of scattered cells. Its members hailed from both Upper and Lower Egypt and many had records of Islamic activism. The group's loose organizational form precluded tight operational control. However two individuals arose to dominate its policies and thinking, 'Abd al-Salam Faraj, a graduate from Cairo University with a degree in engineering, and the Azhari shaykh, 'Umar 'Abd al-Rahman, who was later charged for complicity in the 1993 World Trade Center bombing. Both Faraj and 'Abd al-Rahman upheld the necessity of struggle against the forces of "Western-inspired evil," which Qutb had helped popularize. But differently from Qutb, they pronounced only that the ruler, not society as a whole, was in a state of disbelief. Faraj justified jihad against the Egyptian state by drawing on a juridical decree by the fourteenth-century Damascene scholar Ibn Taymiyya. Ibn Taymiyya had argued that, although the Mongol rulers of the medieval Middle East were nominally Muslim, the fact that they continued to apply pagan Mongol law qualified them as disbelievers who ought to be resisted. In the document above, Faraj condemns Sadat (although not by name) as a ruler who similarly usurped God's prerogative, even while claiming to be a Muslim, and urged Muslims to revive the obligation of jihad, which hitherto Muslims had neglected. In his treatise Faraj argued that apostate leaders (such as Sadat) were the "Near enemy" who must be confronted prior to engagement with "far enemies," such as Israel.

The Jihad Group assassinated Sadat on October 6, 1981. The killing of Sadat was meant to spark a popular uprising against the regime. But it never occurred and many within the jihad's membership consequently suffered imprisonment and execution. Offshoots of the organization survived and continued their clandestine struggle against the central authority, which was by then represented by the government of Husni Mubarak. Alongside the revived jihad emerged the Islamic Group (Jama'a al-Islamiyya), comprising largely Upper Egyptians who resented the political and economic dominance of Cairo and the delta in addition to the Egyptian regime's secularism and purported corruption. To a larger extent than the Jihad Group and other Egyptian radical organizations, the Islamic Group ingratiated itself among the local population, opening its doors widely to recruits. Throughout the 1980s and the first half of the 1990s, Jihad, the Islamic Group, and other smaller organizations such as the short-lived Salvation from Hell attacked the Egyptian government incessantly, ratcheting up the level of violence against it.

The violence and self-righteousness of Egypt's extremist organizations earned them the censure of religious scholars, including even those, such as the Azhari scholar Yusuf al-Qaradawi, sympathetic to the mainstream Islamist movement. According to these scholars, the extremists posed a challenge not only to the state, but more ominously, to the very fabric of Islamic civilization. In the scholars' view, their anathematizing of large numbers of Muslims was a sure recipe for *fitna* ("discord") within the community of believers. Muslims, they said, ought to heed the example of the pious ancestors and postpone judgment on other Muslims. To do otherwise was to follow the nefarious example of the Kharijites who during Islam's formative period seceded from the larger community of Muslims after declaring the caliph of the period to be an infidel for his alleged disregard of Qur'anic principles.

"Islam Needs a Country That Protects Its Creed"

- **Document:** Selection from 'Abud al-Zumur's "Strategy of the Islamic Jihad Group," Translated by Mohammed Zakaria and John Calvert.
- **Date:** 1986.
- **Where:** Tura Prison, Cairo.
- **Significance:** 'Abbud al-Zumur outlines the strategy and ideology of the Jihad Group in the mid-1980s on the eve of a ten-year radical Islamist offensive against the state.

DOCUMENT

Anyone who observes the Islamic nation today as it groans from its wounds and stumbles through illusions, drunk on the false nectar of western civilization, will ask the God of earth and heaven to cure the disease that captured Muslim leaders, the disease that resulted in their separation from religion and dismissal of God's Book. The fall of the Islamic Caliphate was a terrible blow to Muslims, as was the loss of the Islamic holy places and the occupation of Palestine and Afghanistan, and the persecution of Muslim minorities everywhere. All of this and the Muslim leaders still keep themselves from God's Shari'a and fight His followers. Do not take lessons from al-Sadat. As God said: "Have they not traveled through the earth, and see what happened in the end of those before them (who did evil)? Allah brought total destruction on them, and similar (fate waits) the disbelievers." Truth be said, they did not learn the lesson and they did not understand the import of that experience. The current rulers of Egypt were pulled from the stage after the crowd stepped on their faces, yet they have not understood the moral lesson. And God tells the truth as He says: "But it is only the men of understanding that pay heed."

The Current State of the World

After the Islamic Caliphate fell in 1924 at the hands of conspirators, Satan expanded his strength in the world by motivating ignorant people to set their laws in contradiction to what God teaches.... We can show at a glance that all these regimes that govern today's world are western, Marxist, or Zionist. All are far from God and His teachings. The colonists cut the nation of Islam to small countries. It is not surprising that these nations came to be governed by rulers who abandoned God's book and chose democracy, calling for secularism, nationalism, parliamentary life, personal freedom and liberalism. The result was the destruction of the economy, a turning away from ethics, a loss of freedom and hope, with no goal served. Then the rulers turned to socialism and called for unity, development, and the liberation of Palestine. None of these goals came to fruition. We failed in our attempts to unify. Freedom was slaughtered and the opposition was persecuted.... This was the result of our rulers' attempts to rule the nation of Islam by means of democracy and socialism.

We cannot understand what these rulers are trying to accomplish in these ignorant attempts to govern. Islam divides rulers to three categories:

1. Those who govern justly and with God's Book; it is necessary for us to obey such rulers.
2. Those who govern by God's Book but are unjust to their people. Most scholars agree that we should obey such rulers.
3. Those who are disbelievers or who do not govern by God's Book. Scholars agree that people should fight against such rulers and remove them.

The only way for this nation to return to the glory of the Islamic Caliphate is to abandon these rulers and have the people join the Islamic movement, offering to it their money, children, and lives.

Islamic Groups

Within the context of colonialism, cultural decline, and the loss of the caliphate, it has been necessary that groups of enthusiastic Muslims rise up in an attempt to stop the invasion and the accompanying moral decline. And so the fight between right and wrong has started again. In fact, the Islamic movement has taken significant steps in reaching its target. There are however obstacles that prevent it from achieving its goal. One of these relates to the scientific superiority enjoyed by the enemies of Islam. This superiority has scattered the thoughts of the people and deflected them from the correct path. Another obstacle is the absence of solidarity among Muslims to the extent that no one advises or helps anyone else. We hope that people will agree with our movement so that we can progress beyond the point where we are today.

The Alternative

We talked in a previous chapter about the world we live in and how corrupt it is despite attempts made to gloss over the reality. It is like a dying person who is taken to the intensive care unit and is saturated with drugs in an effort to rescue him, although there is no real hope for a cure.

It is clear even for simple people that the ruling regime in Egypt abandoned Islam for liberalism and then for socialism and that these ideologies diminished life and religion. Many modern intellects have recognized that Islam is the correct path that balances both the individual and the society and rights and duties. Having completed their research, they recognize what has been known to us for a long time. So it is clear that Islam is a reasonable and legitimate alternative. It is the path to paradise for a sick and tired world.

Islam needs a country that protects its creed and provides a secure environment for its rituals and raises new generations on a sound basis.... It does not make sense that there should be a separation between an individual's belief and the social system in which he lives. Without a state Muslims will be without vital protection and the instruction necessary to keep them on the straight path.

On such a basis, we refuse the deformed application of Islamic Shari'a, which is present in Sudan and elsewhere. Egypt's government applies only few Islamic regulations in order to prevent the regime from being terminated by the Islamic movement. This attempt will not meet with any success because we do not accept applying portions of Islamic Shari'a. God says: "Is it only part of the book that you believe in? And do you reject the rest? But what is the reward for those among you who behave like this except disgrace in this life? And on the Day of Judgment they shall receive the most painful penalty." We want an Islamic state. But we will not respond to those who ask us for Islamic solutions to complicated cases and issues that crop up in our daily lives, for example, the economic crisis or the crisis in the public transportation system. By not responding to such issues, people imagine that we do not have answers. What they do not understand is that it is the biggest waste of time and resources for the Islamic movement to come up with partial solutions when its real goal is to remove the regime by its roots. In addition, the Islamic method (*manhaj*) is a comprehensive system whose efficiency will only truly be manifested when Islam is adopted in all its many aspects. It should not come as a surprise that the solution to our economic crisis lies not in applying a five year plan to increase the number of loans from foreign countries, or in postponing the payment of interest on loans already contracted. Rather, the solution rests in canceling the entire system of borrowing money with attached interest rates.

The alternative we seek is unique, for it is from God. There is nothing to which it can be compared. It has solid foundations that do not allow for alteration. Yet its inherent flexibility makes it applicable to all circumstances, including those of the modern era.

The Path

In the preceding chapters we presented the basis of our movement, and after detailing our view of the painful reality in which we live presented an alternative program of action. It is incumbent on us to illustrate the path that we should walk in order to reach our noble goal. To this end, our methods must be both appropriate and noble.

Our way is dangerous, but there is no doubt of the gains that accrue to those who choose to follow it. As a movement dealing comprehensively with Islam, we will not limit our methods to only one of the acceptable paths. We are called "the Jihad Group" but that does not mean that jihad is our only activity. Our methods in advising people and guiding them to God are diverse.

Style

Our revolutionary style distinguishes our movement from others and leads it to achieve its noble purpose of Islamic revolution at the expense of the current non-Islamic regime. It aims to make comprehensive changes in all areas of life by putting into practice the Islamic alternative. Our revolutionary style rejects all solutions that aim to apply Islamic boundaries gradually or partially. God said: "Is it only a part of the Book that you believe in? And do you reject the rest? But what is the reward for those among you who behave like this except disgrace in this life? And on the Day of Judgment they shall receive the most painful penalty. And Allah is aware of what you do."

We also refuse to participate in the current governance in the country because it is not legitimate for us to do so. Were we to join an existing political party or by forming an Islamic party call for the application of Shari'a, our message would be swept away by the ignorant majority in the parliament.

Methods

Our methods are based on two important processes that cannot be separated but work in parallel. The movement should grow and build its institutions as it moves towards its goal.

1. Growing and building: this process includes education, to be accomplished by means of the Islamic Jihad Group's schools or by individual training. Here we acknowledge the need for basic knowledge in different fields and the importance of setting strict academic rules and applying modern educational methods. This education is divided to two parts:

   (a) Religious education, in which each member learns his religious duties and the correct understanding of the creed and how to perform worship. The student is provided with the requisite knowledge to protect him from taking the wrong side and to understand Islam in the right—*Salafi*—way.

   (b) Practical education, in which each member is educated to understand the minimum he needs to know of life-related sciences that are acceptable and useful to the Islamic movement.

2. Edification, which involves the spiritual and physical preparation for each individual:

   (a) Spiritual Elevation, which will aid in connecting each member with God through fasting, night prayers, etc. This training will stimulate the member of the group to do his best for God.

   (b) Physical Enhancement, which will tap into each member's physical energy, not for the purpose of exhausting him but to use it constructively. Islam guides men to use their strength in military training and in the strengthening of their bodies, and guides women to channel their energy in carrying out house work, which can be regarded as physical exercise.

   (c) Preparation, which includes measures taken by the group's leadership and its executive branches to prepare all of the members for their tasks and missions, including preparing the appropriate members of the group to carry out military missions within the context of strict security measures; and preparing suitable members to undertake higher education so that they will be ready to manage and govern after the movement takes over the government of the land.

3. Motion, which is the summation of the work accomplished by the movement to reach its goals. This includes preaching, ordering people to command the good and to forbid the wrong, and fighting for the cause of God (*al-jihad*):

   (a) Preaching: It is necessary that that we undertake preaching ourselves on account of the fact that Islam is misrepresented by many Muslims.

   (b) Ordering people to command the good and forbid the wrong, which is ordering people to obey God's orders. Our group sees this as a mission that should be done by all of its members, each according to his ability.

   (c) *Al-jihad*, which is sacrificing one's soul and money to propagate God's word. It is one of the obligations incumbent on believers and it is one of the reasons why God distinguished Muslims from other nations. It is not true that jihad is allowed only to defend Islam; it also has an offensive purpose that allows following disbelievers to their countries. Fighting a disbelieving ruler is a legitimate form of jihad. But prior to commencing hostilities, you should ask your opponent to choose one of three options: accept Islam, pay a yearly fee, or war. It is also allowed to go undercover among the disbelievers and to manipulate them without breaking any agreements signed with them.

We—the Group of Islamic Jihad—believe that jihad will continue until the Day of Judgment, and that it is every one's responsibility until a group decides to take it on. Fighting disbelieving rulers, removing them and setting up a Muslim leader in their place is an obligation imposed by [Shari'a], and all scholars agree on that. Everyone who has the ability to do so must participate by offering himself and his money.

SOURCE: 'Abbud al-Zumur, "The Strategy of the Islamic Jihad Group," in Rifa'at Sayyid Ahmad, ed., *The Militant Prophet: The Rejectionists*, vol.1 [in Arabic] (London: Riad al-Ra'is, 1991), 110–26.

CONTEXT AND ANALYSIS

One of the principal theorists of the Jihad Organization was 'Abbud al-Zumur, an air force colonel whose family hailed from the village of Nahia on the western outskirts of Cairo. Against his colleagues, Khalid al-Islambuli and Karam Zuhdi who were pushing for Sadat's murder, which they hoped would spark a general uprising, al-Zumur argued that the Egyptian Jihad Organization was not yet sufficiently prepared to undertake such an action. He argued that it would take at least two years before the group could move directly from assassination to the revolution that they planned would give birth to the Islamic state. But when the assassination occurred on October 6, 1981, al-Zumur had no choice but to support the coup.

In an effort to take advantage of the chaotic situation that followed the assassination, al-Zumur and two Jihad Organization colleagues, Ayman al-Zawahiri and Esam al-Qamari, made hasty plans to attack government officials gathered at Sadat's funeral. However, the conspirators did not have the opportunity to act. The very next day the police took 'Abbud al-Zumur into custody; al-Zawahiri and al-Qamari were arrested shortly afterward. By that time, too, al-Islambuli and those involved directly in the killing of Sadat were in the custody of the police. The court sentenced al-Islambuli and his accomplices to death. 'Abd al-Salam Faraj, author of *The Neglected Duty*, was also slated for execution. 'Abbud al-Zumur was condemned to life imprisonment. The court deemed al-Zawahiri's and Shaykh 'Umar 'Abd al-Rahman's involvement in the assassination to have been incidental; they were given light sentences. After his release in 1983, Ayman al-Zawahiri traveled to Afghanistan where he befriended a young Saudi named Usama bin Laden.

The prison guards dished out to al-Zumur and his colleagues the same sort of ill treatment experienced by previous Islamist prisoners, such as Sayyid Qutb and Zainab al-Ghazali. Like Sayyid Qutb, al-Zumur channeled his energies into the writing of treatises, although he was not nearly as prolific as Qutb. In the document above he eschews the type of gradualism espoused by the Muslim Brotherhood and presses for the immediate and unqualified establishment in Egypt of an Islamic state. Islam, he says, is a comprehensive system (*manhaj*) that cannot be implemented in stages. It must be imposed in whole at the expense of the pagan order, which must be torn out by its roots.

In the years that followed Sadat's assassination, the Jihad Organization was able to regroup under the leadership of Ayman al-Zawahiri, and by 1987 it was ready to restart the jihad. But by that time a new militant organization had emerged, the Islamic Group (al-Jama'a al-Islamiyya), which believed that militant jihad should be accompanied by a campaign of preaching that should reach into society. In contrast, the Jihad Organization focused solely on violent revolution from above. Responding to the perceived weakness of the Husni Mubarak government, and emboldened by the example of the Islamist fighters in Afghanistan, the two organizations launched gun and bomb attacks against the state and its supporters, which included violence against Egypt's Coptic population and the assassination of public critics of Islamism, such as the intellectual Faraq Fuda in 1992. Clashes between the militants and the police were amplified by local traditions of blood vengeance. As Gilles Kepel notes, the activity of the radicals "was an Islamist version of the putsch scenario that Arab nationalist army officers had used all over the Middle East during preceding decades" (*Jihad*, 282).

However, by 1997 it had become clear to many Islamists that the insurgency was a spent force. Two things happened. First, the state responded with force, wearing the radicals down with massive searches, arrests, and force. For example, in 1992 when militants declared that they had taken over the Cairo district of Imbaba and were running it along Islamist lines, government forces moved in and cleared the area of Islamist elements. Second, the terrorism of the radicals ended up alienating the general population. Especially horrifying to the Egyptian people was the November 1997 massacre of over sixty tourists at Luxor. Popular television preachers, such as Shaykh Mitwali al-Sharawi denounced the savagery of the militants. Combined, these two factors prompted the Islamic Group in 1996 to call for ceasefires and even to denounce violence. Certain members of the Jihad Organization, including 'Abbud al-Zumur, followed suit, although the overall position of the Organization regarding the issue of violence is less clear. Certainly, those leaders of the Jihad Organization who resided outside of Egypt, such as Ayman al-Zawahiri, remained committed to the overthrow of the Egyptian government, although the focus of their attention shifted in the late 1990s to attacks on the "far enemy," namely, the United States.

FURTHER READINGS

Ayubi, Nazih. *Political Islam: Religion and Politics in the Arab World* (London: Routledge, 1991).

Fandy, Mamoun. "Egypt's Islamic Group: Regional Revenge?" *Middle East Journal,* 48 (1994), 607–63.

Goldberg, Ellis. "Smashing Idols and the State: The Protestant Ethic and Egyptian Sunni Radicalism," in Juan Cole (ed.), *Comparing Muslim Societies: Knowledge and the State in a World Civilization* (Ann Arbor: University of Michigan Press, 1992).

Ibrahim, Saad Eddine. "Anatomy of Egypt's Militant Groups: Methodological Note and Preliminary Findings," *International Journal of Middle East Studies,* 12 (1980), 432–53.

Jansen, Johannes J. G. *The Neglected Duty: The Creed of Sadat's Assassins and Islamic Resurgence in the Middle East* (London: Macmillan, 1986).

Kenny, Jeffery Thomas. *Muslim Rebels: Kharijite Rhetoric and the Politics of Extremism in Modern Egypt* (Oxford: Oxford University Press, 2006).

Kepel, Gilles. *Jihad: On the Trail of Political Islam,* translated by Anthony E. Roberts (Cambridge, MA: Harvard University Press, 2002).

Kepel, Gilles. *Muslim Extremism in Egypt: The Prophet and Pharaoh* (Berkeley: University of California Press, 1989).

Ramadan, Abd al-Aziz. "Fundamentalist Influence in Egypt," in M. Martin and S. Appleby (eds.), *Fundamentalisms and the State* (Chicago: University of Chicago Press, 1993), 152–83.

Al-Zayyat, Montasser. *The Road to Al-Qaeda: The Story of Bin Laden's Right-Hand Man,* edited by Sara Nimis and translated by Ahmed Fekry (London: Pluto Press, 2004).

Zeidan, David. "Radical Islam in Egypt: A Comparison of Two Groups," in Barry Rubin (ed.), *Revolutionaries and Reformers: Contemporary Islamist Movements in the Middle East* (Albany, NY: SUNY Press, 2003), 11–22.

"The Junta Is Pursuing the Path of Evil"

- *Document:* English translation of document issued by The Islamic Salvation Front National Provisional Executive Bureau.
- *Date:* November 14, 1993.
- *Where:* Algiers, Algeria.
- *Significance:* The document illustrates the radicalization of sectors within Algeria's Islamic Salvation Front following the generals' cancellation of national elections and suppression of the organization.

DOCUMENT

Allah has stated: "Do not incline toward those who do evil, for hellfire will seize you." And He also said: "This is an announcement to people, so that they be warned by it." "What the illegitimate ruling junta has done in the past, and is still engaged in pursuing, is an open war against Allah and his messenger (may peace be upon him). The junta is pursuing the path of evil, and the forbidding of the good, the destruction of the houses of Allah (mosques), the detention of the free, the scholars and the callers to the good. Its aggression on human dignity, the punishment of thousands of families, the betrayal of the people's and the martyr's covenant, the torture and killings and judicial kidnapping through the use of the courts of shame (special courts)—All are clear evidence of the junta's ideology with regard to its declared war on Islam and the people. It has been especially manifested in the recent period during which the junta and its stooges have opted for a new strategy in their war against the Muslim People of Algeria. This strategy has been manifested through the roundup of dozens of citizens from the safety of their homes and families, just to be killed and thrown in the streets later on. This type of operation has repeated itself in several places in the country. It is in addition to the dozens of victims killed elsewhere in the mountains and in the countryside. The barbaric killings do remind us of the atrocities perpetrated by the Organization of the Secret Army. These atrocities are being carried out at a time in which the junta is calling for dialogue to gain time, reinforce its gains, and attempt to abort the struggle, and shake the unity of the (opponents') ranks.

1. The Islamic Salvation Front (FIS) announces to the Muslim People of Algeria and to the entire world that it rejects any dialogue or reconciliation which the putchist junta calls for. The betraying junta has no observance for agreements or covenants. We shall not accept any alternative to the Islamic State or any other choice except a radical change, in both men, and project of society, according to the exalted Islamic Shari'a.

2. The Algerian people and the Islamic Salvation Front are alert and following very closely the acts of the junta and especially its attempts to mortgage the sovereignty of the country and the future of generations to come in order to satisfy its greed for authority. Exploiting the (economic) difficulties of the population, the junta is engaging in deal-making with some former colonial powers which are seeking privileges to suck the resources of the country, and seize the opportunity to attack the ideological, historical and social makeup of the people. For this the Algerian people and the Islamic Salvation Front will not honor any deal or agreement made with the ruling junta in the absence of the people's true representatives as of the date of January 11, 1992. In addition, we inform the world public that credits and economic aid accorded to the junta are being used specifically to cover the expenses of the repression apparatus and the misinformation campaign currently underway. Therefore the partners of the current regime, whose sole interest is to remain in power, are to be considered as colonizers and partners in the crime against the Algerian people. They have to assume their responsibilities regarding the consequences which would rise against their nationals and interests.

3. The government of a foreign state, which raises the banner of human rights, champions the respect of the will of peoples, just to contradict these tenants by the roundup and detention of dozens of Algerians, and the support (both material and moral) accorded to the fascist junta which is ruling by guns and fire and which has crushed the ballot box with the might of the armored tank. This foreign government is the true killer of its citizens (residing in Algeria), and is a direct danger to its own interests. "Allah truly loves those who fight in His Cause in battle array as if they were a solid cemented structure...." "On that day, shall the believers rejoice with the victory from Allah." For the National Provisional Executive Bureau; in Charge of the Commission on Information SIGNED: Abdelrezak Rajdam. Isf93.txt

SOURCE: Communique no. 42, "The Islamic Salvation Front National Provisional Executive Bureau, "Algiers, November 14, 1993. Translated by C. R. Pennell. Available at: http://historicaltextarchive.com/sections.php?op=viewarticle&artid=19. Reprinted with permission.

CONTEXT AND ANALYSIS

Following the army's coup on January 11, 1992, Algeria's Islamic Salvation Front (FIS) fell apart. The state authorities imprisoned its two leaders, Abbas Madani and the more radical Ali Belhaj, and closed FIS-affiliated mosques and interrogated individuals deemed suspicious, often picking them up off the street. Many FIS affiliates were taken to prison camps in the Sahara Desert.

The above document was written by Abdel Razik Rajjam, the director of communications for the FIS, before he went underground. The document clearly communicates Rajjam's anger over the generals' intervention into politics and subsequent "war against Islam." However, Rajjam and his associates in FIS did not yet translate their bitterness into action, with the result that many Algerians, especially the young *hittistes*—the unemployed "wall leaners" whose interests revolved around Rai music and football—began to gravitate to groups willing effectively to resist the state authorities.

The disaffected elements of society found an outlet for their humiliation and anger in the radical Islamist groups that had either formed or consolidated in the wake of the military takeover, organizations such as the MIA (Armed Islamic Movement) and GIA (Armed Islamic Group). The GIA operated as an amalgam of armed units dispersed throughout the country. At odds with FIS's procedural approach to politics, the amirs of the radical groups took their cues from the jihadist tradition represented by the Egyptian Sayyid Qutb and his disciples, or else from the Salafi outlook imported to Algeria by Arab fighters returning from the anti-Soviet jihad in Afghanistan. The Salafis prioritized imposing "correct Islamic behavior" on the population. Oftentimes, this was done forcefully. "For much of the GIA, this preoccupation tended to take precedence over fighting the state" (International Crisis Group, "Violence and Reform in Algeria"). As many of FIS's more economically well-to-do supporters scurried to avoid the mounting conflict, often abandoning businesses and expensive homes, the more disaffected elements of the society girded themselves for what would amount to "total war" against the government. As in other comparable conflicts in which terrorism and assassination are the norm, the ensuing violence had the effect of polarizing allegiances and choices.

From 1992 until 1997 the militant groups, chiefly the GIA, engaged the state and its representatives in a conflict of exceptional savagery. Initially the armed groups targeted policemen, army troops, regime officials, and secular activists. Then, beginning in March 1993, they extended their attacks to intellectuals, journalists, professionals, and foreigners whose world view was at odds with their own.

IN HISTORY

Armed Islamic Group (GIA): Declaration of Apostasy on Algerian Society, September 8, 1995

This is the dominating Group, the believing faction, and the victorious sect—with the permission of Allah, all of this will come about—and just as it calls all the unjust rulers infidels, it also calls all their families, their followers, and any who render them aid or owe them allegiance infidels. For this reason you will find it following those who owe the apostates allegiance in the cities, the villages, and the deserts in order to extirpate them completely, and to annihilate their green gardens, to loot their possessions, and to take their women captive in order to make them taste their own evil. The explosions in their homes and their protected cities are because of the unjust rulers; also the repeated slaughters and the blood that flows in every place that has robbed them of their sleep. Let not even one of them close his eyes without expecting his head to be cut off from his body, for his possession to be looted and his women taken captive. This is Allah's bounty; He gives it to whomever He wishes.

SOURCE: David Cook, *Understanding Jihad* (Berkeley: University of California Press, 2005), 170.

It was at this stage, in May 1994, that Abdel Razik Rajjam and other prominent former FIS members, including the influential leader Muhammad Sa'id, met with Sharif Gousmi, amir of the GIA, and pledged their allegiance to him. Evidently Rajjam and Muhammad Sa'id had come to the conclusion that confrontational jihad, not simply rhetoric, was necessary if the Islamists were to gain their Islamic state. They agreed with Gousmi to "abide by the Book [Qur'an], the Sunna [Traditions] of the Prophet," not to negotiate with the "apostate" regime, and to pursue jihad until victory. The integration of prominent FIS leaders like Rajjam into the GIA provided the organization with an extra dose of legitimacy against its jihadist competitors. At the same time, with other FIS leaders in prison, the inclusion of these leaders ended any prospect for a negotiated settlement between FIS and the Algerian government.

Other active members of FIS countered the ascendancy of the ultra-extreme GIA by forming the Islamic Salvation Army (French acronym, AIS), which functioned as the armed surrogate for the FIS. The aim of the Army was to provide militant Algerians with a more "principled" option than that offered by the GIA. In contrast to the indiscriminate killing of the GIA, the AIS targeted only those who directly aided the regime against the Islamists. When Rajjam and Sa'id began to show interest in the new organization and question the excessive bloodletting of the GIA, Djamel Zitouni, Gousmi's successor as GIA amir, had them and hundreds of other "deviants" killed.

The GIA's jihad reached a crescendo under Antar Zouabri, Zitouni's successor who condemned anyone who did not directly assist the GIA. Zouabri claimed that ordinary Algerians were tacitly supporting the regime and thus were a danger to Islam. The GIA argued that such behavior qualified them as apostates and thus deserving of death in accordance with the Shari'a. Sayyid Qutb's argument regarding the impiety of the times was thus extended to justify a reign of terror over Algeria's civilian population. Oftentimes, GIA factions massacred entire villages. As was the case with the militant groups in Egypt, the violence perpetrated by the GIA cut it off from society. Deprived of a social base and plagued increasingly by infighting, by 1998 the GIA disappeared from the scene. On the other hand, the AIS, sensing the futility of struggle against a stronger enemy, signed a truce with the government in 1997. The truce paved the way for a series of elections followed by a referendum of "national concord," which effectively ended Algeria's agony. Once again, a government had vanquished a radical Islamist foe.

FURTHER READINGS

Burgat, Francois. *The Islamic Movement in North Africa,* trans. William Dowell. Middle East Monograph Series (Austin: Center for Middle Eastern Studies, University of Texas Press, 1997).

International Crisis Group. "Violence and Reform in Algeria," *Middle East Report,* 29 (July 30, 2004).

Hafez, Mohammed M. "Armed Islamist Movements and Political Violence in Algeria," *Middle East Journal,* 4 (Fall 2000), 572–91.

Malley, Robert. *The Call from Algeria: Third Worldism, Revolution, and the Turn to Islam* (Berkeley: University of California Press, 1996).

Martinez, Luis. *The Algerian Civil War, 1990–1998* (New York: Columbia University Press, 2000).

Roberts, Hugh. *Embattled Algeria, 1988–2002: Studies in a Broken Polity* (London: Verso, 2003).

Stone, Martin. *The Agony of Algeria* (New York: Columbia University Press, 1999).

Willis, Michael. *The Islamist Challenge in Algeria: A Political History* (New York: New York University Press, 1999).

7

ISLAMISM IN SAUDI ARABIA

Gen. H. Norman Schwarzkopf accompanies Saudi Arabian King Fahd as he reviews U.S. troops at an air base in eastern Saudi Arabia, January 7, 1991. This marked the first visit of the king to troops in the field following Iraq's invasion of Kuwait. Many Saudi Arabians blamed the House of Saud for allowing foreign troops to be stationed on Saudi soil. The Gulf War marks the effective beginning of Islamist dissidence in Saudi Arabia. (AP photo/Bob Daugherty. Courtesy of AP Images.)

INTRODUCTION

Islamist dissent in the Kingdom of Saudi Arabia surfaced during the Gulf War of 1990–1991 when large numbers of American troops were stationed in the country, ostensibly to protect the country against the ambitions of Saddam Husayn. To be sure, rebellious groups and dissident individuals acting in the name of Islam existed prior to this event, but they were "rejectionists," rather than Islamists, in so far as they did not address broad social, cultural, or political issues or present a comprehensive program for change. The Bedouin-oriented Ikhwan revolt of the 1920s and 1930s, and the seizure of the Grand Mosque in Mecca in 1979 by Juhayman al-Utaybi and his rebels, fall into this category.

The Gulf War threw ordinary Saudis into contact with hundreds of thousands of American and European soldiers and highlighted the kingdom's dependence on non-Muslim military assistance, despite the billions spent by the Saudi monarch on advanced military equipment. For many Saudis, the presence of "infidel" troops in the land of the two holy mosques (Mecca and Medina) was an affront to Islam. In their view, Saudi Arabia's problems were the consequence of the House of Saud's turning away from Islam, which in Saudi Arabia takes the form of Wahhabism (see sidebar). Not only, they said, did the ruling establishment encourage Western values at the expense of Islamic principles, its princes and officials were morally bankrupt. The royals allowed the United States to determine the shape of the country's foreign policy, and supported the American-led Palestinian-Israeli peace process, which the critics regarded as a sellout of Palestinian rights. Much of the anger was focused on the Sudairi branch of the Al Saud, headed by the king, which, in addition to occupying many of the kingdom's most powerful positions, opponents regarded as the most corrupt and un-Islamic of the royal family.

Nearly all of these critics of the regime formed what came to be called the "Sahwa al-Islamiyya" (Islamic Awakening), the religious revivalist movement that gripped Saudi universities and other elite institutions from the late 1960s onward. The *Sahwa* gave rise to a generation of Saudi Islamists that, broadly speaking, combined the official, conservative Wahhabi outlook on social and cultural issues, with Muslim Brotherhood-style political activism.

The concerns of the *Sahwa* Islamists were initially embodied in two documents that were addressed to the king, the "Letter of Demands" (1991) and the "Memorandum of Advice" (1992). These called for reform, rather than radical change, and were sent through Shaykh 'Abd al-Aziz Bin Baz, the kingdom's Grand Mufti, in the hopes of bringing him and the other state *ulama* aboard. The documents had over a hundred signatures and included the names of shaykhs Safar al-Hawali, Salman al-'Awda, Muhammad al-Mas'ari, Sa'd al-Faqih, and Usama bin Laden, among others. Four of these individuals are represented here by documents.

IN HISTORY

"Those Who Affirm the Unity of God"

The theological foundations of the Wahhabi movement were set by a religious scholar from Nejd, the central region of Arabia, Muhammad Ibn 'Abd al-Wahhab (1703–1792). The son of a *qadi* (religious judge) 'Abd al-Wahhab received his education in Mecca, Medina, and Basra. He followed the Hanbali School of Islamic law and was influenced by the thirteenth-century theologian Ibn Taymiyya. As a serious student of the Qur'an and other Islamic sciences, 'Abd al-Wahhab was appalled by the superstitions and religious practices of the town dwellers and tribesmen of Arabia. In his view, such practices were accretions that had crept into Islam over the centuries. He was particularly aggrieved at the people's practice of seeking the intercession of dead holy men at shrines erected over their graves. For the same reason he condemned the devotion of Shi'i Muslims to their Imams. 'Abd al-Wahhab's strict fundamentalism was at odds with the spirit of doctrinal tolerance that had generally prevailed in Islamic lands throughout history. However, in the view of his followers, his teaching represented nothing less than the revival of authentic Islam after centuries of decadence. The members of the nascent movement did not call themselves "Wahhabis,"… for to do so would have glorified 'Abd al-Wahhab at God's expense. Rather, they called themselves *al-Muwahhidun*, "those who affirm the unity of God."

'Abd al-Wahhab's preaching attracted the support of a local chieftain from Nejd, Muhammad Ibn Saud. With the conversion of Ibn Saud to the Wahhabi cause, Wahhabism became the religious ideology of tribal unification and subsequently the basis of the Saudi state. Today, the official *'ulama*, including the Grand Mufti, draw their pay from government departments where they are employed. In return for government patronage, the *'ulama* ratify and provide legitimacy to the regime's policies.

However, although these figures expressed similar, if not entirely overlapping views, they subsequently went their separate ways with little apparent interest in joining forces organizationally or even working together toward a common program. This is true especially of bin Laden who stood apart form the others because of his internationalist, as opposed to strictly Saudi Arabian, interests and concerns. Alone among these activists, bin Laden turned to terrorism, although significantly he has never targeted the Saudi royal family. Since the late 1990s, most of the representatives of the *Sahwa* have been forced into exile or persuaded by the ruling house to soften their critique of the regime.

"We Are Calling for a Sweeping Reform in Our People's Affairs"

- **Document:** Sermon by Salman al-'Awda, entitled "From Behind the Bars."
- **Date:** 1994.
- **Where:** Saudi Arabia.
- **Significance:** Salman al-'Awda is a *Sahwa* preacher who came to prominence during the Gulf War of 1990–1991. His messages to the Saudi royal family articulate a widespread desire for the reform of the country's religiopolitical establishment.

DOCUMENT

All praises are due to Allah. We praise Him, and seek His Assistance, and ask for His forgiveness. We seek refuge in Allah from the evil in our souls and from our sinful deeds. Whoever Allah guides, no one can deceive. And whoever Allah misguides, no one can guide. I bear witness that there is no one worthy of worship except Allah (SWT). And I bear witness that Mohammed is His servant and messenger.

This letter is titled "From Behind the Bars." It is intended to those who are yearning to know about Muslim activists performing Islamic *Da'wa*.

My beloved, as many of us have heard, the campaign of arrests and detention of leading Muslim intellectuals, shaykhs and doctors has intensified with the arrest of Dr. Shaykh Safar al-Hawali. Furthermore, there is a possibility that I will be joining this select group of Muslims very soon.

Only Allah knows what is in the hearts of His creation, but believe me when I say that I do not mind joining my brothers in prison. This is because whenever a young citizen of this land is detained for his beliefs while I roam the land freely, a feeling of overwhelming shame descends over my soul and makes me wish I were in his place.

And of course all of you know that sometime ago, some oppressive and illegal measures were introduced in this land to prevent the Muslims from making *Da'wa* [i.e., engaging in missionary activity]. The authorities used these measures to dismiss me and my colleagues from our jobs. They prevented us from giving lessons, lecturing, giving Friday sermons and even recording religious talks. There is no doubt in my mind that preventing people from giving *Da'wa* is very dangerous and hence we should not keep silent unless our rights are restored....

To all those honest and loyal Muslims who advocate reform openly or secretly, we must admit that: corruption has taken its roots in our society as well as in nearly all other Muslim societies with varying degrees.... It has engulfed all aspects of our life, from the spiritual to the mundane. Today, we find a deteriorated standard of morals in everything, from the world of commerce and politics to the ministries of education and information. A situation such as this calls for a sweeping reform.

It could be a grave mistake on our part to think that such a reform can be realized with theories and intentions only. This is a wishful thinking.... Reform will not come about until we are ready to bear hardships for the sake of our beliefs....

The existing decadence has become apparent to everyone, yet there are people in positions of power who defend it since their very survival depends on its very existence. These people in power are set dead against any kind of reform. They work days and nights, secretly and publicly waging war and inciting others against the reform movement.

Thus, there is an everlasting struggle between right and wrong, between reform and corruption, between guidance and deviation, between justice and oppression ... That is why it is an obligation upon every reformer to prove his loyalty and truthfulness to Islam. He/She must make it clear on which side he stands. He must prove that he is ready to give and sacrifice for the sake of what he has been calling for. It is essential for him to go to great pains as a proof to others of his truthfulness.

In general, we have to bear in mind that the masses may enjoy listening to our lectures about piety and righteousness, but we have to set an example for them by physically practicing what we preach. Otherwise, how can we prove that we are loyal? How can we prove that we are not driven by our egos?

All of us know that cheating is forbidden and illegal as stated clearly in the Qur'an and the *Sunna* of our prophet Mohammed p.b.u.h. [Peace be upon him]. For example, the prophet questioned severely the faith of a Muslim merchant who cheated others while selling dates. If this was how our prophet handled a case of a single cheater, so what should we do if our whole nation (*Umma*) is engaged in the art of deception and treachery? Therefore, our silence on these matters is a reflection of our faith. Indeed our deafening silence is a testimony to our weak faith. Believe me, we will not be spared the suffering and punishment unless we declare publicly what is right. God says: (God would not have unjustly destroyed the villages had their people been reformers).

So if we are truly reformers then we can save ourselves from the punishment of God, otherwise his punishment befalls us sooner or later.

Therefore, we are calling for a sweeping reform in our people's affairs. We are calling for our rights to give *Da'wa*. We are asking for freedom of expression to every scholar, caller, journalist, writer, poet, and teacher or worker. We are calling for freedom of expression which allows people to express their beliefs and lets them participate in the reform process for this nation (*Umma*), which is surrounded by dangers from all sides. It is an open secret that our society has become analogous to an island in the middle of a restless sea waiting to devour it.

This reform is needed badly because the existing corruption has many advocates who would like to make this area (the Middle East) an open market for the Israelis, who will, consequently, affect the ideology, culture and commerce in this region, not to mention the military aspect. Hence, it is a plan to make us slaves in our own land at the mercy of our enemies.

Meanwhile, no one is allowed to express his/her opinion. We are simply told to agree to everything without objection or risk facing punishment by the security forces. This strong arm tactic is being used to prevent the reformers from continuing their mission. It is meant to discourage anyone who thinks about making the slightest positive change in our society.

Many of us talk among ourselves about the absence of social justice from our society. The problem lies in our failure to apply the rules of our religion (Shari'a) which was sent with a comprehensive reform message that included the spreading of justice, equality and abolishment of state and societal oppression. The message was sent to address our needs and protect our dignity and rights. Under Islamic law, no one will have a right to insult another fellow being, oppress him in any way, spy on him, arrest him without just reason or invade his privacy.... All of these rights would be protected under the Islamic Shari'a. Therefore, the issue here is not a personal one. It is a universal matter that concerns the whole *Umma*. Hence, it is time the reformers declare their message publicly.

We must declare it publicly, that we are not asking for any materialistic reward for these efforts. If the public sees us one day seeking worldly gains, then they have the right to throw dust in our faces. I tell you here and now, that we are callers to the truth where all are invited. We have also to make sure that this banner stays upright no matter what adversity we may face.

So, where are the intellectual leaders of this nation? Where are the thousands of doctors, professors and university students on whom millions of dollars were spent to further their education. These educated people today are being told to stop thinking! They are being told to follow the status quo and to refrain from harboring any political thoughts whatsoever. This is unacceptable.

It is every human's right to exercise his intellect to improve the community surrounding him.

God has honored human beings by blessing them with the ability to think. So why not take advantage of this blessing. Why do we presume that the masses have no opinions of their own and they might want to express them? Who gave us this right to deny the masses of their natural rights.

The prophet Mohammed p.b.u.h. used to mount the pulpit and talk to the people about various matters. He consulted them about the battles of Badr and Uhud [against pagan Mecca] and about other matters such as the distribution of wealth.

Our religion was not meant to be only confined to corners of a particular mosque. It came to teach us how to structure our economy and how to invest our money. Furthermore, as Muslims, we should exert our best efforts in whatever we do, so naturally our industries, our educational and social systems should be governed by the Islamic principle.

Brothers, I can not comprehend our situation when I compare it with the other nations of the world. Now, of course we know that due to the communication revolution, the whole world is reduced to a small village and nothing can be hidden anymore. The East knows what is happening in the West and vice versa. Today, as the rest of the world is acquiring education, we the Muslims do not seem to want a share in it. Why we are acting in such a manner. We do not seem to be benefiting from these radical and crucial changes that are shaping the world.

Let us take the Soviet Union for example. It had disintegrated because it was a one party system run by the (KGB) that ruled with an iron fist by spreading terror in the population. Now we see that Communism is dead forever.

Nowadays, all countries in the world take pride that their people are pleased to be governed by leaders who respond to their needs and engage openly in discussion with them about all affairs.... These people feel they have a right to know what is going on in their lands.

So I ask you why do we have to stand in the way of this historical change and against all other natural forces? Why do we have to cover up our problems with obscure secrets that are not understood by ordinary citizens?

When I and Dr. Safar al-Hawali were called a year ago to go to the Ministry of Interior, we wrote a letter to Shaykh 'Abd al-'Aziz bin Baz [chief Mufti of Saudi Arabia] telling him what went on over at the Ministry. We told him that we were questioned about some statements we said in the past with regard to the illegality of interests and its dealings, our disapproval of the Jewish-Arab peace process, our disclosure of some existent social injustices, our displeasure of some wrongful practices and measures committed against innocent people by the security forces, our talk about the rights of Muslims for protection and the illegality of terrorizing and hurting them.... These were some of the things that we were accused of committing at that time.

I believe that there is someone out there devising a plan to keep this nation of ours in everlasting silence. And that is why if it happens that someone speaks up against any form of oppression, he will be automatically labeled as a power seeker. However, this accusation is a very old one since Pharaoh said it before to Moses, and Quraysh said it to our prophet Mohammed. Thus, it becomes very easy indeed to accuse a Muslim activist of something he/she did not commit because accusations are packed and ready for distribution.... However, a question is left to be asked to those who utter such claims.... Do you have proof for what you claim? Do you have proof that our mission is other than reforming and correcting the distortion and deviation that have befell this nation?

Are we really one single nation? Do we not know that many hands have been extended to make peace with the Israelis? Do we not know that anybody who does not agree with this deal is to be considered an extremist or fundamentalist who must be fought by all means? Do we not know that hands are being extended to the communists, secularists, and to all other groups? The argument used to justify these gestures is that we should have some dialogue and be in harmony with these groups. Simply, we are told to make peace with these groups. So if this [is] the case, why don't we make a dialogue with ourselves before we move to make it with others? It does not make sense to have a discussion with the far ones whereas our society has failed to discuss its own matters and problems with its own people.

As for imprisoning us, I want to tell you that it is not a concern of mine. If I end up there, at least I will have a chance to be alone, to be with my Lord, to test my patience, my worship, my closeness to God, my truthfulness, my readiness to bear some hardships for the sake of delivering our message of reform.... this is the road....

We are in need for huge numbers of activists, reformers, *mujahidin* for this cause. We need those who are pious and ready to take up their designated positions ...

Our nation needs many of those who take it upon themselves to deliver the right message, review and correct their situations and try their utmost to deliver the message of reform.

Our aim and objective is to spread reform in all fields, including the scientific (theoretical) and practical ones. This is a mission that must be carried out by people from amongst us. It must be carried out by people who are ready to endure some hardships for the sake of their mission. We believe that part of our responsibility is to address the important issues that concern our nation (*Umma*) from the east to the west. We have to stand beside our fellow Muslims when disasters and hardships befall them ... We have to inform other Muslims about their brothers' problems ...

We must work hard to revive the notion of brotherhood among Muslims and try to make the necessary correction to various things in their thoughts and lives. Hence, our objective includes helping Islamic associations with everything we have at our disposal, including spiritual, political, and economical support.

We live now with our fellow Muslims in Bosnia, Somalia, Tajikistan, Egypt, Syria, Palestine ... etc. We live with them moment by moment and hour by hour. We consider this to be part of our responsibility. Therefore, it is a betrayal on our part to neglect our fellow Muslims and leave them as easy targets for their enemies.

If we cannot give them a hand, we should at least shed some light at their situation and expose it to the public. We can say a good word about them which may ease their pains and comfort their feelings. We can make them feel that there are brothers out there who are listening to their cries and are very saddened and hurt because of their suffering....

So the issue we are addressing is not a local one. In fact, it has no boundaries because it is an issue that concerns all Muslims, whether they are in China, India, Kashmir, Bangladesh, Kurdistan, Iraq, Turkey, Algeria, Tunisia, Egypt, Palestine, Europe, America, Russia or any other place on earth. God says:

(The believing men and the believing women are the protectors of each other, they enjoin good and forbid evil, and hold their prayers, pay their Zakat and obey Allah and his prophet; those are the blessed ones).

SOURCE: http://www.geocities.com/saudhouse_p/letter2.htm

CONTEXT AND ANALYSIS

Salman al-'Awda (b. 1955) was born and raised in Saudi Arabia's Qasim Province near the city of Burayda. In common with many young Saudis, al-'Awda was affected by the wave of religious activism that swept Saudi Arabia in the 1970s and 1980s. He gained a reputation in the local mosques as a passionate preacher whose sermons, captured on audio cassette, focused on current events. As a leading figure in the *Sahwa* group of Saudi dissidents, he took issue with what he saw as the creeping secularization of Saudi society, especially in education, the blind conservatism of the Wahhabi clerical establishment, and the ruling house's subservience to the United States. All of these factors, in his view, were liabilities that undermined Saudi Arabia's integrity as an Islamic state. His concerns were amplified when the Saudi ruling house granted the United States permission to station its troops in the Kingdom to protect it from a possible attack from Saddam Husyan's Iraq. Al-'Awda was especially unhappy that U.S. troops remained in Saudi Arabia following Saddam Husayn's ouster from Kuwait. Salman al-'Awda shared the view of many in the Kingdom that Saudi Arabia, "the land of the Prophet," was a special place that should be free of non-Muslims, especially foreign troops but also Western expatriates. In his view, Saudi Arabians had a special mission to ensure the continuity of Wahhabi Islam in the Arabian Peninsula. "In al-'Awda's imagination, Saudi Arabia and its two holy mosques represent the center of the universe. [Each] event that takes place in Saudi Arabia has cosmic significance" (Fandy *Saudi Arabia and the Politics of Dissent*, 100). Al-'Awda was a signatory to the "Letter of Demands" (1991) and "Memorandum of Advice" (1992), which the *Sahwa* dissidents presented to King Fahd.

Salman al-'Awda is a religiously conservative man who is critical of the moral laxity he sees in society, for example, of the efforts of liberalizing Saudi women to gain more latitude in their daily lives. According to al-'Awda, women's role in society is mandated from God and cannot be compromised in the name of spurious "freedom." He is critical of the judicial system, which he says is too closely tied to the power of the ruling house. As a result, he says, legal judgments are skewed in favor of the princes. And he believes the ruling house is mismanaging the country's economy, refusing to engage seriously in a program of restructuring and privatization.

However, his biggest complaint, one highlighted in the above document, is the lack of consensual government and freedom of expression in the Kingdom. According to al-'Awda, "Shura," (consultation) has been an integral part of Islam since the time of the Prophet Muhammad. Looking at the historical record, he makes the point that Muslim states prospered as long as the rulers consulted with representatives of the society. Al-'Awda is not arguing for democracy, which, in his view, compromises God's sovereignty, but he does believe that decisions pertaining to the state and society should not be the monopoly of a dynastic clique. Although al-'Awda has little good to say about Western civilization, he does applaud Western countries for the political and press freedoms they extend to their citizens.

In 1994 Saudi authorities cracked down on the *Sahwa* dissidents. As the document indicates, Safar al-Hawali was first to be arrested, followed shortly after by al-'Awda, whose arrest sparked a small riot in his hometown of Burayda. The crushing of the so-called "Burayda Intifadha," and similar crackdowns by Saudi security forces, created deep divisions between the regime and Islamists that resulted in turning some eventually to terrorism. In 1999 the Saudi ruling house released al-'Awda and al-Hawali, in return for which they tacitly agreed to soften their criticism of the Saudi regime. Al-'Awda has gone so far as to rhetorically attack exiled Saudi opposition figures in London and broker deals between the House of Saud and its jihadi enemies.

The Betrayal of Palestine

- **Document:** "An Open Letter to Shaykh 'Abd al-'Aziz Bin Baz Refuting His Fatwa Concerning the Reconciliation with the Jews," Communication no. 11, Advice and Reform Committee, by Usama bin Laden.
- **Date:** December 29, 1994.
- **Where:** Khartoum, Sudan.
- **Significance:** In the wake of the 9/11 attacks, it is often forgotten that Usama bin Laden emerged from within the movement of reform in Saudi Arabia. In this document he chastises Grand Mufti bin Baz for endorsing the 1993 Oslo Accords between Israel and the Palestinians.

DOCUMENT

"The best *jihad* against a despotic sultan is the word of truth."

You are well aware what a great status the scholars, the men of knowledge, have been given by God. It is no wonder that He has given them this distinguished standing, since theirs is the legacy of the Prophets, from whom they have inherited this religion. They protect it from the corruption of fanatics, from the false ascriptions of liars, from the interpretations of the ignorant, and from the dilutions of profligate oppressors. They represent the model exemplars of our *umma* in promoting the victory of truth, despite all its burdens and preferring it to a worldly life.

The virtuous scholars who were the forefathers of our *umma*, and their successors, undertook these missions admirably. Sa'id bin Jubayr's stance in the face of al-Hajjaj's tyranny, when he stood up for the truth, Imam Ahmad bin Hanbal's challenge to the power of the sultan and his presence in the struggle over the nature of the Qu'ran, and ibn Taymiyya's heroic endurance of prison for the victory of the traditions of the Prophets—all these are examples of people who embraced their duty so that truth would be victorious and out of zeal for their religion. May God bless them all.

Honorable Sheikh, by mentioning all this we wanted to remind you of your duty to your religion and to our *umma*, and to bring your attention back to your enormous responsibility. For recalling this will be of benefit to the believers. We wanted to remind you at this time, an age in which falsehood has spread, in which corrupt and wayward people have caused controversy, and in which the truth has been buried, preachers have been imprisoned and reformists silenced. What is even more curious is that this has not only happened in your knowledge and with your silence, but as a result of your juridical decrees and opinions. We would remind you, honorable sheikh, of some of these juridical decrees and opinions to which you may not be giving your full attention, even though our *umma* might fall into seventy years of error because of these decrees. We do this in order that you might appreciate along with us even a fraction of the serious consequences that follow from them. Here are some examples:

1. No one can be unaware of the tremendous spread of corruption, which has penetrated all aspects of life. It can no longer be a secret to anyone that various evils have spread, as detailed in the advisory memo submitted by a select group of scholars and reformists. Among the most serious things the scholars highlighted in this memo was the setting up of rival authority to God. This can be seen in the enactment of man-made laws that deem illegal acts to be permissible, the worst of which is the practice of usury, which is now widespread in the country thanks to the usurious state institutions and banks, whose towers are competing with the minarets of the two Holy Sanctuaries. The length and breadth of the country is positively teeming with them. It is surely well known that the usurious regimes and laws with which these banks and institutions are working are legitimate in the eyes of the ruling regimes and officially certified by it. We have heard from you only to the effect that practicing usury is absolutely prohibited, although this position ignores the fact that your words deceive people because you do not distinguish in your judgment between those who merely practice usury and those who legitimize it and make it legal. In fact, the distinction between these two issues is very clear: he who makes usury legal, in doing so he becomes an apostate and an infidel who has placed himself outside the religious community, because he has considered himself an equal and a partner to God in deciding what is permissible and what is not. (This is something we have detailed in an independent study, which will be published soon, God willing.)

   Although he who practices usury to the utmost degree has declared war on God and on His Prophet, yet still we hear you expressing praise and commendation for this regime, which is not satisfied merely with its addiction to usury, but has also legalized and justified it. The Prophet has said, as related by al-Hakim: "There are 73 easier ways to offend God than usury, such as to marry your own mother."

   And Ibn 'Abbas said, as related by Ibn Jarir: "Committing usury is a serious offence, so the leader of the Muslims should call the offender to repent, and punish him if he fails to do so." This is just for those who practice usury, so what about those who legalize it?

   The political and economic crises that the country is suffering, and the crimes of all varieties that have spread through it like wildfire, are a punishment from God. They are part of the war that God Almighty has declared on those who have not ceased to practice usury and similar evils, and of the eradication of usury that He has ordained: "God blights usury, but blessed charitable deeds with multiple increase."

2. When the king hung the cross around his neck and showed it to the world, happy and smiling, you excused his deed and justified this terrible act, despite the fact that it clearly constitutes unbelief and that it shows pleasure and preference for the perpetrator of the deed, rather than for knowledge.

3. When the forces of the aggressive Crusader-Jewish alliance decided during the Gulf War—in connivance with the regime—to occupy the country in the name of liberating Kuwait, you justified this with an arbitrary juridical decree excusing this terrible act, which insulted the pride of our *umma* and sullied its honor, as well as polluting its holy places. You considered this to be a way of seeking help from the infidels in your time of need, neglecting the curbs and restrictions such a call for help necessarily imposed.

4. When the ruling Saudi regime undertook to help and support the leaders of apostasy, the Communist Socialists in Yemen, against the Muslim Yemen people in the last war there, you kept a committed silence. But when the tide turned against the Communists you issued—no doubt under pressure from this regime—advice calling on everyone to agree to peace and reconciliation on the basis that they are all Muslims! It is ludicrous to suggest that Communists are Muslims whose blood should be spared. Since when were they Muslims? Wasn't it you who previously issued a juridical decree calling them apostates and making it a duty to fight them in Afghanistan, or is there a difference between Yemeni Communists and Afghan Communists? Have doctrinal concepts and the meaning of God's unity become so confused? The regime is still sheltering some of these leaders of unbelief in a number of cities in the country and yet we have heard no disapproval from you. The Prophet said, as related by Muslim [hadith scholar]: "God cursed him who accommodates an innovator."

5. When the regime decided to attack Sheikhs Salman al-'Awda and Safar al-Hawali, who had stood up for the truth and suffered much harm, you issued a juridical decree condoning everything suffered by the two sheikhs, as well as justifying the attacks and punishments suffered by the preachers, sheikhs, and you of our *umma* who were with them. May God break their fetters and relieve them of the oppressors' injustice.

These are only some—by no means all—examples. It has become necessary to mention them in light of your latest astonishing juridical decree justifying peace with the Jews, which is a disaster for Muslims. This was clearly a response to the political wishes of the regime, which decided to reveal what it previously had in mind and enter into this farce of capitulation to the Jews. You issued a juridical decree wholly endorsing this peace, which was praised and lauded by the prime minister of the Zionist enemy and his parliament, after which the Saudi regime announced its intent for more normalization with the Jews.

And it seemed as if you were not satisfied with abandoning Saudi Arabia, home of the two Holy Sanctuaries, to the Crusader-Jewish forces of occupation, until you had brought another disaster upon Jerusalem, and the third of the Sanctuaries, by conferring legitimacy on the contracts of surrender to the Jews that were signed by the traitorous and cowardly Arab tyrants. These contracts constitute a serious and dangerous calamity containing deceit and deception from a number of different perspectives. We raise the following points:

1. The current Jewish enemy is not an enemy settled in his own original country fighting in its defense until he gains a peace agreement, but an attacking enemy and a corrupter of religion and the world, for whom the words of the Sheikh of Islam Ibn Taymiyya apply: "There is no greater duty after faith than unconditionally fighting the attacking enemy who corrupts religion and the world. He must be resisted as hard as possible, as stipulated by our companions the scholars and others."

   The legal duty regarding Palestine and our brothers there—these poor men, women, and children who have nowhere to go—is to wage *jihad* for the sake of God, and to motivate our *umma* to *jihad* so that Palestine may be completely liberated and returned to Islamic sovereignty. Palestine could do without this kind of juridical decree, which abandons the *jihad* and lets things be, which accepts the enemy's occupation of the holiest of the Muslims' holy places after the two Holy Sanctuaries, and which confers legitimacy on this occupation. The kind of decree that fully supports the enemy's attempts to face down the zealous Islamic efforts to liberate Palestine by means of *jihad*, which the operations of the heroes and the youth of Muslim *jihad* in Palestine have shown to be the only useful way to confront the enemy and guarantee the country's liberation, God willing.

   We might remind you at this point of your previous juridical decree on this issue. When you were asked how to liberate Palestine, you said that it was impossible to reach a solution unless this was considered an Islamic issue, and unless we stand shoulder to shoulder in solidarity with Muslims in order to save them, and unless we wage an Islamic *jihad* against the Jews until the land is returned to its people and these deviant Jews return to their country.

2. Given that this false place with the Jewish enemy, to which defeatist Arab tyrannies and regimes are committing themselves, comes full of conditions, can it really be allowed to happen? Everyone knows that is not the case. For this alleged peace that the rulers and tyrants are falling over themselves to make with the Jews is nothing but a massive betrayal, epitomized by their signing of the documents of capitulation and surrender of the Holy City of Jerusalem and all of Palestine to the Jews, and their acknowledgment of Jewish sovereignty over Palestine for ever.

3. These apostate rulers who are fighting against God and His Messenger have no legitimacy or authority over Muslims, and they are not acting in the interests of our *umma*. But through these juridical decrees of yours you are giving legitimacy to these secular regimes and acknowledging their authority over Muslims, in contradiction of the fact that you have previously pronounced them to be infidels. This has been made clear to you by a select group of scholars and preachers in their appeal to you to refrain from issuing such juridical decrees. We enclose a copy of this appeal to remind you and bring it to your attention once again.

This juridical decree of yours was deceitful, as it contained shamefully misleading generalizations. It is not even valid as a juridical decree on the authority of a just peace, let alone this fake peace with the Jews, which is a huge betrayal of Islam and Muslims. No normal Muslim would accept it, let alone a scholar like you who is obliged to show zeal for our religious community and our *umma*.

Anyone who undertakes to issue a juridical decree concerning the serious issues of our *umma* has a duty to be knowledgeable about all its dimensions, and the dangers and detrimental effects that might ensue from it. Such knowledge is one of the indispensable conditions of becoming a jurist. The Imam Ibn al-Qayyim says: "Neither the jurist nor the ruler can issue a juridical decree and rule in truth without two kinds of knowledge: first, material, tangible knowledge and true understanding of the surrounding context, and secondly, the duty of understanding God's judgment that he has laid down in his book and on the tongue of His Messenger. He then has to apply the one to the other."

If these are the general conditions necessary for any juridical decree to be issued, then they are certainly necessary for any juridical decree pertaining to *jihad* and making peace and the like. The Imam Ibn Taymiyya says: "When it comes to *jihad*, we must take into consideration the correct opinion of religious scholars who have experienced what is confronting the worldly men, except for those who focus solely on the ritual aspects of religion; their opinion should not be taken, nor should the opinion of religious scholars who have no experience in the world."

The falsehood in previous juridical decrees, even if not issued by you, were knowingly uttered by their authors and had dangerous consequences, but when they come from you, it is certain that the fault in them should not be ascribed to a lack of legal knowledge on your part, but rather to a lack of understanding of the truth of reality. The necessary conditions of such juridical decrees cannot be fulfilled, so they are therefore unfit to be issued in the first place. This makes it necessary for the issuer to stop issuing juridical decrees, and to leave it to the specialists who can bring together knowledge of legal judgments and knowledge of reality. For example, when the Imam Malik ibn Anas was asked about different readings he deferred to the Imam Nafi, may God bless them both.

Honourable Sheikh, our considerable concern at the state of our *umma* and of scholars such as you is what motivated us to remind you of all this. For we esteem you and those like you too highly to think that the ruling regime would exploit you in such a terrible way and throw you in the face of every preacher and reformist, or that every word of truth and call to honesty would fall silent at your juridical decrees and opinions, as happened with your response to the Memorandum of Advice and the Committee for the Defense of Legal Rights, and others.

Honorable Sheikh, you have reached a good age, and you have achieved much in the service of Islam, so fear God and distance yourself from these tyrants and oppressors who have declared war on God and His Messenger, and stand with the righteous men. The forefathers of our *umma* and their successors have set a good example, and one of the most prominent characteristics of these righteous scholars was the way they disassociated themselves from the sultans. The Imam Abu Hanifa and others, with their great integrity in matters of religion, avoided working with the rulers of their age, even though those sultans cannot be compared to the rulers of today, whose degeneracy and corruption of religion is no secret. And in our time, when Sheikh 'Abdallah bin Hamid has realized the danger of the course that the ruling Saudi regime is taking, and the damaging consequences for those who participate or are implicated in it and desert their religion, he resigned from the Supreme Council of Judges. The Imam al-Khattabi warned of getting involved with these rulers: "I wish I knew who is getting involved with them today but does not believe their lies and who is speaking justly when he sees their councils, and who is advising them and who is taking advice from them."

And the Prophetic saying is true: "Whoever enters the sultan's door has been led astray." So beware, honorable sheikh, of relying on these men, whether in word or in deed, "and do not rely on those who have been oppressive or else the fire will befall you—for what other protectors do you have than God?—and you will not be victorious."

He who is unable to proclaim the truth can at least refuse to proclaim what is not true. The Prophet said, as related by al-Bukhari: "He who believes in God, let him say something good on the Last Day or be silent."

And finally, we pray that you do not take these words out of turn or consider them to overstep the limits of etiquette. We could not be silent or fail to speak out, for the matter is too serious to justify turning a blind eye.

What we have mentioned is known by the men of knowledge, and a select group of the *umma*'s scholars and preachers has previously brought it to your attention, presenting to you several appeals in this regard. They included the one made a while back asking you to refrain from the juridical decree justifying this alleged peace with the Jews, which is no more than capitulation. They showed that this juridical decree did not meet the necessary conditions of legality and they warned of the many dangers—both religious and worldly—that would follow from it. The signatories of this appeal included the honorable Sheikhs ibn Jarbin, Abdallah al-Qa'ud, Hammud al-Tuwijri, Hammud al-Shu'aybi, al-Barrak, al-'Awda, al-Khudairi, al-Tariri, al-Dabyan, 'Abdalla al-Tuwijri, Abdallah al-Jalali, A'id al-Qarni, and many others.

In conclusion, we ask God Almighty to respond to our striving for truth and provide for us, his followers. We ask Him to show the liar his lies, and help us avoid them, and to establish an order of guidance from our *umma* in which those who obey Him will be proud and those who disobey him will be humbled, and in which good is enjoined and evil rejected, and in which justice is done and the truth is spoken, in which the banner of *jihad* is raised up high to restore to our *umma* its pride and honor, and in which the banner of God's unity is raised once again over every stolen Islamic land, from Palestine to al-Andalus and other Islamic lands that were lost because of the betrayals of rulers and feebleness of Muslims. We ask Him to direct our affairs for the best and to take away our sins. We ask Him to help us to say and to do the right things, and for success in what He loves and what pleases Him in life, and for the best outcome when we die. He is our protector and enabler. Our final prayer is praise be to God, Lord of the worlds.

SOURCE: Bruce Lawrence, ed. "The Betrayal of Palestine," translated by James Howarth in *Messages to the World: The Statements of Osama Bin Laden* (New York and London: Verso, 2005), 3–14.

CONTEXT AND ANALYSIS

Usama bin Muhammad bin Awad bin Laden was born in Riyadh in 1957, the seventeenth of fifty-two children fathered by Muhammad Bin Laden, Saudi Arabia's wealthiest construction magnate. Shortly after graduating in 1979 from King 'Abd al-'Aziz University in Jedda with a degree in civil engineering, bin Laden left Saudi Arabia to join the Afghan resistance (*mujahidin*) against the Soviet invasion. From Pakistan's border region, he raised funds for the *jihad* and provided in-coming volunteers from around the Muslim world with logistical support. It was during this period, the mid-1980s, that bin Laden came under the influence of the Palestinian *jihadi* 'Abdallah 'Azzam. In 1988 bin Laden established a formal network of the jihadis who had passed through his training camps, which was given the name "Al Qaeda"—"the Base." This was the foundation of the organization that would soon lead the global *jihad*.

After the Soviets pulled out of Afghanistan in 1989, bin Laden returned to Saudi Arabia a hero. When it became clear to him that Saddam Husayn was going to launch an invasion of Kuwait and possibly other Arab Gulf countries, bin Laden offered King Fahd the services of the *jihadi* network that had come together in Afghanistan. When the king refused and instead invited the troops of the U.S.-led coalition to protect Saudi Arabia from possible Iraqi aggression, bin Laden joined Safar al-Hawali, Salman al-'Awda and others in vehemently opposing the "occupation of the land of the two Holy Mosques." Feeling pressured by the Saudi regime, bin Laden fled Saudi Arabia, first to Pakistan and Afghanistan and then to Khartoum, Sudan. By 1992 Sudan had become a magnet for Islamists from around the world. Hundreds of experienced and would-be jihadis came to Sudan where Hasan al-Turabi, ideologue of Sudan's Islamist government, sought to create his own international Islamist front.

Bin Laden was one of Turabi's Islamist "stars." Under Turabi's and Sudan President Bashir's protection, he set up legitimate businesses, including a tannery, two large farms, and a major road construction company. In 1994, bin Laden, working from Khartoum, set up a media information office in London called the Advice and Reform Committee, which was designed to publicize his statements and provide a cover for Al Qaeda's activities. It was about this time that Saudi Arabia stripped bin Laden of his citizeship, ostensbily for supporting Islamist radicals in Saudi Arabia, Sudan, and elsewhere. According to bin Laden, the committee was formed in response to the imprinment of the *Sahwa* shaykhs, al-Hawali and al-'Awda. Although the committee's concerns were increasingly international, its chief focus was Saudi politics. Bin Laden addresses his letter (reproduced above)

IN HISTORY

Juhayman al-Utaybi

For Saudi Arabia, 1979 was the year during which the Grand Mosque in Mecca was seized by a group of religious rebels commanded by Juhayman al-Utaybi, seeking to overthrow the Saudi dynasty. The takeover was a landmark event in the history of the young kingdom. The group's spiritual leader, Muhammad Ibn 'Abdullah al-Qahtani, called himself the Mahdi (the "guided one")—the messianic figure whose appearance, many Muslims believe, will usher in the Last Days. Most of Juhayman's and al-Qahtani's followers came from tribes that had spearheaded the Ikhwan revolts against 'Abd al-'Aziz Ibn Saud fifty years earlier, although support for the movement also came from students, the urban lower classes, and from foreign laborers. On November 20, the last day of the pilgrimage and the first year of Hijri year 1400, the rebels, numbering between four and five hundred, struck. They used the mosque's public address system to broadcast their demands. Blending the old Ikhwan "zeal for *jihad* with a strand of millenarianism altogether foreign to Wahhabism," they called for a return to the society of the first centuries of Islam, which the royal family, they said, had corrupted. They demanded the elimination of Western influences in the kingdom, including such things as photography, and the severing of economic and political ties with Western nations. In addition, the rebels blamed the *ulama* for failing to condemn policies that betrayed Islam.

The House of Saud understood that it had to take decisive action against Juhayman and al-Qahtani. Its legitimacy hinged on its ability to protect the holy places. On November 24 King Khalid received from Grand Mufti Ibn Baz a *fatwa* authorizing the use of force against the insurgents. The *fatwa* was necessary because in normal circumstances the spilling of blood was not allowed on the holy ground of the Meccan sanctuary. For two weeks the Saudi armed forces, aided by French commandos, battled the rebels. In the course of the fighting al-Qahtani, the "Mahdi," was killed. Juhayman and the surviving rebels surrendered. Afterwards Juhayman and sixty-two others were publicly beheaded in accordance with Shari'a law.

to 'Abd al-'Aziz bin Baz, Grand Mufti of Saudi Arabia between 1993–1999. Bin Laden respectfully reprimands the Mufti for issuing the *fatwa* allowing the entry of U.S. and coalition troops into the kingdom. But the focus of his message is bin Baz's endorsement of the Oslo Accords between Israel and the Palestinian Authority, which were finalized on August 20, 1993. Bin Laden and the Advice and Reform Committee accuse bin Baz of providing Islamic sanction to a process that, in their view, was clearly illegitimate. He advises bin Baz to do what is right and distance himself from the "tyrants and oppressors who have declared war on God and His Messenger."

In 1995, bin Laden was linked to a car bomb explosion in Riyadh and to an assassination attempt in Ethiopia against Egyptian President Husni Mubarak. Consequently, the Saudis and the United States put pressure on al-Turabi and Bashir to expel bin Laden and his followers. Early in 1996 bin Laden started making contacts with his colleagues in Afghanistan to prepare for his reception. In summer 1996 he and his followers slipped out of Sudan for Jalalabad, Afghanistan.

A Saudi Oppositionist's View

- **Document:** A telephone interview conducted by Mahan Abedin with the head of the London-based Saudi opposition group, Committee for the Defense of Legitimate Rights (CDLR), Dr. Muhammad al-Mas'ari. (Note: TM=Terrorism Monitor and MM=Dr. Muhammad al-Mas'ari.)
- **Date:** November 26, 2003.
- **Where:** London.
- **Significance:** Muhammad al-Mas'ari was a founding member of the *Sahwa* organization, the Committee for the Defense of Legitimate Rights. His subsequent emphasis on transnational issues illustrates the easy confluence in many Islamist discourses between local and global concerns.

DOCUMENT

TM: What kind of Islamic ideology does the Committee for the Defense of Legitimate Rights promote? Do you consider yourself a Wahhabi organization?

MM: The word Wahhabi has become a misnomer. The U.S., for example, uses it to denote Jihadists. They called the Taliban Wahhabists, but this was not true. Wahhabism has several essential ingredients, and we don't consider ourselves to be Wahhabi. We do, however, share the Jihadi spirit.

TM: Then in what way does your version of Islam differ from the official religious establishment in Saudi Arabia?

MM: The official clergy are basically a government party. They are well organized. Their view is that the regime has flaws but these can be corrected from the "inside." They basically believe that the regime is Islamic and thus legitimate.

TM: How about the dissident clerics. Do your views differ from theirs?

MM: The radical forces can roughly be divided into two branches: First, there are the Jihadists, who say the regime is *Kufr* (i.e., belonging to the realm of the disbelievers), therefore it has to be fought and destroyed.

Secondly, there are people [who] say indeed the regime is *Kufr*, but this does not mean that everybody who serves the regime is a disbeliever. They say the regime has to be overthrown but not necessarily through violent means alone. This is the view of the CDLR.

TM: I take that to mean you believe violence is needed to engineer the collapse of the regime.

MM: We believe that any way to remove the regime is legitimate. However, we are more inclined to move the masses toward some kind of revolt or popular uprising, perhaps along the lines of the French and Iranian revolutions. We also do not rule out winning over powerful factions in the military and subsequently convince them to move against the regime. This will minimize bloodshed. But I should add that the legal and moral issues are exceedingly complex!

TM: There are of course dissident forces both inside and outside the country who do not want the regime to go in its entirety.

MM: There is an in-between group. They are mostly from a Salafi background, [who] have been influenced by the "Muslim Brotherhood." Most of them take inspiration from Muhammad Surur and hence they are called the Sururi Group. They are reluctant to move against the regime. They believe it has many faults, but they hesitate before calling for its overthrow. They possibly have the best intentions, but they lack any coherent program or efficient methodology. I do not believe that they will ever be a real threat to the regime.

TM: There are of course those who say the Saudi royal family has become so embedded as an institution that it now represents Saudi national consciousness. Therefore, getting rid of it would cause an enormous amount of harm to the country. How do you respond to these people?

MM: It is mostly an issue of symbolism. And of course, symbolism is important in understanding the behavior of the wider masses towards the political realities. But never forget that the al-Sauds were once a small and irrelevant tribe. By aligning themselves with the Wahhabi movement they evolved, over two and a half centuries, into the powerful establishment we see today. The legitimacy of the regime has always rested on its claim to be Islamic. That has been undermined, so everything else is coming under question. And most people are aware of this. The whole structure of the regime is now in peril. What you call Saudi national consciousness never existed although the regime tried to create something in that direction in the last thirty years, albeit to no avail.

TM: Are the people really that critical of the regime?

MM: There was a recent poll in Kuwait, which is regarded as much more secular and pro-Western than Saudi Arabia, in which 74.5 percent of respondents said that they sympathized with bin Laden and consider him to be a hero. If a similar poll was conducted in Saudi Arabia, I am sure that over 85 percent would register approval with bin Laden.

TM: What tactics does CDLR use to engineer the collapse of the regime? Do you follow the so-called Horizontal Trend Movement of MIRA [Movement of Islamic Reform in Arabia]?

MM: Yes we are very strong horizontally. But we have also developed strong theoretical and scholarly capabilities. We admire Hizb al-Tahrir because they have developed a constitution of the Islamic state. They have worked out all the characteristics of the Islamic state, from women's rights to elections. Clearly their constitution contains certain scholarly and theological biases, but the important point is that nobody else has done this before. Of course we disagree with many aspects and details of Hizb-al-Tahrir's constitution, but at least they have put something on the table. So we are very strong theoretically. We do have some vertical capabilities, but our activist network and organization is not properly structured. We are hoping to improve this in the future through the formal establishment of a properly organized and well-structured political party.

TM: How do your views differ from those of Osama bin Laden?

MM: Osama bin Laden is a military leader. He was appointed by the Afghans as Amir of the Arab *Mujahdin*. Because he has been engaged in fighting for decades, OBL and his followers have not had time to study recent developments and innovations in Islamic politics and philosophy. They have no detailed theory of the Islamic state in whose cause they are fighting. They believe in the Islamic state in a very general sense, and they have no real program. This is the essential difference between OBL and CDLR. Moreover, bin Laden's obsessive concentration on the U.S. is not really wise. Bin Laden forgot or neglected for tactical reasons that the U.S. did not invade Saudi Arabia. It was invited in by the Saudi royal family. The regime invited the U.S. and it has to pay the price.

TM: There are some people in the U.S. who claim that bin Laden receives support from certain quarters in the Saudi regime.

MM: There are two types of people in the regime who support bin Laden:

1. Some are sincerely fed up with the corruption and lack of respect for Islam.
2. The others hope to use the Jihadis for their "power game" inside the royal family. Turki Al-Faisal, the ex-intelligence chief and current Saudi ambassador in London, is one of the prime suspects.

TM: There have been suggestions that CDLR, and in particular Dr. Muhammad Mas'ari, are increasingly promoting a pan-Islamic agenda and are no longer exclusively focused on Saudi Arabia. How do you respond to these charges?

MM: Any Islamic movement worth its salt has to become international. When the Saudis passed the Saudi citizenship law in 1932, the regime ceased to be an Islamic order. An Islamic state has to be internationalist and inclusive. Islamic tenets demand nothing less. But really we at CDLR remain focused on Saudi Arabia. We may publish an article against Musharaf or any other leader from time to time, but on the whole our focus is on Saudi Arabia.

TM: You have mentioned Hizb-al-Tahrir and said you admire them. Is it not the case that Hizb-al-Tahrir is primarily a British Islamic party?

MM: No, this is a misconception. Hizb-al-Tahrir is still a prime party in Jordan, Palestine and even Pakistan. The Pakistanis are so terrified of them that they have recently moved against the party. In fact they are thinking of banning it. The party is also very strong in Uzbekistan. And of course Hizb-al-Tahrir was the mother of most Jihadi groups in Egypt.

....

TM: I want to focus on the wider region now. What do you make of the United States' war on terrorism?

MM: (Chuckles)

TM: Do you believe it is a war against Islam?

MM: Yes, there is no question about that. But they will sooner or later realize that their aggressive policies will fail. They will kill a lot of Muslims in the process because they have advanced technology and they bomb from high up in the air, but they will blink first. Take Iraq for example; everybody is surprised that the resistance has started so quickly. I thought it would take a year or two before the resistance would start in earnest. But it has happened much more quickly than that. And in Afghanistan as well there is now rigorous resistance.

TM: Do you think the U.S. will eventually fail in Iraq?

MM: It will take a few years but they will fail. They will begin to make blunders, like bombing whole cities, the kind of things they are doing in Afghanistan right now. But of course Iraq is much more sophisticated and they will not be able to cover up their crimes there.

TM: Was al Qaeda behind the recent bombings in Turkey?

MM: Al Qaeda has now become a jackass suitable for carrying any load. They are blamed for everything. There may be a hard core group called al Qaeda, but most of these bombings are by local groups.

TM: But don't you think there are connections between these local groups and a wider international network?

MM: The connections are ideological and mostly informal. It is very difficult to forge operational connections. The real point is that Western intelligence can not penetrate these groups. We are talking about two divorced worlds with diametrically opposed cultures. Western intelligence is used to using bars, prostitutes and dancing clubs to entrap people, and of course the Jihadists have nothing to do with these things. Even Saudi intelligence, many of whose officers are devout classic Wahhabists, has a hard time penetrating these groups. I knew someone in Kabul, and he told me that almost everyone in Kabul knew, just before 9/11, that something big was going to happen in America. But of course Western intelligence had no clue. The best way to think of al Qaeda is by using the cluster bomb analogy. A large bomb is aimed at a target but before it hits the target, it divides into hundreds of small and independent bomblets.

TM: And the targets are Western interests and corrupt local governments?

MM: Exactly! Take this bombing in Istanbul. The MOSSAD was hiding in these synagogues and they were bombed.

TM: Are you sure about this?

MM: The Jews have been living in Istanbul for centuries. Why have they become a target now? Also this recent bombing in Kirkuk targeted a center used by MOSSAD operatives. The bombing of this MOSSAD center precipitated Bremer's recent trip to Washington.

TM: That is very interesting! Going back a few years now, after the Khobar bombing in June 1996, you said that you understood on an "intellectual level" the motives and grievances of the bombers. What exactly did you mean by this?

MM: The bombers wanted these *Kufr* forces to leave the country in which they do not belong and from which they were performing acts of war against Iraq, a Muslim country. The bombing was intended to force their withdrawal.

TM: You recently took part in a dialogue (which was later compiled into a book) with Ayatollah Araki, the UK representative of Iran's supreme leader, Ayatollah Khamenei. Do you think the Islamic regime in Iran could serve as a model for the future Arabia?

MM: No, I don't. Also that dialogue was on purely philosophical issues.

TM: What are your views on the Islamic Republic?

MM: That regime has never been able to surpass nationalism and sectarianism. I also find the *Vilayat al-Faqih* doctrine abhorrent. It smells and tastes like the Catholic Church!

TM: But some say the Velayat-e-Faqih doctrine is Sunni in origin.

MM: No, it is not. It is a principle to substitute for the infallible hidden Imam during his "great absence" and now it has just become a tool to ensure the continuation of that regime. The regime in Iran is much better than the others in that region, but ultimately it is, strictly speaking, not an Islamic state. It is an Iranian and sectarian state with some Islamic orientation and plenty of empty Islamic rhetoric very much similar to Saudi Arabia. No wonder that Iran and Saudi Arabia recently have become friends!

SOURCE: Mahan Abedin, "A Saudi Oppostionist's View: An Interview with Dr. Muhammad al-Massari," Terrorism Monitor, The Jamestown Foundation, 1, no. 7 (December 4, 2003). At: http//www.jamestown.org

---

CONTEXT AND ANALYSIS

The Committee for the Defense of Legitimate Rights (CDLR) was founded on May 3 1993 by a group of Saudi professionals with strong Islamist leanings. Two of the leading figures in the new group were Muhammad al Mas'ari and Sa'd al-Faqih, eloquent men well-practiced in the art of crafting arguments. Immediately, they issued a communiqué and circulated a cassette tape explaining to the Saudi public that the CDLR was a human rights group opposed to the "corrupt" and increasingly "un-Islamic" rule of the House of Saud. Then the Council of the Higher 'Ulama denounced the group and the Saudi state cracked down on the *Sahwa* movement. After brief imprisonment, al-Mas'ari and al-Faqih relocated to London where they assumed direct control of the group. In London they joined a variety of other exiled Muslim organizations and individuals. Taking advantage of Great Britain's press freedoms and media infrastructure, they continued to propagate their message of reform in Saudi Arabia. Each week the CDLR faxed its newsletter to hundreds of distribution points in the Kingdom and transmitted the same information through e-mail and its World Wide Web home page, a form of communication that was virtually impossible for the Saudi authorities to control. However, in 2007 their influence in Saudi Arabia is difficult to measure. Regardless, Saudi authorities keep close watch on them.

In 1996 Sa'd al-Faqih split with al-Mas'ari to form another Islamist organization called the Movement for Islamic Reform in Arabia (MIRA). The disagreement between the two Islamist reformers hinged on al-Mas'ari's interest in forging links with other, transnational Islamist organizations at the expense of focusing solely on Saudi issues. These organizations were Hizb al-Tahrir (the Liberation Party), which calls for a universal caliphate, and the Muhajirun, a radical Salafi group based in the United Kingdom. Against CDLR, MIRA presented itself as the legitimate representative of the Islamist reform in Saudi Arabia that began after the Gulf War.

With other *Sahwa* dissidents, al-Mas'ari believes that the House of Saud deviates from the true principles of Islam. Rather than encourage Islam as a force capable of lifting Muslims from their relative backwardness, the ruling house uses Islam and the Wahhabi clerics simply to legitimize its rule. As a result, establishment Islam is drained of value, and the Kingdom slides into morally-generated decline. According to al-Mas'ari, one sign of the ruling house's skewed ethic is Saudi Arabia's membership in the United Nations, an international organization that is premised on the idea of the nation-state, not on the ideal of Islamic universalism (the Caliphate). Another indication is the ruling house's dependence on the United States for protection. Especially in his more recent speeches and writings, al-Mas'ari accuses the ruling establishment of forging secret contacts with Israel and the Jews whom he accuses of conspiracies of every kind.

CDLR withered after the break with al-Faqih. Al-Mas'ari went on to oppose the Saudis under different banners, including the Party of Islamic Renewal. His effectiveness in gaining Saudi followers has been blunted by pan-Islamism and extremism. Also at issue is his family background, which puts him at a disadvantage. In order to be taken seriously as a legitimate Islamist critic of the royal family, one must have a good family pedigree, in addition to solid religious credentials. According to Mamoun Fandy, historian of the *Sahwa* movement, al-Mas'ari's grandmother was an Ethiopian, making his family *khadiri*, unable to marry into tribal families.

IN HISTORY

Hizb al-Tahrir al-Islami

Hizb al-Tahrir al-Islami (The Islamic Liberation Party) was founded in 1952 in Jordan by Shaykh Taqi al-Din al-Nabahani (1909–1977). Shaykh Nabahani was a graduate of al-Azhar University, a schoolteacher, and a religious judge (*qadi*) before being forced to flee Palestine after the 1948 Arab-Israeli War. The Party has a strong *Salafi* orientation, for example, as in its strong opposition to Sufism and Shi'ism. Al-Nabahani's concept of *jahilyya* was less far reaching than that of Sayyid Qutb, casting aspersion upon the leaders of a state but not necessarily its population. The organization is currently most active in Central Asia (Uzbekistan, Kyrgyzstan, and Tajikistan), where it aims to unite Central Asia, Western China, and eventually all Muslims worldwide under a new caliphate modeled after the Rashidun, the exemplary Rightly Guided Caliphs who ruled Islamdom following the death of the Prophet Muhammad. Hizb al-Tahrir has a strong presence in Europe, especially the United Kingdom, where it has attracted attention as a result of alleged anti-Semitic remarks made by some of its members. Operating in secret, the party does not divulge its leaders. Like other Islamist groups in the global age, it propagates its message using modern technologies.

See Suha Taji-Farouki, *A Fundamental Quest: Hizb al-Tahrir and the Search for the Islamic Caliphate* (London: Grey Seal, 1996). See the party's Web site: http://www.hizb-ut-tahrir.org

Al-Mas'ari encourages Western human rights organizations to put pressure on the House of Saud for its abuses, but his own understanding of rights is based on the strict application of Shari'a, which differs from the Universal Declaration on key points. Thus, in his writings he condemns the Universal Declaration of Human Rights for its emphasis on the equality of men and women and freedom of belief and freedom of expression. According to al-Mas'ari's Islamist worldview, the rights of those who disagree with true Islam are necessarily circumscribed by Shari'a.

"The State of Saudi Arabia Is Facing a Dire Crisis"

- **Document:** Interview conducted by Mahan Abedin with Dr. Sa'd al-Faqih, Head of the Movement for Islamic Reform in Arabia (MIRA).
- **Date:** 2003.
- **Where:** London.
- **Significance:** Dr. Sa'd al-Faqih's eloquent rebuttal of the current Saudi system illustrates the far-reaching changes demanded by the *Sahwa* dissidents. The uncompromising nature of his and others' dissent has forced them to flee to the West where they enjoy freedom of expression.

DOCUMENT

You frequently state that Saudi Arabia is facing a dire crisis. What do you mean by this? What are the roots of this crisis?

The regime is facing several major challenges that it is incapable of dealing with. The challenge of violence has already started and is increasing. Once it shifts towards the royals, rather than Westerners, the collapse will be imminent. In addition, there are mounting socioeconomic problems: increasing poverty, unemployment, domestic crime, social disintegration and sky-high national debt. In the background, there is the crumbling of the regime's Islamic legitimacy since the 1991 Gulf War, which has significantly weakened its foundations.

To make matters worse, the regime does not have the proper command system to deal with these crises. There is neither a central, powerful figure in the royal family [to impose his will] or a collective decision-making mechanism, so the regime is not capable of surmounting these challenges. The dispute within the royal family about succession is kept artificially hidden by the living body of the king. Once King Fahd dies, the dispute will flare up.

How did the Gulf War precipitate the breakdown of the regime's religious legitimacy?

Since the time of King 'Abd al-'Aziz Ibn Saud [founder of the Saudi Arabian state], the regime has understood that it cannot, on its own, convince the public that it is a legitimate government—legitimacy had to be conferred by the *'ulama* [clerics]. 'Abd al-'Aziz wanted people to obey him as the representative of God's will. It is well known in Islamic discourse that when the ruler is implementing Islam, he should be obeyed. 'Abd al-'Aziz was not implementing Islam in the proper political sense, but he knew that he could convince the people by securing the loyalty of the *'ulama*. 'Abd al-'Aziz's successors followed the same principle and hence were very tolerant towards the *'ulama*, even though their own behavior and the way they have run the country is un-Islamic.

During the 1990-1991 Gulf crisis, the official *'ulama* sanctioned the entry of 500,000 non-Muslim forces into the kingdom, a decision that led dissident clerics to challenge the regime after the war. Many were arrested or silenced during the nineties. After 9/11, the regime provided the Americans with air bases to attack the Taliban, creating further strains. Shaykh Hamud bin Uqla al-Shu'aybi, a respected independent cleric, challenged the regime and said that its support for America deprived it of Islamic legitimacy. The support provided by the regime to the Americans in the current war on Iraq was the straw that broke the camel's back. Interestingly, the official *'ulama* remained as loyal to the regime as ever, to the degree that they appeared as mere officers implementing instructions. That destroyed their credibility and hence their ability to provide legitimacy to the regime.

What kind of Islamic ideology does MIRA promote? Are you a Wahhabi organization?

I do not like to use this description. I would describe myself as a Muslim. I derive my teachings straight from the Qur'an and Sunna—understanding them through the original interpretations without deviation. In terms of implementation, however, I believe very much in practicality and flexibility.

How does your interpretation of Islam differ from that of the Saudi religious establishment?

The official *'ulama* preach that Islam means absolute obedience to the leader. There is no room for accountability, transparency, or freedoms. This is the way they sell Islam. We say Islam is power sharing, accountability, transparency, and freedom of expression. This is the main difference. Their interpretation is always what the regime wants.

What about women's rights?

This is a very intricate issue in Saudi Arabia. The problem is that there is a mixture between social habits and real Islamic teachings. It is very difficult to underline the differences between the two.

Should women have the right to drive?

Again social habits dictate this. In Islam there is no clear justification for denying these rights. In Islam only activities that are explicitly prohibited are *haram* [forbidden]. In MIRA, we want women to be active and many women take part in our radio shows and Internet service. But we are reluctant to explore this issue in detail until proper platforms for debate and discussion have been established in the country since it might backfire.

MIRA has called for a consultative council directly elected by the people and empowered to appoint the head of the executive branch. Are you essentially calling for the overthrow of the Saudi regime?

Well … to put it simply, I would say yes. We are demanding changes in the country and these change are simply incompatible with the survival of the regime. I don't expect the regime to bring about comprehensive reforms on its own. It cannot tolerate even minimal freedoms of expression and assembly. If these freedoms were allowed, people would demand an accounting of the many billions of dollars stolen by the royals and, if they were not stopped, they would then encircle the princes' palaces, demanding the return of these billions. People would demand that those behind the abuse of thousands of prisoners be prosecuted and, if not stopped, would attack the prisons or the Interior Ministry. The regime is instinctively aware of this and will not allow it to happen.

What is your strategy for engineering the regime's collapse?

We are working to inform, empower, and mobilize the people through radio and television broadcasts and other means of communication. The first test [of this strategy] came in

October, when we succeeded in organizing an unprecedented demonstration in Riyadh. However, while we're working to change the regime ourselves if necessary, we anticipate that it will fall on its own from internal problems. And our role then would be to prevent the chaos rather than remove the regime.

How is it likely to fall?

The regime is very weak and divided. There is no central figure or collective decision-making mechanism. The four most powerful royals—Abdullah, Sultan, Nayif and Salman—rarely meet together. There is a deep rift in the royal family and the only thing preventing it from coming out into the open is the living body of King Fahd. Although the king is mentally incapacitated, his physical survival is actually protecting the royal family. Once Fahd dies, they will have to deal with two points of disagreement. The first is who will become the next crown prince. They have no problem with Abdullah becoming king, but there is division over who will be next in line. Abdullah does not want Sultan to become Crown Prince. Even if he initially appoints him as a crown prince to avoid turmoil, he will remove him later.

The second point of disagreement is how much authority Abdullah will exercise. Abdullah insists that he will have complete authority as king—he will not accept power sharing within the royal family. The other three want him to have no more authority than what is has now.

So there will be a confrontation between the royals?

Yes, there is likely to be an armed confrontation between the different factions sooner or later. Abdullah may temporarily accept some form of settlement after his ascension, but when he gets more confident he will try to sideline people like Sultan and Nayif, who will then resist in a fierce manner.

The second problem, which is no less dangerous, is the challenge by al-Qaeda and other groups who believe in violence. Their target is not only America but the royals as well. If they go ahead with that the aura of the regime will disappear and the country will sink into chaos.

Saudi officials claim a ten-man terrorist cell that fought security forces in August at a rest stop north of Riyadh was linked to MIRA. Is this allegation true?

It is rubbish. The Saudi regime is unable to defeat us politically, so they resort to these lies, exploiting the current views in the West.

They want to smear you?

Of course. We are their public enemy number one. MIRA is probably more dangerous to them than Al Qaeda. Al Qaeda is still preoccupied with America, while we are dedicated only to fighting the Saudi regime.

Do you advocate violence against the regime?

We are totally dedicated to peaceful means and we think we can achieve change by that.

What points of disagreement do you have with Osama bin Laden?

I think bin Laden is more concerned with America and hence see no logic in the question itself.

You suffered a stabbing attack in June …

A kidnapping attempt.

You claimed that they were acting on behalf of Saudi intelligence.

The people who came were English, but apparently sponsored by the Saudis …

Did they come here to this house?

Yes, they came here. And their intention, judging from the way they conducted the fight, was clearly to kidnap me.

Were you alone in the house?
I was with my family.

You have no protection here, do you?
Well, now I have added some protection.

Isn't this place under surveillance by British security?
Now it is, but it wasn't before.

Why would they want to kidnap you?
To take me back home. Kidnapping is better than elimination ...

It would give them a chance to interrogate you.
Yes. Also, they would paralyze all the potential leaders behind me who are still in the country. After torturing me they would arrest them and get rid of them. But if they eliminate me they will not be able to identify potential leaders.

How would they manage to kidnap you here in London and smuggle you out of the country?
They kidnapped a member of the royal family, Sultan bin Turki, from Geneva earlier this year. So it is not impossible.

You were once a leading figure in the Committee for the Defense of Legitimate Rights (CDLR), headed by Muhammad al-Mas'ari. Why did you break away from the committee and found MIRA in 1996?
Well, there are things that we have agreed not to speak about. So I will speak about the things that we can speak about, which have to do with policies and strategy.

When we came to Britain, our original mission consisted of four principles, which I felt Dr. Mas'ari had later shifted from. The first principle was that CDLR should be focused on Saudi Arabia. It should not involve itself with any other country. The second was that CDLR should be a discreet and independent group. It would respect other groups and might even exchange ideas and experience, but it would not make an alliance or affiliate itself with any other group. The third principle was that decision-making in CDLR should be based on collective consultation. The fourth was we saw our role as ambassadors and messengers. We don't sell or promote ourselves as the future presidents or future leaders of the country. The real action is inside the country. We are only a media window or communications platform. And then came the straws that broke the camel's back. But these are the ...

These are the things you do not want to discuss.
Yes.

Why did the British government want to deport Mas'ari?
To please the Saudis. This is the same reason why I have not been *officially* given asylum.

But you are not pressured here. You can act freely.
Nobody can pressure you here in the UK. Even if you are a visitor for six months you can do anything in terms of media and press like any British citizen. The law protects you.

Have you ever felt under surveillance here?
Well, the Saudis are trying to convince the government here that we have links to terrorism.

Have they succeeded?
No. We are careful to remain within legal boundaries and recently they [the British] have discovered that betting on strategic relations with the [Saudi] regime is dangerous. It is better to have relations with the people and I assume they know how much public support we have.

One scholar recently wrote that Saudi opposition leaders are more interested in preserving the identity of their separate voices as critics of the regime than in undertaking coordinated action. Is that an accurate assessment?

If he means that we are not working with other opposition groups, then yes, he is correct. We are not very keen to work with other groups. We don't want to confront them either. We have a very clear and sensitive program and we want to control this program completely. It is in our interest currently to keep our program to ourselves. We want to see what is happening in the country. This idea of cooperation does not preoccupy us. But if he means that we are preoccupied with that, then he is wrong.

How extensive is your network inside Saudi Arabia?

We extend everywhere horizontally, but we are relatively weak vertically. We have huge numbers of followers inside the country, but we have to admit that the command and control network is not equivalent to the horizontal spread.

How are instructions transmitted to your followers in Saudi Arabia?

We use the mass media and communications technology to reach the followers and enable them to reach us.

How are these satellite broadcasts routed into the Kingdom?

We send the signal to a land station, which beams it to the satellite, which then beams it to a wide area, including Saudi Arabia.

How successful have the Saudis been in jamming these broadcasts?

They have had some success. It can be jammed by directing a jamming beam from anywhere in North Africa, Europe, the Middle East, eastern parts of the Atlantic and the Mediterranean.

How do they do this?

They identify the satellite, uplink the frequency (which is not coded) and then send a signal to the transponder using the same frequency as our uplink frequency. Since they are conscious of the illegality of this kind of jamming, they conceal the source of the jamming by using multiple sites.

What kind of relationship should Saudi Arabia have with the United States?

Like its relationship with other countries. There should be no special relationship. This domination and huge influence should stop.

Are you alarmed by growing U.S. involvement in the region?

Obviously I loathe a U.S. invasion of a Muslim country, but I think this invasion and all the troubles it has caused will help the American public better appreciate the shortcomings of the Bush administration.

By invading Iraq, has the U.S. gained greater leverage to change the region for the better?

This is just not happening. The Americans are not pressuring the Saudi regime to change at all. All the pressure is either to cooperate in terms of security or to force a cultural change to remove what they believe are the foundations for terrorism.

SOURCE: *Middle East Intelligence Bulletin* (November 2003). Available at: http://www.meib.org/articles/0311_saudii.htm

CONTEXT AND ANALYSIS

Sa'd al-Faqih (b. 1958) is the head of the Movement for Islamic Reform in Arabia (MIRA). He founded the movement after breaking with Muhammad al-Mas'ari and the CDLR in 1996. Al-Faqih spent his formative years in Iraq and trained as a surgeon in Riyadh. At an early age he read the works of the Muslim Brotherhood, including Sayyid

Qutb's seminal treatise *Milestones,* which introduced him to a more politicized understanding of the Qur'anic message. The advent of the Gulf War and the ensuing presence of U.S. troops on Saudi soil prompted him to act in accordance with this understanding. Al-Faqih was one of the signatories of the Memorandum of Advice, which remained for him his touch-stone in all of his subsequent efforts to reform the Saudi monarchy and religious establishment. Over the years he has spent both with the CDLR and MIRA, his goals have remained more or less constant. Since 1994 he has resided in London from where he disseminates his call for change.

In his writings and broadcasts, al-Faqih criticizes the royal house on two main points. First, he argues that all of Saudi Arabia's problems—national indebtedness, corruption, religious hypocrisy, nepotism—trace back to the house of Saud's monopoly of power. In a political system devoid of checks and balances, the royal house does what it pleases, even to the extent of twisting Shari'a to suit its purposes. Worse, the 'ulama, including the late 'Abd al-'Aziz bin Baz, the Grand Mufti, support the House of Saud uncritically, bowing to royal whims and passions without calling the Saudi royals to account. The unwillingness of the 'ulama to "speak truth to power" is the second major theme in his pronouncements. The connivance between the state and the clerics, al-Faqih says, is due to the fact that the latter owe their positions in education and government to the Al Saud. When faced with the choice between supporting the ruling house and following the truth of religion, invariably they back the state.

Al-Faqih admits that his organization does not yet have a fully blown blueprint of the kind of state he and his supporters would want to set up in place of the current regime. Nor is he entirely clear to the extent he would support the violent overthrow of the monarchy. Nevertheless, he does put forward a number of ideas, the most important of which is the institutional separation of the religious establishment from the state. This separation, he says, would take the form of an independent body of 'ulama, which would ensure that all laws in the Kingdom were in keeping with basic Islamic principles. Positions in such a body would be determined by election to reflect the consensus of the Islamic community. Further, a reformed Saudi state would have freedom of expression within limits set by the Shari'a. It would also have a leader (*imam*) chosen on the basis of merit rather than tribal or family affiliation.

Al-Faqih acknowledges that some things in the West are superior to institutions in Saudi Arabia, especially when it comes to efficiency and organization, and sees no problem with adopting them if they do not conflict with Islam. However, in common with most Islamists, he chides the West for its emphasis on individualism and materialism at the expense of the collective good and spiritual value.

FURTHER READINGS

Abedin, Mahan. "Saudi Dissent More Than Just Jihadis." Online at: http://www.saudidebate.com/index.php?option=com_content&task=view&id=162&Itemid=119.

Aburish, Said. *The Rise, Corruption, and Coming Fall of the House of Saud* (New York: Palgrave/Macmillan, 1996).

Commins, David. *The Wahhabi Mission and Saudi Arabia* (London: I. B. Tauris, 2006), chapters 5 and 6.

Cordesman, Anthony. "Saudi Arabia: Opposition, Islamic Extremism, and Terrorism," in *Saudi Arabia Enters the Twenty-First Century: Politics, Economics, and Energy* (Westport, CT: Praeger, 2003).

Delong-Bas, Natana. *Wahhabi Islam: From Revival and Reform to Jihad* (Cambridge: Oxford University Press, 2004), chapter 5.

Fandy, Mamoun. *Saudi Arabia and the Politics of Dissent* (New York: St. Martin's Press, 1999).

International Crisis Group. "Saudi Arabia Backgrounder: Who Are the Islamists," *Middle East Report,* 31 (September 21, 2004).

Kechichian, Joseph A. "Islamic Revivalism and Change in Saudi Arabia: Juhayman Al-'Utaybi's 'Letters' To the Saudi People," *Muslim World*, 80, no. 1 (January 1990), 1–6.

Kepel, Gilles. *The War for Muslim Minds* (Cambridge, MA: Belknap Press, 2004), chapter 5.

Okruhlik, Gwenn. "Networks of Dissent: Islamism and Reform in Saudi Arabia," *Current History* 101, no. 651 (January 2002), 22–28.

Al-Rasheed, Madawi. *Contesting the Saudi State: Islamic Voices from a New Generation* (Cambridge: Cambridge University Press, 2007).

8

THE LIBERATION OF
MUSLIM LANDS

Mujahidin, "warriors of the faith," are shown as they rest high in the mountains in the Kunar province in Afghanistan, May 1980. The struggle of the Mujahidin against the Soviet Red Army captured the imagination of Muslims around the world. Thousands of volunteers from the Arab countries and from as far away as Indonesia flocked to Afghanistan in the 1980s to aid in the anti-Soviet jihad. (Courtesy of AP Images.)

INTRODUCTION

Until the 1980s, Islamism was chiefly focused establishing Islamic polities in majority Muslim countries that had, to greater or lesser extents, secularized in the course of the nineteenth and twentieth centuries. As we have noted, some Islamists adopted a bottom-up gradualist approach to change, while others adopted the tactics of violence and revolution from above.

However, during the 1980s and 1990s, some Islamists began actively to concentrate on redeeming Muslim lands ruled by non-Muslims or under occupation. The most notable examples of this kind of "irredentist" Islamism include the Islamist campaign against the Soviet Union in Afghanistan (1979–1989) and Hamas' role in the first Palestinian *Intifadha* (uprising) against the Israeli occupation (1987–1991). But there are other instances. During this period, the Moro Islamic Liberation Front drew on the works of Sayyid Qutb to call for jihad in Mindanao and the Sulu Archipelago against the "colonial Philippine occupation armies." Over the 1990s, Chechen forces battled Russian troops in the Caucasus in order to secede from Russia and create an independent Chechen state. At the same time, Islamist liberationists were active in the Muslim majority Indian state of Kashmir, and in the Balkan state of Bosnia-Herzegovina. Some radical Islamists have even dreamed of redeeming Spain, the fabled Al-Andalus of medieval times, for Islam. The young men responsible for the March 2004 Madrid train bombings were evidently fired up by such dreams.

In some ways, contemporary Islamist efforts to liberate Muslim territorries from "infidel" rule are reminiscent of the jihads of the colonial era. During the eighteenth and nineteenth centuries, and continuing in the early decades of the twentieth century, charismatic Muslim leaders rallied Muslim populations against European encroachment and imperialist rule throughout the Islamic world. In this regard, names such as Muhammad Ahmad, the Mahdi of the Sudan, Imam Shamil (1797–1871) who led a jihad against Russian expansion in the Caucasus, and the woman jihadist, Tjoet Njak Dien (1848–1908) who fought Dutch colonialism in Aceh, stand out. However, despite the common feature of rolling back foreign, un-Islamic rule and occupation, today's Islamist irredentists operate within a totalizing ideological framework that was quite unknown to earlier, anti-foreign jihadists.

Irredentist Islamists sometimes compete with secular nationalist forces in their struggle to redeem the homeland. For example, in the Palestinian Territories of Gaza and the West Bank the Islamist organization Hamas vies for control of the Palestinian liberation movement against Fatah and other secular nationalist Palestinian organizations. At other times the effort to liberate lost lands is shared between local Islamist fighters and jihadists who have a global agenda, such as those who subscribe to Al Qaeda's brand of radical Islamism. Such pairings were evident in Afghanistan in the 1980s and in Bosnia-Herzegovina between 1992 and 1996. Today in Iraq religiously-inspired domestic insurgents sometimes cooperate with transnational jihadists. An important distinction is between the resort to struggle that is primarily determined by the context (foreign rule or military occupation) and that which arises primarily out of a radical doctrine expressing a preference for violence over nonviolent strategies despite the possibility of engaging in the latter.

"The Entire Islamic Land Is Like a Single Country"

- *Document:* Selection from *Join the Caravan* by 'Abdullah 'Azzam (1941–1989).
- *Date:* 1987.
- *Where:* Pakistan.
- *Significance:* 'Azzam formulated much of the ideology for the war against the Soviets in Afghanistan, recruited Arab fighters for the jihad, and established the foundation of the international network that his disciple, Usama bin Laden, would inherit and turn into Al Qaeda.

DOCUMENT

Oh Muslims! Upon you be peace, and Allah's mercy and His blessings.

The enormous sacrifices apportioned to the Afghan Muslim people are no secret to you. To date, nine years and some have passed since the start of the illustrious revolution against the Communist invasion. During this time, the Muslims in Afghanistan have endured as much as mortals can endure in the course of protecting their religion, honor and children. Not a single house remains in Afghanistan that has not been transformed into a funeral home or an orphanage.

These people have an excuse before Allah, and have called to Allah to bear witness, on the basis of the skulls, cripples, souls and blood, that there has not remained a single arrow in the bow, and the arrows of the quiver have almost broken through.

Through the course of this long period of time, the Afghans had expectations of their Muslim brethren in case their numbers became decreased, and also so that the Muslim brotherhood could be aroused in their depths. Yet, until now, the Muslims have not heeded their call. In the ears of the Muslims is a silence, rather than the cries of anguish, the screams of virgins, the wails of orphans and the sighs of old men. Many well-off people have deemed it sufficient to send some of the scraps from their tables and crumbs from their food.

But the situation is more serious, and gravely momentous, and the Muslims in Afghanistan are in severe distress and definite, menacing peril. This blessed jihad was established by a handful of youths who were nurtured in Islam, and by a group of scholars who devoted themselves to Allah. But most of this first generation has fallen in martyrdom, and the second generation has advanced. This second generation has not been fortunate enough to receive the same share of upbringing and guidance, and have not come across a stretched-out hand showing an interest in teaching and training them. Such people are in dire need of somebody who can live amongst them to direct them toward Allah and teach them religious regulations.

According to our modest experience and knowledge, we believe that jihad in the present situation in Afghanistan is individually obligatory (*fard 'ayn*), with one's self and wealth as has been confirmed by the jurists of the four schools of Islamic jurisprudence, without any exception. Along with them, the same opinion has been given by the majority of exegetes (*mufassirin*), hadith-scholars and scholars of religious principles (*usul*). Ibn Taymiyya said, "When the enemy has entered an Islamic land, there is no doubt that it is obligatory on those closest to the land to defend it, and then on those around them, for the entire Islamic land is like a single country. Also, (it is compulsory) to go forth to meet the enemy without permission from parents or people to whom one is in debt. The texts of (Imam) Ahmad are quite explicit regarding this."

He also said, "When the enemy wants to attack the Muslims, defense becomes obligatory on all those upon whom the attack is intended, and on others besides them, just as Allah has said, (translated)

'And if they seek your help in the matter of religion, then you must help them.'"

This is just as the Prophet (may Allah bless him and grant him peace) has ordered the individual to help Muslims, whether or not he has been recruited for fighting. It is obligatory on every individual according to his capability and wealth, little or plenty, whether walking or riding. When the enemy proceeded towards the Muslims in the Year of the Trench, Allah did not excuse anybody. The texts of the four juristic schools are explicit and definite in this respect, and leave no room for interpretation, ambiguity or uncertainty.

Ibn 'Abidin, the Hanafi scholar says,

"(Jihad is) *fard 'ayn* when the enemy has attacked any of the Islamic heartland, at which point it becomes *fard 'ayn* on those close to the enemy … As for those beyond them, at some distance from the enemy, it is *fard kifaya* for them unless they are needed. The need arises when those close to the enemy fail to counter the enemy, or if they do not fail but are negligent and fail to perform jihad. In that case it becomes obligatory on those around them—*fard 'ayn*, just like prayer and fasting, and they may not abandon it. (The circle of people on whom jihad is *fard 'ayn* expands) until in this way, it becomes compulsory on the entire people of Islam, of the West and the East."

Verdicts in the same vein were issued also by the Hanafi scholars al-Kasani in "Bada'i' al-Sanai'," "Ibn Nujaym in "al-Bahr al-Ra'iq," and Ibn al-Humam in "Fath al-Qadir."

If you wish, you may also peruse the Maliki al-Dasuqi's "Hashiyah," "Nihayah al-Muhtaj" by the Shafi'i al-Ramali, and "al-Mughni" by the Hanbali Ibn Quddamah.

....

The Russians have taken five thousand two hundred Afghan Muslim children to rear them on the Communist ideology, and to sow heresy deep within them. The Americans have confirmed the opening of six hundred schools, and they are maintaining, educating and raising one hundred fifty thousand Afghan children inside and outside the country.

Where then are the propagators of Islam? Where are the Muslim educators, and what have they prepared for saving this Muslim generation, and for safeguarding this great and blessed people?

The jurists have documented that the lands of the Muslims are like a single land, so that whichever region of the Muslims' territory is exposed to danger, it is necessary that the whole body of the Islamic *umma* rally together to protect this organ which is exposed to the onslaught of the microbe. What is the matter with the scholars that they do not arouse the youths for jihad, especially since arousal is compulsory?

"And arouse the believers."

What is the matter with the propagators that they do not dedicate a year of their lives to live amongst the *Mujahidin*, giving guidance and direction? What is the matter with the students that they do not take a year off from their studies in order to attain the distinction of jihad, and contribute with their own selves to the establishment of Allah's religion on earth?

> They are content to be among the women who remain behind, and their hearts have been sealed, so that they do not comprehend.
>
> However, the Messenger and those who believe with him perform jihad with their selves and their wealth; they are the ones for whom there are blessings and reward, and they are the successful ones.

What is the matter with the Imams, that they do not sincerely advise those who seek counsel from them regarding going out with blood and soul in the Path of Allah? For how long will the believing youths be held back and restrained from jihad? These youths, whose hearts are burning with a fire, spurting forth enthusiasm, and blazing with zeal that their pure blood may irrigate the earth of the Muslims. The one who forbids a young man from jihad is no different from the one who forbids him from prayer and fasting. Does the one who forbids people from jihad not fear that he falls under the implication (albeit indirectly) of the noble verse in which Allah says, (translated):

> Perhaps Allah knows those among you who restrain others, and those who say to their brethren, "Come to us," while they show only a little courage. They are miserly toward you. Then, when fear comes, you see them looking toward you, their eyes rolling like one who has been enshrouded on account of death. Then, when the fear departs, they lash you with sharp tongues, envious of the good. They have not believed, so Allah has rendered their deeds void, and that is easy for Allah.

What is the matter with the mothers, that one of them does not send forward one her sons in the Path of Allah, that he might be a pride for her in this world, and a treasure for her in the Hereafter through his intercession? And what is the matter with the fathers that they do not urge one of their sons, so that he can grow up in the rearing-ground of heroes, and the lands of men, and the grounds of battle? He should consider that Allah created him infertile, and part of giving thanks for the blessing of children is to submit the charity from his children as thanks to his Lord. Did he create himself? Or provide himself with wealth?

Why then, the stinginess towards the Lord of the Worlds?

Stinginess towards the King with respect to what He owns, notwithstanding the fact that we believe "A soul will not die until its life span and sustenance have been depleted."

What is the matter with the Muslims that they do not record some days of frontier-guarding, and some hours of battle in the books of their deeds, and the chronicles of their virtues? It has been confirmed in an authentic hadith that,

"Guarding the frontier for a day in the Path of Allah is better than the fasting and prayer of a month."

And in a *hasan* [good, reliable] hadith,

"Guarding the frontier for a day in the Path of Allah is better than a thousand days spent in other abodes, during which the nights are spent in prayer and the days in fasting."

And in the authentic hadith narrated by Imam Ahmad and Tirmidhi,

"Standing for an hour in the ranks of battle is better than standing (in prayer) for sixty years."

Oh brothers of Islam! Come, therefore, to the defense of your religion, and the victory of your Lord, and the elevation of the way of your prophet! Beloved brother! Draw your sword, climb onto the back of your horse, and wipe the blemish off your *umma*. If you do not assume the responsibility, who then will?

Kind friend!
The dream of disgrace has gone on long enough
Where, then, is the roar of lions?
The party of the small birds have become eagle-like
And we are under the subjugation of slaves-
The subjugation of slaves out of submissiveness
And not as a result of military defeat.
Dear friend!
"Surely, in their stories is a moral for intelligent people."

So, the bloody tale of Bukhara, the narrative of mutilated Palestine, and blazing Eden, and enslaved peoples, the sorry stories of Spain, the terrible accounts of Eritrea, sore Bulgaria, the tragedy of Sudan, the devastated remnants of Lebanon, Somalia, Burma, Caucasia and its deep wounds, Uganda, Zanzibar, Indonesia, Nigeria. All these slaughters and tragedies are the best lesson for us. Will we take admonishment from the past before we lose the present? Or will history repeat itself over us while we swallow degradation, fall into oblivion as those before us did, and lose just as they lost?

We hope that Allah defeats the Russians in Afghanistan, and that they turn back on their heels in failure. If the latter occurs, then I wish I knew what catastrophe will befall the Muslims.

Abu Dawud has reported, with a strong chain of narration, on the *marfu'* authority of Abu Umama,

"Whoever did not go out for jihad, nor helped equip a fighter, nor treated a *mujahid's* family well in his absence, Allah will afflict him with a calamity before the Day of Judgment."

"Surely, therein is a reminder for anybody with a heart, or who listens while bearing witness (to the truth)."

Have I not conveyed the message? Oh Allah, bear witness then.
Have I not conveyed the message? Oh Allah, bear witness then.
Have I not conveyed the message? Oh Allah, bear witness then.

SOURCE: Join the Caravan, by Imam Abdullah Azzam, Downloaded from the Web site www.al-haqq.org http://www.religioscope.com/info/doc/jihad/azzam_caravan_1_foreword.htm in December 2001

CONTEXT AND ANALYSIS

'Abdullah 'Azzam was born in 1941 in the village of Silat al-Harithiyya near Jenin in what was then British Mandate Palestine. His childhood unfolded against the dramatic backdrop of Israel's creation in 1948 and the absorption of his native West Bank into the Hashimite Kingdom of Jordan in 1950. Possessed of a scholarly disposition, he studied agriculture and taught school in villages in Jordan and the West Bank. But a growing interest in religion prompted him to enroll at the faculty of law at Damascus University, and later, at Al-Azhar in Cairo to study Shari'a. Distraught by the circumstances of Palestinian dispossession and inspired by Islamic learning, he joined the local branch of the Muslim Brotherhood, whose Islamic focus and activism he admired.

While serving in 1980 as a teacher in Saudi Arabia, 'Azzam learned about the ravages inflicted on the people of Afghanistan by the Soviet Red Army. The Soviets had invaded Afghanistan in December 1979 in order to prop up a faltering regime of indigenous communists in Kabul. Moved by the plight of the Afghans, 'Azzam relocated to Peshawar, Pakistan, the external base of the Afghan resistance, and there established the Maktab al-Khadamat (The Services Office) to provide lodging and logistical support for the foreign, mostly Arab volunteers who streamed into Pakistan to aid the Afghan fighters in their anti-Soviet jihad. Among the volunteers was Usama bin Laden who deferred to the older and wiser 'Azzam.

For the fighters in Afghanistan, the war was a source of heroism, solidarity, and total devotion to Islam defined in terms of the Shari'a. Although caught up in the immediacy of the conflict, 'Azzam looked ahead to the period of liberation. He was aware that the struggle against the Red Army was a school in which he and his fellow fighters might learn tactics and strategy useful to the recovery of other lands lost to Islam. The list of such lands was long and included Palestine, Kashmir, the Southern Philippines, and even Spain. In 'Azzam's vision, the foreign fighters comprised the vanguard of an army of Muslim liberation.

'Azzam spelled out his vision of jihad in two treatises, which he crafted as *fatawa* (juridical opinions): *Defense of Muslim Lands* and *Join the Caravan*. An excerpt from the latter work is provided above; "caravan" refers to the stream of jihadis then pouring into Afghanistan. Both writings appeared in the mid-1980s. Although written from an Islamist perspective, the appeal of these documents was, and remains, broad, providing legitimacy to the contention that the Afghan jihad was not a radical venture but one that spoke to the concern of Muslims everywhere. In them, 'Azzam made the point that in contrast to the Muslims of old, recent generations have neglected the obligation of jihad. This was a point already made famous by 'Abd al-Salam Faraj in *The Neglected Duty*.

According to 'Azzam, the obligation to jihad is of two kinds: jihad as *fard kifaya*, a collective obligation carried out by a sufficient number of Muslims on behalf of the community at large, and jihad as *fard 'ayn*, which is incumbent on all Muslims, not simply representatives of the community. Jihad becomes a *fard 'ayn* when Muslim territory is threatened or occupied by infidels. 'Azzam believed that in his own day the Muslim world was in a state of emergency that required activation of jihad as an individual duty required of all. Afghanistan required immediate assistance. But once Afghanistan was liberated Muslims should turn their attention to Palestine and other occupied Muslim lands.

In 1989 Abdullah 'Azzam and two of his sons were killed in a car bomb explosion as they drove to the mosque in Peshawar. No solid evidence exists linking the assassination with any particular group, although Pakistan's and Saudi Arabia's intelligence services and a number of mujahidin factions were all held in suspicion. But there is another suspect: Ayman al-Zawahiri. It is notable that soon after 'Azzam's death, the Egyptian al-Zawahiri made a move to exert his influence over 'Azzam's erstwhile disciple, bin Laden, and change the direction of the jihad. No longer would the jihadis focus their energies on liberating the "lost lands" of Islam. Following al-Zawahiri, they would aim their guns at the "corrupt" Muslim regimes and, more famously, at the "Far Enemy"—the United States.

FURTHER READINGS

Abou Zahab, Mariam, and Olivier Roy. *Islamic Networks: The Afghan-Pakistan Connection* (London: Hurst, 2004).

Calvert, John. "The Striving Shaykh: Abdullah Azzam and the Revival of Jihad," *Journal of Religion and Society*, Supplement Series 1 (2004), 83–103. Online at: http://moses.creighton.edu/JRS/toc/Supplement.html.

Coll, Steve. *Ghost Wars: The Secret History of the CIA, Afghanistan, and Bin Laden from the Soviet Invasion to September 10, 2001* (New York: Penguin, 2004).

Kepel, Gilles. *Jihad: On the Trail of Political Islam* (Cambridge, MA: Harvard University Press, 2002).

Kepel, Gilles, ed. *Al-Qaida dans le texte: Ecrits d'Oussama ben Laden, Abdallah Azzam, Ayman al-Zawahiri et Abou Moussab al-Zarqawi* (Paris: Presses Universitaires de France, 2005).

Roy, Olivier. *Islam and Resistance in Afghanistan* (Cambridge: Cambridge University Press, 1986).

Wright, Lawrence. *The Looming Tower: Al Qaeda and the Road to 9/11* (New York: Alfred A. Knopf, 2006).

"We Were Looking for Jihad"

- *Document:* Interview with Comm. Abu 'Aziz "Barbaros."
- *Date:* August 1994.
- *Where:* Bosnia.
- *Significance:* Bosnia-Herzegovina beckoned as a viable front for jihad following the conclusion of the war in Afghanistan.

DOCUMENT

To begin with, we would like to welcome the Mujahid Abu Abdel Aziz. We would like him to give us a brief overview of how he came to know Jihad. What are in your opinion the characteristics of the Mujahid in this time and era?

... Now, concerning the beginning of Jihad in my case, I was one of those who heard about Jihad in Afghanistan when it started. I used to hear about it, but was hesitant about (the purity and intention of) this Jihad. This—and Allah knows best—is most probably because we forgot the concept of Jihad in Islam. We became part of those who subscribe to the conception that Islam means *istislam* (submission) and *Salam* (peace), and that Jihad was only prescribed at the dawn of Islam, and now it is history and that the present forum is one of call and propagation of the faith (*Da'wa*). This credo reached the point that the lights of Jihad, its rules and prescriptions (as detailed in the coded Islamic legal text), faded (and disappeared) from our daily reality in the *Umma* (World Muslim Community). But Allah—in His infinite wisdom and planning—made it such that these brothers in Afghanistan declared Jihad (against the communist government and the Russian intruders) and revived this important element of Islam to teach people anew that Jihad means "to fight to make the word of Allah supreme and the word of the disbelievers low and despised" (Qur'an).

One of those who came to our land (presumably Saudi Arabia) was sheikh Dr. 'Abdallah 'Azzam—may his soul rest in peace—I heard him rallying the youth to come forth and (join him) to go to Afghanistan. This was in 1984—I think. I decided to go and check the matter for myself. This was, and all praise be to Allah, the beginning (of my journey with) Jihad. I am still following this same path. I have found that the best sacrifice we can offer for the sake of Allah, is our souls, then our possession. This is because Allah said in his holy book, "Behold, God has bought from the believers their lives and their possession, promising them paradise in return, (and so) they fight in God's cause, slay, and are slain: a promise which in truth He has willed on Himself in (the words of) the Torah, the Gospel and the Qur'an. And who could be more faithful to his bond than God? Rejoice, then, in the bargain which you have made with Him: for this, this is the triumph supreme!" (At-Tawbah 9:111)

Then the conquest of Kabul came, and we thanked Allah, praised be He. The joy of Jihad overwhelmed our hearts. The Prophet, peace be upon him, said, "The highest peak of Islam is Jihad." We were looking for Jihad (after Afghanistan). We found it in the Philippines, and in Kashmir. Only fifteen days lapsed (after the conquest of Kabul) and the crisis of Bosnia began. This confirmed the saying of the Prophet (of Islam), peace and blessings be upon him, who said, "Indeed Jihad will continue till the day of Judgment." A new Jihad started in Bosnia, (we moved there), and we are with it, if Allah wills.

As to your question about the characteristics needed for someone to be a *Mujahid*, I say: Belief in Allah, praised be He (comes first). He should be in our sight, heart and mind. We have to make Jihad to make His word supreme, not for a nationalistic cause, a tribal cause, a group feeling or any other cause. This matter is of great importance in this era, especially since many groups fight and want to see to it that their fighting is Jihad and their dead ones are martyrs. We have to investigate this matter and see under what banner one fights.

In short, how did (your) Jihad start in Bosnia, and what is the truth to the existence of an Arab Mujahidin Brigade under your command? What is its role and what are its relations with the Bosnian government?

As I told you before, when Jihad in Afghanistan was over, with the conquest of Kabul, I went with four of those who participated in Afghanistan to Bosnia to check out the landscape. We wanted to see things with a closer eye. I wanted to find out the truth to what is reported by the Western media. And surely, as was reported, there was persecution of Bosnian Muslims. Many were slaughtered, others were killed, while others were forced to exile. The chastity of their women was infringed upon for the simple reason that they were Muslims. The Christians took advantage of the fact that the Muslims were defenseless with no arms. They recalled their age-old hatred. As to Arab *Mujahidin* (in Bosnia), they do not have a separate battalion. There is a battalion for non-Bosnian fighters. Arabs are a minority compared to those of the *Mujahidin* (gathered from around the World). This battalion is under a unified command and is called *Katibat al-Mujahidin* (Mujahideen Battalion), *Odred "El-Mudzahidin"* as they call them in Bosnian. Militarily, it has a link to the Bosnian government under the general command of the Bosnian Armed Forces. It is in fact part of the seventh battalion (SEDMI KORPUS, ARMIJA REPUBLIKE BH) of the Bosnian Army.

I am a field commander under the "General Unified Armed Command." We have—and all grace be to Allah—full jurisdiction in the region we are responsible for (Editor's note: mostly central Bosnia). The general command of the Muslim forces wants to see results, it does not dictate strategy or action.

We heard, and many brothers heard, that you met with prominent ulama and scholars in the Muslim world and discussed with them the question of Jihad in Bosnia. Can you tell us some of their views and the issues you discussed?

First, we consider our scholars the light and guidance of Islam. They are the heirs of prophets (as the Hadith says, "*warathat al-Anbiya*"). Our duty is to seek knowledge from them and guidance from their scholarly light [sic]. I—*alhamdulillah* [praise to God]—met several prominent *ulama*. Among them Shaykh Nasir ad-Din al-Albani, Shaykh Abdel Aziz Bin Baz and Shaykh Salih Ibn Uthaymin and others in the Gulf area. *Alhamdulillah*, all grace be to Allah, they all support the religious dictum that "the fighting in Bosnia is a fight to make the word of Allah supreme and protect the chastity of Muslims." It is because Allah said (in his holy book), "Yet, if they ask you for succor against religious persecution, it is your duty to give [them] this succor." (Lit. "to succor them in religion," Qur'an, al-Anfal, 8:72). It is then our (religious) duty to defend our Muslim brethren wherever they are, as long as they are persecuted because they are Muslims and not for any other reason.

...

We heard that you have strong connections in Kashmir. What is the latest from that battle front?

Jihad in Kashmir is still going on. It is healthy—*alhamdulillah*. Our Kashmiri brothers have achieved a lot. Some of our *Mujahidin* brethren, whether Arab or (*Ajam*, non-Arab), such as the Pakistanis and our brethren from South-East Asia, have also helped. Their actions have been very successful, especially in the lands under Indian government control. *Mujahidin* execute hit-and-run operations. However there is a lack of support by Islamic governments and a lack of media coverage by Islamic outlets, on the level of atrocity and destruction by the non-believers in those lands: From killings to bulldozing to the burning of Muslims, sometimes alive, in public squares. Action is slow. There is also a lack of trained Jihadist cadres to stand to this dire situation. We ask Allah to give them and us success.

How do you perceive the future of Jihad in Bosnia, based on what has happened in the past and what is going on now? What are the best and worst case scenarios there?

Of course, knowledge of the future is with Allah. As to what we foresee based on our expertise and participation, in the past and now, I see that the future is for Jihad. Yes, Jihad in Bosnia should continue. This is because Westerners do not want Jihad to find a launching-board. We say to them what Allah said in His holy book, "If you champion Allah, Allah shall assuredly champion you and ground your feet." And He said, "It is our prerogative to champion the believers."

We have to strengthen our belief and the belief of our brethren the Bosnians by all means: through training, through education, through awareness programs and other means.

Now as to the best and worst case scenarios that things might turn out to: The best is the establishment of a state for the Muslims by any means and under any rule (religious or secular). When we went there, we did not go to train state employees and create cadres for it. We went to defend and champion our Muslim Brethren. The worst scenario is to have a mixed state or a mixed parliament or a mixed government between the Muslims and Christians as the case that happened in some Arab countries of having a Muslim president and a Christian vice-president or the opposite (Editor's note: the only such state in the Arab world is Lebanon).

Based on your participation and long stay in Bosnia, how do you perceive the Bosnian Muslim people? What about their government? Do you think that the Christian onslaught has strengthened their attachment to their religion?

Concerning the Bosnian People, and this is not my view, but what our Muslim Brethren themselves say: They say that this is not a crisis (*azma*), but a blessing (*Rahma*). "If it were not for this, we would not have known Allah, glorious be He. We would not have known the road to the Mosque. Our men, women and children were loose morally and in their appearance, one could not distinguish the Muslim from the Christian. Muslim women were dressed, but were really exposed (*kasiyat-ariyat*). But now *alhamdulillah*, all grace be to Allah, our Mosques are full. Our women are wearing the complete *Hijab*" (Editor's note: commonly known as Niqab whereby women cover the body and face, as in Saudi Arabia and some Arab and Muslim countries). That is, they cover their faces completely. They are proud when they parade in the market-place or bazaar in it. The complete Hijab is something natural now. This, *alhamdulillah*, is due to da'wa that our youth, the freelance *Mujahidin*, do in their spare time.

In general, commitment to religious doctrine and the return to Allah is fast in the midst of these Bosnians.

Now as to your question about the (Bosnian) government, I say: After my meeting with President Ali Izzet (Begovic) in the past, and according to what we hear and gather, the members of his government perform the five (obligatory) prayers. We, in general, do not expect them to be like the *Sahaba* (Prophet's Companions), may Allah be pleased with them. These (Bosnian) people lived and knew nothing of the *Din* (system and religion) and creed of Islam, except the name.

Qur'an and religious studies were absent during the communist days (of General Tito).

The Christian onslaught strengthened their attachment to their religious values. This is what they say: "Our return to the *Din* was caused by this onslaught."

A lot of noise and rambling is made when one talks of material support. Whether it is officially given by different governments or that offered by different philanthropic Islamic institutions. People question whether such money reaches the Mujahidin or those who need it most. Can you shed some light on this issue? What is the best way, in your view, to send help to fighters there?

Yes, dear brother! Many Muslim states collected material help, aired what is happening in Bosnia, created relief agencies in all Arab and Muslim lands. But did these agencies deliver this money or send it to fighters? I can assure you that no Muslim or Arab state delivered money or food for *Mujahidin*. Where did this money go? What is delivered to the Bosnian government directly? Did these agencies open their own refugee camps and offer food services for the needy in different regions? This, I can neither confirm nor deny. As for *Mujahidin*, it is a pity that no Muslim state wants to help or even deal with them. They are fought by these states and are considered terrorists. This is what they say. (Official) heads of relief agencies say that they do not want to deal with *Mujahidin* because they are terrorists. "All power and glory are to Allah" (for such accusations)!

Does any help reach us? Yes, from individuals. Our good brothers collect donations for us and bring them directly to us. We use these donations to buy food and clothing. May Allah reward them the best, *Jazakum Allah Khayran*. The best way to send donations—in my view—is for Islamic centers to deliver them directly, in the person of their *Iman* or Mosque official. He collects these donations and sends them personally to the *Mujahidin* (as a religious duty). Donations through relief agencies or governments do not necessarily make it to *Mujahidin*, even if they are collected in their name (as is done in some countries).

Do you have a final issue you would like to address?

May Allah reward you the best. And this is not a final word, but a request and announcement. (I would like to say) that the number of *Mujahidin* in Bosnia is small. A very small number of brethren came from Muslim countries and despite their Islamic commitment, they have little religious knowledge to do *da'wa* in the midst of these brothers and sisters. We need—and this is unfortunate—*ulama*, scholars of Islam, in Bosnia. Believe me dear brother, until now, two years since we established our base there, there isn't a single scholar in our midst for us to seek his religious judgment. For the small number of youth that make it here, we ask them do *da'wa*, and they reply, "We came seeking martyrdom. We did not come to sit in Mosques and public squares to teach people and educate them. We want the word of Allah to be supreme and the word of the disbelievers to be low and despised. All we wish for is a bullet that hits our chests through which we reach *Shahada* (the state of witness and martyrdom)." The other issue I would like to address is the question of material support. Again, I say that collections made in the name of *Mujahidin*, through official means, I have no knowledge of. You should consult with such institutions and agencies as to where the money goes. (Again) many relief agencies do not like to deal with the *Mujahidin*. They are afraid of "helping and assisting terrorists" as the saying goes.

Finally, I ask Allah to make you and me successful (in this world and the hereafter). I ask Him to help the workers and those who support this newsletter to perform their religious duty of *da'wa*, to publicize *Mujahidin* news and Jihad, not just in Bosnia, but also in Kashmir, Tajikistan, Philippines and Armenia. Again thank you for your interest. Our final prayer, *alhamdulillah*, all grace to Allah, Lord of the Worlds.

SOURCE: *Al-Sirat al-Mustaqeem* (*The Straight Path*), no. 33, Safar 1415, August 1994. Translation: MSANEWS http://www.seprin.com/laden/barbaros.html

CONTEXT AND ANALYSIS

War broke out on Bosnian territory in April 1992, the month following Bosnia's declaration of independence. The Bosnian-Serb offensive against the Muslims was marked by atrocities and attacks on religious property, including mosques and cultural institutions like the historical national library in Sarajevo, which was shelled. In much of the Islamic world, the Serbian aggression was viewed entirely as a Christian assault on a Muslim population, even though most Bosnian Muslims did not strongly identify with Islam.

As the war wore on, Bosnian Muslim leaders turned to Islamic states for support. Iran sent humanitarian assistance and weapons to the Bosnian Muslims, and announced its readiness to contribute troops as part of an international peace keeping force. Saudi Arabia likewise stepped in with millions of dollars of financial aid, mostly channelled through the offices of the Muslim World League.

But the conflict in Bosnia also attracted the notice of foreign jihadis. In 1992 the *Mujahidin* and their Islamist supporters concluded their campaign in Afghanistan by capturing Kabul. While many veterans of the war in Afghanistan returned to their respective countries—where they took up arms against their home governments, as in Egypt and Algeria—others saw the Bosnian war as an opportunity to liberate yet another Muslim population from oppressive "infidel" rule. Throughout the Muslim world, but especially from Afghanistan, Pakistan, the Sudan, Saudi Arabia, and Yemen, jihadis made their way to Bosnia, concentrating in the town of Zenica. Estimates put the number of jihadi volunteers at 1,500 to 5,000.

The primary leader of the jihadis in Bosnia was Abu 'Abd al-'Aziz, called "Barbaros" "on account of his carefully combed, two-foot long beard, which he dyed red in imitation of the Prophet" (Kepel *Jihad*, 250). Barbaros was a Saudi national of Indian extraction who had fought the Soviet Red Army in Afghanistan with 'Abdullah 'Azzam. After he departed Afghanistan in 1992, Barbaros considered making either Kashmir or the southern Philippines his new field of operations. But the news out of Bosnia was particularly bad, and so he made the decision to make that country the new theatre of combat. Impressed by the possibility of establishing a jihadi springboard in the heart of the Balkans, he urged other Muslim fighters, especially veterans of Afghanistan, to join him. Seeking sanction for the cause, he petitioned and received *fatawa* from Grand Mufti Shaykh 'Abd al-'Aziz Ibn Baz and the Saudi cleric Salih Ibn 'Uthaymin, who blessed the new venture.

Many of the volunteers fought as members of the Seventh Islamic Brigade of the Bosnian army, which was formed in September 1992. But the ideological differences between them and the secular-minded Bosnians were great, prompting many jihadis eventually to enrol in their own El-Mudzahidin regiment, which was formed in 1993. Barbaros, the "Commandant," was in charge of this regiment and led it into battle against the Serb militias. They were as cruel as their Serb opponents. Photographs taken of the jihadis on the battlefield portray them with the severed heads of their enemies, or else standing astride corpses.

In addition to their military activities, Barbaros and his colleagues attempted to spread their jihadi-*salafi* ideas among the Bosnian Muslim population. Specifically, they undertook the "reform" of Bosnian Islam, attempting to impose the veil on women and beards on men. In the end, however, the jihadis were unable either to transform the nature of the indigenous Islam of the Balkans or turn the war generally into a jihad, because the Islamism of the foreigners struck no chord in the majority of Bosnian Muslims, as it had done among some Afghans.

IN HISTORY

In the Hearts of Green Birds

In the Hearts of Green Birds: The Martyrs of Bosnia, a book by various anonymous authors about the war in Bosnia-Herzegovina, focuses on the martyrdom of foreign Muslims who had gone to Bosnia to serve as fighters. The association of martyrdom with "green birds" comes from the prophetic hadith: "The Prophet (SAWS) said: 'The souls of martyrs reside in the bodies of green birds that perch on chandeliers suspended from the throne and fly about paradise whenever they please.'" (Ahmad and Tirmidhi). See Faisal Devji, *Landscapes of the Jihad* (Ithaca, NY: Cornell University Press, 2005), 87, 110. The following is from *In the Hearts of Green Birds*:

A member of the Qatar National Handball team, he came to Bosnia at the end of 1992. He used to love doing double guard duty shifts for 4 hours in the cold weather. He was a very humble and very pious brother. He was of black descent but brothers described his face like a glowing lamp because of the shine and Noor [light] on his face. He had two large marks of prostration on his face due to prolonged prostration, as he used to pray all night long. Once he was asked,

"When will you return back to your country, Abu Khalid?" And he replied,

"I want to be Shaheed [martyr] here." Abu Khalid once said to a brother,

"Back in Qatar, I bought some fighting clothes to go and fight in Afghanistan, but my mother prevented me from going. But, Insha-Allah, this time, with these same clothes, I will be killed in Bosnia."

Before one operation against the Croats, as soon as he was picked by the Ameer, he said to the brother next to him, "Insha-Allah, this time ALLAH will take me as Shaheed."

As he was traveling in a car with five other brothers, of them Wahiudeen al-Misree, the Ameer of the Mujahideen (RA), they took a wrong turning and ventured 7km into enemy territory. The Croats shot at the car with anti-aircraft weapons and it blew 20 feet into the air. All of the five brothers got out and fought until they were killed. When their bodies were returned to the Mujahideen after two months, the brothers were able to identify four of them but they could not identify the body of Abu Khalid Al-Qatari. When the Bosnian army general said to them "This is your last man," they looked at the body and saw that this body was that of a white person with a white face, and they replied,

"This is not our brother: our brother had black skin."

Upon looking carefully at this body, they pulled down his shirt and noticed that from below the neck downwards, its skin was black. They pulled up his sleeve and they found that above the elbows it was black and below the elbows it was white. Then they pulled up his trousers, where they found that his feet were white but the skin above his ankles was black. One of the brothers commented on this, saying that as the Hadith of Rasoolullah (SAWS) goes about the signs of the believers on the Day of Resurrection, the marks of Wudu [ritual washing] were shining white on the body of Abu Khalid al-Qatari. May ALLAH (SWT) accept him amongst the Shuhadaa'.

SOURCE: http://www.islamicawakening.com/viewarticle.php?articleID=200&

The Mudzahidin brigade was disbanded after the Dayton Accords, which put an end to the three-year long conflict, were signed in 1995 in Paris. The Accords stipulated that Bosnia and Herzegovina, Croatia, and the Federal Republic of Yugoslavia were fully to respect the sovereign equality of one another and to settle disputes by peaceful means.

FURTHER READINGS

Burr, J. Millard, and Robert O. Collins. *Alms for Jihad: Charity and Terror in the Islamic World* (Cambridge: Cambridge University Press, 2006), chapter 6.

Gvosdev, Nikolas K., and Ray Takeyh. *The Receding Shadow of the Prophet: The Rise and Fall of Political Islam* (Westport, CT: Praeger/Greenwood, 2004), chapter 5.

Kepel, Gilles. *Jihad: On the Trail of Political Islam* (Cambridge, MA: Belknap Press, 2002), chapter 10.

Kohlmann, Evan. *Al-Qaida's Jihad in Europe: The Afghan-Bosnian Network* (London: Berg Publishers, 2004).

LeBor, Adam. *A Heart Turned East: Among the Muslims of Europe and America* (New York: St. Martin's Press, 2001), chapter 2.

"The Movement's Program Is Islam"

- **Document:** Covenant of the *Islamic Resistance Movement* (HAMAS).
- **Date:** 1988.
- **Where:** Occupied Palestinian Territories.
- **Significance:** The Hamas Covenant communicates the organization's double-pronged effort to Islamize the Palestinian Territories and end Israel's occupation by means of jihad.

DOCUMENT

In the Name of the Most Merciful Allah

Introduction

Praise be unto Allah, to whom we resort for help, and whose forgiveness, guidance and support we seek; Allah bless the Prophet and grant him salvation, his companions and supporters, and to those who carried out his message and adopted his laws—everlasting prayers and salvation as long as the earth and heaven will last. Hereafter:

O People:

Out of the midst of troubles and the sea of suffering, out of the palpitations of faithful hearts and cleansed arms; out of the sense of duty, and in response to Allah's command, the call has gone out rallying people together and making them follow the ways of Allah, leading them to have determined will in order to fulfill their role in life, to overcome all obstacles, and surmount the difficulties on the way. Constant preparation has continued and so has the readiness to sacrifice life and all that is precious for the sake of Allah.

Thus it was that the nucleus (of the movement) was formed and started to pave its way through the tempestuous sea of hopes and expectations, of wishes and yearnings, of troubles and obstacles, of pain and challenges, both inside and outside.

When the idea was ripe, the seed grew and the plant struck root in the soil of reality, away from passing emotions, and hateful haste. The Islamic Resistance Movement emerged to carry out its role through striving for the sake of its Creator, its arms intertwined with those of all the fighters for the liberation of Palestine. The spirits of its fighters meet with the spirits of all the fighters who have sacrificed their lives on the soil of Palestine, ever since it was conquered by the companions of the Prophet, Allah bless him and grant him salvation, and until this day.

This Covenant of the Islamic Resistance Movement (HAMAS), clarifies its picture, reveals its identity, outlines its stand, explains its aims, speaks about its hopes, and calls for its support, adoption and joining its ranks. Our struggle against the Jews is very great and very serious. It needs all sincere efforts. It is a step that inevitably should be followed by other steps. The Movement is but one squadron that should be supported by more and more squadrons from this vast Arab and Islamic world, until the enemy is vanquished and Allah's victory is realized …

Article One

The Islamic Resistance Movement: The Movement's program is Islam. From it, it draws its ideas, ways of thinking and understanding of the universe, life and man. It resorts to it for judgment in all its conduct, and it is inspired by it for guidance of its steps.

Article Two

The Islamic Resistance Movement is one of the wings of Moslem Brotherhood in Palestine. Moslem Brotherhood Movement is a universal organization which constitutes the largest Islamic movement in modern times. It is characterized by its deep understanding, accurate comprehension and its complete embrace of all Islamic concepts of all aspects of life, culture, creed, politics, economics, education, society, justice and judgment, the spreading of Islam, education, art, information, science of the occult and conversion to Islam.

Article Three

The basic structure of the Islamic Resistance Movement consists of Moslems who have given their allegiance to Allah whom they truly worship—"I have created the jinn and humans only for the purpose of worshipping"—who know their duty towards themselves, their families and country. In all that, they fear Allah and raise the banner of Jihad in the face of the oppressors, so that they would rid the land and the people of their uncleanliness, vileness and evils.…

Article Four

The Islamic Resistance Movement welcomes every Moslem who embraces its faith, ideology, follows its program, keeps its secrets, and wants to belong to its ranks and carry out the duty. Allah will certainly reward such one.

Article Five

Time extent of the Islamic Resistance Movement: By adopting Islam as its way of life, the Movement goes back to the time of the birth of the Islamic message, of the righteous ancestor, for Allah is its target, the Prophet is its example and the Koran is its constitution.…

Article Six

The Islamic Resistance Movement is a distinguished Palestinian movement, whose allegiance is to Allah, and whose way of life is Islam. It strives to raise the banner of Allah over every inch of Palestine, for under the wing of Islam followers of all religions can coexist in security and safety where their lives, possessions and rights are concerned. In the absence of Islam, strife will be rife, oppression spreads, evil prevails and schisms and wars will break out....

Article Seven

As a result of the fact that those Moslems who adhere to the ways of the Islamic Resistance Movement spread all over the world, rally support for it and its stands, strive towards enhancing its struggle, the Movement is a universal one. It is well-equipped for that because of the clarity of its ideology, the nobility of its aim and the loftiness of its objectives....

The Islamic Resistance Movement is one of the links in the chain of the struggle against the Zionist invaders. It goes back to 1939, to the emergence of the martyr 'Izz al-Din al-Qassam and his brethren the fighters, members of Muslim Brotherhood. It goes on to reach out and become one with another chain that includes the struggle of the Palestinians and Moslem Brotherhood in the 1948 war and the Jihad operations of the Moslem Brotherhood in 1968 and after.

Moreover, if the links have been distant from each other and if obstacles, placed by those who are the lackeys of Zionism in the way of the fighters obstructed the continuation of the struggle, the Islamic Resistance Movement aspires to the realization of Allah's promise, no matter how long that should take. The Prophet, Allah bless him and grant him salvation, has said: "The Day of Judgment will not come about until Moslems fight the Jews (killing the Jews), when the Jew will hide behind stones and trees. The stones and trees will say O Moslems, O 'Abdulla, there is a Jew behind me, come and kill him. Only the Gharkad tree, (evidently a certain kind of tree) would not do that because it is one of the trees of the Jews." (related by al-Bukhari and Muslim [in their canonical hadith collections]).

Article Eight

Allah is its target, the Prophet is its model, the Koran its constitution: Jihad is its path and death for the sake of Allah is the loftiest of its wishes.

Article Nine

The Islamic Resistance Movement found itself at a time when Islam has disappeared from life. Thus rules shook, concepts were upset, values changed and evil people took control, oppression and darkness prevailed, cowards became like tigers: homelands were usurped, people were scattered and were caused to wander all over the world, the state of justice disappeared and the state of falsehood replaced it. Nothing remained in its right place. Thus, when Islam is absent from the arena, everything changes. From this state of affairs the incentives are drawn.

As for the objectives: They are the fighting against the false, defeating it and vanquishing it so that justice could prevail, homelands be retrieved and from its mosques would the voice of the *mu'azen* [caller to prayer] emerge declaring the establishment of the state of Islam, so that people and things would return each to their right places and Allah is our helper....

Article Ten

As the Islamic Resistance Movement paves its way, it will back the oppressed and support the wronged with all its might. It will spare no effort to bring about justice and defeat injustice, in word and deed, in this place and everywhere it can reach and have influence therein.

Article Eleven

The Islamic Resistance Movement believes that the land of Palestine is an Islamic *Waqf* [pious endowment] consecrated for future Moslem generations until Judgment Day. It, or any part of it, should not be squandered: it, or any part of it, should not be given up. Neither a single Arab country nor all Arab countries, neither any king or president, nor all the kings and presidents, neither any organization nor all of them, be they Palestinian or Arab, possess the right to do that. Palestine is an Islamic *Waqf* land consecrated for Moslem generations until Judgment Day. This being so, who could claim to have the right to represent Moslem generations till Judgment Day?

This is the law governing the land of Palestine in the Islamic Sharia (law) and the same goes for any land the Moslems have conquered by force, because during the times of (Islamic) conquests, the Moslems consecrated these lands to Moslem generations till the Day of Judgment.

It happened like this: When the leaders of the Islamic armies conquered Syria and Iraq, they sent to the Caliph of the Moslems, 'Umar bin al-Khatab, asking for his advice concerning the conquered land—whether they should divide it among the soldiers, or leave it for its owners, or what? After consultations and discussions between the Caliph of the Moslems, 'Umar bin al-Khatab and companions of the Prophet, Allah bless him and grant him salvation, it was decided that the land should be left with its owners who could benefit by its fruit. As for the real ownership of the land and the land itself, it should be consecrated for Moslem generations till Judgment Day. Those who are on the land, are there only to benefit from its fruit. This *Waqf* remains as long as earth and heaven remain. Any procedure in contradiction to Islamic Shari'a, where Palestine is concerned, is null and void....

Article Twelve

Nationalism, from the point of view of the Islamic Resistance Movement, is part of the religious creed. Nothing in nationalism is more significant or deeper than in the case when an enemy should tread Moslem land. Resisting and quelling the enemy become the individual duty of every Moslem, male or female. A woman can go out to fight the enemy without her husband's permission, and so does the slave: without his master's permission....

Article Thirteen

Initiatives, and so-called peaceful solutions and international conferences, are in contradiction to the principles of the Islamic Resistance Movement.... The Islamic Resistance Movement does not consider these conferences capable of realizing the demands, restoring the rights or doing justice to the oppressed. These conferences are only ways of setting the infidels in the land of the Moslems as arbitrators. When did the infidels do justice to the believers? "But the Jews will not be pleased with thee, neither the Christians, until thou follow their religion; say, The direction of Allah is the true direction. And verily if thou follow their desires, after the knowledge which hath been given thee, thou shalt find no patron or protector against Allah." (The Cow—verse 120).... There is no solution for the Palestinian question except through Jihad.

Article Fourteen

The question of the liberation of Palestine is bound to three circles: the Palestinian circle, the Arab circle and the Islamic circle. Each of these circles has its role in the struggle against Zionism. Each has its duties, and it is a horrible mistake and a sign of deep ignorance to overlook any of these circles. Palestine is an Islamic land which has the first of the two

Qiblas (direction to which Moslems turn in praying), the third of the holy (Islamic) sanctuaries, and the point of departure for Mohamed's midnight journey to the seven heavens (i.e. Jerusalem). "Praise be unto him who transported his servant by night, from the sacred temple of Mecca to the farther temple of Jerusalem, the circuit of which we have blessed, that we might show him some of our signs; for Allah is he who heareth, and seeth." (The Night-Journey—verse 1).

Article Fifteen

The day that enemies usurp part of Moslem land, Jihad becomes the individual duty of every Moslem. In face of the Jews' usurpation of Palestine, it is compulsory that the banner of Jihad be raised. To do this requires the diffusion of Islamic consciousness among the masses, both on the regional, Arab and Islamic levels....

Article Sixteen

It is necessary to follow Islamic orientation in educating the Islamic generations in our region by teaching the religious duties, comprehensive study of the Koran, the study of the Prophet's *Sunna* (his sayings and doings), and learning about Islamic history and heritage from their authentic sources.... Side by side with this, a comprehensive study of the enemy, his human and financial capabilities, learning about his points of weakness and strength, and getting to know the forces supporting and helping him, should also be included....

Articles Seventeen and Eighteen (see chapter 3)

Article Nineteen

Art has regulations and measures by which it can be determined whether it is Islamic or pre-Islamic (*Jahili*) art. The issues of Islamic liberation are in need of Islamic art that would take the spirit high, without raising one side of human nature above the other, but rather raise all of them harmoniously and in equilibrium....

Article Twenty

... In their Nazi treatment, the Jews made no exception for women or children. Their policy of striking fear in the heart is meant for all.... To counter these deeds, it is necessary that social mutual responsibility should prevail among the people. The enemy should be faced by the people as a single body which if one member of it should complain, the rest of the body would respond by feeling the same pains.

Article Twenty-One

Mutual social responsibility means extending assistance, financial or moral, to all those who are in need and joining in the execution of some of the work. Members of the Islamic Resistance Movement should consider the interests of the masses as their own personal interests....

Article Twenty-Two

For a long time, the enemies have been planning, skillfully and with precision, for the achievement of what they have attained. They took into consideration the causes affecting the current of events. They strived to amass great and substantive material wealth which they devoted to the realization of their dream. With their money, they took control of the world media, news agencies, the press, publishing houses, broadcasting stations, and others. With their money they stirred revolutions in various parts of the world with the purpose of achieving their interests and reaping the fruit therein....

The imperialistic forces in the Capitalist West and Communist East, support the enemy with all their might, in money and in men. These forces take turns in doing that. The day Islam appears, the forces of infidelity would unite to challenge it, for the infidels are of one nation.

> O true believers, contract not an intimate friendship with any besides yourselves: they will not fail to corrupt you. They wish for that which may cause you to perish: their hatred hath already appeared from out of their mouths; but what their breasts conceal is yet more inveterate. We have already shown you signs of their ill will towards you, if ye understand. (The Family of Imran—verse 118).

It is not in vain that the verse is ended with Allah's words "if ye understand."
....

SOURCE: http://www.yale.edu/lawweb/avalon/mideast/hamas.htm

CONTEXT AND ANALYSIS

Al-Haraka al-Muqawama al-Islamiya (the Islamic Resistance Movement, known by the acronym Hamas), was established in Gaza on December 14, 1987, during the Palestinian uprising, *Intifadha*, against Israel's occupation of the West Bank and Gaza Strip. The organization grew out of the Muslim Brotherhood's Palestinian branch, which Sa'id Ramadan, son-in-law of Hasan al-Banna, opened in Jerusalem in 1945. Until the outbreak of the *Intifadha*, the Palestinian Muslim Brotherhood did not actively resist the State of Israel. Nor did it position itself among Palestinians as a political alternative to the secular-oriented Palestine Liberation Organization (PLO). Rather, it focused on establishing educational institutions, bookstores, and libraries.

However, the scale and intensity of the *Intifadha* encouraged the Palestinian Muslim Brotherhood to attempt to take charge of the situation. By assuming an active role, it aimed to channel the rage of the young protesters toward the liberation of all Palestine and the creation of an Islamic state. The Brotherhood established Hamas as its armed wing, although it very quickly came to represent Brotherhood interests in Palestine as a whole. Like other grassroots Islamist movements, Hamas offers the Muslim community social services, schools, and health care, but it also openly maintains military wings that carry out attacks against Israel. The Hamas tactic offers to Palestinians a quasi-state and helps endear the population to Hamas, as well as providing a source of recruitment. Since its founding, Hamas has challenged PLO as the sole political force and legitimate representative of the Palestinian people. Consequently, the secular Palestinian leadership regards Hamas as its chief rival.

Hamas' chief founder and its principle theoretician was Shaykh Ahmad Yasin (1937–2004) who grew up in the period of the British Mandate. Paralyzed at the age of sixteen due to an accident, he turned to religion for solace. His passion for Islamic studies took him to Cairo where, influenced by the Muslim Brothers, he formed the belief that Palestine was "consecrated land"—a *waqf*. As Yasin came to understand, Palestine was God-given to all

Muslim generations, and no one had the right to take away any part of it. Muslims had an obligation to liberate Palestine from Zionist control.

Back in Gaza, Yasin worked as a teacher of Arabic and Islamic studies, gaining the reputation of being one of the strip's most respected preachers. In 1989, with the *Intifadha* in full swing, the Israelis arrested Yasin and sentenced him to prison. Released in 1997 as a part of a prisoner swap with Jordan, he reassumed his position of moral authority over the organization. He was killed in an Israeli attack in March 2004. But his ideas as regards the retaking of Palestine for Islam live on in the Hamas Charter, which was issued in 1988 soon after the *Intifadha* commenced. Although the author(s) of the charter remain unknown, the document bears the imprint of Yasin's thought and writing style.

In contrast to the PLO Charter, which is formulated in legal, civil, and nationalist terms, the Hamas Charter is ideological in nature, positing Islam as the chief marker of Palestinian identity. All of the articles in the Hamas charter are underpinned by notions of holiness, divinity, and religious purpose. Differently from the PLO charter, it does not allow amendment, because God's will is absolute. In keeping with Islamism's comprehensive vision, the Charter deals with all manner of issues, such as the status of women in society, the need for cross-sectional unity among Muslims (including the practical, political need for surrounding Arab states to open their borders to Hamas fighters), and support for the poor. As authors Mishal and Sela note, "The Hamas Charter is saturated with historic examples of the continued clash of Western and Islamic civilizations and the central role of Judaism and Zionism in the West's offensive against the Islamic world in modern times" (Mishal and Sela, 45). The Charter sometimes adopts language and symbols drawn from the repertoire of European anti-Semitism. In keeping with its ideological position of intransigence, Hamas does not recognize the legitimacy of the state of Israel, and its militant operations against the Jewish state include terrorist attacks against civilians.

FURTHER READINGS

Abu Amr, Ziad. *Islamic Fundamentalism in the West Bank and Gaza: The Muslim Brotherhood and Islamic Jihad* (Bloomington: Indiana University Press, 1994).

Hroub, Khaled. *Hamas: Political Thought and Practice* (Washington, DC: Institute for Palestine Studies, 2000).

Human Rights Watch. *Erased n a Moment: Suicide Bombing Attacks against Israeli Civilians* (New York: Human Rights Watch, 2002).

Levitt, Matthew. *Hamas: Politics, Charity, and Terrorism in the Service of Jihad* (New Haven, CT: Yale University Press, 2006).

Milton-Edwards, Beverley. *Islamic Politics in Palestine* (London: I. B. Tauris, 1999).

Mishal, Shaul, and Avraham Sela. *The Palestinian Hamas: Vision, Violence, and Coexistence* (New York: Columbia University Press, 2000).

Nusse, Andrea. *Muslim Palestine: The Ideology of Hamas* (London: Routledge Curzon, 2006).

Paz, Rueven. "The Development of Palestinian Islamist Groups," in Barry Rubin (ed.), *Revolutionaries and Reformers: Contemporary Islamist Movements in the Middle East* (Albany, NY: SUNY Press, 2003).

Tamimi, Azzam. *Hamas: A History* (Ithaca, NY: Olive Branch Press, 2007).

"A Ruling Pertaining to the Participation of Palestinians in Government Institutions in the Occupied Land"

- **Document:** *Fatwa* (juridical opinion) of the Syrian-Kurdish scholar Dr. Muhammad Sa'id Ramadan al-Buti, Chairman of the Department of Doctrines and Religions in the University of Damascus; on behalf of Israel's Islamic Movement; on the question of Palestinian Muslims participating in Israel's national elections. Translated by Marion Boulby.

- **Date:** 2000.

- **Where:** Damascus, Syria.

- **Significance:** Dr. Buti's *fatwa* points to the dilemma that faced members of the Islamic Movement in Israel: whether or not to participate in Israel's national elections. The controversy points to Islamism's ideological flexibility and practical bent.

DOCUMENT

In the name of God, the Compassionate, the Merciful

It is pertinent, before enunciating this ruling, to be reminded of the following:

Firstly: The Territory of Islam (*Dar al-Islam*) does not change into a territory of Infidelity (*Dar al-Kufr*) as a result of occupation or similar reasons, according to the opinion of the majority of legists [scholars]. The condition that needs to be realized for such a change to be possible does not exist in the occupied land of Palestine, according to the opinion of the Hanafi Gentlemen. It remains, therefore, a territory of Islam, according to the unanimity of Muslims.

Secondly: On the basis of this, Muslims are not permitted to vacate their territory of Islam, especially those citizens who enjoy the right of citizenship, and who own in it land and properties. This is to say that they must remain in it and work toward terminating occupation through all possible means. In answer to the question: In what manner should their stay be? Should it be the stay of peaceful citizens, who conform with the reality of occupation, accepting its rule, or should it be the stay of fighter warriors [who] chase the occupying enemy, the aggressor, out of the occupied land?

In answer to this question we say: It is not permissible that staying be a form of submission to the rule of occupation and its reality, but it should be a form of working toward terminating occupation through every possible means.

And to say "possible means" entails the point that needs to be scrutinized, and the meaning of which be recognized, in order that implementation will be congruent with the canonical legal ruling. The criterion of "possible means" is not confined to the Muslim people who live under the domination of occupation. It rather takes into consideration the means at the disposal of all Muslims, whether they are inside the land, or out of it. Abu Bakr Ibn al-'Arabi [12th c. jurisprudent of Maliki School] says, "When the Muslims are captives or down-trodden, assisting them is pertinent, and supporting them physically is an obligation, so that until we cease to have an eye that flickers, we have to go out to deliver them if our numbers warrant that, or we have to expend all our money to relieve them until not one dirham of that will remain with anyone." (1) I am not aware of any contradiction to this ruling of Ibn al-'Arabi. Based on this ruling, responsibility for failing to act on this obligation rests equally on both, those who languish under occupation, and on their brethren who are dipersed outside of its domination. Justification for procrastinating and waiting is also a legitimate matter in favor of both these parties, as long as the excuse is valid and as long as the capablities are not available.

Al-Mu'iz Ibn 'Abd al-Sallam enunciated the circumstances that justify this excuse, he said: "If routing [the enemy] did not materialize, fleeing is obligatory, because victory will elaspse while the infidels become gratified and the people of Islam subdued; staying has become a restricted evil in the fold of which there is no good." (2)

Issuing from this clear enunciation, we say:

When the Muslims who are out of the occupied land are in a position that does not enable them to resist occupation and support their brethren who suffer under its yoke in the inside, it is more appropriate [to say] that those who are under its domination and who move inside its grip are incapable all by themselves of supporting themselves and shaking the nightmare of occupation off their backs. That is why the license that applies to the Muslims on the outside would certainly apply more appropriately to their brethren who live in the inside.

However, what are the boundaries of the license which the Muslims in the occupied land can use and benefit from? The boundaries of the license is entailed in enduring the unavoidable least amount of harm that emanates from the reality of subordination and subjugation to the enemy and the occupier; and in the need to endeavor to achieve to the maximum extent their legitimate rights and their livelihood interests. The grounds on which all this rests is the principle which is quoted from the saying of God Almighty, "Except for the down-trodden ones among men, women and children, who cannot devise a plan nor are they able to direct their way."

This text, though it pertains to those who were not able to migrate from the territory of infidelity to the territory of Islam, yet the exclusion entails, according to the legists, a comprehensive principle [that is part] of the principles that are observed in all similar situations. Those down-trodden people in the occupied land have to study their conditions and their relationship with the enemy and the occupier, and the extent of material and moral assistance that can reach them from their brethren outside this land; if they find that the closest way for them to protect their rights and foster their interests, wholly or partially, is to participate in the official institutions which revolve around the state such as parliamentary councils, union establishments, administrative committees and the like, they are entitled— perhaps they are obligated—to impose their presence in them, to pursue achieving the optimum level of their rights which they should defend in any possible manner. And when, by refraining from involvement in these institutions, they face isolation that only increases their humiliation and exhaustion, and the loss of their interests and rights, then the known canonical rules may openly disallow this isolation, which may well be a source of tremendous comfort and pleasure for the occupying enemy.

Those who send them stinging criticism from the outside of the occupied land, and who urge them to resist instead of participating in these institutions, should know that the down-trodden who suffer from the nightmare of occupation in the inside, are not more deserving of

---

IN HISTORY

Hawa Barayev, Chechen "Black Widow"

Beginning in 1994, Russia waged a number of fierce campaigns against the Muslim break-away republic of Chechnya. For the Chechens, the conflict was the latest in an ongoing struggle to redeem their homeland from foreign rule and occupation. Quickly, the struggle took on an Islamist tone. On June 9, 2000, a Chechen woman named Hawa Barayev drove a truck laden with explosives into a Russian barracks at Alkhan-Kala, a large village that lies on the western outskirts of Grozni. After the dust settled, 27 Russian soldiers, many of them senior Special Forces officers, lay dead. Barayev was the first of the Chechen "Black Widows"—female suicide bombers whose husbands had been killed in the war. Fellow Chechen fighters commemorated her memory in the following way:

Allah legislated Jihad for the dignity of the *umma*, knowing that it is abhorrent to us. People today have neglected this great duty, and pursued what they love, thinking good lies in what they love, and failing to realize that good lies in that which Allah has legislated.

Allah has blessed us, here in Chechnya, by allowing us to fight unbelief— represented by the Russian army, and we ask Allah to strengthen and assist us. We praise Allah for allowing us to have scored victories over the enemy. Some of us have fulfilled their pledges; others are still waiting. Verily, Allah has fulfilled His promise to us, and granted us dignity through jihad. Our martyred brothers have written, with their blood, a history that we can be proud of, and their sacrifices only increase us in eagerness for our own martyrdom, so as to meet Allah, and be resurrected with the Prophet (peace and blessings be upon him), his companions and all the other prophets, martyrs, and righteous ones.

The *umma* has become used to hearing, through its history, about men who sacrifice their lives for the religion, but they are not familiar with women doing the same. The young woman who was—*inshaa-Allah*—martyred, Hawa Barayev, is one of the few women whose name will be recorded in history. Undoubtedly, she has set the most marvelous example by her sacrifice. The Russians may well await death from every quarter now, and their hearts may appropriately be filled with terror on account of women like her. Let every jealous one perish in his rage! Let every sluggish individual bury his head in the dirt! She has done what few have done. Every supporter of the truth should prepare to give the like of what she has given. The *umma* may well be proud that such a paragon has appeared in our midst. We are certain that an *umma* that contains people like her will never—by Allah's leave become devoid of good.

SOURCE: http://journal.maine.com/pdf/martyrdom.pdf

---

this taunting and blame than their brethren who do not extend any help to them from the outside.

And God is the Guardian of victory and design.

1. Ibn al-Arabi, *Ahkam al-Qur'an* [Rulings of the Qur'an] (2/876).
2. *Qawid al-Ahkam fi Masalah al-Anam* [The Bases of the Rulings in the Interest of the People], 1/95.

SOURCE: Dr. Muhammad Sa'id Ramadan al-Buti, *Fatwa on the Question of Palestinian Muslims Participating in Israel's National Elections*. Reprinted with permission of the translator, Marion Boulby.

CONTEXT AND ANALYSIS (CO-WRITTEN WITH MARION BOULBY)

While Hamas speaks for many Palestinians in Gaza and the Israeli administered West Bank, it has little popularity among the Arab citizens of Israel who number about one million—just under 20 percent of Israel's total population. Historically, Arab Israelis have been secular in their political outlook. Around 80 percent of them are Muslims; the rest divide almost equally between Christians and Druze. In contrast to the Arabs who fled Palestine in the course of the 1948-1949 Arab-Israeli War, these Arabs remained in their ancestral villages and towns. The Arabs of Israel enjoy political rights unmatched by many in the region. They are allowed to form political parties and to contest elections for seats in Israel's parliament (Knesset). Nevertheless, the Arabs of Israel are a relatively socially isolated, politically marginalized, and economically disadvantaged population, at least compared to Jewish Israelis. While many Jewish Israelis question the loyalty of the Arab population to the State of Israel, Arab Israelis point to the covert and overt forms of discrimination that are leveled against them at the hands of the Israeli state (for a balanced view on the Israeli Arabs see "Identity Crisis: Israel and its Arab Citizens," International Crisis Group).

Despite the secular political allegiances of many Arab Israelis, a popular Islamist stream has emerged in Israel that is separate from Hamas, although it shares broad ideological characteristics with the Muslim Brotherhood. The Islamic Movement was founded by Shaykh 'Abdullah Nimr Darwish in 1983. Darwish, a former Communist, was concerned with the need of the Muslim minority to reassert its Islamic identity against secularism and Israeli national identity. He also determined that the Muslims of Israel must not be quiescent but must take action, not only to become better Muslims but also to advance their rights in the Jewish state in the face of persecution and oppression. Reflecting on the unique position of the Muslim minority in Israel, Darwish decided that it should work within the legal parameters of the Israeli State. In 1989 the Islamic Movement contested municipal elections and swept to victory winning five mayoralties in Arab towns which have since evolved as Islamist enclaves characterized by the proliferation of mosques, banning of alcohol and western music and widespread wearing of conservative Islamic dress. Darwish believed the Islamic Movement should take participation a step further to the extent of running in Israel's 1996 national elections. Only thus, opined Darwish, would the Arab Muslims of Israel gain the rights that they deserved, and push forward pragmatically to eventual liberation. In support of his position, he pointed to the minority status of the Prophet and Companions in Mecca, where the Muslims, despite persecution, continued to struggle for Islam's implementation within the constraints of the existing system.

But not all in the Islamic Movement agreed with Darwish. The northern wing of the movement led by Shaykh Ra'id Salah, mayor of Umm al-Fahm, argued that national versus municipal participation "would be tantamount to recognizing Israel's legitimacy and require the movement to make partisan deals that risked compromising its moral authority" ("Identity Crisis: Israel and its Arab Citizens" p. 23). In support of their contention they received a juridical opinion (*fatwa*) from the Egyptian-Qatari Shaykh Yusuf al-Qaradawi who agreed that all forms of cooperation with an occupying enemy should be banned, for "preventing evil" supercedes any short term interest that might be gained by participating in an election.

Not to be outdone, Shaykh Abdullah Nimr Darwish and his supporters, chief among them Shaykh Ibrahim Sarsur, head of the southern wing and currently a Knesset member, received a countervailing legal opinion from Dr. Muhammad Sa'id Ramadan al-Buti, Chairman of the Department of Doctrines and Religions at the University of Damascus, which is reproduced above. Although not an Islamist, Dr. al-Buti agreed that it is not only admissible but necessary that Muslims participate in Israel's Knesset. Muslims, he says, must attain the best situation for themselves, while continuing to work toward ending the occupation by various means of Arab Muslim empowerment.

The use of al-Buti's *fatwa* not only points to the desire among Islamists to participate in a democratic forum such as the Knesset, it is also an indication of Islamism's potential for elasticity and pragmatism. Although the overwhelming majority of Islamist groups and movements refuse diplomatically to deal with Israel, significant elements within the Islamic Movement in Israel have adopted a realistic approach, saying that if political participation will improve the minority's situation, it should be condoned. Not every Islamist effort to recover lost Islamic space is grounded in violent jihad.

FURTHER READINGS

Aburaiya, Issam. "The 1996 Split of the Islamic Movement in Israel: Between the Holy Text and Israeli-Palestinian Context," *International Journal of Politics*, 17, no. 3 (Spring 2004), 439–55.

Amara, Muhammad Hasan. "The Nature of Islamic Fundamentalism in Israel," in Bruce Maddy-Weitzman and Efraim Inbar (eds.), *Religious Radicalism in the Greater Middle East* (London: Routledge, 1997), 155–70.

Christmann, Andreas. "Islamic Scholar and Religious Leader: A Portrait of Muhammad Sa'id Ramadan al-Buti," in J. Cooper, R. Nettler, and M. Mahmoud (eds.), *Islam and Modernity: Muslim Intellectuals Respond* (London: I. B. Tauris, 1998), 57–81.

International Crisis Group. "Identity Crisis: Israel and Its Arab Citizens," *Middle East Report*, 25 (March 4, 2004).

Tal, Nachman. "The Islamic Movement in Israel," *Strategic Assessments*, 2, no. 4 (February 2000). Online at: http://www.tau.ac.il/jcss/sa/v2n4p5.html.

9

GLOBAL JIHAD

The iconic portrait of Usama bin Laden on display in Jakarta, Indonesia, January 1, 2003. Since the terror attacks of 9/11, the Al Qaeda ideology of bin Laden and Ayman al-Zawahiri has galvanized Islamist radicalism around the world. Although many Al Qaeda-inspired groups, such as Indonesia's Jemaah Islamiyah, act locally, they espouse a utopian vision of global conquest. (AP photo/John Stanmeyer. Courtesy of AP Images.)

INTRODUCTION

Over the 1970s, 1980s, and into the 1990s, Islamist jihadis were concerned either with liberating lands lost to Islam (for instance, Palestine, Afghanistan, Bosnia, and Chechnya) or, more commonly, attacking state regimes in the Muslim world they considered corrupt and unworthy. Only after they had restored the political integrity of Dar al-Islam, the Islamists said, would they target the United States, Israel, and the West generally. Islamists of all kinds accepted Ayman al-Zawahiri's dictum that "the road to Jerusalem passes though Cairo." Their vision of Islam's rebirth took the form of concentric circles of Muslim power radiating outward from a core.

However, by the mid-1990s, these primarily local priorities began to change for some Islamists. Militant Islamists, who previously had targeted "apostate" governments and populations, transferred much of their odium to the "far away" enemies in the West. As a result, radical Islamist violence was now applied to world cities like New York, Madrid, London, and to international enclaves in Casablanca, Istanbul, Dhahran, and Amman. The reason for this shift in strategy was largely strategic. The failure of the savagely fought jihads in Egypt and Algeria to mobilize Muslim populations, prompted activists like Egypt's Ayman al-Zawahiri and Saudi Arabia's Usama bin Laden to think in terms of striking directly at the Great Powers of the West, whose harsh response, they calculated, would shake Muslims out of their complacency and reignite the jihad. By raising the stakes in this way, the leaders of Al Qaeda aimed to precipitate nothing less than a clash of civilizations between the West and Islam—a cosmic war between the forces of good and evil.

Among the first to answer the call to the new global jihad were Muslim fighters from around the world who in the 1980s had come to the rescue of Afghanistan. In Afghanistan, these men developed networks based on personal loyalty and adherence to a common cause. In the early 1990s many of these men returned to their home countries to fight the enemy at home. Others participated in the irredentist jihads in Bosnia, Kashmir, Chechnya, and the southern Philippines. Still others returned to Afghanistan with bin Laden in 1996, where they were trained in camps. Under the protection of the new, fundamentalist Taliban regime, bin Laden and his transnational cadre of jihadis planned to use Afghanistan as a base from which to mount raids against the West and its regional allies.

Although in 2002 Coalition forces succeeded in relegating Al Qaeda to the geographical margins of Afghanistan, bin Laden's goal of globalizing the jihad appears to have paid him dividends. In the years following the 9/11 attacks on the twin towers and the Pentagon, a second generation of jihadis has emerged that, if not directly controlled by Al Qaeda, is at least inspired by its ideology of confrontation on a global scale. Hailing from a variety of national backgrounds, these men join comrades in jihad operations around the world. They may target "apostate" Muslim regimes and populations or they may attack civilians and governments in the West, but always their prime target is the Western-dominated World Order.

A good example of this globalizing trend is the Salafist Group of Preaching and Combat (GSPC), an Algeria-based group that claims to be the local franchise operation for Al Qaeda. Long categorized as part of a strictly domestic insurgency against Algeria's military government, since 2004 the GSPC has carried out a number of terrorist attacks in the wider North African region, declared its intention to attack Western targets, sent a squad of jihadis to Iraq, and has declared solidarity with Islamists in the Palestinian territories, Iraq, Somalia, and Chechnya. "Experts believe these actions suggest widening ambitions within the group's leadership, now pursuing a more global, sophisticated and better-financed direction" (http://www.cfr.org/publication/12717/#3Andrew Hansen). Below we trace the development of the global jihad from the early *fatwas* of bin Laden to the more recent declarations of the Jordanian terrorist Abu Mu'sab Zarqawi in Iraq.

Declaration of Jihad

- *Document:* The following are excerpts of a *fatwa*, or juridical opinion, by Usama bin Laden first published in *Al Quds Al Arabi*, a London-based newspaper. Dubbed the "Ladenese Epistle," the *fatwa's* full title is "Declaration of War against the Americans Occupying the Land of the Two Holy Places."
- *Date:* Sometime between August and October, 1996.
- *Where:* Afghanistan.
- *Significance:* This "fatwa" did much to alert the people of Western countries to the existence of Usama bin Laden. In the document, bin Laden continues his ongoing tirade against the House of Saud, but now broadens his angry critique of the situation in Arabia to include the peninsula's "occupation" by American "crusader" forces. In addition, bin Laden highlights the suffering of Muslims in other countries. The document illustrates bin Laden's move toward a global agenda.

DOCUMENT

It should not be hidden from you that the people of Islam had suffered from aggression, iniquity and injustice imposed on them by the Zionist-Crusaders alliance and their collaborators; to the extent that the Muslims' blood became the cheapest and their wealth as loot in the hands of the enemies. Their blood was spilled in Palestine and Iraq. The horrifying pictures of the massacre of Qana, in Lebanon are still fresh in our memory. Massacres in Tajikistan, Burma, Kashmir, Assam, Philippine, Fatani, Ogaden, Somalia, Eritrea, Chechnya and in Bosnia-Herzegovina took place, massacres that send shivers in the body and shake the conscience. All of this and the world watch[ed] and hear[d], and not only didn't respond to these atrocities, but also with a clear conspiracy between the USA and its allies and under the cover of the iniquitous United Nations, the dispossessed people were even prevented from obtaining arms to defend themselves.

The people of Islam awakened and realized that they are the main target for the aggression of the Zionist-Crusaders alliance. All false claims and propaganda about "Human

Rights" were hammered down and exposed by the massacres that took place against the Muslims in every part of the world.

The latest and the greatest of these aggressions, incurred by the Muslims since the death of the Prophet (ALLAH'S BLESSING AND SALUTATIONS ON HIM) is the occupation of the land of the two Holy Places—the foundation of the house of Islam, the place of the revelation, the source of the message and the place of the noble Ka'ba, the Qibla [direction of prayer] of all Muslims—by the armies of the American Crusaders and their allies. (We bemoan this and can only say: "No power and power acquiring except through Allah.")

Under the present circumstances, and under the banner of the blessed awakening which is sweeping the world in general and the Islamic world in particular, I meet with you today. And after a long absence, imposed on the scholars ('ulama) and callers (da'is) of Islam by the iniquitous crusaders movement under the leadership of the USA; who fears that they, the scholars and callers of Islam, will instigate the umma [world-wide community] of Islam against its enemies as their ancestor scholars—may Allah be pleased with them—like Ibn Taymiyya and al-'Izz Ibn 'Abd al-Salam did. And therefore the Zionist-Crusader alliance resorted to killing and arresting the truthful 'ulama and the working da'is (We are not praising or sanctifying them; Allah sanctify whom He pleaseth). They killed the mujahid Shaykh 'Abdullah 'Azzam, and they arrested the mujahid Shaykh Ahmad Yasin and the mujahid Shaykh 'Umar 'Abd al-Rahman (in America).

By orders from the USA they also arrested a large number of scholars, da'is and young people—in the land of the two Holy Places—among them the prominent Shaykh Salman Al-'Awda and Shaykh Safar Al-Hawali and their brothers; (We bemoan this and can only say: "No power and power acquiring except through Allah"). We, me and my group, have suffered some of this injustice ourselves; we have been prevented from addressing the Muslims. We have been pursued in Pakistan, Sudan and Afghanistan, hence this long absence on my part. But by the Grace of Allah, a safe base is now available in the high Hindu Kush Mountains in Khurasan; where—by the Grace of Allah—the largest infidel military force of the world was destroyed [i.e. the Soviets]. And the myth of the super power was withered in front of the Mujahidin cries of Allahu Akbar (God is greater). Today we work from the same mountains to lift the iniquity that had been imposed on the umma by the Zionist-Crusader alliance, particularly after they have occupied the blessed land around Jerusalem, route of the journey of the Prophet (ALLAH'S BLESSING AND SALUTATIONS ON HIM) and the land of the two Holy Places. We ask Allah to bestow us with victory, He is our Patron and He is the Most Capable.

From here, today we begin the work, talking and discussing the ways of correcting what had happened to the Islamic world in general, and the Land of the two Holy Places in particular. We wish to study the means that we could follow to return the situation to its normal path. And to return to the people their own rights, particularly after the large damages and the great aggression on the life and the religion of the people. An injustice that had affected every section and group of the people; the civilians, military and security men, government officials and merchants, the young and the old people as well as schools and university students. Hundreds of thousands of the unemployed graduates, who became the widest section of the society, were also affected.

Injustice had affected the people of the industry and agriculture. It affected the people of the rural and urban areas. And almost everybody complains about something. The situation at the land of the two Holy places became like a huge volcano at the verge of eruption that would destroy the Kufr [disbelief] and the corruption and its sources. The explosion at Riyadh and Al-Khobar is a warning of this volcanic eruption emerging as a result of the severe oppression, suffering, excessive iniquity, humiliation and poverty.

People are fully concerned about their every day livings; everybody talks about the deterioration of the economy, inflation, ever increasing debts and jails full of prisoners. Government employees with limited income talk about debts of tens of thousands and hundreds of thousands of Saudi Riyals. They complain that the value of the Riyal is greatly and continuously deteriorating among most of the main currencies. Great merchants and contractors speak about hundreds and thousands of million Riyals owed to them by the government. More than three hundred forty billions of Riyal owed by the government to the people in addition to the daily accumulated interest, let alone the foreign debt. People wonder whether we are the largest oil exporting country?! They even believe that this situation is a curse put on them by Allah for not objecting to the oppressive and illegitimate behavior and measures of the ruling regime: Ignoring the divine Shari'a law; depriving people of their legitimate rights; allowing the American to occupy the land of the two Holy Places; imprisonment, unjustly, of the sincere scholars. The honorable *'ulama* and scholars as well as merchants, economists and eminent people of the country were all alerted by this disastrous situation.

Quick efforts were made by each group to contain and to correct the situation. All agreed that the country is heading toward a great catastrophe, the depth of which is not known except by Allah. One big merchant commented: "the king is leading the state into 'sixty-six' folded disaster," (We bemoan this and can only say: "No power and power acquiring except through Allah"). Numerous princes share with the people their feelings, privately expressing their concerns and objecting to the corruption, repression and the intimidation taking place in the country. But the competition between influential princes for personal gains and interest had destroyed the country. Through its course of actions the regime has torn off its legitimacy:

(1) Suspension of the Islamic Shari'a law and exchanging it with manmade civil law. The regime entered into a bloody confrontation with the truthful *'ulama* and the righteous youths (we sanctify nobody; Allah sanctify whom He pleaseth).

(2) The inability of the regime to protect the country, and allowing the enemy of the *umma*—the American crusader forces—to occupy the land for the longest of years. The crusader forces became the main cause of our disastrous condition, particularly in the economical aspect of it due to the unjustified heavy spending on these forces. As a result of the policy imposed on the country, especially in the field of oil industry where production is restricted or expanded and prices are fixed to suit the American economy ignoring the economy of the country. Expensive deals were imposed on the country to purchase arms. People asking what is the justification for the very existence of the regime then?

SOURCE: http://www.pbs.org/newshour/terrorism/international/fatwa_1996.html

Jihad against Jews and Crusaders

- **Document:** Usama bin Laden's World Islamic Front Statement, published in *al-Quds al-Arabi* [Arab Jerusalem]. Translation slightly modified by the editor of this volume.
- **Date:** 23 February 1998.
- **Where:** Afghanistan.
- **Significance:** The declaration condemns the U.S. policies in the Middle East and calls on Muslims to "kill Americans and their allies." Citing juridical sources, he argues that such attacks are incumbent on individual Muslims.

DOCUMENT

Shaykh Usama Bin-Muhammad Bin-Laden
Ayman al-Zawahiri, amir of the Jihad Group in Egypt
Abu-Yasir Rifa'i Ahmad Taha, Egyptian Islamic Group
Shaykh Mir Hamzah, secretary of the Jamiat-ul-Ulama-e-Pakistan
Fazlur Rahman, amir of the Jihad Movement in Bangladesh

Praise be to Allah, who revealed the Book, controls the clouds, defeats factionalism, and says in His Book: "But when the forbidden months are past, then fight and slay the pagans wherever ye find them, seize them, beleaguer them, and lie in wait for them in every stratagem (of war)" [Qur'an 9:5]; and peace be upon our Prophet, Muhammad Bin 'Abdallah, who said: "I have been sent with the sword between my hands to ensure that no one but Allah is worshipped, Allah who put my livelihood under the shadow of my spear and who inflicts humiliation and scorn on those who disobey my orders" [from the hadith collection of Ahmad Ibn Hanbal].

The Arabian Peninsula has never—since Allah made it flat, created its desert, and encircled it with seas—been stormed by any forces like the crusader armies spreading in it like locusts, eating its riches and wiping out its plantations. All this is happening at a time in which nations are attacking Muslims like people fighting over a plate of food. In the light of the grave situation and the lack of support, we and you are obliged to discuss current events, and we should all agree on how to settle the matter.

No one argues today about three facts that are known to everyone; we will list them, in order to remind everyone:

First, for over seven years the United States has been occupying the lands of Islam in the holiest of places, the Arabian Peninsula, plundering its riches, dictating to its rulers, humiliating its people, terrorizing its neighbors, and turning its bases in the Peninsula into a spearhead through which to fight the neighboring Muslim peoples.

If some people have in the past argued about the fact of the occupation, all the people of the Peninsula have now acknowledged it. The best proof of this is the Americans' continuing aggression against the Iraqi people using the Peninsula as a staging post, even though all its rulers are against their territories being used to that end, but they are helpless.

Second, despite the great devastation inflicted on the Iraqi people by the crusader-Zionist alliance, and despite the huge number of those killed, which has exceeded 1 million … despite all this, the Americans are once again trying to repeat the horrific massacres, as though they are not content with the protracted blockade imposed after the ferocious war or the fragmentation and devastation.

So here they come to annihilate what is left of this people and to humiliate their Muslim neighbors.

Third, if the Americans' aims behind these wars are religious and economic, the aim is also to serve the Jews' petty state and divert attention from its occupation of Jerusalem and murder of Muslims there. The best proof of this is their eagerness to destroy Iraq, the strongest neighboring Arab state, and their endeavor to fragment all the states of the region such as Iraq, Saudi Arabia, Egypt, and Sudan into paper statelets and through their disunion and weakness to guarantee Israel's survival and the continuation of the brutal crusade occupation of the Peninsula. All these crimes and sins committed by the Americans are a clear declaration of war on Allah, his messenger, and Muslims. And *ulama* have throughout Islamic history unanimously agreed that the jihad is an individual duty if the enemy destroys the Muslim countries. This was revealed by Imam Bin-Qadama in "Al- Mughni" (*The Resource*), Imam al-Kisa'i in "Al-Bada'i (*The Marvels*)," al-Qurtubi in his Qur'an Interpretation, and the Shaykh of Islam [i.e., Ibn Taymiyya] in his *fatwas*, where he said: "As for the fighting to repulse [an enemy], it is aimed at defending sanctity and religion, and it is a duty as agreed [by the *ulama*]. Nothing is more sacred than belief except repulsing an enemy who is attacking religion and life."

On that basis, and in compliance with Allah's order, we issue the following fatwa to all Muslims:

The ruling to kill the Americans and their allies—civilians and military—is an individual duty for every Muslim who can do it in any country in which it is possible to do it, in order to liberate the al-Aqsa Mosque [in Jerusalem] and the holy mosque [in Mecca] from their grip, and in order for their armies to move out of all the lands of Islam, defeated and unable to threaten any Muslim. This is in accordance with the words of Almighty Allah, "and fight the pagans all together as they fight you all together" [Qur'an 2:193], and "fight them until there is no more tumult or oppression, and there prevail justice and faith in Allah" [Qur'an 8:39].

This is in addition to the words of Almighty Allah: "And why should ye not fight in the cause of Allah and of those who, being weak, are ill-treated (and oppressed)?—women and children, whose cry is: 'Our Lord, rescue us from this town, whose people are oppressors; and raise for us from thee one who will help!'" [Qur'an 4:75].

We—with Allah's help—call on every Muslim who believes in Allah and wishes to be rewarded to comply with Allah's order to kill the Americans and plunder their money wherever and whenever they find it. We also call on Muslim ulema, leaders, youths, and soldiers to launch the raid on Satan's U.S. troops and the devil's supporters allying with them, and to displace those who are behind them so that they may learn a lesson.

Almighty Allah said: "O ye who believe, give your response to Allah and His Apostle, when He calleth you to that which will give you life. And know that Allah cometh between a man and his heart, and that it is He to whom ye shall all be gathered" [Qur'an 8:24].

Almighty Allah also says: "O ye who believe, what is the matter with you, that when ye are asked to go forth in the cause of Allah, ye cling so heavily to the earth! Do ye prefer the life of this world to the hereafter? But little is the comfort of this life, as compared with the hereafter. Unless ye go forth, He will punish you with a grievous penalty, and put others in your place; but Him ye would not harm in the least. For Allah hath power over all things" [Qur'an 9:38–39].

Almighty Allah also says: "So lose no heart, nor fall into despair. For ye must gain mastery if ye are true in faith" [Qur'an 3:139].

SOURCE: http://www.fas.org/irp/world/para/docs/980223-fatwa.htm

---

IN HISTORY

Sulayman Abu Ghaith: "Why We Fight the U.S."

Sulayman Abu Ghaith, an Al Qaeda spokesman of Kuwaiti origins, posted a three-part article on the Internet in June 2002, "In the Shadow of the Lances," in which he condemned America for its "tyranny" and made the case for the domination of the world by Islam. Here are excerpts from that article:

Why is the world surprised?! Why were millions of people astounded by what happened to America on September 11? Did the world think that anything else would happen? That something less than this would happen?

What happened to America is something natural, an expected event for a country that uses terror, arrogant policy, and suppression against the nations and the peoples, and imposes a single method, thought, and way of life, as if the people of the entire world are clerks in its government offices and employed by its commercial companies and institutions.

Anyone who was surprised and did not expect [the events of September 11] did not [understand] the nature of man, and the effects of oppression and tyranny on man's emotions and feelings. They thought that oppression begets surrender, that repression begets silence, that tyranny only leaves humiliation. Perhaps they also thought that this [oppressive] atmosphere is sufficient to kill man's virility, shatter his will, and uproot his honor. These people erred twice: once when they ignored [the consequences of] treating man with contempt, and again when they were unaware of man's ability to triumph.

How can he possibly [accept humiliation and inferiority] when he knows that his nation was created to stand at the center of leadership, at the center of hegemony and rule, at the center of ability and sacrifice. How can [he] possibly [accept humiliation and inferiority] when he knows that the [divine] rule is that the entire earth must be subject to the religion of Allah—not to the East, not to the West—to no ideology and to no path except for the path of Allah?

SOURCE: MEMRI, Special Dispatch Series, no. 388. Available at http://memri.org/bin/opener.cgi?Page=archives&ID=SP38802

CONTEXT AND ANALYSIS

In the summer of 1996, Usama bin Laden left Sudan [see Chapter 7] and returned to Afghanistan where he shored up his Al Qaeda organization. In August he issued a self-declared *fatwa* (juridical opinion) called "Declaration of Jihad against the Americans Occupying the Land of the Two Holy Places," an eleven-page tract full of references to medieval Hanbali jurists such as Ibn Taymiyya. In the document, bin Laden draws attention to the plight of Muslims around the world, including the April 18, 1996 killing of 106 civilians at Qana, Lebanon, by an Israeli shell in the course of fighting between Israel and the Shi'i Islamist organization Hizbullah. He lambastes the sanctions regime imposed on Saddam Husayn's Iraq by "the crusader-zionist alliance," which caused great numbers of Iraqi civilians to die. He castigates the House of Saud for mismanaging the economy, suspending the Shari'a in favor of "man-made law," and especially for allowing the United States to station troops on Saudi soil following the 1990–1991 Gulf War, which for him is an illegal occupation of infidel troops. He writes that Muslim anger is mounting over these and other injustices, as is evident from the June 1996 bombing of Khobar Towers near Dhahran, which killed 19 American servicemen. (Although bin Laden approves of this bombing, it appears that he was innocent of it; members of a Saudi-Shi'i group were later charged with the crime.) In February 1998 bin Laden composed the founding document of "World Islamic Front against Jews and Crusaders," a spinoff of Al Qaeda, which was signed by Ayman al-Zawahiri, Abu-Yasir Rifa'i Ahmad Taha of Egypt's Islamic Group (al-Jama'a al-Islamiyya), and leaders of two South Asian Islamist organizations.

This short document draws attention to the "Zionist-Crusader" occupation of the Arabian Peninsula and demands that Muslims respond vociferously to it.

In the document's criticism of the Saudi Royal family, bin Laden had at his disposal the various articulations of anathema that had earlier been developed by Sayyid Qutb and the extremist organizations in Egypt. Precedents for rebuke were also available in the very Wahhabi tradition in which he had been raised. In the 1920s the Ikhwan, the Bedouin forces that had spearheaded the Saudi takeover of the Hijaz, revolted against 'Abd al-'Aziz Ibn Saud for, among other things, allowing the Shi'is of Hasa to persist in their "disbelief." Yet while bin Laden was willing in the tradition of Wahhabi dissent severely to reprimand the ruling house, he chooses in these documents to focus his rage on the American power that he saw lurking behind the throne. In so doing, he reversed the order theorized by other Islamist groups, which advocated as a first step the eradication of the perceived corruption at home. According to this standard view, the Western "other" should be engaged only once the Muslim world had been strengthened by the creation of a true, transnational Islamic state. Bin Laden, on the other hand desired global confrontation sooner, rather than later. This is the new twist. Behind this stance we may detect the influence of bin Laden's lieutenant Ayman al-Zawahiri.

Like 'Abdullah 'Azzam and 'Abd al-Salam Faraj (author of *The Neglected Duty*), Bin Laden contends that jihad is an individual duty (*fard 'ayn*), which in the context of infidel occupation and invasion, must target "Americans and their allies … in any country in which it is possible to do it." In support of this contention he cites the unanimous opinion among 'ulama of every age.

Bin Laden's statements provided the doctrinal underpinnings of the violence that followed. On August 7, 1998, two explosions simultaneously destroyed the U.S. embassies in Nairobi, Kenya, and Dar-es-Salaam, Tanzania. On October 12, 2000, Al Qaeda operatives attacked the USS *Cole* at Aden, Yemen. Al Qaeda organized other attacks on Western targets, but none matched the scale and ferocity of the operation mounted against the World Trade Center and Pentagon on September 11, 2001, which killed close to 3,000 people. In mounting their attack, the hijackers sought to underscore the same point that Qutb and other radical Islamists had made previously—that the West and its regional surrogates constituted a conceptual realm of irreligion and vice that had to be resisted in the name of God. Taking this point to the extreme, bin Laden and his operatives defined the attacks as the ultimate expression of jihad, designed to have a searing effect of the consciousness of a global television audience.

Knights under the Prophet's Banner

- **Document:** Selections from Ayman al-Zawahiri's book *Fursan Taht Rayah al-Nabi* (*Knights under the Prophet's Banner*), published in the London-based Saudi newspaper *Al-Sharq Al-Awsat*.
- **Date:** Unknown; written probably at some point between September 2000 and December 2001.
- **Where:** Unknown; probably the tribal lands of western Pakistan.
- **Significance:** The Egyptian Ayman al-Zawahiri (b. 1951) is Al Qaeda's chief theorist. In this passage he clearly articulates Al Qaeda's goal of global jihad against the West and its allies in the Muslim world.

DOCUMENT

Emerging Phenomena

Any neutral observer could discern a number of phenomena in our Islamic world in general and Egypt in particular:

A. The universality of the battle:

The western forces that are hostile to Islam have clearly identified their enemy. They refer to it as Islamic fundamentalism. They are joined in this by their old enemy, Russia. They have adopted a number of tools to fight Islam, including:

1. The United Nations.
2. The friendly rulers of the Muslim peoples.
3. The multinational corporations.
4. The international communications and data exchange systems.
5. The international news agencies and satellite media channels.
6. The international relief agencies, which are being used as a cover for espionage, proselytizing, coup planning, and the transfer of weapons.

In the face of this alliance, a fundamentalist coalition is taking shape. It is made up of the jihad movements in the various lands of Islam as well as the two countries that have been liberated in the name of jihad for the sake of God (Afghanistan and Chechnya).

If the coalition is still at an early stage, its growth is increasingly and steadily accelerating.

It represents a growing power that is rallying under the banner of jihad for the sake of God and operating outside the scope of the new world order. It is free of the servitude for the dominating western empire. It promises destruction and ruin fort the new Crusades against the lands of Islam. It is ready for revenge against the heads of the world's gathering of infidels, the United States, Russia, and Israel. It is anxious to seek retribution for the blood of the martyrs, the grief of the mothers, the deprivation of the orphans, the suffering of the detainees, and the sores of the tortured people throughout the land of Islam, from Eastern Turkistan to Andalusia [Islamic state in Spain].

This age is witnessing a new phenomenon that continues to gain ground. It is the phenomenon of the *mujahid* youths who have abandoned their families, country, wealth, studies, and jobs in search of jihad arenas for the sake of God.

...

Small Groups Could Frighten the Americans

Through this jihad the stances of the rulers, their henchmen of *'ulama* of the sultan [reference to pro-government clerics], writers, and judges, and the security agencies will be exposed. By so doing, the Islamic movement will prove their treason before the masses of the Muslim nation and demonstrate that the reason for their treason is a flaw in their faith. They have allied themselves with the enemies of God against His supporters and antagonized the *mujahidin*, because of their Islam and jihad, in favor of the Jewish and Christian enemies of the nation. They have committed a violation of monotheism by supporting the infidels against the Muslims.

Tracking down the Americans and the Jews is not impossible. Killing them with a single bullet, a stab, or a device made up of a popular mix of explosives or hitting them with an iron rod is not impossible. Burning down their property with Molotov cocktails is not difficult. With the available means, small groups could prove to be a frightening horror for the Americans and the Jews.

....

The jihad movement must adopt its plan on the basis of controlling a piece of land in the heart of the Islamic world on which it could establish and protect the state of Islam and launch its battle to restore the rational caliphate based on the traditions of the Prophet.

....

Moving the Battle to the Enemy

The Islamic movement and its jihad vanguards, and actually the entire Islamic nation, must involve the major criminals—the United States, Russia, and Israel—in the battle and do not let them run the battle between the jihad movement and our governments in safety. They must pay the price, and pay dearly for that matter.

The masters in Washington and Tel Aviv are using the regimes to protect their interests and to fight the battle against the Muslims on their behalf. If the shrapnel from the battle reach their homes and bodies, they will trade accusations with their agents about who is responsible for this. In that case, they will face one of two bitter choices: either personally wage the battle against the Muslims, which means that the battle will turn into clear-cut jihad against infidels, or they reconsider their plans after acknowledging the failure of the brute and violent confrontation against Muslims.

Therefore, we must move the battle to the enemy's grounds to burn the hands of those who ignite fire in our countries.

The struggle for the establishment of the Muslim state cannot be launched as a regional struggle:

It is clear from the above that the Jewish-Crusade alliance, led by the United States, will not allow any Muslim force to reach power in any of the Islamic countries. It will mobilize all of its power to hit it and remove it from power. Toward that end, it will open a battle-front against it that includes the entire world. It will impose sanctions on whoever helps it, if it does not declare war against them altogether. Therefore, to adjust to this new reality we must prepare ourselves for a battle that is not confined to a single region, one that includes the apostate domestic enemy and the Jewish-Crusade external enemy.

The struggle against the external enemy cannot be postponed:

It is clear from the above that the Jewish-Crusade alliance will not give us time to defeat the domestic enemy then declare war against it thereafter. The Americans, the Jews, and their allies are present now with their forces, as we explained before.

Unity before the single enemy:

The jihad movement must realize that half the road to victory is attained through its unity, rise above trivial matters, gratitude, and glorification of the interests of Islam above personal whims.

The importance of the unity of the *mujahid* Islamic movement is perhaps clear now more than any time before. The movement must seek this unity as soon as possible if it is serious in its quest for victory.

Rallying around and supporting the struggling countries:

Backing and supporting Afghanistan and Chechnya and defending them with the heart, the hand, and the word represent a current duty, for these are the assets of Islam in this age. The Jewish-Crusade campaign is united to crush them. Therefore, we must not be content with safeguarding them only. We must seek to move the battlefront to the heart of the Islamic world, which represents the true arena of the battle and the theatre of the major battles in defense of Islam.

In this regard, these two steadfast castles may not help us much because of many circumstances, the tremendous pressure, and the apparent weakness. Therefore, we must solve this problem ourselves without exposing them to pressure and strikes. This could pose a dilemma for the jihad movement, but it is not impossible to handle. It may be difficult, but it is possible, God willing. "And whosoever keepeth his duty to Allah, Allah will appoint a way out for him." [Koranic verse]

Choosing the Targets and Concentrating on the Martyrdom Operations

Changing the method of strikes:

The *mujahid* Islamic movement must escalate its methods of strikes and tools of resisting the enemies to keep up with the tremendous increase in the number of its enemies, the quality of their weapons, their destructive powers, their disregard for all taboos, and disrespect for the customs of wars and conflicts. In this regard, we concentrate on the following:

1. The need to inflict the maximum casualties against the opponent, for this is the language understood by the west, no matter how much time and effort such operations take.

2. The need to concentrate on the method of martyrdom operations as the most successful way of inflicting damage against the opponent and the least costly to the *mujahidin* in terms of casualties.

3. The targets as well as the type and method of weapons used must be chosen to have an impact on the structure of the enemy and deter it enough to stop its brutality, arrogance, and disregard for all taboos and customs. It must restore the struggle to its real size.

4. To reemphasize what we have already explained, we reiterate that focusing on the domestic enemy alone will not be feasible at this stage.

The battle is for every Muslim:

An important point that must be underlined is that this battle, which we must wage to defend our creed, Muslim nation, sanctities, honor, values, wealth, and power, is a battle facing every Muslim, young or old. It is a battle that is broad enough to affect every one of us at home, work, in his children, or dignity.

In order for the masses to move, they need the following:

1. A leadership that they could trust, follow, and understand.
2. A clear enemy to strike at.
3. The shackles of fear and the impediments of weakness in the souls must be broken.

These needs demonstrate to us the serious effects of the so-called initiative to end the violence and similar calls that seek to distort the image of the leadership and take the nation back to the prison of weakness and fear.

To illustrate this danger, let us ask ourselves this question: what will we tell the future generations about our achievements?

Are we going to tell them that we carried arms against our enemies then dropped them and asked them to accept our surrender?

What jihad value could the future generation benefit from such conduct?

We must get our message across to the masses of the nation and break the media siege imposed on the jihad movement. This is an independent battle that we must launch side by side with the military battle.

Liberating the Muslim nation, confronting the enemies of Islam, and launching jihad against them require a Muslim authority, established on a Muslim land that raises the banner of jihad and rallies the Muslims around it. Without achieving this goal our nations will mean nothing more than mere and repeated disturbances that will not lead to the aspired goal, which is the restoration of the caliphate and the dismissal of the invaders from the land of Islam.

This goal must remain the basic objective of the Islamic jihad movement, regardless of the sacrifices and the time involved.

SOURCE: Al-Sharq al-Awsat (in Arabic), London, December 12, 2001. Translated by Foreign Broadcast Information Service, Document Number: FIBIS-NES-2001-1212. Online at: http://faculty.msb.edu/murphydd/ibd/MiddleEast-Islam/Zawahiri's%202001%20book%20extracts.htm

CONTEXT AND ANALYSIS

No Islamist ideologue is as important as Ayman al-Zawahiri (b. 1951) in overturning the logic of struggle against the "near enemy" (the regimes that held power in the Muslim world), in favor of an immediate war against the "far enemy" (the United states, Israel, Russia, and the West in general). Zawahiri grew up in Maadi, a suburb of Cairo notable for the Anglophile ways of its Egyptian inhabitants and large community of Western expatriates. Zawahiri, however, stood aloof from Maadi's liberal social scene. He was the product of a religiously conservative Muslim home that enjoyed considerable status in traditional social circles. His father's uncle, Rabi'a al-Zawahiri, was the grand imam of Cairo's al-Azhar University, and his maternal grandfather had served as the president of Cairo University and founded King Saud University, in Riyadh, Saudi Arabia.

Ayman al-Zawahiri was a diligent student determined to follow his father into the medical profession. But he was also attracted to Egypt's Islamist movement, and when the

IN HISTORY

Sayyid Qutb's Influence on Ayman al-Zawahiri

"The martyr Sayyid Qutb was one of the most important figures in terms of his impact on Zawahiri. Qutb's writing was important in shaping Zawahiri's principles. His book *Fi Dilal al-Qur'an* [meaning *Under the Umbrella of the Koran*] formed the framework for Zawahiri's ideology and his approach to effecting change.... Zawahiri's love for Qutb is clear in that he quotes him in almost everything he publishes.

In his book *Knights under the Banner of the Prophet*, Zawahiri wrote:

Sayyid Qutb underscored the importance of monotheism in Islam, and that the battle between it and its enemies is at core an ideological difference over the issue of the oneness of God. It is the issue of who has the power: God and his *shari'a* ... or man-made, materialistic laws.

Zawahiri expresses his admiration for Qutb, saying:

Although the Qutb group was oppressed and tortured by Nasser's regime, the group's influence on young Muslims was paramount. Qutb's message was and still is to believe in the oneness of God and the supremacy of the divine path. The message fanned the fire of Islamic revolution against the enemies of Islam at home and abroad. The chapters of this revolution are renewing one day after another."

Source: Montasser al-Zayyat, *The Road to Al-Qaeda: The Story of Bin Laden's Right-Hand Man*, translated by Ahmed Fekry, edited by Sara Nimis (London: Pluto Press, 2004), 24–25.

'Abd al-Nasser regime hanged Sayyid Qutb in 1966 the teenaged al-Zawahiri responded by forming a small, clandestine Islamist group, the Jihad Organization (*Tanzim al-Jihad*), which eked out a meagre, shadowy existence throughout the 1970s. In 1980, after graduating from medical school, al-Zawahiri made two trips to Afghanistan with the Red Crescent Society, the Islamic correlate of the Red Cross, to provide medical aid to the *Mujahidin* who were fighting the Soviets. On returning to Egypt, he was caught up in the whirlwind of arrests that followed President Anwar al-Sadat's assassination at the hands of his colleagues. Although not directly involved in the killing, his membership in the Jihad Organization earned him a three-year prison sentence during which he was subjected to torture, an experience that hardened his attitude toward the Egyptian regime and its U.S. backers.

After he was released in 1985, al-Zawahiri left Egypt for Saudi Arabia and then Afghanistan where he rebuilt the severely weakened Jihad Organization. His goal remained the toppling of Egypt's pro-Western government. During this period he wrote a book called *Sixty Years of the Muslim Brothers Bitter Harvest*, in which he criticized the Brotherhood's gradualist approach to change. He also met Usama bin Laden and gained influence over him at the expense of bin Laden's first mentor, 'Abdullah 'Azzam. In the cementing of this relationship, Egyptian Qutbism merged with strict Saudi Salafism. In 1992, Zawahiri followed bin Laden to Sudan and from there planned attacks against the Egyptian regime. But by 1996 the local jihads in Egypt, Algeria, and Bosnia, which al-Zawahiri had hoped would change the political landscape, had lost ground. In addition, there was the expanded U.S. presence in the region following the defeat of Saddam Husayn in the Gulf War of 1990–1991. In response to these reversals of fortune al-Zawahiri, in agreement with bin Laden, began to concoct the strategy that would lead to 9/11. Instead of striking at the "near enemy," al-Zawahiri and bin Laden would take their fight to the Americans, whose power undergirded the region's state system. In 1998 bin Laden and al-Zawahiri relocated once again to Afghanistan. As a movement, Al Qaeda, which first appeared in rudimentary form in the late 1980s, was coming into its own.

Al-Zawahiri wrote *Knights under the Prophet's Banner* as Al Qaeda's sanctuary in Afghanistan came under assault from U.S.-led ground and air forces in the winter of 2001. The word "knights" in the title refers to the cadre of dedicated and trained jihadists whose task is to inspire the Muslim masses by undertaking heroic actions that will be propagated through the international media. According to al-Zawahiri, the battle is global in scope, and ongoing, and pits the "young jihad combatants" against the United States, Israel, Russia, and the "apostate" regimes. Because of the asymmetry of power, the jihadists ought to strike at the infidels any way they can: "It is entirely possible to kill Americans and Jews with a single bullet, a knife, an ordinary explosive device, and iron bar." The goal, al-Zawahiri says, is to take the struggle to the "far enemy's" own territory.

FURTHER READINGS

Abukhalil, As'ad. *Bin Laden, Islam, and America's New "War on Terrorism"* (New York: Seven Stories Press, 2002).

Bergen, Peter. *The Osama Bin Laden I Know* (New York: Simon and Schuster, 2006).

Devji, Faisal. *Landscapes of the Jihad* (Ithaca, NY: Cornell University Press, 2005).

Gerges, Fawaz. *The Far Enemy: Why Jihad Went Global* (Cambridge: Cambridge University Press, 2005).

Greenberg, Karen. *Al Qaeda Now: Understanding Today's Terrorists* (Cambridge: Cambridge University Press, 2005).

Gunaratna, Rohan. *Inside Al Qaeda: Global Network of Terror* (New York: Columbia University Press, 2002).

Kepel, Gilles. *The War for Muslim Minds: Islam and the West* (Cambridge, MA: Belknap Press, 2004).

Roy, Olivier. *Globalized Islam: The Search for a New Ummah* (New York: Columbia University Press, 2004).

Wright, Lawrence. *The Looming Tower* (New York: Alfred A. Knopf, 2006).

al-Zayyat, Montasser. *The Road to Al-Qaeda: The Story of Bin Laden's Right-Hand Man*, edited by Sara Nimis and translated by Ahmed Fekry, with an introduction by Ibrahim Abu Rabi (London: Pluto Press, 2004).

"Muslims Can Legitimately Kill Disbelievers"

- **Document:** Selection from the book *The Truth about the New Crusader War*, by Yusuf al-Ayiri, former leader of the global jihadist group Al Qaeda on the Arabian Peninsula. Translated by Mohammed Zakaria and John Calvert.
- **Date:** 2003.
- **Where:** Saudi Arabia.
- **Significance:** Al-Ayiri dispassionately justifies the killing of innocents in the course of the September 11 attacks against America with reference to the Qur'an and Islamic Tradition. His interpretation of these sources is colored by the Al Qaeda ideology of global combat to which he adheres.

DOCUMENT

In the name of God, the Merciful

Before beginning our reasoned argument on the permissibility of killing non-believing women and children in America, we must clarify an important point: Is America a country of peace, or is it at war with us?

We choose to say that America is not and has never been a country of peace. Our contention on this point is supported by the fact that fifty years ago America helped the Jews to occupy Palestine and expel and kill its people. Therefore America is a nation of war that recently has lashed out at Iraq, Sudan, and Afghanistan, and Muslims in every place over the past decades.

It is agreed that America is a country at war with us. As such, Muslims are allowed to fight back, just as the Prophet fought those who were against him. To provide but a few examples, the Prophet took captive a man from the Bani 'Aqil in response to the kidnapping by that tribe of two of the Prophet's companions; he cut off supplies to the Banu Quraysh, and killed Ka'b al-Ashraf and Salama bin Abi al-Haqiq [for their slander against him]. He burned the land of Bani al-Nadir [Jewish tribe of Medina], and destroyed forts as he did at al-Ta'if [City near Mecca; in Prophet's time, idolatrous].

As for the Blessed Tuesday operations [9/11] in the United States, we ask people who condemn these operations to calm down because it has not been proven with certainty that Muslims were the perpetrators. These critics claim that Muslims are to blame, but we do not accept their investigations on the matter because they are not based on the Qur'an and the Prophet's teachings. Besides that, the people who make such judgments are our enemy. Thus, we ask people to calm down and not rush to conclusions based on these faulty investigations.

Everyone should know that, basically, one cannot shed the blood of a Muslim or confiscate his property except in cases sanctioned by law. On the other hand, disbelievers do not enjoy such treatment except in cases of treaty, when they are allowed refuge, or if they live among Muslims. As for those disbelievers who dwell in the Abode of War, their blood may be legally shed and their money taken, with the exception of women, children and the elderly.

Thus, even if one accepts that Muslims carried out the [9/11] operations, these operations would be acceptable according to the Shari'a, because the attacks were aimed at a nation that was at war with us.

Some might say that among the victims were children, women, and elderly persons who, as fore mentioned, are not allowed to be killed. So, how could the Shari'a allow such an operation?

We say that the killing of these [categories of people] is not absolutely forbidden, and that there are special cases when it is allowed to kill them, if they are part of a nation at war. It is true that during the Blessed Tuesday operations some casualties occurred among people who ordinarily should not be killed. But those people were, in fact, killed in circumstances that made it permissible, which we will now mention. Any one of these reasons provides sufficient justification. These then are the circumstances:

1. Muslims can legitimately kill disbelieving innocents under the "eye for an eye" rule. So, if disbelievers kill Muslim women, children, and the elderly, then Muslims are allowed to avenge such hostility and kill equal numbers of the disbelievers' women, children, and elderly. God said: "Thus, whoever commits aggression against you, retaliate against him in the same way" [2:194], and other proofs. The Americans and their allies are trying to destroy the Muslims, for instance, in Palestine, in Jenin, Nablus, Ramallah, and other places in which massacres of children, women, and the elderly have taken place with American support. Should not then Muslims treat them the same way as the Muslims were killed? By God, it is the Muslims' right to do so.

2. Muslims can legitimately kill these categories of people if they are not able to distinguish between them and the enemy fighters. This is sanctioned by the word of the Messenger when he was asked about the families of the polytheists who were sleeping, whether they could target women and families. He said, "They are the same." This proves that it is allowed to kill women and children who are in harms way, when it is difficult to tell them apart from their fathers.

3. Muslims can legitimately kill such people if they have contributed to the war effort against Islam in any way, whether by action, word, or opinion. Thus, the Prophet ordered the killing of Durayd Ibn al-Simma who was part of Hawazin, though he was one hundred and twenty years old. He advised them against the Muslims, and therefore could no longer count on the protection of the Muslims; he had to be killed. Is it not right, then, that someone who votes for an unjust, criminal government that persecutes Muslims should be killed?

4. Muslims are allowed to kill [infidels] in cases in which the burning of forts and farms is necessary to weaken the enemy, as the Prophet did with regard to the Bani al-Nadir [Jewish tribe of Medina].

5. Muslims are allowed to undertake such killings in situations in which they need to bombard the enemy with heavy weapons, which do not distinguish between fighters

IN HISTORY

Al-Ayiri's Views on the Fall of Saddam Husayn and the War in Iraq

In another of his books, *The Future of Iraq and the Peninsula after the Fall of Baghdad*, al-Ayiri comments on what the war means for the region. Following are excerpts:

The collapse of the Ba'th government is a blessing for Islam and Muslims as the fall of the Arab Ba'th signals the collapse of the infidel pan-Arab slogans that swept the Islamic nation. After Communism, pan-Arabism, secularism, and modernism, the Iraqi Arab Ba'th (Party) has fallen to be replaced by the Islamic banner, which has remained steadfast throughout history to serve as an alternative for the nation, which has realized the failure of the non-Islamic calls regardless of their principles.

Had the Ba'th achieved victory, this victory would have contributed to the spread and the promotion of its ideology among the Muslims. It would have been difficult for members of the nation to turn down the ideas of a party that achieved a major victory. In addition, the party had recently started to pursue marriage with Islam. It changed its terminology from a purely Ba'thist line that rejected the Islamic slogans to one that embraced Islamic Ba'thist slogans.... A victory by the Ba'th would have caused a major crack in the true concept of Islam within the Islamic nation. A Ba'th military victory certainly would have been less dangerous than the advance of the Crusades [i.e., Americans], but still it would have constituted a threat to the nation in its creed that would have made it difficult for the nation to revolt against at a later stage, unless it started to threaten the rest of the Muslim countries militarily.

Undoubtedly one of the biggest threats to the domination of Islam and the rule of the Shari'ah in the nation is the US secularism, which will be imposed on the nation by force. The people of the Cross want this secularism to be applied throughout the Islamic world. After the occupation of Iraq, the application of this plan in the Islamic world is more likely. As a result, the Islamic world will move from dictatorship to democracy, which means paganism in all aspects of life.

SOURCE: http://www.why-war.com/news/read.php?id=3782&printme

and non-combatants, as the Prophet did at al-Ta'if when he bombarded the city with mangonels.

6. Muslims are allowed to kill [women, children, and old persons] in cases where the enemy is using them as human shields, and Muslims cannot get at the enemy and the evil they do without harming them. License for this is provided by most Islamic scholars and clerics.

7. Muslims are allowed to kill these categories when disbelievers have broken a treaty. In such cases, the Muslim leader needs to kill the women, children, and old people of the treaty-breakers for reasons of revenge, as the Prophet did with respect to the Bani Qurayza [Jewish tribe of Medina].

Someone might ask about the legitimacy for the killing of Muslims who happened to be in the World Trade Center at the time of the attacks, if indeed there were any. We will provide six answers to this question, any one of which is enough to justify this loss.

1. If it turns out that some Muslims were present, then we need to know the justifications of the attackers, if they were Muslim. If the attackers were forced by emergency to undertake the attack, then it is acceptable. If there was no circumstance of emergency, then we offer the following:

2. If to the best of the attackers' knowledge the World Trade Center contained only disbelievers, then the deaths of Muslims is acceptable, because the odds were against Muslims being killed. This is according to the Shari'a.

3. The jurist al-Shafi'i [d. 820] and al-Jassas [d. 982] from the Hanafi school of law believed that it is acceptable to burn, ravage and destroy the properties of people who fight you, even if accidental Muslim casualties will result. Calling a halt to warfare against infidels because of the risk to Muslims who live in the area, would obstruct jihad....

4. Prohibiting the killing of Muslims would lead to the cessation of jihad, because in every nation today there are considerable numbers of Muslims, and it is the nature of modern warfare that there are large numbers of casualties.

5. If the attacks were carried out by a Muslim and he knew that Muslims were in danger, he would have only to pay blood money to the family of each Muslim killed, as did the Prophet in the case of the Muslims of the Bani Khath'am. In

that case, the Prophet paid half the blood money from the treasury and did not blame the army because the victims were living amongst disbelievers.

6. It is acceptable to treat any Muslim who works in the countries of the disbelievers and strengthens them and helps them, as a disbeliever, just as God caused the army that attacked the Ka'ba to destroyed when there were among them those who were not guilty.

SOURCE: Shaykh Yusuf al-Ayiri, *The Truth about the New Crusader War* (hijri 1422), 6–8.

"Physical Fitness of the *Mujahid*"

- *Document:* An article attributed to al-Ayiri that outlines a schedule of physical exercises and training for the Mujahidin of Al Qaeda on the Arabian Peninsula.
- *Date:* Between 2001–2003.
- *Where:* Kingdom of Saudi Arabia.
- *Significance:* Since the time of Hasan al-Banna, Islamist groups have emphasized physical, in addition to spiritual and moral training. Al Qaeda is no different in this regard.

DOCUMENT

A *Mujahid*'s Fitness Training

Indeed, the physical fitness of the *Mujahid*, his ability to run long distances, carry heavy loads and exert a lot of bodily effort for extended periods of time is the primary factor that determines his usefulness on the battlefield. A *Mujahid* can be skilled in the use of weapons, but due to his lack of physical fitness, he is unable to determine the proper position to fire his weapon from, or to scale a wall in order to find a better position to shoot from, etc. This can all happen due to a lack of physical fitness, and the *Mujahid* that has the luxury of a high level physical fitness is able to carry out all of the tasks required of him in the best manner possible, even if he is not an expert in the use of weapons. This is because he is able to maneuver and position himself in the best manner to shoot, and he is able to do all of this in the quickest and lightest manner possible, as tiredness and fatigue do not overtake him and occupy his thoughts and affect his speed. Because of this, we can conclude that physical fitness is an essential asset to the *Mujahid*, especially in the case of street-fighting.

....

The level of physical fitness that is required of the *Mujahid* consists of him being able to do the following:

1. Jog for 10 kilometers (about 6.2 miles) without stopping, and this should take him no more than 70 minutes in the worst of cases.

2. Run a distance of 3 kilometers (roughly 2 miles) in about 13.5 minutes.

3. Run for a distance of 100 meters with only 12–15 seconds of rest.

4. Walk a long distance without stopping once for at least 10 hours.

5. Carry a load of 20 kilograms (around 44 pounds) for at least 4 hours straight.

6. Perform at least 70 pushups in one shot without stopping (one can start by performing 10 pushups at once, then increasing the number by 3 every day until eventually reaching 70).

7. Perform 100 sit ups in one shot without stopping (one can start by performing 10 sit ups at once, then increasing the number by 3 every day until eventually reaching 100).

8. Crawl using his arms for a distance of 50 meters in 70 seconds at most.

9. Perform the Farat like run (an exercise that combines walking, speed walking, jogging and running), and it is as follows:

The *Mujahid* begins by walking normally for 2 minutes, then he walks quickly for 2 minutes, then he jogs for 2 minutes, then he runs for 2 minutes, then he runs fast for a distance of 100 meters, then he returns to walking, and so on and so forth until he does this 10 times non-stop. And normal walking differs from quick walking, which differs from jogging, which differs from running. Normal walking is known to all, while quick walking is that one walks at a greater speed while making sure not to raise his feet from the ground for a greater amount of time than he would while walking normally. As for jogging, then this is that one covers a distance of 1 kilometer (roughly 0.6 miles) in less than 5.5 minutes. As for running, then it is that one covers a distance of 1 kilometer in less than 4.5 minutes.

This level of physical fitness can be achieved by the *Mujahid* in one month if he exerts great effort, with the condition that he advances gradually and does not damage his muscles or expose them to tearing. For example, if one begins at the start of the month by jogging for 15 minutes, and increased this time by 2 minutes every day, then this would mean that in a month's time, he would be able to jog for an entire hour without stopping (assuming that the number of days in the month in which he exercises would be 20 if the exercise program was 5 days a week). Likewise, if he begins with 10 pushups at the start of the month and increases the number by 3 everyday, then this means that he would be able to perform 70 pushups nonstop in the space of one month. So, advancing gradually and continuously has a great effect on one's fitness level. Also, during one's physical program, there must be some strength training included to strengthen and tone one's muscles, and the *Mujahid* must concentrate specifically on those types of weight training that can be performed without heavy exercise equipment, so that he can continue his physical program in any location. Exercise equipment has the effect of making one's body inactive if he is away from them for a long period of time. The best type of exercises are those that can be performed easily and rely on the body's own strength.

SOURCE: http://forums.islamicawakening.com/archive/index.php/t-2326.html
Accessed at: http://www.jarretbrachman.com/research.php

CONTEXT AND ANALYSIS

The Saudi face of jihadi militancy was manifested most visibly in 2003–2004, when a network of hardened militants operating under the name of "Al Qaeda on the Arabian Peninsula" began to target U.S. and other Western personnel and interests. The organization is typical of Al Qaeda's "second wave" in so far as it operated more or less autonomously of bin Laden and al-Zawahiri while adhering to its basic ideology. Although Al Qaeda on the Arabian Peninsula is a component of Al Qaeda's global jihad, its specific aim is to eradicate the U.S. presence in and influence over the countries of the Arabian Peninsula, chiefly Saudi Arabia. According to the organization's theorists, the "cleansing" of the peninsula of American power would weaken the "corrupt" House of Saud, thus rendering it vulnerable to Al Qaeda. The conquest of Saudi Arabia would be the first step in the reestablishment of the global Caliphate. However, there is some debate over whether Al Qaeda in the Arabian Peninsula is seriously interested in overthrowing the regime. Some have argued that it merely wants to weaken the regime and force its Western backers to flee, by attacking the oil industry and Western targets.

Al Qaeda on the Arabian Peninsula's call for jihad in Saudi Arabia is found in its publications, *Sawt al-Jihad* (*The Voice of Jihad*) and *Mu'askar al-Battar* (*The Camp of the Sabre*), which make only passing references to the jihads in Bosnia, Chechnya, Kashmir, and Afghanistan. At its height in 2003, the organization included no more than 500 hardcore militants (International Crisis Group 2004, 16).

Al Qaeda on the Arabian Peninsula's first leader was Yusuf al-Ayiri (1973-2003). Al-Ayiri was born in Damam and as a youth was influenced by the *Sahwa* movement that appeared among religion-minded Saudi dissidents in the 1990s. In 1991 he left for Afghanistan and received training at the al-Faruq camp outside Kandahar. Thereafter, he was incorporated into bin Laden's entourage in Sudan and in this role visited a number of the jihad's that were underway in the mid-1990s, including those in Bosnia, Kosovo, the Philippines, and in Afghanistan waged by the Taliban against the Northern Alliance.

Over this period al-Ayiri established himself as a knowledgeable and dedicated Islamist militant. When asked by bin Laden to establish an Al Qaeda "branch" in Saudi Arabia, he obliged. He ran Al Qaeda's Web site, *al-Nida*, which carried coded directives about Al Qaeda's motives and plans. He also set up training camps in remote areas of Saudi Arabia that were modeled on the al-Faruq camp in Afghanistan. The second document in this section details the physical training and exercise that recruits were to receive in these camps. Al-Ayiri understood that the success of the jihad was contingent on the physical as well as the mental discipline of its practitioners. Al Qaeda is in need of individuals capable of mounting operations in the most difficult of circumstances.

But it is al-Ayiri's "political" treatises that deserve the most attention. He was a prolific writer who churned out hundreds of pages of text, much of it posted on the Internet. In these writings, al-Ayiri "comes across as a well-informed, clear headed, and down to earth analyst" [Meijer 2006, 16]. In his online book *The Future of Iraq and the Arabian Peninsula After the Fall of Baghdad*, written as the United States prepared its attack, he wrote that an American invasion of Iraq would be in Al Qaeda's best interests, in that it would encourage militant anti-Westernism throughout the Islamic world and achieve in Iraq the radical environment that bin Laden had hoped would occur in Afghanistan. In another book, *The Truth about the New Crusader War*, an excerpt of which appears above, al-Ayiri takes pains to legitimize the killing of innocents in the 9/11 attacks by combing the Qur'an and especially the traditions of the Prophet for precedents and justifications. However, al-Ayiri's selection of religious texts is highly selective, and his interpretation of them goes against the grain of legitimate Islamic scholarship.

In April 2003 operatives within the organization, chief among them Ali 'Abd al-Rahman al-Faqasi al-Ghamdi, argued that the time was right to launch a massive strike against the Saudi state. They were supported in their judgment by Ayman al-Zawahiri. But Yusuf al-Ayiri said no. He said it was too soon—that the organization had not yet sufficiently matured. Nevertheless, the attacks took place. Throughout May Riyadh and other Saudi cities were rocked by bomb blasts and gun battles between Al Qaeda militants and Saudi security forces. On May 31, al-Ayiri and other members of the organization were cornered in a house and killed by Saudi government troops. He was succeeded as leader of the organization by 'Abd al-'Aziz al-Muqrin, who was killed by security forces in 2005—a psychological blow that still resonates among members of the group. Since al- Muqrin's death, Al Qaeda in the Arabian Peninsula has launched other attacks, both against Saudi and U.S. personnel and interests in the kingdom. However, these attacks were met by force, to the extent that by late 2005 the organization was effectively defeated. However, manifestations of Al Qaeda militancy in Saudi Arabia continue to linger.

FURTHER READINGS

Cordesman, Anthony, and Nawaf E. Obaid. *National Security in Saudi Arabia: Threats, Responses, and Challenges* (Westport, CT: Praeger/Greenwood, 2005).

International Crisis Group. "Saudi Arabia Backgrounder: Who Are the Islamists," *Middle East Report*, 31 (September 21, 2004).

Meijer, Roel. "Re-Reading al-Qaeda: Writings of Yusuf al-Ayiri," *International Institute for the Study of Islam in the Modern World*, 18 (Autumn 2006), 16–17.

"The Land of Those Who Reside in Paradise"

- **Document:** Excerpt from *Aku Melawan Terroris!* (*I Oppose Terrorists!*) By Imam Samudra, the "Bali Bomber." Translated from Bahasa Indonesia by Fachrizal Halim.
- **Date:** 2004.
- **Where:** Indonesia.
- **Significance:** The document illustrates how local jihad movements gained a global outlook through interaction in Afghanistan with Al Qaeda. It also provides an intimate look at the formation and worldview of a jihadi operative.

DOCUMENT

Snow Has Arrived: The Incarnation of Memory

But that was only a painting that once hung on the walls of the room where I studied, the room of a third grade student, I.D. No. 84851027, Junior high school Negeri 4 Serang, Jl. Juhdi No. 18, Serang Banten West Java Indonesia. I forget the postal code, but my wife would remember. She was my classmate and we used to sit beside each other in one of the front desks of the class.

Beside that impressive painting was stacks of paper and scribbles of numerical equations; these were, indeed, despondent equations. Under the pile of paper were books, one of which was entitled *Ayat al-Rahman fi Jihadi Afghanistan* (*The Signs of Allah's Sovereignty in Jihad in Afghanistan*), written by a certain Dr. 'Abdullah 'Azzam. Those who had time to read the book would, God willing, have their hearts moved to pick up arms and pursue jihad in Afghanistan. But at the time I was only sixteen, when all I could do was think about it, and then seriously reflect about it, before I found myself staring at empty blankness.

I read that book several times, and each time I finished it I prayed that God would take me to Afghanistan, the land of the martyrs, the land of those who reside in paradise.

Plastered on the door of my study room was a map of Afghanistan—it looked much like the map of Kalimantan. The last time I saw it was in 1995. And when I got married, the map was still plastered on the door.

Since the time I got my hands on this "enchanting" book, I never ceased entreating God to unite me with the other *mujahidin*—to make me one of them. In order that my supplications would be more acute and polished, I ceased watching television and listening to music. I became somewhat of an introvert. My only associates were the Qur'an and other religious texts. Occasionally, I would read the hand-written letters of a friend who became the mother of my children and the grandmother of their children.

The Intifadha in Palestine and the jihad in Afghanistan often left me irritated and distraught. I wanted to finish school quickly and work so that I could afford the fare to go to Afghanistan. But how can it be? For a Lebaran [the Eid celebration at the end of Ramadan] greeting card and a diary I wanted to send to the president of the student council, I had to dig a hole in my savings—money from a scholarship I received from the Ministry of education and culture. That president of the student council was now "Prime Minister" in a kingdom of soldiers and tears in paradise. (My son's name means "soldier of Allah," and my daughter's "tears in paradise.") The king of that kingdom is named Imam Samudra.

Praise to God. God Knows and Sees All. Three years later my wishes were finally granted. On 1990, I graduated from MAN (Madrasah Aliyah Negeri) in Cikulur, Serang. In a mosque of the Dewan Dakwah Islamiyah Indonesia, known as Masjid Al-Furqan Kramat Raya 45 Jakarta, I listened to a sermon from a da'i [missionary] whose name was a relative unknown. It was then that I met a certain Jabir (who died a martyr in the Antapani Bandung Bombing). Talking in Indo-Sundanese, we introduced ourselves and began conversing amicably. Then, I cannot recall how, our conversation arrived at the topic of jihad. I told him about the books I had been reading and he seemed interested and enthusiastic.

Then he ran a sort of background check and asked, "This year a group is taking off for jihad. Do you want to come?" I asked, "You mean to Afghanistan?" He replied, "listen brother, quickly get yourself Rp. 300 000, with God's Will, if your intentions are sincere, He'll make it easy for you."

Ciaoooo!!! I immediately bade him farewell and headed for home. There, I found whatever was left of my savings: remnants of the honorarium for an article I wrote for Panji Masharakat and the money I had received from my mother. I felt uncomfortable receiving money from her, but what could I do? After I announced that I would be departing for abroad, she gave me the rest of the money I needed. That was the money from her business; she sold jilbab and Muslim women's apparel. I occasionally helped her by purchasing materials in the Tanah Abang market.

After three days I joined up with Kang Jabir. We received our passports from Jakarta the same week and left for Dumai where we spent the night. The following day, we continued to Malaka, Malaysia. At that time, the Dumai-Malaka route was famous for the masses of migrant-workers who used it to go to Malaysia. Many were rejected by Malaysian immigration, even though they had completed documents and were able to show they had enough money for their first months in the country.

Maybe I did not have the look of a migrant worker. Praise to God, with ease we were able to pass through the waiting line, where hundreds of Indonesian "tourists" were set to cross the border. We had only one more day in Malaysia. The following evening, we left for Subang-Jaya airport in Selangor Darul-Ehsan. Once the Malaysian airliner took off, it struck me that I was truly leaving behind the land of my birth. At that instant, I felt distant from my old self—the ex-president of the Student council SMPN-4, graduating year 84/85 Serang. Anyway! Forget that. I aptly remembered these verses from the Qur'an (At-Taubad: 24):

Say: If your fathers, your sons, your brothers, your wives, your kindred, the wealth that you have gained, the commerce in which you fear a decline, and the dwellings in which you delight ... are dearer to you than Allâh and His Messenger, and striving hard and fighting in His Cause, then wait until Allâh brings about His Decision (torment). And Allâh guides not the people who are Al-Fâsiqûn (the rebellious, disobedient to Allâh).

In the plane, the flight attendant offered us a free postcard, an envelope and a booklet on which was written the name of the Malaysian Airline. I busied myself during the eight hour flight from Kuala Lumpur to Karachi writing to the only woman with whom I shared my life, apart from my mother and sisters. That woman was that same ex-president of the student council who had previously graduated from senior high school. If I recall correctly, I wrote on that postcard a translation of Surat Al-Baqara, verse 214:

> Or think you that you will enter Paradise without such (trials) as came to those who passed away before you? They were afflicted with severe poverty and ailments and were so shaken that even the Messenger and those who believed along with him said, "When (will come) the Help of Allâh?" Yes! Certainly, the Help of Allâh is near!
>
> ....

Truly, this was one chapter of my life in which I can say I was happy. Our "music" was that of guns and bullets, the explosion of mortars, and the hammering sound of the Zigoyak and Da-sha-ka (anti-aircraft artillery). Our "Songs" were those that roused us to the spirit of jihad. Our "melodies" were the never-silent verses of the Qur'an. There were no voices of women, no tantrums of babies, and no decadent music to invoke Satan.

The ground was flat and surrounded by mountains stretching to the four corners of the earth. Truly, this landscape eased the heart. Truly it was "paradise" for those who yearn for the everlasting paradise in the hereafter. None had enough courage to come to that place except he who was truly ready to sacrifice his life in the path of God. None would endure living there unless he was ready to fight the infidels, both the communists of the Soviet Union and the communists of northern Afghanistan—the group of ['Abd al-Rashid] Dustum—which is now in coalition with Karzai under the armpit of America and its cowardly allies.

Those who came to this "unusual" place were the few who were prepared to kill and be killed by infidels, ready to wage jihad in order to vindicate the Word of God. And this unqualified mental resolve could only be realized with the mercy and ordinance of God. All Praise to God.

Khost. That was the name of the place. The sundry zaitun leafs were immutable, they held on through the cold. The leaves of the Afghani *caparkat* and cactus had withered; only its thorns and corpse remained, which was burned as firewood for heat and cooking. The Anor no longer beget any fruit. All its leaves had fallen. Wolves howled woefully during the night. A thick layered jacket was necessary to protect against the cold. Those were the conditions when I arrived during the autumn.

Khost is no ordinary place. It is not like European or American university campuses where people fill their lives with the lasciviousness of the world. Khost is a piece of land on the wide expanse of earth.... At any time, the enemy could attack, setting off mortars, vomiting bullets, launching a spectacular battle. In such a situation, the End is truly in the hands of God. In Khost, and on other fronts in Afghanistan where jihad was pursued, one could feel the imminence of death. Enemies were everywhere. At any moment one could be visited by death.

....

Islam is Truth. Islam is God's straight path. So follow this path, and not others. All that finds its source in the Qur'an is truth, because it, in turn, finds its source in God, the supreme Truth. There is no truth other than the Qur'an, other than Islam.

The reality is that the Islamic community is divided, and not unified. The Islamic community has dispersed into various groups, sects, and parties. Each belongs to a particular circle, society or organization, thinking that it alone is right. Those outside their circle, outside their society, outside their organization, are considered to be wrong. Indeed, there is even a "science" of heresiology (*takfir*) that condemns all who are outside one's circle as infidels. Tragic!

Now, I will outline the method that I followed to understand Islam—something I learned from my studies here and there. If one is caught up in the method of the Khawarij

[Kharijites], then he will easily condemn another as an infidel simply on account of a single sin. Conversely, if one is caught by the method of the Murji'a, he will disregard major sins, however dire, even though that sin causes a person to be a disbeliever (*murtad*) or someone who associates another with God (*mushrik*).

The Khawarij are too severe, while the Murji'a is too lenient. Both are extreme (*ghuluw*) attitudes that are forbidden in Islam. Someone who commits fornication is deemed an infidel by the Khawarij. On the other hand, in the Murjia's view, someone who worships a rock and whose disbelief is evident, or someone who deliberately replaces Islamic Law with another law, is not taken as a problem. There are other methods that are extreme and excessive.

There is a method that approaches an understanding of the Qur'an and Sunna based on the model of the Salafiyya, which is just, moderate, and not extreme. All the imams of the four schools of Islamic law (Shafi'i, Hanbali, Hanafi and Maliki) use this method.

The Qur'an and the Sunnad (*sahih hadiths*) comprise the absolute truth. All Muslims have understood this. The problem is that as civilization develops, the human population grows, and as one generation passes on to the next, the antics of Satan have become more sophisticated. The return to the Qur'an and Sunna demands interpretation or exegesis (*tafsir*). In reading the Qur'an, one thousand minds can produce more than one exegesis. If an error in interpretation occurs in something that concerns branches of religion, perhaps it can be tolerated. But if the error is in things that concern the essentials of religion, of course this could damage doctrine (*aqida*). And if this is the case, it is not rare that it destroys one's adherence to Islam.

In this era, no one has the right to claim that his interpretation of the Qur'an and Sunna is the most correct. This also applies to previous generations. Those whose interpretation is the truest are the ones who have received an assurance from God and his Messenger. They are the people who are blessed by Allah, and they are open to that blessing. They are the people to whom Allah has promised Paradise.

Who are they?

They are the Prophet's Companions and Muslims of the succeeding generation.

The Qur'an is absolute truth. But to err in one's interpretation is to cause wrong understanding, an understanding that will create wrong beliefs. And a wrong belief will conceive wrong actions. This is what is called deviant corruption.

This is why the Qur'an should not be open for anyone to interpret. Only those who have certain credentials have the right to interpret the Qu'ran and Sunna. Of course, the task of interpreting and explaining the Qur'an to fellow human beings should be given to those who understand when, where, why and to whom the verses of the Qur'an were revealed. The Prophet Muhammad was a human being who truly apprehended the Qur'an, and who had the right, the competency and the capability to interpret it to others. The Sunna of the Prophet is a living embodiment of the Qur'an. The Prophet interpreted the Qur'an with his life. And this is Truth.

The Messenger is dead, but the chain of prophecy was fulfilled and perfected. The Qur'an and the Sunna are available to us. The generation of the Salaf has long passed away. Their bodies and souls no longer reside among us. But they have left their written works. Their opinions were immortalized by the generation closest to them.

The Islamic world is familiar with the names of those companions and the scholars of the people of the Sunna. They are the imams of the four schools of Islamic law: Imam Qatada, Imam Mujahid, Imam Sufyan bin Uyayna (the eminent Imam Shafi'i), Imam Muqatil, Imam Ibn Taymiyya, Imam Ibn al-Qayyim Al-Jauziya, and thousands of other great names that are impossible to mention here.

SOURCE: Imam Samudra, *Aku Melawan Terroris! (I Oppose Terrorists!)*, Bambang Sukiron, ed. (Solo: Jazera, 2004), 41–50; 57–61.

IN HISTORY

Abu Bakr Ba'asyir, Amir of Jemaah Islamiyah

Following the Bali bombings Abu Bakr Ba'asyir was jailed. After his early release in July 2005, he made the following points to Malaysian academic and commentator Farish Noor:

There is not a single Muslim leader today who has the courage and commitment to defend Islam and the Muslims, they are all in awe of the United States and other Western powers, and indebted to them. This is what we call "wahn" [lifelessness and enervation]. Our Prophet warned that this would be the case in the future, that the Muslim ummat would be great in numbers, but weak in spirit—until they are trampled upon again and again.

The Arab leaders and other Muslim leaders in Asia all suffer from this disease called "wahn," this weakness brought about by wealth and privilege, and thus they have become soft. That is why they cannot stand up to the kafirs and they cannot be firm in their statements and policies....

The only model to follow is pure Islam. Because Islam in its original form was tough and hard, not weak and pliable. Islam is fixed, stable, ordered and disciplined, and so are the Muslims.

If we return to the real practice of true Islam we would be much stronger and that is when the kafirs will fear us. That is why we need to uphold the Shari'a and return to real Islam. But the West is trying to weaken Islam from outside and inside. They attack our people and invade our countries from outside, and they weaken us from within with ideas like secularism, liberalism, and democracy. That is all designed to contaminate our pure Islam.

SOURCE: Aljazeera, 8/21/2006.

CONTEXT AND ANALYSIS

The emergence of violent Islamist groups mobilizing followers for *jihad* is one of the most conspicuous new phenomena in contemporary Indonesian Islam. Certainly the most significant of these Indonesian jihadist organizations is the Jemaah Islamiyah, which carried out the bombings in Bali on October 12, 2002. The attack killed more than two hundred people. One of the ringleaders of this attack was Imam Samudra. Born into a conservative family, he attended a religiously-oriented high school in Serang in Banten Province and moved to the West Java city of Bandung in 1990 on a scholarship to the State Islamic Studies Institute. It was there, as noted in the autobiographical statement excerpted above, that his imagination was inflamed by visions of jihad in far-away Afghanistan and Palestine. 'Abdullah 'Azzam's writings, in particular, had an effect on him. In 1991 he moved to Jakarta and met Enjang Bustaman who fulfilled his dreams of becoming a holy warrior.

Bustaman, known by his *nom de guerre* "Jabir," had fought the Soviets in Afghanistan in the late 1980s alongside Riduan Isammudin—another Indonesian, who would become famous under the alias "Hambali." Both men had passed through 'Abdullah 'Azzam's "Services Center" (*Maktab al-Khidmat*) in Peshawar and had trained at camps run by bin Laden. "Jabir" advised Samudra to join a Qur'an reading session at the Islamic Propagation Council, a group concerned with an alleged externally generated plot to "Christianize"Indonesia. In 1991, Jabir approached Samudra and told him it was time for him to go to Afghanistan and prepare for jihad. After arriving in Malaysia, Samudra flew to Karachi, Pakistan and from there took a bus to the Afghan border, where he was met by one of Jabir's contacts, who guided Samudra through the cold and unfamiliar landscape to the Al Qaeda training camp at Khost. Samudra was in Afghanistan from 1991 to 1993, and received training in the handling of assault rifles and rudimentary bomb construction. By the time he arrived, the Soviets had departed and in-fighting among the *Mujahidin* factions had begun.

Following the setting up of the *Mujahidin* coalition government in Kabul, Samudra left Afghanistan. In order to avoid arrest at the hands of Indonesia's Suharto regime, he and other returning Indonesian Jihadis went to Malaysia. Two of these exiles, Abu Bakr Ba'asyir and 'Abdullah Sungkar, then gathered a network of contacts among committed Islamists in Malaysia, Singapore, and the Philippines, including Imam Samudra, to form the Jemaah Islamiyah, the only true transnational Islamist group in South East Asia. Sungkar was set up as the organization's amir. Upon his death in 1998, he was succeeded by Ba'asyir. Under the stewardship of its amirs, Jemaah Islamiyah aimed to establish an Islamic state in Indonesia, which would form the basis of an encompassing Caliphate in South East Asia, governed by Shari'a.

In 1998 Imam Samudra took an oath of allegiance to Abu Bakir Ba'asyir. When that same year President Suharto died, he and the radical Islamists of Jemaah Islamiyah saw an opportunity to make their mark. The organization's first targets were the scattered Christian communities of the Indonesian Archipelago. Imam Samudra assisted Jemaah Islamiyah's operations chief, Hambali, in organizing and financing the bombings of twenty-four churches on December 24, 2000; during these attacks his old friend Jabir was killed. In order to whip up support for the anti-Christian jihad, he traveled to Muslim schools and talked about alleged Christian atrocities in Maluku. At the same time, he helped organize attacks against Indonesia's secular establishment, for example, providing explosives and detonators to the two men who carried out the attack on a Jakarta shopping mall on August 1, 2001. Adopting key aspects of bin Laden's philosophy, he and his colleagues also targeted the interests of the "far enemy," the United States and its allies, which included the bombing of Westerners in the tourist district of Kuta on the Indonesian island of Bali, which he planned with Amrozi bin Haji Nurhasyim. An Indonesian court sentenced both men to death in 2003.

Imam Samudra wrote *I Oppose Terrorists!* in prison. The book, which attracted great interest among Indonesia's public, is notable for the insight it provides into Samudra's, and the Jemaah Islamiyah's, world view. In it, he castigates America as the "real center" of international terrorism, and calls on Muslims to avenge the blood of Muslims who perished in Afghanistan, Sudan, Palestine, Kashmir, Bosnia, and Iraq as a result of Western policies and military interventions. He portrays himself and his colleagues as acting in accordance with the demands of their faith, which, as the above excerpt indicates, he defines in strictly Salafi-jihadi terms. It is interesting also, that the book includes an exposition on cyber terrorism, which Samudra believes to be a key tactic in bringing the Western-dominated world order to its knees. "It would not be America if the country were secure. It would not be America if its computer network were impenetrable," he writes in his computer-hacking chapter. He urges fellow militants to take advantage of this vulnerability: "Any man-made product contains weakness because man himself is a weak creature. So it is with the Americans, who boast they are a strong nation."

FURTHER READINGS

Abuza, Zachary. *Militant Islam in South East Asia* (London: Lynne Rienner, 2003).

Barton, Greg. *Indonesia's Struggle: Jamaah Islamiyya and the Soul of Islam* (Sydney: University of New South Wales Press, 2004).

International Crisis Group. "Jemaah Islamiyah in South East Asia: Damaged But Still Dangerous," *Asia Report*, no. 63 (August 26, 2003).

Lim, Merlyna. *Islamic Radicalism and Anti-Americanism in Indonesia: The Role of the Internet* (Washington, DC: East-West Center, 2005).

Ramakrishna, Kumar, and See Seng Tan, eds. *After Bali: The Threat of Terrorism in South East Asia* (Singapore: World Scientific Publishing, 2003).

Ressa, Maria. *Seeds of Terror: An Eyewitness Account of Al-Qaeda's Newest Center of Operations in Southeast Asia* (New York: Free Press, 2003).

Zarqawi's Letter

- *Document:* Letter to senior Al Qaeda leaders, allegedly written by Abu Mus'ab al-Zarqawi. Translated by the Coalition Provisional Authority.
- *Date:* Seized in January 2004.
- *Where:* Baghdad, Iraq.
- *Significance:* The letter, written by Al Qaeda's principal affiliate in Iraq, clearly communicates the jihadis' strategy of creating sectarian violence in Iraq. Zarqawi's group aims to topple the Shi'a-led government in Iraq by attacking Shi'a civilians.

DOCUMENT

In the name of God, the Merciful, the Compassionate,

From——to the proudest of persons and leaders in the age of the servants,

To the men on the mountain tops, to the hawks of glory, to the lions of [the] Shara [Mountains], to the two honorable brothers, …

Peace and the mercy and blessings of God be upon you.

Even if our bodies are far apart, the distance between our hearts is close.

Our solace is in the saying of the Imam Malik. I hope that both of us are well. I ask God the Most High, the Generous, [to have] this letter reach you clothed in the garments of health and savoring the winds of victory and triumph…. Amen.

I send you an account that is appropriate to [your] position and that removes the veil and lifts the curtain from the good and bad [that are] hidden in the arena of Iraq.

As you know, God favored the [Islamic] nation with jihad on His behalf in the land of Mesopotamia. It is known to you that the arena here is not like the rest. It has positive elements not found in others, and it also has negative elements not found in others. Among the greatest positive elements of this arena is that it is jihad in the Arab heartland. It is a stone's throw from the lands of the two Holy Precincts and the al-Aqsa [Mosque]. We know from God's religion that the true, decisive battle between infidelity and Islam is in this land, i.e., in [Greater] Syria and its surroundings. Therefore, we must spare no effort and strive urgently to establish a foothold in this land. Perhaps God may cause something to happen thereafter. The current situation, o courageous shaykhs, makes it necessary for us to examine this matter deeply, starting from our true Law and the reality in which we live....

....

Here is the current situation as I, with my limited vision, see it. I ask God to forgive my prattle and lapses. I say, having sought help from God, that the Americans, as you know well, entered Iraq on a contractual basis and to create the State of Greater Israel from the Nile to the Euphrates and that this Zionized American Administration believes that accelerating the creation of the State of [Greater] Israel will accelerate the emergence of the Messiah. It came to Iraq with all its people, pride, and haughtiness toward God and his Prophet. It thought that the matter would be somewhat easy. Even if there were to be difficulties, it would be easy. But it collided with a completely different reality. The operations of the brother mujahidin began from the first moment, which mixed things up somewhat. Then, the pace of operations quickened. This was in the Sunni Triangle, if this is the right name for it. This forced the Americans to conclude a deal with the Shi'a, the most evil of mankind. The deal was concluded on [the basis that] the Shi'a would get two-thirds of the booty for having stood in the ranks of the Crusaders against the mujahidin.

The Work Plan

After study and examination, we can narrow our enemy down to four groups.

1. The Americans

These, as you know, are the most cowardly of God's creatures. They are an easy quarry, praise be to God. We ask God to enable us to kill and capture them to sow panic among those behind them and to trade them for our detained shaykhs and brothers.

2. The Kurds

These are a lump [in the throat] and a thorn whose time to be clipped has yet to come. They are last on the list, even though we are making efforts to harm some of their symbolic figures, God willing.

3. Soldiers, Police, and Agents

These are the eyes, ears, and hands of the occupier, through which he sees, hears, and delivers violent blows. God willing, we are determined to target them strongly in the coming period before the situation is consolidated and they control arrest[s].

4. The Shi'a

These in our opinion are the key to change. I mean that targeting and hitting them in [their] religious, political, and military depth will provoke them to show the Sunnis their rabies ... and bare the teeth of the hidden rancor working in their breasts. If we succeed in dragging them into the arena of sectarian war, it will become possible to awaken the inattentive Sunnis as they feel imminent danger and annihilating death at the hands of these Sabeans. Despite their weakness and fragmentation, the Sunnis are the sharpest blades, the most determined, and the most loyal when they meet those Batinis [Shi'a; originally the term designates Shi'a, especially Isma'ilis who looked to the inner, esoteric meaning of the Qur'an], who are a people of treachery and cowardice. They are arrogant only with the weak and can attack only the broken-winged. Most of the Sunnis are aware of the danger of these people, watch their sides, and fear the consequences of empowering them. Were it not for the enfeebled Sufi shaykhs and [Muslim] Brothers, people would have told a different tale.

This matter, with the anticipated awaking of the slumberer and rousing of the sleeper, also includes neutralizing these [Shi'a] people and pulling out their teeth before the inevitable battle, along with the anticipated incitement of the wrath of the people against the Americans, who brought destruction and were the reason for this miasma. The people must beware of licking the honeycomb and enjoying some of the pleasures from which they were previously deprived, lest they surrender to meekness, stay on the[ir] land, prefer safety, and turn away from the rattle of swords and the neighing of horses.

The Work Mechanism

Our current situation, as I have previously told you, obliges us to deal with the matter with courage and clarity and to move quickly to do so because we consider that [unless we do so] there will be no result in which religion will appear. The solution that we see, and God the Exalted knows better, is for us to drag the Shi'a into the battle because this is the only way to prolong the fighting between us and the infidels. We say that we must drag them into battle for several reasons, which are:

1. —They, i.e., the Shi'a, have declared a secret war against the people of Islam. They are the proximate, dangerous enemy of the Sunnis, even if the Americans are also an archenemy. The danger from the Shi'a, however, is greater and their damage is worse and more destructive to the [Islamic] nation than the Americans, on whom you find a quasi-consensus about killing them as an assailing enemy.

2. —They have befriended and supported the Americans and stood in their ranks against the *mujahidin*. They have spared and are still sparing no effort to put an end to the jihad and the *mujahidin*.

3. —Our fighting against the Shi'a is the way to drag the [Islamic] nation into the battle. We speak here in some detail. We have said before that the Shi'a have put on the uniforms of the Iraqi army, police, and security [forces] and have raised the banner of preserving the homeland and the citizen. Under this banner, they have begun to liquidate the Sunnis under the pretext that they are saboteurs, remnants of the Ba'th, and terrorists spreading evil in the land. With strong media guidance from the Governing Council and the Americans, they have been able to come between the Sunni masses and the *mujahidin*. I give an example that brings the matter close to home in the area called the Sunni Triangle—if this is the right name for it. The army and police have begun to deploy in those areas and are growing stronger day by day. They have put chiefs [drawn] from among Sunni agents and the people of the land in charge. In other words, this army and police may be linked to the inhabitants of this area by kinship, blood, and honor. In truth, this area is the base from which we set out and to which we return. When the Americans disappear from these areas—and they have begun to do so—and these agents, who are linked by destiny to the people of the land, take their place, what will our situation be?

If we fight them (and we must fight them), we will confront one of two things. Either:

1. —We fight them, and this is difficult because of the gap that will emerge between us and the people of the land. How can we fight their cousins and their sons and under what pretext after the Americans, who hold the reins of power from their rear bases, pull back? The real sons of this land will decide the matter through experience. Democracy is coming, and there will be no excuse thereafter.

2. —We pack our bags and search for another land, as is the sad, recurrent story in the arenas of jihad, because our enemy is growing stronger and his intelligence data are increasing day by day. By the Lord of the Ka'ba, [this] is suffocation and then wearing down the roads. People follow the religion of their kings. Their hearts are with you and their swords are with Bani Umayya (the Umayyads), i.e., with power, victory, and security. God have mercy.

I come back and again say that the only solution is for us to strike the religious, military, and other cadres among the Shi'a with blow after blow until they bend to the Sunnis. Someone may say that, in this matter, we are being hasty and rash and leading the [Islamic] nation into a battle for which it is not ready, [a battle] that will be revolting and in which blood will be spilled. This is exactly what we want, since right and wrong no longer have any place in our current situation. The Shi'a have destroyed all those balances. God's religion is more precious that lives and souls. When the overwhelming majority stands in the ranks of truth, there has to be sacrifice for this religion. Let blood be spilled, and we will soothe and speed those who are good to their paradise. [As for] those who, unlike them, are evil, we will be delivered from them, since, by God, God's religion is more precious than anything and has priority over lives, wealth, and children. The best proof [of this] is the story of the Companions of the Ditch, whom God praised. [Imam] al-Nawawi said that this story contained proof that, if the city and the desert fought each other until all without exception perished unless they professed belief in the oneness of God, this would be good. Persons live, blood is saved, and honor is preserved only by sacrifice on behalf of this religion. By God, o brothers, with the Shi'a, we have rounds, attacks, and dark nights that we cannot postpone under any circumstances. Their danger is imminent, and what we and you feared is most certainly a reality. Know that those [Shi'a] are the most cowardly of God's creatures and that killing their leaders will only increase their weakness and cowardice, since with the death of one of their leaders the sect dies with him. It is not like when a Sunni leader dies. If one dies or is killed, a sayyid arises. In their fighting, they bring out courage and hearten the weak among the Sunnis. If you knew the fear [that exists] among the Sunnis and their masses, your eyes would cry over them in sadness. How many mosques have been converted into Husayniyyas (Shi'i mosques), how many houses have they demolished on the heads of their occupants, how many brothers have they killed and mutilated, and how many sisters have had their honor defiled at the hands of these depraved infidels? If we are able to strike them with one painful blow after another until they enter the battle, we will be able to [re]shuffle the cards. Then, no value or influence will remain to the Governing Council or even to the Americans, who will enter a second battle with the Shi'a. This is what we want and, whether they like it or not, many Sunni areas will stand with the *mujahidin*. Then, the *mujahidin* will have assured themselves land from which to set forth in striking the Shi'a in their heartland, along with a clear media orientation and the creation of strategic depth and reach among the brothers outside [Iraq] and the *mujahidin* within.

1. —We are striving urgently and racing against time to create companies of *mujahidin* that will repair to secure places and strive to reconnoiter the country, hunting the enemy—Americans, police, and soldiers—on the roads and lanes. We are continuing to train and multiply them. As for the Shi'a, we will hurt them, God willing, through martyrdom operations and car bombs.
2. —We have been striving for some time to observe the arena and sift the those [sic] who work in it in search of those who are sincere and on the right path, so that we can cooperate with them for the good and coordinate some actions with them, so as to achieve solidarity and unity after testing and trying them. We hope that we have made good progress. Perhaps we will decide to go public soon, even if in a gradual way, so that we can come out into the open. We have been hiding for a long time. We are seriously preparing media material that will reveal the facts, call forth firm

intentions, arouse determination, and be[come] an arena of jihad in which the pen and the sword complement each other.

3. —This will be accompanied by an effort that we hope will intensify to expose crippling doubts and explain the rules of Shari'a through tapes, printed materials, study, and courses of learning [meant] to expand awareness, anchor the doctrine of the unity of God, prepare the infrastructure, and meet [our] obligation.

    ....

What about You?

You, gracious brothers, are the leaders, guides, and symbolic figures of jihad and battle. We do not see ourselves as fit to challenge you, and we have never striven to achieve glory for ourselves. All that we hope is that we will be the spearhead, the enabling vanguard, and the bridge on which the [Islamic] nation crosses over to the victory that is promised and the tomorrow to which we aspire. This is our vision, and we have explained it. This is our path, and we have made it clear. If you agree with us on it, if you adopt it as a program and road, and if you are convinced of the idea of fighting the sects of apostasy, we will be your readied soldiers, working under your banner, complying with your orders, and indeed swearing fealty to you publicly and in the news media, vexing the infidels and gladdening those who preach the oneness of God. On that day, the believers will rejoice in God's victory. If things appear otherwise to you, we are brothers, and the disagreement will not spoil [our] friendship. [This is] a cause [in which] we are cooperating for the good and supporting jihad. Awaiting your response, may God preserve you as keys to good and reserves for Islam and its people. Amen, amen.

Peace and the mercy and blessings of God be upon you.

SOURCE: http://www.state.gov/p/nea/rls/31694.htm.

CONTEXT AND ANALYSIS

Abu Mus'ab Zarqawi was born Ahmad Fadil Nazal al-Khalaylah in October 1966 in the Jordanian town of Zarqa, some sixteen miles north of Amman, into a working class family. As an adolescent he dropped out of school and entered into a life of petty crime and drug abuse. However, he was exposed to the ideas of radical Salafi preachers operating in the nearby Palestinian refugee camp and so changed his behavior. He gave up drugs, married a cousin, and found a job as an office worker.

Seeking an outlet for his religious passion, in 1989 he abandoned both family and job and traveled to Afghanistan to join the jihad. But he arrived just as the Soviet troops were pulling out and thus saw little action. In Peshawar, the Pakistani headquarters of the Arab volunteers, he met Muhammad al-Maqdisi, a well-known militant Islamist with family roots in Palestine, and came under his influence. After the *Mujahidin* commanders captured Kabul from the Soviet puppet Muhammad Najibullah in 1992, Maqdisi returned with Zarqawi to Jordan to prepare for a jihad closer to home. Zarqawi's vocal denunciation of Jordan's Hashimite political and religious establishment earned him a stiff prison sentence, but he was released following the ascension of King Abdullah II as part of a general amnesty. He returned to Afghanistan and at Herat established a network of radical Islamists called *al-Tawhid wa al-Jihad* (Monotheism and Holy War), which was closely allied with Usama bin Laden's Al Qaeda organization.

The American-led attack on Al Qaeda and the Taliban following 9/11 prompted Zarqawi to relocate, first to Iran and then to a remote corner of northern Iraq controlled by the

Kurdish Islamist group Ansar al-Islam. Believing that an American invasion to oust Saddam Husayn was inevitable, Zarqawi began preparing the groundwork for the battle ahead. In cooperation with Al Qaeda, he began to facilitate the entry of Arab Islamists into Iraq through Syria. Foreign jihadis in Iraq, including many whose first allegiance was to Usama bin Laden, came to recognize Zarqawi as their *de facto* leader in Iraq. Soon Zarqawi was in charge of a new organization, *Tanzim al-Qa'ida fi Bilad al-Rafidayn* ("Al Qaeda's Organization in Mesopotamia"), which incorporated elements of his old network.

Some observers have questioned the authenticity of Zarqawi's letter. They say that the letter's educated style is not consistent with Zarqawi's lack of formal education. Others say there is no reason to doubt the stated identity of the author. Regardless of who within the jihadi camp wrote the letter, it appears accurately to reflect the jihadi strategy for destabilizing Iraq to the advantage of radical Sunni Islamists. In the letter, Zarqawi encourages his operatives to attack Americans, foreign contractors, and especially Iraqi police and military units; for it is essential, writes the author, to deter Iraqis from supporting the U.S.-led transition. Indeed, beginning in 2004 Zarqawi's followers carried out numerous car bomb attacks on police stations and recruitment centers, killing hundreds, and have assassinated Iraqi politicians.

But Zarqawi's most important point is the necessity of attacking Iraq's majority Shi'i population. In various communications Zarqawi calls the Shi'is *Rawafid* ("Rejectors"), a term of opprobrium, common among *Salafis*, that castigates the Shi'i refusal to accept the legitimacy of the Sunni Caliphs following the Prophet Muhammad's death. But over and above his *Salafi*-oriented prejudice, Zarqawi has a strategic purpose in mind. Violence against the Shi'is, he suggests, will encourage a Shi'i backlash against the Sunni minority, which in turn will "awaken the sleepy Sunnis" and spur them to action. Clearly, Zarqawi's chief aim was to create in Iraq the conditions for a sectarian battle that would empower the Sunni minority and destroy U.S. plans for the country's political and economic development. To this end, Zarqawi's Al Qaeda Organization in Mesopotamia attacked the Golden Mosque in Samarra in February 2006, the site of the Shi'i Twelfth Imam's Occultation, which ignited the wave of sectarian killings that followed. Zarqawi appears to have desired Iraq to become the new base for the global jihad against the West and its supporters in the Muslim world.

The letter is interesting for other reasons. In it, Zarqawi hints that his organization has been weakened by U.S. and Iraqi countermeasures. It also points to the relative autonomy of Zarqawi's "Al Qaeda in Mesopotamia" from bin Laden's parent organization. The letter suggests that in Iraq and elsewhere, the Al Qaeda movement for several years had comprised groups that, although sharing the basic ideology and strategic vision of al-Zawahiri and bin Laden, operate more or less autonomously of the parent organization in their respective "theaters" of operation.

On June 7, 2006, coalition forces killed Abu Mus'ab al-Zarqawi in an air strike north of Baghdad. Evidence suggests that his location was betrayed by Sunnis who reacted against Zarqawi's targeting of innocent Shi'i and Sunni Muslim civilians.

FURTHER READINGS

Brisard, Jean-Charles, in collaboration with Damien Martinez. *Zarqawi: The New Face of Al-Qaeda* (New York: Other Press, 2005).

International Crisis Group. "The Next Iraqi War? Sectarianism and Civil Conflict," *Middle East Report*, 52 (February 27, 2006).

Napoleoni, Loretta. *Insurgent Iraq: Al-Zarqawi and the New Generation* (New York: Seven Stories Press, 2005).

Rosen, Nir. *In the Belly of the Green Bird: The Triumph of the Martyrs in Iraq* (New York: Free Press, 2006).

BIBLIOGRAPHY

BOOKS AND ARTICLES

General Works on Islamism

Al-Azmeh, Aziz. *Islams and Modernities* (London: Verso, 1993).

Ayubi, Nazih. *Political Islam: Religion and Politics in the Arab World* (London: Routledge, 1991).

Beinin, Joel, and Joe Stork (eds.). *Political Islam: Essays from Middle East Report* (Berkeley: University of California Press, 1997).

Binder, Leonard. *Islamic Liberalism* (Chicago: University of Chicago Press, 1988).

Brown, L. Carl. *Religion and State: The Muslim Approach to Politics* (New York: Columbia University Press, 2000).

Calvert, John. "The Islamist Syndrome of Cultural Confrontation," *Orbis*, 46 (Spring 2002), 333–49.

Choueiri, Youssef M. *Islamic Fundamentalism* (rev. ed.) (London: Pinter/Cassell, 1997).

Davidson, Lawrence. *Islamic Fundamentalism: An Introduction* (Westport. CT: Greenwood Press, 2003).

Dekmejian, R. Hrair. *Islam in Revolution: Fundamentalism in the Arab World* (Syracuse, NY: Syracuse University Press, 1995).

Dessouki, Ali Hilal. *Islamic Resurgence in the Arab World* ((New York: Praeger, 1982).

Eickelman, Dale, and James Piscatori. *Muslim Politics* (Princeton, NJ: Princeton University Press, 2004).

Enayat, Hamid. *Modern Islamic Political Thought* (Austin: University of Texas Press, 1982).

Esposito, John. *Voices of Resurgent Islam* (New York: Oxford University Press, 1983).

Euben, Roxanne. *Enemy in the Mirror: Islamic Fundamentalism and the Limits of Modern Rationalism* (Princeton, NJ: Princeton University Press, 1999).

Fuller, Graham. *The Future of Political Islam* (New York: Palgrave Macmillan, 2003).

Gerges, Fawaz. *America and Political Islam: Clash of Culture or Clash of Interests* (Cambridge: Cambridge University Press, 1999).

Guazzone, Laura (ed.). *The Islamist Dilemma: The Political Role of Islamist Movements in the Contemporary Arab World* (Reading, UK: Ithaca Press, 1995).

Hafez, Mohammed. *Why Muslims Rebel: Repression and Resistance in the Islamic World* (Boulder, CO: Lynne Rienner Publishers, 2003).

Halliday, Fred. *Nation and Religion in the Middle East* (Boulder, CO: Lynne Rienner Publishers, 2000).

Hoffman, Valerie. "Muslim Fundamentalists: Psychosocial Profiles," in Martin E. Marty and R. Scott Appleby (eds.), *Fundamentalisms Comprehended* (Chicago: University of Chicago Press, 1995).

Huband, Mark. *Warriors of the Prophet* (Boulder, CO: Westview Press, 1998).

International Crisis Group. "Understanding Islamism," *Middle East/North Africa Report*, 37 (March 2, 2005).

Ismail, Salwa. *Rethinking Islamist Politics: Culture, the State, and Islamism* (London: I. B. Tauris, 2003).

Jansen, Johannes. *The Dual Nature of Islamic Fundamentalism* (Ithaca, NY: Cornell University Press, 1997).

Kepel, Gilles. *Jihad: On the Trail of Political Islam* (Cambridge, MA: Harvard University Press, 2002).

Lawrence, Bruce. *Defenders of God: The Fundamentalist Revolt against the Modern Age* (San Francisco: Harper and Row, 1989).

Mousalli, Ahmed. *Moderate and Radical Islamic Fundamentalism: The Quest for Modernity, Legitimacy and the Islamic State* (Gainesville: University Press of Florida, 1999).

Rahnama, Ali (ed.). *Pioneers of Islamic Revival* (New York: Palgrave/Macmillan, 1994).

Roy, Olivier. *The Failure of Political Islam* (Cambridge, MA: Harvard University Press, 1994).

Roy, Olivier. *Globalized Islam: The Search for a New Ummah* (New York: Columbia University Press, 2004).

Rubin, Barry (ed.). *Revolutionaries and Reformers: Contemporary Islamist Movements in the Middle East* (Albany, NY: SUNY Press, 2003).

Ruthven, Malise. *A Fury of God: The Islamist Attack on America* (London: Granta Books, 2002; revised 2004).

"Shades of Islamism." *ISIM Review* (Autumn 2006).

Takeyh, Ray, and Nikolas K. Gvosdev. *The Receding Shadow of the Prophet: The Rise and Fall of Radical Political Islam* (Westport, CT: Praeger, 2004).

Tibi, Bassam. *Islam between Culture and Politics* (New York: Palgrave, in association with the Weatherhead Center for International Affairs, Harvard University, 2001).

Wiktorowicz, Quintan (ed.). *Islamic Activism: A Social Movement Theory Approach* (Bloomington: Indiana University Press, 2004).

Islamism in the Sunni Arab East (Mashriq)

Abd Allah, Umar. *The Islamic Struggle in Syria* (Berkeley, CA: Mizan Press, 1983).

Abu Amr, Ziad. *Islamic Fundamentalism in the West Bank and Gaza: The Muslim Brotherhood and Islamic Jihad* (Bloomington: University of Indiana Press, 1994).

Abu Rabi, Ibrahim. *Intellectual Origins of Islamic Resurgence in the Modern Arab World* (Albany, NY: SUNY Press, 1996).

Aburish, Said. *The Rise, Corruption and Coming Fall of the House of Saud* (New York: Palgrave/Macmillan, 1996).

Ajami, Fouad. *The Arab Predicament* (Cambridge: Cambridge University Press, 1999 [1981]).

Amara, Muhammad Hasan. "The Nature of Islamic Fundamentalism in Israel," in Bruce Maddy-Weitzman and Efraim Inbar (eds.), *Religious Radicalism in the Greater Middle East* (London: Routlege, 1997), 155–70.

Ayubi, Nazih. *Political Islam: Religion and Politics in the Arab World* (London: Routledge, 1991).

Batatu, Hanna. "Syria's Muslim Brethren," in Fred Halliday and Hamza Alavi (eds.), *State and Ideology in the Middle East and Pakistan* (New York: Monthly Review Press, 1988).

Boulby, Marion. *The Muslim Brotherhood and the Kings of Jordan* (Atlanta, GA: Scholars Press, 1999).

Christmann, Andreas. "Islamic Scholar and Religious Leader: A Portrait of Muhammad Sa'id Ramadan al-Buti," in J. Cooper, R. Nettler, and M. Mahmoud (eds.), *Islam and Modernity: Muslim Intellectuals Respond* (London: I. B. Tauris) 1998, 57–81.

Commins, David. *The Wahhabi Mission and Saudi Arabia* (London: I. B. Tauris, 2006).

Cordesman, Anthony. "Saudi Arabia: Opposition, Islamic Extremism and Terrorism," in *Saudi Arabia Enters the 21st Century: Politics, Economics and Energy* (Westport, CT: Praeger, 2003).

Davis, Joyce. *Between Jihad and Salaam* (Palgrave Macmillan, 1997).

Dekmejian, R. Hrair. *Islam in Revolution: Fundamentalism in the Arab World* (Syracuse, NY: Syracuse University Press, 1995).

Delong-Bas, Natana. *Wahhabi Islam: From Revival and Reform to Jihad* (Cambridge: Oxford University Press, 2004).

Dessouki, Ali Hilal. *Islamic Resurgence in the Arab World* ((New York: Praeger, 1982).

Fandy, Mamoun. "Egypt's Islamic Group: Regional Revenge?" *Middle East Journal*, 48 (1994), 607–63.

Fandy, Mamoun. *Saudi Arabia and the Politics of Dissent* (New York: St. Martin's Press, 1999).

Fisher, Ian. "Women, Secret Hamas Strength, Win Votes at Polls and New Role," *New York Times*, February 3, 2006.

Ghabra, Shafeeq. "Balancing State and Society: The Islamic Movement in Kuwait," in Barry Rubin (ed.), *Revolutionaries and Reformers: Contemporary Islamist Movements in the Middle East* (Albany, NY: SUNY Press, 2003).

Hanna, Sami A., and George H. Gardner. *Arab Socialism: A Documentary Survey* (Salt Lake City: University of Utah Press, 1969).

Hinnebusch, Raymond. *Authoritarian Power and State Formation in Ba'thist Syria: Army, Party, and Peasant* (Boulder, CO: Westview Press, 1990) [see chapter 9, "Political Islam: Sectarian Conflict and Urban Opposition under the Ba'th"].

Hroub, Khaled. *Hamas: Political Thought and Practice* (Washington, DC: Institute for Palestine Studies, 2000).

Human Rights Watch. *Erased in a Moment: Suicide Bombing Attacks against Israeli Civilians* (New York: Human Rights Watch, 2002).

International Crisis Group. "Identify Crisis: Israel and Its Arab Citizens," *Middle East Report*, 25 (March 4, 2004).

International Crisis Group. "Saudi Arabia Backgrounder: Who Are the Islamists," *Middle East Report*, 31 (September 21, 2004).

Ismael, Tareq. *The Arab Left* (Syracuse, NY: Syracuse University Press, 1976).

Kechichian, Joesph A. "Islamic Revivalism and Change in Saudi Arabia: Juhayman Al-'Utaybi's 'Letters' To the Saudi People," *The Muslim World*, 80, no. 1 (January 1990), 1–16.

Levitt, Matthew. *Hamas: Politics, Charity, and Terrorism in the Service of Jihad* (New Haven, CT: Yale University Press, 2006).

Meyer, Tamar. *Women and the Israeli Occupation: The Politics of Change* (London: Routledge, 1994).

Milton-Edwards, Beverley. *Islamic Politics in Palestine* (London: I. B. Tauris, 1999).

Mishal, S., and A. Selah. *The Palestinian Hamas: Vision, Violence, and Coexistence* (New York: Columbia University Press, 2000).

Nusse, Andrea. *Muslim Palestine: The Ideology of Hamas* (London: Routledge Curzon, 2006).

Okruhlik, Gwenn. "Networks of Dissent: Islamism and Reform in Saudi Arabia," *Current History*, 101, no. 651 (January 2002), 22–28.

Paz, Rueven. "The Development of Palestinian Islamist Groups," in Barry Rubin (ed.), *Revolutionaries and Reformers: Contemporary Islamist Movements in the Middle East* (Albany, NY: SUNY Press, 2003).

al-Qaradawi, Yusuf. *The Lawful and the Prohibited in Islam (Al-Hala wal Haram Fil Islam)*, trans. Kamal El-Helbawy, M. Moinuddin Siddiqui, and Seyed Shukry (Plainfield, IN: American Trust Publications, 1994).

Al-Rasheed, Madawi. *Contesting the Saudi State: Islamic Voices from a New Generation* (Cambridge: Cambridge University Press, 2007).

Tal, Nachman. "The Islamic Movement in Israel," *Strategic Assessments*, 2, no. 4 (February 2000), online at: http://www.tau.ac.il/jcss/sa/v2n4p5.html.

Tamimi, Azzam. *Hamas: A History* (Northampton, MA: Olive Branch Press, 2007).

Wathaiq Haraka al-Muqawama al-Islamiyya "Hamas": Min Wathaiq al-Intifadha al-Mubaraka (Documents of the Islamic Resistance Movement "Hamas": Documents of the Blessed Uprising (Gaza: Palestine: Hamas Media Office, 1991).

Wiktorowicz, Quintan. "Islamist Activism in Jordan," in Donna Bowen and Evelyn Early (eds.), *Everyday Life in the Middle East* (Bloomington: Indiana University Press, 2002).

Islamism in Egypt and Sudan

Abu Rabi, Ibrahim. *Intellectual Origins of Islamic Resurgence in the Modern Arab World* (Albany, NY: SUNY Press, 1996).

El-Affendi, Abdelwahab. *Turabi's Revolution: Islam and Power in Sudan* (London: Grey Seal, 1991).

Auda, Gehad. "The 'Normalization' of the Islamic Movement in Egypt from the 1970s to the Early 1990s," in Martin E. Marty and R. Scott Appleby (eds.), *Accounting for Fundamentalisms: The Dynamic Character of Movements* (Chicago: University of Chicago Press, 1994), 374–412.

Baker, Raymond. *Islam without Fear: Egypt and the New Islamists* (Cambridge, MA: Harvard University Press, 2003).

al-Banna, Hasan. *Five Tracts of Hasan al-Banna*, translated and annotated by Charles Wendell (Berkeley: University of California Press, 1978).

al-Banna, Imam Hasan. *Letter to a Muslim Student* (Leicester, UK: The Islamic Foundation, 1995).

al-Banna, Hasan. *Mudhakkirat al-Da'wawa al-Da'iya* (Cairo: Dar al-Tawzi' wa al-Nashr al-Islamiyya, 1986 [1947]).

Calvert, John. "'The World Is an Undutiful Boy!': Sayyid Qutb's American Experience," *Islam and Christian-Muslim Relations*, 11, no.1(2000), 87–103.

Commins, David. "Hasan al-Banna (1906–1949)," in Ali Rahnema (ed.), *Pioneers of Islamic Revival* (London: Zed Press, 1994).

al-Ghazali, Zainab. *Return of the Pharaoh: Memoir in Nasir's Prison*, trans. Mokrane Guezzou (Leicester, UK: The Islamic Foundation, 1994/1415 AH).

Goldberg, Ellis. "Smashing Idols and the State: The Protestant Ethic and Egyptian Sunni Radicalism," in Juan Cole (ed.), *Comparing Muslim Societies: Knowledge and the State in a World Civilization* (Ann Arbor: University of Michigan Press, 1992).

Haddad, Yvonne. "Sayyid Qutb: Ideologue of Islamic Revival," in John L. Esposito (ed.), *Voices of Resurgent Islam* (New York: Oxford University Press, 1983), 67–98.

Hamdi, Mohamed Elhacmi. *The Making of an Islamic Political Leader: Conversations with Hasan a-Turabi*, trans. Ashur A. Shamis (Boulder, CO: Westview Press, 1998).

Harris, Christina Phelps. *Nationalism and Revolution in Egypt: The Role of the Muslim Brother-hood* (Stanford, CA: Hoover Institute on War, Revolution and Peace, 1964).

Heyworth-Dunne, J. *Religious and Political Trends in Modern Egypt* (Washington, DC: author, 1950).

Husayni, I. M. *The Muslim Brethren: The Greatest of Modern Islamic Movements*, trans. J. F. Brown and J. Racy (Beirut: Khayat's College Book Cooperative, 1956).

Ibrahim, Saad Eddine. "Anatomy of Egypt's Militant Groups: Methodological Note and Preliminary Findings," *International Journal of Middle East Studies*, 12 (1980), 432–53.

International Crisis Group. "Islamism in North Africa I: The Legacies of History," *Middle East/North Africa Briefing*, 12 (April 20, 2004).

Ismail, Salwa. "Confronting the Other: Identity, Culture, Politics, and Conservative Islamism in Egypt," *International Journal of Middle East Studies*, 30 (1998), 199–225.

Jansen, Johannes J. G. *The Neglected Duty: The Creed of Sadat's Assassins and Islamic Resurgence in the Middle East* (London: Macmillan Publishers, 1986).

Jansen, Johannes. *The Dual Nature of Islamic Fundamentalism* (Ithaca, NY: Cornell University Press, 1997).

Kenny, Jeffery Thomas. *Muslim Rebels: Kharijite Rhetoric and the Politics of Extremism in Modern Egypt* (Oxford: Oxford University Press, 2006).

Kepel, Gilles. *Muslim Extremism in Egypt: The Prophet and the Pharaoh*, trans. Jon Rothschild (Berkeley: University of California Press, 1982).

Khatab, Sayed. *The Political Thought of Sayyid Qutb: The Theory of Jahiliyya* (London: Routledge, 2006).

Lia, Brynjar. *The Society of the Muslim Brothers in Egypt: The Rise of an Islamic Movement, 1928–1942* (Reading, UK: Ithaca, 1998).

Mitchell, Richard P. *The Society of the Muslim Brothers* (New York: Oxford University Press, 1993 [1969]).

Moussalli, Ahmad. *Radical Islamic Fundamentalism: The Ideological and Political Discourse of Sayyid Qutb* (Beirut: American University of Beirut Press, 1992).

Moussalli, Ahmad S. "Hasan al-Turabi's Islamist Discourse on Democracy and Shura," *Middle Eastern Studies* 30, no. 1 (January 1994), 52–63.

Musallam, Adnan. *From Secularism to Jihad: Sayyid Qutb and the Foundations of Radical Islam* (Westport, CT: Praeger/Greenwood, 2005).

Qutb, Sayyid. *Milestones*, revised translation (Indianapolis, IN: American Trust Publications, 1990).

Ramadan, Abd al-Aziz. "Fundamentalist Influence in Egypt," in Martin E. Marty and R. Scott Appleby (eds.), *Fundamentalisms and the State* (Chicago: University of Chicago Press, 1993), 152–83.

Rifa'at Sayyid Ahmad (ed.). *The Militant Prophet: The Rejectionists* (vol. 1) [in Arabic] (London: Ri'ad al-Ra'is Books, 1991).

Rosefsky, Carrie. *Mobilizing Islam: Religion, Activism and Political Change in Egypt* (New York: Columbia University Press, 2002).

Shepard, William E. *Sayyid Qutb and Islamic Activism: A Translation and Critical Analysis of Social Justice in Islam* (Leiden, New York, Koln: E. J. Brill, 1996).

Shepard, William. "Sayyid Qutb's Doctrine of Jahiliyya," *International Journal of Middle East Studies*, 35 (2003), 521–45.

Sullivan, Dennis J., and Sana Abed-Kotob. *Islam in Contemporary Egypt: Civil Society vs. the State* (Boulder, CO: Lynne Rienner, 1999).

Voll, John O. "Fundamentalism in the Sunni Arab World: Egypt and the Sudan," in Martin E. Marty and R. Scott Appleby (eds.), *Fundamentalisms Observed* (Chicago: University of Chicago Press, 1991), 345–402.

Warburg, Gabriel R., and Uri M. Kupferschmidt (eds.). *Islam, Nationalism, and Radicalism in Egypt and the Sudan* (New York: Praeger, 1983).

Zeidan, David. "Radical Islam in Egypt: A Comparison of Two Groups," in Barry Rubin (ed.), *Revolutionaries and Reformers: Contemporary Islamist Movements in the Middle East* (Albany, NY: SUNY Press, 2003), 11–22.

Al-Zumur, Abbud. "The Strategy of the Islamic Jihad Group," in Rifa'at Sayyid Ahmad (ed.), *The Militant Prophet: The Rejectionists* (vol.1) [in Arabic] (London: Riad al-Ra'is, 1991), 110–26.

Islamism in North Africa (Maghrib)

Al-Ahnaf, M., B. Bottiveau, and F. Fregosi. *L'Algerie par ses Islamistes* (Paris: Editions Karthala, 1991).

Burgat, Francois. *The Islamic Movement in North Africa*. Trans. William Dowell. Middle East Monograph Series. (Austin: Center for Middle Eastern Studies, University of Texas Press, 1997).

Burgat, Francois. *Face to Face with Political Islam* (London: I. B. Tauris, 2003).

Dunn, Michael Collins. "The Al-Nahda Movement in Tunisia: from Renaissance to Revolution," in John Ruedy (ed.), *Islamism and Secularism in North Africa* (New York: St. Martin's Press, 1994).

Emad Eldin, Shahin. *Political Ascent: Contemporary Islamic Movements in North Africa* (Boulder, CO: Westview Press, 1997).

Esposito, John, and John Obert Voll. *Makers of Contemporary Islam* (Oxford: Oxford University Press, 2001).

Hafez, Mohammed M. "Armed Islamist Movements and Political Violence in Algeria," *Middle East Journal*, 4 (Fall 2000), 572–91.

Hermassi, Abdelbaki. "The Rise and Fall of the Islamist Movement in Tunisia," in Laura Guazzone (ed.), The *Islamist Dilemma: The Political Role of Islamist Movements in the Contemporary Arab World* (Ithaca, UK: Reading Press, 1995).

Howe, Marvine. *Morocco: The Islamist Awakening and Other Challenges* (New York: Oxford University Press, 2005).

International Crisis Group. "Violence and Reform in Algeria," *Middle East Report*, 29 (July 30, 2004).

Jourchi, Slaheddine. "Authenticity, Modernity, and the Islamic Movement in Tunisia," in Roel Meijer (ed.) *Cosmopolitanism, Identity and Authenticity in the Middle East* (Surrey, UK: Curzon Press, 1999).

Maddy-Weitzman, Bruce. "Islamism, Moroccan-Style: The Ideas of Sheikh Yassine," *Middle East Quarterly* (Winter 2003); online at: http://www.meforum.org/article/519.

Maddy-Weitzman, Bruce, and Meir Livak. "Islamism and the State in North Africa," in Barry Rubin (ed.), *Revolutionaries and Reformers: Contemporary Islamist Movements in the Middle East* (Albany, NY: SUNY Press, 2003).

Malley, Robert. *The Call from Algeria: Third Worldism, Revolution, and the Turn to Islam* (Berkeley: University of California Press, 1996).

Martínez, Luis. *The Algerian Civil War, 1990–1998*, with a preface by John P. Entelis; translated from the French by Jonathan Derrick (New York: Columbia University Press, in association with the Centre d'Etudes et de Recherches Internationales, Paris, 2000).

Munson, Henry. *Religion and Power in Morocco* (New Haven, CT: Yale University Press, 1993).

Roberts, Hugh. *Embattled Algeria, 1988–2002: Studies in a Broken Polity* (London: Verso, 2003).

Ruedy, John (ed.). *Islamism and Secularism in North Africa* (Washington, DC: Center for Contemporary Arab Studies, Georgetown University; New York: St. Martin's Press, 1994).

Scheele, Judith. "Recycling *Baraka*: Knowledge, Politics, and Religion in Contemporary Algeria." *Comparative Studies in Society and History*, 49, no. 2 (April 2007), 304–28.

Tamimi, Azzam S. *Rachid Ghannuchi: A Democrat within Islam* (Oxford: Oxford University Press, 2001).

Waltz, Susan. "Islamist Appeal in Tunisia," *Middle East Journal*, 40, no. 4 (Autumn 1986).

Willis, Michael. *The Islamist Challenge in Algeria: a Political History* (London: Ithaca Press, 1996).

Islamism in Turkey

Gole, Nilufer. "The Quest for the Islamic Self within the Context of Modernity," in Sibel Bozdogan and Resat Kasaba (eds.), *Rethinking Modernity and National Identity in Turkey* (Seattle: University of Washington Press, 1997).

Gole, Nilufer. "Secularism and Islamism in Turkey: The Making of Elites and Counter-Elites," *Middle East Journal*, 51, no. 1 (Winter 1997).

Karmon, Ely. "Radical Islamist Movements in Turkey," in Barry Rubin (ed.), *Revolutionaries and Reformers: Contemporary Islamist Movements in the Middle East* (Albany, NY: SUNY Press, 2003).

Lapidot, Anat. "Islamic Activism in Turkey Since the 1980 Military Takeover," in Bruce Maddy-Weitzman and Efraim Inbar (eds.), *Religious Radicalism in the Greater Middle East* (London: Frank Cass, 1997).

Mardin, Serif. "Religion and Politics in Modern Turkey," in James Piscatori (ed.), *Islam in the Political Process* (Cambridge: Cambridge University Press, 1983).

Margulies, Ronnie, and Ergin Yildzoglu. "The Resurgence of Islam and the Welfare Party in Turkey," in Joel Beinin and Joe Stork (eds.), *Political Islam: Essays from Middle East Report* (Berkeley: University of California Press, 1997).

Silverstein, Brian. "Islamist Critique in Modern Turkey: Hermeneutics, Tradition, Genealogy." *Comparative Studies in Society and History*, 47, no. 1 (January 2005), 134–60.

Vertigans, Stephen. *Islamic Roots and Resurgence in Turkey: Understanding and Explaining the Muslim Resurgence* (Praeger/Greenwood, 2003).

White, Jenny. *Islamist Mobilization in Turkey: A Study in Vernacular Politics* (Seattle: University of Washington Press, 2002).

Yarvuz, M. Hakam. *Islamic Political Identity in Turkey* (New York: Oxford University Press, 2003).

Yavuz, M., and John Esposito (eds.). *Turkish Islam and the Secular State: The Gulen Movement* (Syracuse, NY: Syracuse University Press, 2003).

Islamism in South Asia

Adams, Charles, J. "Mawdudi and the Islamic State," in John L. Esposito (ed.), *Voices of Resurgent Islam* (New York: Oxford University Press, 1983), 99–103.

Abou Zahab, Mariam, and Olivier Roy. *Islamic Networks: The Afghan-Pakistan Connection* (London: Hurst, 2004).

Ahmad, Khurshid. *The Religion of Islam* (Lahore: Islamic Publications, 1967).

Ahmad, Khurshid. *Mawlana Mawdudi: An Introduction to His Life and Thought* (Islamic Foundation Limited, 1979).

Ahmad, Mumtaz. "Islamic Fundamentalism in South Asia: The Jamaat-i-Islami and the Tablighi Jamaat," in Martin E. Marty and R. Scott Appleby (eds.), *Fundamentalisms Observed* (Chicago: University of Chicago Press, 1991), 457–530.

Ahmed, Rafiuddin. "Redefining Muslim Identity in South Asia: The Transformation of Jama 'at-i Islami," in Martin E. Marty and R. Scott Appleby (eds.), *Accounting for Fundamentalisms: The Dynamic Character of Movements* (Chicago: University of Chicago Press, 1994), 669–705.

Esposito, John, and John Voll. "Khurhid Ahmad: Muslim Activist-Economist," in *Makers of Contemporary Islam* (New York: Oxford University Press, 2001), 39–53.

Hasan, Masudul. *Sayyid Abul A'ala Maududi and His Thought* (Lahore: Islamic Publications, 1984).

Marsden, Peter. *The Taliban: War, Religion, and the New Order in Pakistan* (New York: St. Martin's Press, 1998).

Maududi, Sayyid Abul A'la. *The Islamic Movement: Dynamics of Values, Power and Change*, Khurram Murad (ed.). (London: The Islamic Foundation, 1984). The original Urdu: *Tehrik Islami Ki Akhlaq Bunyadain.*

McDonough, Sheila. *Muslim Ethics and Modernity: A Comparative Study of the Ethical Thought of Sayyid Ahmad Khan and Mawlana Mawdudi* (Waterloo, Canada: Wilfred Laurier University Press, 1984).

Nadwi, Abul Hasan Ali, *Islam and the World* (Lucknow: Academy of Islamic Research and Publications, 1967 [1959]).

Nasr, Seyyed Vali Reza. *The Vanguard of the Islamic Revolution: The Jama'at-i Islami of Pakistan* (Berkeley: University of California Press, 1994).

Nasr, Sayyed Vali Reza. *Mawdudi and the Making of Islamic Revivalism* (New York: Oxford University Press, 1996).

Roy, Olivier. *Islam and Resistance in Afghanistan* (Cambridge: Cambridge University Press, 1986).

Weiss, Anita. *Islamic Reassertion in Pakistan: The Application of Islamic Laws in a Modern State* (Syracuse, NY: Syracuse University Press, 1986).

Shi'i Islamism: Iran, Lebanon, and Iraq

Abdo, Geneive, and Jonathan Lyons. *Answering Only to God: Faith and Freedom in Twenty-First Century Iran* (New York: Henry Holt, 2003).

Abedi, Mehdi, and Gary Legenhausen (eds.). *Jihad and Shahadat: Struggle and Martyrdom in Islam. Essays and Addresses by Ayatollah Mahmud Taleqani, Ayatollah Murtada Mutahhari, and Ali Shariati* (Houston, TX: Institute for Research and Islamic Studies, 1986).

Abidi, A. H. H. "Shariati's Social Thought," in Nikkie Keddie (ed.), *Religion and Politics in Iran, Shi'ism from Quietism to Revolution* (New Haven, CT: Yale University Press, 1983), 124–44.

Abrahamian, Evrand. *Iran between Two Revolutions* (Princeton, NJ: Princeton University Press, 1992).

Abrahamian, Evrand. *The Iranian Mojahidin* (New Haven, CT: Yale University Press, 1992).

Aghaie, Kamran Scot. *The Martyrs of Karbala: Shi'i Symbols and Rituals in Modern Iran* (Seattle: University of Washington Press, 2004).

Ansari, Ali. *Confronting Iran: The Failure of American Foreign Policy and the Next Great Crisis in the Middle East* (New York: Basic Books, 2006).

Arjomand, Said Amir. *The Turban for the Crown: The Islamic Revolution in Iran* (New York: Oxford University Press, 1989).

Aziz, Talib. "Fadlallah and the Remaking of the Marja'iya," in Linda Walbridge (ed.), *The Most Learned of the Shi'a: The Institution of the Marja Taqlid* (New York: Oxford University Press, 2001).

———. "The Role of Muhammad Baqir al-Sadr in Shi'i Political Activism in Iraq, 1958–1980," *International Journal of Middle East Studies*, 25 (1993), 209–19.

Bakhash, Shaul. The *Reign of the Ayatollahs: Iran and the Islamic Revolution* (New York: Basic Books, 1990).

Baram, Amatzia. "From Radicalism to Radical Pragmatism: The Shi'ite Fundamentalist Opposition Movements of Iraq," in James Piscatori (ed.), *Islamic Fundamentalisms and the Gulf Crisis* (Chicago: The Fundamentalism Project, 1991).

Batatu, Hanna. "Iraq's Underground Shi'a Movements: Characteristics, Causes and Prospects," *Middle East Journal*, 35, no. 4 (1981), 578–94.

Beeman, William. *The Great Satan vs the Mad Mullahs* (Westport, CT: Praeger/Greenwood, 2005).

Boroujerdi, Mehrzad. *Iranian Intellectuals and the West: The Tormented Triumph of Nativism* (Syracuse, NY: Syracuse University Press, 1996).

Brumberg, Daniel. *Reinventing Khomeini: The Struggle for Reform in Islam* (Chicago: University of Chicago Press, 2001).

Chehabi, Houchang. *Iranian Politics and Religious Modernism: The Liberation Movement of Iran under the Shah and Khomeini* (London: I. B. Tauris, 1990).

Clawson, Patrick, and Michael Rubin. *Eternal Iran* (New York: Palgrave/Macmillan, 2005).

Dabashi, Hamid. *Theology of Discontent: The Ideological Foundation of the Islamic Revolution in Iran* (New Brunswick, NJ: Transaction Books, 2006).

Davari, Mahmood. *The Political Thought of Ayatollah Murtaza Mutahhari: An Iranian Theoretician of the Islamic State* (London: Routledge, 2005).

De Bellaigue, Christopher. *The Struggle for Iran* (New York: Random House, 2007).

Ehteshami, Anoushiravan. *After Khomeini: The Second Iranian Republic* (London: Routledge, 1995).

Fisher, Michael M. J. "Imam Khomeini: Four Levels of Understanding," in John L. Esposito (ed.), *Voices of Resurgent Islam* (New York: Oxford University Press, 1983), 150–74.

Hamzeh, Ahmad Nizar. *In the Path of Hizbullah* (Syracuse, NY: Syracuse University Press, 2004).

Hiro, Dilip. *The Iranian Labyrinth: Journeys through Theocratic Iran and Its Furies* (New York: Nation Books, 2005).

Khalil, Laleh. "'Standing with My Brother': Hizbullah, Palestinians, and the Limits of Solidarity." *Comparative Studies in Society and History*, 49, no. 2 (April 2007), 276–303.

Khomeini, Ruhollah. *Islam and Revolution: Writings and Declarations of Imam Khomeini*. Trans. and annotated by Hamid Algar (Berkeley, CA: Mizan Press, 1981).

Mallat, Chibli. *The Renewal of Islamic Law: Muhammad Baqer al-Sadr, Najaf and the Shi'i International* (Cambridge: Cambridge University Press, 1993).

Moin, Baqer. *Khomeini: Life of the Ayatollah* (London: I. B. Tauris, 1999).

Mottahedeh, Roy. *The Mantle of the Prophet: Religion and Politics in Iran* (New York: Simon and Schuster, 1985).

Nasr, Seyyed Hossein, Hamid Dabashi, and Seyyed Vali Reza Nasr (eds.). *Expectation of the Millennium: Shi'ism in History* (Albany, NY: SUNY Press, 1989).

Naser, Sayyed Vali Reza. *The Shi'a Revival: How Conflicts within Islam Will Shape the Future* (New York: W. W. Norton, 2006).

Norton, Augustus Richard. Hezbollah (Princeton, NJ: Princeton University Press, 2007).

Qassem, Naim. *Hizbullah: The Story from Within* (London: Saqi Books, 2005).

Rahnama, Ali. *An Islamic Utopian: A Political Biography of Ali Shariati* (London: I. B. Tauris, 2000).

Saad-Ghorayeh, Amal. *Hizbu'llah: Politics and Religion* (London: Pluto Press, 2002).

Sachedina, Abdulaziz A. *Islamic Messianism: The Idea of the Mahdi in Twelver Shi'ism* (Albany, NY: SUNY Press, 1981).

Sachedina, Abdulaziz. "Ali Shariati: Ideologue of the Iranian Revolution," in John L. Esposito (ed.), *Voices of Resurgent Islam* (New York: Oxford University Press, 1983), 191–214.

Sachedina, Abdulaziz A., and Hamid Enayat. "Martyrdom," in Seyyed Vali Reza and Hamid Dabashi (eds.), *Expectation of the Millennium: Shi'ism in History* (Albany, NY: SUNY Press, 1989), 44–57.

al-Sadr, Ayatollah Baqir, and Ayatollah Muratda Mutahhari. *The Awaited Savior* (Karachi, Islamic Seminary Publications, n.d.).

Al-Sadr, M. B. *Iqtisaduna* [Dar al-Fikr, Beirut, 1974]. Translated by John J. Donohue in John J. Donohue and John L. Esposito, *Islam in Transition: Muslim Perspectives*, 2nd ed. (New York: Oxford University Press, 2007), 254–59.

Sakari, Jamal. *Fadlallah: The Making of a Radical Shiite Leader* (London: Saqi Books, 2005).

Tabataba'i, Allamah, Jassim M. Hussaini, and Abdulaziz A. Sachedina. "Messianism and the Mahdi," in Seyyed Vali Reza and Hamid Dabashi (eds.), *Expectation of the Millennium: Shi'ism in History* (Albany, NY: SUNY Press, 1989).

Vahdat, Farzin. "Mohammad Khatami: The Philosopher President," *International Institute for the Study of Islam in the Modern World Review*, 18 (Autumn 2006), 21.

Walbridge, John. "Muhammad Baqir al-Sadr: The Search for New Foundations," in Elizabeth Walbridge (ed.), *The Most Learned of the Shi'a: The Institution of the Marja Taqlid* (New York: Oxford University Press, 2001).

Wilson, Rodney. "The Contribution of Muhammad Baqir al-Sadr to Contemporary Islamic Economic Thought," *Journal of Islamic Studies*, 9, no. 1 (1998), 46–59.

Wright, Robin. *The Last Great Revolution: Turmoil and Transformation in Iran.* (New York: Alfred A. Knopf, 2000).

Zanganeh, Lila Azam (ed.). *My Sister, Guard Your Veil, My Brother, Guard Your Eyes: Uncensored Iranian Voices.* (Boston: Beacon Press, 2006).

Islamism in Southeast Asia

Abuza, Zachary. *Militant Islam in South East Asia* (London: Lynne Rienner, 2003).

Ali, Mustafa. "The Islamic Movement and the Malaysian Experience," in Azzam Tamimi (ed.), *Power-Sharing Islam?* (London: Liberty Publications, 1993).

Anwar, Zaina. *Islamic Revivalism in Malaysia: Dakwah among the Students* (Petaling Jaya: Pelanduk Publications, 1987).

Barton, Greg. *Indonesia's Struggle: Jamaah Islamiyya and the Soul of Islam* (Sydney: University of New South Wales Press, 2004).

Esposito, John, and John Voll. "Anwar Ibrahim: Activist Moderate," in *Makers of Contemporary Islam* (New York: Oxford University Press, 2001), 177–98.

Federspiel, Howard M. *Islam and Ideology in the Emerging Indonesian State: The Persatuan Islam (Persis), 1923–1957* (Leiden: E. J. Brill, 2001).

Giora, Eliraz. *Islam in Indonesia: Modernism, Radicalism, and the Middle East Dimension* (Eastbourne, UK: Sussex Academic Press, 2004).

Gunaratna, Rohan (ed.). *Terrorism in the Asia Pacific: Threat and Response* (Singapore: Eastern Universities Press, 2003).

Hefner, Robert W. (ed.). *Islam in an Era of Nation-States: Politics and Religious Renewal in Muslim Southeast Asia* (Honolulu: University of Hawaii Press, 1997).

Hefner, Robert W. *Civil Islam: Muslims and Democratization in Indonesia.* (Princeton, NJ: Princeton University Press, 2000).

Hefner, Robert W. "Civic Pluralism Denied? The New Media and *Jihadi* Violence in Indonesia," in Dale F. Eickelman and Jon W. Anderson (eds.), *New Media in the Muslim World: The Emerging Public Sphere* (Bloomington: Indiana University Press, 2003), 158–79.

International Crisis Group. "Jemaah Islamiyah in South East Asia: Damaged but Still Dangerous," *Asia Report*, 63 (August 26, 2003).

International Crisis Group. "Indonesia Backgrounder: Why Salafism and Terrorism Mostly Don't Mix," *Asia Report*, 83 (September 13, 2004).

Laffan, Michael Francis. *Islamic Nationhood and Colonial Indonesia: The Umma below the Winds* (London: Routledge, 2003).

Lim, Merlyna. *Islamic Radicalism and Anti-Americanism in Indonesia: The Role of the Internet* (Washington, DC: East-West Center, 2005).

Millard, Mike. *Jihad in Paradise: Islam and Politics in Southeast Asia* (Armonk, NY: M. E. Sharpe, 2004).

Nagata, Judith. *The Reflowering of Malaysian Islam* (Vancouver: University of British Columbia Press, 1984).

Nash, Manning. "Islamic Resurgence in Malaysia and Indonesia," in Martin E. Marty and R. Scott Appleby (eds.), *Fundamentalisms Observed* (Chicago: University of Chicago Press, 1991), 691–739.

Nasr, Vali. *The Islamic Leviathan: Islam and the Making of State Power* (Oxford: Oxford University Press, 2001).

Ramakrishna, Kumar, and See Seng Tan (eds.). *After Bali: The Threat of Terrorism in South East Asia* (Singapore: World Scientific Publishing, 2003).

Ressa, Maria. *Seeds of Terror: An Eyewitness Account of Al-Qaeda's Newest Center of Operations in Southeast Asia* (New York: Free Press, 2003).

Samudra, Imam. *Aku Melawan Terroris! (I Oppose Terrorists!* (ed.). Bambang Sukiron (Solo: Jazera, 2004).

Subkahn, Imam. "Islam and Democracy Cannot Meet: Irfan Awwas Sets Out His Vision of Islamic Law in Indonesia," *Inside Indonesia* (July–September 2004). At: http://www.insideindonesia.org.

Von der Mehden, Fred R. Malaysian and Indonesian Islamic Movements and the Iranian Connection," in John Esposito (ed.), *The Iranian Revolution: Its Global Impact* (Miami: Florida International University Press, 1990).

Islamism in Europe

International Crisis Group. Bin *Laden and the Balkans: The Politics of Anti-Terrorism* (Brussels: author, 2001).

Izetbegovic, Alija Ali. *Islam between East and West* (Indianapolis, IN: American Trust Publications, 1984).

Izetbegovic, Alija. *Izetbegovic of Bosnia and Herzegovina: Notes from Prison, 1983–1988* (Westport, CT: Praeger/Greenwood, 2001).

Kepel, Gilles. *Allah in the West* (Palo Alto, CA: Stanford University Press, 1997).

Kohlmann, Evan. *Al-Qaida's Jihad in Europe: The Afghan-Bosnian Network* (London: Berg Publishers, 2004).

LeBor, Adam. *A Heart Turned East: Among the Muslims of Europe and America* (New York: St. Martin's Press, 2001).

Pederson, Lars. *New Islamic Movements in Western Europe* (Aldershot, UK: Ashgate, 1999).

Pinson, Mark (ed.), *The Muslims of Bosnia-Herzegovina: Their Historic Development from the Middle Ages to the Dissolution of Yugoslavia* (Cambridge, MA: Harvard University Press, 1994).

Roy, Olivier. *Globalized Islam: The Search for a New Ummah* (New York: Columbia University Press, 2004).

Sells, Michael Anthony. *The Bridge Betrayed: Religion and Genocide in Bosnia* (Berkeley: University of California Press, 1998).

Wiktorowicz, Quintan, *Radical Islam Rising: Muslim Extremism in the West* (New York: Rowman & Littlefield, 2005).

Islamism and Gender

Afshar, Haleh. *Islam and Feminisms: An Iranian Case-Study* (New York: St. Martin's Press, 1998).

Ahmed, Leila. *Women and Gender in Islam: Historical Roots of a Modern Debate* (New Haven, CT: Yale University Press, 1992).

Chistiansen, Connie. "Women's Islamic Activism: Between Self-Practices and Social Reform Efforts," in John L. Esposito and Francois Burgat (eds.), *Modernizing Islam: Religion in the Public Sphere in the Middle East and Europe* (New Brunswick, NJ: Rutgers University Press, 2003).

Clark, Janine. "Islamist Women in Yemen: Informal Nodes of Activism," in Quintain Wiktorowicz (ed.), *Islamic Activism: A Social Movement Theory Approach* (Bloomington: Indiana University Press, 2004).

Cooke, Miriam. *Women Claim Islam: Creating Islamic Feminism through Literature* (New York: Routledge, 2001).

Fernea, Elizabeth (ed.). *Women and the Family in the Middle East: New Voices of Change* (Austin: University of Texas Press, 1985).

Fernea, Elizabeth Warnock. *In Search of Islamic Feminism: One Woman's Global Journey* (New York: Doubleday, 1998).

Hale, Sondra. "The Women of Sudan's National Islamic Front," in Joel Beinin and Joe Stork (eds.), *Political Islam: Essays from Middle East Report* (Berkeley: University of California Press, 1997), 234–49.

Hammami, Rema. "From Immodesty to Collaboration: Hamas, the Women's Movement, and National Identity in the Intifada," in Joel Beinin and Joe Stork (eds.), *Political Islam: Essays from Middle East Report* (Berkeley: University of California Press, 1997).

Hatem, Mervet. "Secularist and Islamist Discourse on Modernity in Egypt and the Evolution of the Postcolonial Nation-State," in Yvonne Haddad and John L. Esposito (eds.), *Islam, Gender, and Social Change* (Baltimore: Oxford University Press, 1998).

Hoffman, Valerie. "An Islamic Activist: Zaynab al-Ghazali," in Elizabeth W. Fernea (ed.), *Women and the Family in the Middle East: New Voices of Change* (Austin: University of Texas Press, 1985).

Joseph, Suad (ed.). *Gender and Citizenship in the Middle East* (Syracuse, NY: Syracuse University Press, 2000).

Joseph, Suad, and Susan Slymovics (eds.). *Women and Power in the Middle East* (Philadelphia: University of Pennsylvania Press, 2000).

Karram, Azza M. *Women, Islamism, and the State: Contemporary Feminisms in Egypt* (London: MacMillan, 1998).

Mahmood, Saba. *Politics of Piety: The Islamic Revival and the Feminist Subject* (Princeton, NJ: Princeton University Press, 2005).

Moghissi, Haideh. *Feminism and Islamic Fundamentalism: The Limits of Postmodern Analysis* (London: Zed Books, 1999).

Rugh, Andrea B. "Reshaping Family Relations in Egypt," in R. Scott Appleby and Martin E. Marty (eds.), *Fundamentalisms and Society: Reclaiming the Sciences, the Family and Education* (Chicago: University of Chicago Press, 1993), 151–80.

Sabbagh, Suha (ed.). *Palestinian Women of the West Bank and Gaza* (Bloomington: Indiana University Press, 1998).

Shehadah, Lamia Rustam. "Women in the Discourse of Sayyid Qutb," *Arab Studies Quarterly* (Summer 2000).

Wiley, Joyce. "Alima Bint al-Huda, Women's Advocate," in Elizabeth Walbridge (ed.), *The Most Learned of the Shi'a: The Institution of Marja Taqlid* (New York: Oxford University Press, 2003).

Yassine, Nadia. *Full Sails Ahead*, translated by Farouk Bouasse (Iowa City, IA: Justice and Spirituality Publishing, 2006).

Democracy and Economy

Abootalibi, Ali. "Islam and Democracy," in Barry Rubin (ed.), *Revolutionaries and Reformers: Contemporary Islamist Movements in the Middle East* (Albany, NY: SUNY Press, 2003).

Abou El Fadl, Khaled. "Islam and the Challenge of Deomocracy," *Boston Review* (April/May 2003). Online at: http://bostonreview.net/BR28.2/abou.html.

Collins, Elizabeth Fuller, and Ihsan Ali Fauzi. "Islam and Democracy: The Successful New Party PKS Is a Moderate Alternative to Radical Islamism," *Inside Indonesia* (January–March 2005). Online at: http://www.insideindonesia.org.

Feldman, Noah. *After Jihad: America and the Struggle for Islamic Democracy* (New York: Farrar, Straus and Giroux, 2003).

Kramer, Gudrun. "Islamist Notions of Democracy," *Middle East Research and Information Project (MERIP)*, 23, no. 183 (July–August 1993), 2–8.

Kuran, Timur. *Islam and Mammon: The Economic Predicaments of Islamism* (Princeton, NJ: Princeton University Press, 2004).

Miles, Hugh. *Al Jazeera: The Inside Story of the Arab News Channel That Is Challenging the West* (New York: Grove Press, 2005).

Moussalli, Ahmad S. "Hasan al-Turabi's Islamist Discourse on Democracy and Shura," *Middle Eastern Studies* 30, no. 1 (January 1994), 52–63.

Moussalli, Ahmad S. *The Islamic Quest for Democracy, Pluralism, and Human Rights* (Gainesville: University Press of Florida, 2001).

Pfeifer, Karen. "Is There an Islamic Economics?" Joel Beinin and Joe Stork (eds.), *Political Islam: Essays from Middle East Report* (Berkeley: University of California Press, 1997), 154–65.

Poole, Elizabeth, and John E. Richardson. *Muslims and the News Media* (London: I. B. Tauris, 2006).

Robinson, Glenn E. "Can Islamists Be Democrats? The Case of Jordan," *Middle East Journal*, 51, no. 3 (Summer 1997).

Tripp, Charles. *Islam and the Moral Economy: The Challenge of Capitalism* (New York: Cambridge University Press, 2006).

Turabi, Hasan. "The Islamic State," in John L. Esposito (ed.), *Voices of Resurgent Islam* (New York: Oxford University Press, 1983).

Turabi, Hasan. *Islam, Democracy, the State and the West: A Round Table with Dr. Hasan Turabi, May 10, 1992.* Edited by Arthur L. Lowrie; transcribed by Maria Schone. WISE monograph series; no. 1 (Tampa, FL: World and Islam Studies Enterprise, 1993).

Wilson, Rodney "The Contribution of Muhammad Baqir al-Sadr to Contemporary Islamic Economic Thought," *Journal of Islamic Studies*, 9, no. 1 (1998), 46–59.

Al Qaeda, the Jihad, and Radical Islamist Networks

Abukhalil, As'ad. *Bin Laden, Islam and America's New "War on Terrorism"* (New York: Seven Stories Press, 2002).

Anonymous. *Through Our Enemies' Eyes: Osama Bin Laden, Radical Islam and the Future of America* (Washington, DC: Brassey's, 2002).

Benjamin, Daniel, and Steven Simon. *The Age of Sacred Terror* (New York: Random House, 2002).

Bergen, Peter. *The Osama Bin Laden I Know* (New York: Simon and Schuster, 2006).

Berman, Paul. *Terror and Liberalism* (New York: W. W. Norton, 2003).

Bloom, Mia. *Dying to Kill: The Allure of Suicide Terror* (New York: Columbia University Press, 2005).

Brisard, Jean-Charles, in collaboration with Damien Martinez. *Zarqawi: The New Face of Al-Qaeda* (New York: Other Press, 2005).

Bunt, Gary R. *Islam in the Digital Age: E-Jihad, Online Fatwas and Cyber Islamic Environments* (London: Pluto Press, 2003).

Burns, Vincent, and Kate Dempsey Peterson. *Terrorism: A Documentary and Reference Guide* (Westport, CT: Greenwood Press, 2005).

Burr, J. Millard, and Robert O. Collins. *Alms for Jihad: Charity and Terror in the Islamic World* (Cambridge: Cambridge University Press, 2006).

Calvert, John. "The Striving Shaykh: Abdullah Azzam and the Revival of Jihad," *Journal of Religion and Society*, Supplement Series 1 (2004), 83–103. Online at: http://moses.creighton.edu/JRS/toc/Supplement.html.

Coll, Steve. *Ghost Wars: The Secret History of the CIA, Afghanistan, and Bin Laden, from the Soviet Invasion to September 10, 2001* (New York: Penguin, 2004).

Cooley, John. *Unholy Wars: Afghanistan, America and International Terrorism* (London: Pluto Press, 2000).

Davis, Joyce. *Martyrs: Innocence, Vengeance and Despair in the Middle East* (New York; Palgrave/Macmillan, 2003).

Devji, Faisal. *Landscapes of the Jihad* (Ithaca, NY: Cornell University Press, 2005).

Furnish, Timothy. *Holiest Wars Islamic Mahdis, Their Jihads, and Osama Bin Laden* (Westport, CT: Praeger/Greenwood, 2005).

Gerges, Fawaz. *The Far Enemy: Why Jihad Went Global* (New York: Cambridge University Press, 2005).

Gray, John. *Al Qaeda and What It Means to Be Modern* (New York: New Press, 2003).

Greenberg, Karen. *Al Qaeda Now: Understanding Today's Terrorists* (Cambridge: Cambridge University Press, 2005).

Gunaratna, Rohan. *Inside Al Qaeda: Global Network of Terror* (New York: Columbia University Press, 2002).

Habeck, Mary. *Knowing the Enemy: Jihadist Ideology and the War on Terror* (New Haven, CT: Yale University Press, 2006).

Kepel, Gilles (ed.). *Al-Qaida dans le texte: Ecrits d'Oussama ben Laden, Abdallah Azzam, Ayman al-Zawahiri et Abou Moussab al-Zarqawi* (Paris: Presses Universitaires de France, 2005).

Lawrence. Bruce (ed.). *Messages to the World: The Statements of Osama Bin Laden*, translated by James Howarth (New York: Verso, 2005).

Meijer, Roel. "Re-Reading al-Qaeda: Writings of Yusuf al-Ayiri," *International Institute for the Study of Islam in the Modern World*, 18 (Autumn 2006), 16–17.

Napoleoni, Loretta. *Insurgent Iraq: Al-Zarqawi and the New Generation* (New York: Seven Stories Press, 2005).

Randal, Jonathan. *Osama: The Making of a Terrorist* (New York: Alfred A. Knopf, 2004).

Rosen, Nir. *In the Belly of the Green Bird: The Triumph of the Martyrs in Iraq* (New York: Free Press, 2006).

Sageman, Marc. *Understanding Terror Networks* (Philadelphia: University of Pennsylvania Press, 2004).

Taji-Farouki, Suha. *A Fundamental Quest: Hizb al-Tahrir and the Search for the Islamic Caliphate* (London: Grey Seal, 1996).

Wright, Lawrence. *The Looming Tower: Al Qaeda and the Road to 9/11* (New York: Alfred A. Knopf, 2006).

Al-Zayyat, Montasser, Trans. Ahmed Fekry, Sara Nimis (ed.). *The Road to Al-Qaeda: The Story of Bin Laden's Right-Hand Man* (London: Pluto Press, 2004).

WEB SITES

A great deal of information relating to Islamism exists on the Internet. What follows is a list of selected Web sites that (1) provide information about Islamist activists and movements from analytical and critical perspectives, (2) provide document collections, and (3) are published by Islamists of various persuasions themselves.

Analytical and Critical Perspectives

http://counterterrorismblog.org
Information and links related to radical Islamism for policymakers and researchers.

http://counterterror.typepad.com/the_counterterrorism_blog/Library/9-11%20Comm%20Report.pdf
Full text of the 9/11 Commission Report.

http://ctc.usma.edu
The Combating Terrorism Center at West Point leverages the operational and academic expertise of its staff to provide cadets with experiential opportunities for studying terrorism, counterterrorism, homeland security, and weapons of mass destruction.

http://religion.info/english.shtml
Religioscope is an independent, nonsectarian Web site that provides news and analysis of current developments and trends in religion, including Islamism.

http://www.e-prism.org
The Project for the Research of Islamist Movements conducts academic and field research on new developments in radical Islam and Islamist movements. The project is affiliated with the GLORIA Center and is based in Hertziliya, Israel.

http://www.futureofmuslimworld.com/research/ctID.8/ctrend.asp
The Center on Islam, Democracy, and the Future of the Muslim World was founded by the Hudson Institute "to analyze the ideological dynamic of Islam around the world and to examine how the political and theological debate within Islam impacts both Islamist radicalism as well as the Islamic search for moderate and democratic alternatives." It publishes the journal *Current Trends in Islamist Ideology*.

http://www.jamestown.org/index.php
The Jamestown Foundation is an American think tank whose mission is to "inform and educate policymakers and the broader policy community about events and trends in

those societies which are strategically or tactically important to the United States." Originally focused on the eastern bloc countries, the current focus of the foundation is Islamism.

http://www.memri.org
The Washington, DC-based Middle East Media Research Institute provides translations of Arabic and Persian media as well as original analyses of political, ideological, intellectual, social, cultural, and religious trends in the Middle East. MEMRI denies the claims of critics that its choice of material reflects a pro-Israel bias and agenda.

http://www.nytimes.com/2001/09/26/international/BINLADEN-INDEX.html?ex=1179806400&en=8459986da19839a8&ei=5070
Compilation of articles from the archives of the *New York Times* on bin Laden.

http://www.pbs.org/wgbh/pages/frontline/shows/saudi
A series of articles and links from the PBS documentary *Saudi Time Bomb?* that explores Islamist developments in Saudi Arabia.

http://www.siteinstitute.org
Founded in 2004, the Search for International Terrorist Entities is a nonprofit organization that tracks the online activity of terrorist organizations.

http://www.washingtonpost.com/wp-srv/world/binladen/front.html
Special coverage by the *Washington Post* of Bin Laden, his network, and his goals.

Document Collections and Bibliographies

http://al-islam.org
Digital library. Collection of translated works on Shi'i Islam, including many Islamist writings.

http://archives.cnn.com/2001/US/09/11/chronology.attack/index.html
Chronology of the 9/11 attack.

http://watch.windsofchange.net/themes_30.htm
News and articles relating to the 2002 Bali bombing.

http://www.gwu.edu/~nsarchiv/NSAEBB/NSAEBB97/index.htm
A collection of declassified U.S. documents covering the rise to power of Osama bin Laden's former hosts in Afghanistan, the Taliban. From the National Security Archive at George Washington University.

http://www.library.cornell.edu/colldev/mideast/algeria.htm
A bibliography of events in Algeria between 1991 and 2004. Monographs, essays, articles, and audiovisual sources.

http://www.shariati.org
Collected speeches and writings of Iranian thinker and activist Ali Shariati.

http://www.witness-pioneer.org
Collection of primary texts by notable Muslim authors, including Islamist writers such as Sayyid Qutb and Abu Ala Mawdudi.

http://www.youngmuslims.ca/online%5Flibrary
An Islamic organization working for and through Muslim youth in Canada. The site includes a comprehensive online library of Islamist documents and readings.

English-Language Web Sites of Islamist Activists and Movements

http://jamaat.org/indexe.html
Web site of Central Information Department of Pakistan's Jama'at-e Islami.

http://kavkazcenter.com/eng
Web site of the Chechen independent international Islamic Internet news agency. It covers events in the Islamic world, Caucasus, and Russia from an Islamist perspective.

http://www.ikhwanweb.com
Official Web site of Egypt's Muslim Brotherhood, featuring news, statements, and interviews with MB leaders.

http://www.islamonline.net/english/index.shtml
Shaykh Yusuf al-Qaradawi's Web site. The site is administered in Doha, Qatar, and its contents managed from Cairo, Egypt. The site addresses variety of issues of concern to contemporary Muslims and invites Muslims from around the world to submit their questions regarding Islam.

http://www.islamtoday.com/library1.cfm
Web site of Saudi "Sahwa" preacher Salman al-Auda.

http://www.moqawama.org/english/index.php
Official Web site of the Lebanese Shi'i movement Hizbullah, offering news and analysis of current events.

http://www.palestine-info.info
Web site of the Palestinian Hamas (Islamic Resistance Movement).

http://yassine.net/en
Web site of Abdessalam Yassine, leader of the Moroccan Islamist organization Justice and Charity.

Select Jihadi Documents

http://counterterrorismblog.org/newslinks/upload/2006/09/Atiyah%20Letter%20to%20Zarqawi.pdf
Letter from Al Qaeda leader "Atiyah" to Abu Musab al-Zarqawi, released September 25, 2006, by the Combating Terrorism Center at West Point. The letter "sheds new light on the friction between al-Qa'ida's senior leadership and al-Qa'ida's commanders in Iraq over the appropriate use of violence."

http://counterterrorismblog.org/site-resources/images/DickeysTalibanRules.doc
Translation of Mullah Omar's nine-page pamphlet of rules by Christopher Dickey for MSNBC and *Newsweek*.

http://islamic-world.net/youth/shaheed_stories.htm
Biographies of martyrs who were killed in Afghanistan.

http://mypetjawa.mu.nu/archives/184836.php
Al Qaeda videos of 9/11 hijackers. Obtained by the *Sunday Times* and available on the Jawa Report Web site.

http://www.ctc.usma.edu/Management_of_Savagery.pdf
"The Management of Savagery," by jihadi theorist Abu Bakr Naji, translated by William McCants of the Combating Terrorism Center at West Point. "Naji explains how al-Qaeda

plans to defeat the U.S. and its allies in the Middle East, establish sanctuaries for Jihadis, correct organizational problems, and create better propaganda."

http://www.odni.gov/press_releases/letter_in_english.pdf

Letter to Abu Mu 'sab al-Zarqawi from Ayman al-Zawahiri, dated July 9, 2005. Link to and English version posted by Director of National Intelligence John Negroponte's office.

Documentaries

Al Qaeda's New Front: An Investigation into the Threat Radical Islamists Pose to Western Europe and its Allies—Including the United States. PBS Frontline documentary. http://www.pbs.org/wgbh/pages/frontline/shows/front

America at a Crossroads. PBS documentary series "that explores the challenges confronting the post-9/11 world—including the war on terrorism; the conflicts in Iraq and Afghanistan; the experience of American troops serving abroad; the struggle for balance within the Muslim world; and global perspectives on America's role overseas." http://www.pbs.org/weta/crossroads

Brotherhood of Terror. History Channel documentary focusing on the "secret apparatus" of Egypt's Muslim Brotherhood. http://www.thehistorychannel.co.uk/site/tv_guide/full_details/Conflict/programme_2953.php

The Power of Nightmares: The Rise of the Politics of Fear. BBC series of documentary films written and produced by Adam Curtis that compares the rise of the American neoconservatives and radical Islamists. The films argue that both movements have benefitted from exaggerating the scale of the terrorist threat. http://news.bbc.co.uk/1/hi/programmes/3755686.stm

Sayyid Qutb's America. National Public Radio documentary on Sayyid Qutb's 1948–1949 visit to the United States. http://www.npr.org/templates/story/story.php?storyId=1253796

INDEX

About the Author

JOHN CALVERT is an associate professor of history at Creighton University. He is the translator and editor of an English translation of Sayyid Qutb's *A Child from the Village*, the editor of a special issue of *Historical Reflections* on "Islam and Modernity," and the translator of several entries in *Terrorism: A Documentary and Reference Guide* (Greenwood, 2005), among other works.